A Canary's Tale

Volume 1

Jacob B. Berkson

Wake up! They're Here!

A Canary's Tale

The Final Battle

Politics, Poisons, and Pollution

vs.

The Environment and the Public Health

Volume I

The Odyssey

(1988 - 1996)

by Jacob B. Berkson

Drawings by Jack Garver

Foreword by Norman E. Rosenthal, M.D.

(Library of Congress Cataloging in Publication Data)

Berkson, Jacob B.
A Canary's Tale

Permissions, Acknowledgements, and Credits appear on pages 296-302.

DISCLAIMER

The material in this book is for information only and is not to be construed as medical, legal, or other professional advice. Inclusion herein does not constitute endorsement of any product or service. The use of this book is not a substitute for medical, legal, or other professional services. Consult a competent professional for answers to your specific questions.

Printed with soy ink on recycled paper.

to Eloise

"We need a Bill of Rights against the 20th-century poisoners of the human race. The book is a call for immediate action and for effective control of all merchants of poison."

Table of Contents

Year Two - 1989 A.D.

Year Four - 1991 A.D.

Year Five - 1992 A.D.

Year Six - 1993 A.D.

Year Seven - 1994 A.D.

Year Eight - 1995 A.D.

Year Nine - 1996 A.D.

Foreword

It was a great privilege for me to have Mr. Jack Berkson as a patient for many years. Besides being a man of principle and integrity, he is one of those rare individuals who has used his illness as a window into a vast area of inquiry that I believe will enlighten and assist many people. I have certainly been one of those people.

Before Mr. Berkson was poisoned in his own home by a routine application of a pesticide, the illness of multiple chemical sensitivity was unknown to me. Alas, it has now become too familiar. The concept that a single intoxication could somehow disable the body's capacity to deal with subsequent chemical exposures was completely novel to me then, as it is to many people even at the present time. There is no generally agreed upon mechanism for how such a process might unfold biologically, though speculations about this question abound. One speculation is that patients with this problem are neurotics, hypochondriacs and malingerers. In my view, this is frequently an erroneous explanation for a complicated biological phenomenon and an injustice to many people who suffer from a legitimate, albeit ill-understood, affliction.

At one point, maintaining an attempt at scientific skepticism, I put Mr. Berkson to the test. My office had recently been treated for ants with the very chemical with which Mr. Berkson had been poisoned. When I walked into the waiting room of my office the day after the treatment, shortly before I was to see Mr. Berkson, I detected no smell indicating the recent pesticide application. Many exterminators pride themselves on the odorlessness of the chemicals they use, as though that were a guarantee that these substances were non-toxic. I elected not to tell Mr. Berkson about this treatment, to determine whether he would in fact experience the symptoms which he had previously reported. The results of this uncontrolled experiment, which lasted all of five minutes, are detailed on page 99 of Mr. Berkson's book. I needed no further proof of the authenticity of his illness. I went on to publish his case as a letter in the *American Journal of Psychiatry* and from that time on, we always met out of doors.

My experience with Mr. Berkson has been of direct assistance to other patients whose complaints would not have been recognized or taken seriously by someone who had not been educated as I had, initially by Mr. Berkson, though I have subsequently learned of an extensive body of literature on the subject of chemical sensitivity. Two individuals from my practice who come to mind as direct beneficiaries of Mr. Berkson's education include a psychologist who was working in a sick building and a physician whose office was permeated by the fumes of a fast food restaurant on the floor below. I have come to understand that chronic exposure to even low dosages of toxic chemicals, especially in poorly ventilated surroundings, can be as detrimental as one-shot exposures to high doses of toxins.

By writing *A Canary's Tale*, Mr. Berkson brings his own experience and a wealth of important information to a general readership. He carries his knowledge lightly and has written an engrossing and thoroughly readable book that should fascinate as well as educate the reader. I hope it is widely read and heeded.

NORMAN E. ROSENTHAL, M.D.

Preface

The purpose of A *Canary's Tale* is to pick up the torch lit by Rachel Carson more than thirty years ago in her *Silent Spring* and to sound a clarion call to every citizen to get involved in the War to preserve and protect the environment and the public health.

A *Canary's Tale* is about a very real, but little understood, danger, to the public health, safety and welfare; indeed, to the very survival of man, on the planet Earth, in the last decade of the twentieth century.

The danger comes from man's daily exposure to thousands of toxic chemicals expelled into the air he breathes, the water he drinks, the soil in which he grows his food, and the food he eats. Despite warnings from thousands of reputable scientists and daily accounts in the media and the press, the public has failed to recognize that toxic chemicals to which they are exposed nearly everywhere on a daily basis may be the cause of their medical problems or the aggravating trigger of a preexisting illness.

People get sick from exposure to toxic chemicals in the home, in the workplace, indoors and outdoors. They sometimes suffer silently while the joy of life is diminished, while their careers are ended, and the body mechanisms become dysfunctional. And they do not realize there is a link between chemical exposure and disease. Many of these illnesses are preventable. Education is the key to prevention.

The author, a trial lawyer who was poisoned in his own home by exposure to a so called "safe pesticide," takes the reader on an eight year Odyssey of experience, study, and research about the effect the environment has upon the people on this planet. He produces clear and convincing evidence that there is a link between what is called "low level" exposure to thousands of chemicals, indoors and outdoors, and adverse health effects, between chemical exposure and disease, including cancer, asthma, emphysema and other respiratory diseases, and multiple chemical sensitivity (MCS). MCS is controversial and the American Medical Association does not recognize it as a disease. A *Canary's Tale* was written to help establish recognition of MCS as a valid disease, syndrome, or illness.

Just how large a problem exists is not known at this time. But everyone is at risk. No one is safe. Not the author. Not the reader. Not anyone. The patient with MCS is like the canary in the coal mine. The canary is warning humanity that the environment is polluted and as a sentinel sounds the Call for Action.

The enemies are real—industry has failed to protect the public. The Congress has rallied to protect the polluters who are their big campaign contributors, the Environmental Presidents have failed to use the influence of their bully pulpit to educate the public, and the public has failed to protect itself.

To read A *Canary's Tale* is to recognize the danger, especially to our children and future generations, and do something about it before it is too late. No cause is more important.

Introduction

Multiple chemical irritants never made me ill (so far as I knew) prior to my being poisoned by a termiticide in March of 1988 as described in *A Canary's Tale, Volume I*.

Subsequent to the poisoning of March '88 nearly every system in my body reacted adversely to exposure to toxic chemicals ubiquitous in the environment. My body had become sensitized from the poisoning and I was diagnosed as having Multiple Chemical Sensitivity (MCS). I found that MCS is a very controversial illness, syndrome, or disease. Boiled down to its simplicity, the issue is whether MCS is "real" or psychosomatic, i.e. is MCS a mental illness or a "real disease"? I am convinced that it is real. When I met other victims of toxic poisoning who developed symptoms similar to mine and who were diagnosed with MCS by reputable medical doctors I was urged to write a book about my experiences as an MCS patient. I had never written a book before. But I considered this a challenge and a duty. To help the present disabled victims it would be necessary to heighten the awareness of the public and public officials to their plight and to the vulnerability of the entire populace especially the children and the elderly. No one is safe. Everyone is at risk from pollution of the environment on this planet. This book is a Call to Action to recognize, deal with, and come up with solutions to the problem.

The problem is bigger than the present victims I met in my early days. I find it now includes thousands of disabled Gulf War veterans, disabled veterans of the Vietnam War, poisoned by Agent Orange, and people from all walks of life. So while Volume I is mostly My Odyssey from 1988-1996, it includes tales about other people I met, places to which I travelled, doctors who treated me, books I read and so forth. It is a chronology of events

xvii

pretty much as I learned about them and not arranged by topics.

That is where Volume II comes in. At the same time as things were happening to me I kept a scrapbook of articles about other people who were poisoned, injured, damaged, or killed by chemical pollution. Stories began popping up without my seeking them out. Like most people, I never paid much attention to them before.

My scrapbook developed into a reference and resource manual which is now titled *A Canary's Tale, Volume II, Research, References and Resources*. It goes well beyond my personal story, education, and development contained in Volume I.

Volume II is divided into 12 major topics which are listed in the Outline in the beginning of Volume II. The short Outline is followed by an expanded Topical Outline divided and subdivided into many topics. I have attempted to arrange the topics in a logical sequence to heighten the awareness of the reader as to how each topic is connected to the next topic. It is my hope that by following the topics from beginning to end the reader will develop a clear understanding of the link between environmental pollution everywhere and the adverse health consequences to everyone.

Year One
1988
A.D.

"In the days before sophisticated sensing technology, miners often took canaries with them as they ventured down into the bowels of the earth. The canaries were their early warning system for poisonous gases. Simple and expedient, if a bit grisly, the health of the canaries mirrored the health hazards posed to the miners themselves."

Niles Eldredge, Curator, Department of Invertebrates, American Museum of Natural History, The Miner's Canary: Unraveling the Mysteries of Extinction, *(New York: Prentice Hall Press, 1991). Reprinted with permission.*

1

Infestation - Extermination - Odor - Nausea - and Irritation

It was March of 1988. Eloise and I were planning to celebrate our retirement with a trip across the country. We expected to spend our golden years walking hand in hand along a sandy beach, watching waves break and smelling salty sea air. We were two ordinary, small-town folks in our early 60s, looking forward to a future of good health and happiness. It was time to relax and smell the roses.

It was not roses that we would soon be smelling.

Eloise noticed the insects first.

They were on the window sill below the picture window. They were on the living room carpet and the wall.

"We need an exterminator," she said.

"I know one." I dialed the number listed in the yellow pages.

"Able, this is Jack Berkson. We need your help."

Able came to the house, took one look at the swarm of black insects in our living room and den, and identified them as subterranean termites. He inspected our house and told us he found evidence of termites in the basement.

"They have not caused any serious damage yet. I can get rid of them in a day or so. No sweat. You are in good hands. Thanks for calling me."

Early a few days later, two men came to the kitchen door. They said Able sent them to get rid of the termites. Baker was a young man in green coveralls and a baseball cap. Charlie was much older and huskier. Their truck had Able's name, address, and phone number on it. They started unloading equipment and went to work. We received no instructions.

That day, Eloise was in and out of the house doing chores. I was completing some legal work in my home office. I didn't pay any attention to what the exterminators were doing. Able had a good reputation, and in my 40 years of practicing law, I had never heard of anyone having a problem with an exterminator. I had complete confidence in Able and relied on him to do the job.

That afternoon, Baker and Charlie came into my office, said they were finished and gave me a bill. I wrote out a check to Able, and thanked them, and they left.

They left behind a distinct odor, like kerosene or diesel oil or some sort of petroleum, but it did not seem unusual for such workmen to smell that way. I recalled how the "gas man" always left behind an unpleasant odor when he came to our house to repair the pilot light on our gas stove when I was a kid.

Eloise and I went out to supper. We came home, watched television and went to bed. Then I began to notice a foul odor in my bedroom. It was reminiscent of the navy ships I had served aboard during World War II and the Korean War.

I began to feel bad. My eyes were tearing. My nose was irritated. My head hurt. I became nauseated.

I got up and opened the two windows in my bedroom. It was March and still plenty cold outside. I unlocked the storm windows and propped them open with a clothes hanger. Cold, fresh air blew into the room.

I ran down the hall to Eloise's room. She was out of bed and coughing.

"What is it?" she asked. "What's making me cough? My eyes are tearing and my head hurts. We never had such a smell in the house before."

"The exterminators," I replied. "There is a definite link

between what those guys did here and this stinking odor and what is happening to us. The house didn't smell like this before they worked here. I don't know what they did, but we'll open your windows and get some fresh air in your room. Or you can sleep in my room. There is a nice, cool, fresh breeze blowing in there ventilating my bedroom. We're lucky we weren't asphyxiated. I'll call Able first thing in the morning."

2

Notification - Investigation - Explanation - Misapplication - and Denunciation

As the sun rose early the next morning, I opened more windows and doors and made a courteous call to Able's place of business.

"This is Jack Berkson calling. Will you please tell Able that there is a foul odor in my house from your extermination? Both Eloise and I became nauseous and ill last night. Ask Able to come out and check the work your men did yesterday."

Able arrived at the kitchen door as the sun began to set.

"Just got your message. What's the problem?"

"Thanks for coming, Able. We have an unusual odor in the house which we didn't have before your men worked here yesterday. Both of us were pretty sick last night."

Able toured the house, sniffing in each room. After several minutes he looked over at me and said, "Yeah, I smell it. This odor is stronger than usual but there is nothing to be concerned about. The treatment we used was perfectly safe and all you have to do is open the windows and all this odor will go away in a couple of hours."

Able and I spent the next two hours replacing storm windows and doors with screens. It was cold when we finished. The oil furnace was running. Able told me to leave all the windows open.

"By tomorrow morning the smell will be gone," he said.

The smell didn't disappear and my stomach was in an uproar. I phoned Able the next day and told him what was happening.

"Don't worry, Jack. I'll be out with a fan and we'll blow that odor out of the house."

Able arrived later with a square industrial-type fan.

He suggested putting the fan in the basement and opening the windows.

"Okay, Able. You know more about this than I do. In fact, I don't remember your ever telling me that there would be any kind of an odor connected with this treatment."

"Well, this is very unusual. Most of the time there isn't any odor or it disappears in a matter of hours."

"How do you account for the fact that we still have the odor?"

"Gee, I don't know. Let's try the fan."

A few days later Able arrived with more fans. By then I was not only sick on my stomach but starting to get nervous, irritable and upset.

"Able, this house smells like a diesel ship. I served in the Navy and I know this smell. The smell isn't dissipating. As a matter of fact, it appears to be worse. Where in the hell is it coming from?"

"Well, jeez, I really don't smell anything, Jack. Whatever you are smelling may be from mothballs, clothes that were dry cleaned—in fact, from anything in your house that gives off odors, like laundry detergent."

Able then began opening closet doors in various bedrooms, sniffing each as if he were trying to locate mothballs or some other odor-causing pollutant.

"Able, I don't buy that. You know we did not have that smell here before your men did their extermination. It started that very evening. The first couple of times you came here you admitted that you smelled a strong familiar odor. You had no doubt it was from whatever your people used in their extermination. As a matter of fact, you told me what they used was perfectly safe. By the way, Able, what did they use?"

"They used Dursban TC, an EPA-approved, safe chemical. It's perfectly safe. But this is kind of a mystery to me. I don't know where the odor is coming from."

"I've been in the basement several times, and the smell seems to be stronger there."

"Okay. I'll check that out."

I followed Able into the basement and he agreed the odor was stronger as we approached the crawlspace. He climbed into the crawlspace and moved to the front foundation wall.

"I'll be a son of a bitch! Those dummies forgot to plug the holes!"

Able shined his flashlight on the unplugged holes and said, "Take a look at that. Can you imagine? Those guys forgot to plug the holes. I'll be damned!"

I was being overcome by the odor. I became light-headed and confused and went outside. Able followed me and said, "Well, we certainly solved that mystery."

"What mystery is that, Able?"

"Well, that's where the smell is coming from."

"Where?"

"The holes."

"What holes are those, Able?"

"Well, when we do our work we drill holes in the ground around the house and sometimes we drill holes in the foundation blocks of the crawlspace and the basement. And if you don't plug up those holes, the chemicals you put in the holes give off odors and those odors come right back into the crawlspace."

"So they should have plugged the holes?"

"Yep. If they had plugged the holes, you wouldn't have this odor."

"What do we do now? Is it too late to plug the holes?"

"Well, I also noticed that the crawlspace didn't have any vents in it."

"So?"

"You never drill holes in an unvented crawlspace. The smell in there is heavy."

"Able, I have never been in the crawlspace. How did the smell get into the house? I don't even know what your guys did. Explain it to me as simply as you can."

"Well, you remember you had a lot of termites in your house and you asked me to get rid of them for you. Now the method we used was a chemical treatment with Dursban, a very safe chemical approved by the EPA. Now those termites are subterranean termites, and if they are in the house, they have to go outside the house once every 24 hours to stay alive. So our strategy is to make a complete chemical barrier around the perimeter of your house. We inject this chemical, which is poisonous to the termites, into the soil about every 18 inches completely around your house. That way, when the termites either go in or go out they have to go through this poison barrier and it kills them. Now we did not stay outside of your house all the way. At certain points we injected these holes into the foundation blocks in your crawlspace and in your basement. Now we just discovered that the holes were unplugged."

"What does that mean, Able?"

"Well, it means that the odors from the chemicals came right back out of the unplugged holes into the crawlspace. Since the crawlspace was not vented, the odors went through the floor into your house and also went from the crawlspace into your basement and into your house. Now do you understand?"

"Yeah, Able. I think I understand what happened. Now what can we do about it?"

"Well, Jack, if you'll give me permission, I'll get a contractor to come out here and put vents in. Then I'll have him plug the holes, and then I'll put a fan in the crawlspace and one in the basement and we'll turn those suckers on, let them blow until all the foul air has disappeared. Simple."

A week later, Dog (not his real name), a husky, handsome contractor arrived at the house and, with a big smile, on his face told me he was there to plug the holes and vent the crawlspace.

A helluva lot of noise followed.

I did not realize that venting the crawlspace meant using sledge hammers and other equipment to knock a hole in the front foundation wall and another hole in the rear foundation wall.

We chatted after he finished his work and Dog told me he used to work for Able.

"Why did you quit?" I asked.

"I couldn't stand the stink of the chemicals! I got sick every day. I became confused, light-headed, nauseous, and then I had trouble with my vision and I started getting tremors. I decided to get the hell out of that kind of business. That extermination shit sucks."

"Dog, you mean to tell me those chemicals are dangerous to the people who work with them?"

"You bet your sweet ass! Those suckers are poison. They not only kill the bugs but they'll knock out your nervous system and make you sick as hell."

"I had no idea."

"I'm surprised a smart lawyer like you don't know that exposure to toxic chemicals can make you sick. Now I know everybody don't get sick. Everybody's different. But I sure did and you don't look too hot to me either. Boy, your house really stinks. That's from the damn solvent."

"What solvent?"

"Well, no disrespect, but I ain't being paid to teach you a chemistry lesson. Why don't you just get some literature on the stuff Able used and read all about it. I'm just a blue-collar worker and I don't read much, but I know that chemicals give off odors and sometimes make people very sick."

"Able told me it was safe and approved by the EPA."

"Bullshit! What did you expect him to say? That's how he makes his living. Next time he comes around he'll tell you the odor is from your dry cleaning or from mothballs or laundry detergent. I'm getting the hell out of here. It's Miller time!"

3

Medication

The vents, the plugs, the fans—nothing helped. The odor remained and I was becoming ill. My nose was stuffed, my eyes burned and my head hurt. Difficulty breathing, fatigue and nervousness followed one after the other. I thought the symptoms would disappear in a day or two, but they didn't.

A few days after the treatment, I went to the Veterans' Administration Center. As usual, there was a long wait. I felt guilty seeing the many veterans with obvious disabilities, some in distress and some in wheelchairs. Their problems made mine seem trivial. I had not lost an arm or a leg or an eye. I could walk and talk and function without assistance. But I was in distress and pain.

It is difficult to quantify pain. In my mind, what was happening to me required medical treatment, but my battle scars were not visible. I looked like the healthiest man in the waiting room.

The VA doctor, a very competent practitioner who had my confidence, listened to my history and complaints, gave me a routine examination and prescribed some medication. He did not seem concerned about the chemical fumes or that I remained in the house.

A few days later I went to my family doctor with the same history and complaints. He also prescribed medication. No one suggested that I get out of the house.

My instinct told me to get out of the house until the odor was tolerable.

I left many times during the day and night. I usually felt better after spending time outside, but nothing sudden or dramatic. It took a long time to clear my head when it ached. And then I would return to the house because I felt okay.

I had a dilemma. On the one hand, it was obvious that I was not feeling well in the house, but I was not feeling well anywhere. And I was assured that the chemical was safe. No one told me to get out of the house. Eloise was in the house and she was not complaining of anything, except the hacking cough she never had before.

It was nothing new for me to have a headache or a stomachache. What was different was the failure of the medications to provide relief. I was nervous and depressed, frustrated and angry.

To make matters worse, the damned termites returned two weeks after the extermination.

Why was this happening to me?

4

Return of the Termites
Dursban Literature

I notified Able that we were blessed with more termites.
"No shit!" he said.

"No, termites," I replied.

Able returned and gave me a few brochures published by Dow Chemical, the manufacturer of Dursban. One was entitled "Dursban TC: Peace of Mind Termite Control." Another was "Dursban TC: The Subterranean Termite Problem and Solution." And the third was "Selecting a Termiticide." The brochures contained quite a bit of material on Dursban and on termites, none of which I had ever seen before. The information was comforting and reassuring. Here is what "Selecting a Termiticide" said:

"HERE'S WHY YOU SHOULD SELECT
DURSBAN* TC TO CONTROL
THE TERMITE THREAT IN YOUR HOME.

It works fast and for a long time!

National Forest Service tests show DURSBAN TC is still effective sixteen years after application. And all indications are that it will keep working for a long time to kill all species of subterranean termites.

You can breathe easy.

DURSBAN TC applications conform to airborne guidelines for safe levels within dwellings as set by the National Academy of Sciences.

You can forget it's there.

DURSBAN TC is biodegradable when exposed to light and air. But, in the soil around and under your house it lasts for years and years.

It only smells for a little while.

DURSBAN TC has an odor which comes from the solvent used in the formulation. You'll know when DURSBAN TC has been used. To many people this odor isn't even objectionable and coupled with the proven safety record of DURSBAN TC it's nothing to be concerned about. In two or three days the odor will be gone.

Only DURSBAN TC can be deactivated.

We can't guarantee against accidents. But we can say that if there was spillage or error during application, DURSBAN TC can easily be deactivated from surfaces, air systems and water sources. That's exclusive with DURSBAN TC. Deactivation procedures and residue removal should be conducted only by your Pest Control Operator.

DURSBAN TC—the worry-free, peace-of-mind termiticide.

Your home is your biggest investment. Your family is your greatest love. You'll have to agree that both deserve the best protection possible. DURSBAN TC offers proven termite protection, plus an excellent safety record.

DURSBAN TC
Termiticide Concentrate

*Trademark of The Dow Chemical Company"

• • •

If you can't believe Dow Chemical, one of the largest inter-national petrochemical corporations in the world, who can you believe?

5

"If Dursban wasn't safe,
they wouldn't be allowed to use it."

I went to the public health officer in the community, a medical doctor I respected and whom I had known for years. I explained my predicament and how it had followed the treatment of my house for termites.

"Doc, I'm really worried about what is happening to me and to my home. I was told the chemical used was perfectly safe and the odor would disappear in a matter of hours. This has been going on for several weeks. What can you tell me about this situation?"

I can still see the warm and affectionate smile on his face. If he were wearing a red suit, he would look exactly like Santa Claus, right down to the beard and jovial demeanor.

"Well, Jack, I don't see that you have anything to worry about. In all my years of practicing medicine and as a public health officer, I have never heard of anyone getting ill from chemicals used to treat a house for termites. I don't believe there is any cause for alarm. As a matter of fact, we don't even deal with this kind of problem. Pesticide operators are licensed by the Department of Agriculture and they regulate those guys. I just don't think you have anything to worry about. If Dursban wasn't safe, they wouldn't be allowed to use it. You know, Dursban has only been on the market a short time."

"What did they use before that?"

"Chlordane."

"Why did they stop using chlordane?"

"They found out it was a carcinogen. People were getting cancer from it. They banned chlordane from the market, but there is still a lot of it around. Anyway, let's get together for lunch one of these days when you feel better. You look like you lost some weight."

"Yeah. Twelve pounds."

"Maybe I ought to have my house sprayed," he laughed as he patted his ample belly.

6

The Furnace Filter

Despite the many glorious advantages and benefits of using Dursban, Able decided to go after the new termites with a different concoction which he said was called Demon TC. He said Demon TC would not have any odor and was much less toxic than Dursban. I found that to be a strange statement, coming from one who had never identified Dursban as being toxic. And, I hate to admit, I really didn't understand that these chemicals were hazardous to people. "Toxic," to me, was just another adjective. It took a long time for me to get it. "Cide" means "to kill." "Pesticide" means "to kill pests." But I had never made the connection that pesticides were harmful to people. Like the public health doctor said, "If it wasn't safe, they wouldn't be allowed to use it."

Able completed the treatment with Demon TC, and another odor—a combination of the Dursban and the Demon TC—was left behind.

I left the house and wandered around the neighborhood to look at other houses with people living normal lives inside. I wondered if a homeless person and I shared feelings.

I made another call to Able.

"Able, this is Jack. Another 911. On the double, please."

Able came right over.

"Able, this is worse than before. What in the hell is going on?"

"Well, Jack, I will take another trip through your house and basement. I never had any experience like this before."

He went through the house again and this time came out with

what he said was a filter. We were outside on the rear patio.

"This is about the filthiest filter I have ever seen in my life, and I'll bet this is what's causing your problem."

"Where did you get that filter?"

"From your furnace."

"What has that got to do with this odor?"

"Well, all the air that goes into your furnace goes through this filter first. Look how dirty it is. Smell it!"

He stuck it under my nose. I backed away.

"No, thanks, Able. I can smell it from here."

"Watch this," he said as he struck the filter against the brick patio wall. Black soot and filth enveloped both of us as Able banged the filter time and again against the wall.

"What in the hell are you doing?"

"Getting this shit out of the filter. This is contaminated with all that crap."

"What are you telling me, Able?"

"When I was down in your basement I noticed your furnace for the first time. I said to myself, 'I'll bet there is an air intake on Jack's furnace. And since it has been cold, Jack's furnace has been running and sucking all this foul air into his intake.' And I noticed you have a duct system with vents throughout your house. So it's really very simple. The mystery is finally solved."

"It's not simple to me, Able. Go on."

"Well, the furnace sucked the foul air through the intake into the duct system and the blowers in the furnace blow this foul air through the ducts. The foul air eventually went through all of your vents into all of your rooms. The odors which should have remained in the concrete blocks, had they been plugged, escaped and were blown throughout your entire house. That's why it stinks in there. Now do you understand?"

"Yeah, Able. That is quite a tale. Now what can we do about it?"

"Well, I suggest we go over to Sears and get a new filter. They only cost a dollar or two. I can't believe you had such a dirty filter in your furnace."

"Hell, I never even knew there was a filter in the furnace. At this point I am not sure I have a furnace or a basement. But I am sure of one thing. I have got 'Tsorus.' Do you know what Tsorus is, Able?"

"No."

"It is a Yiddish word for trouble. That is one thing I am sure of. I have Tsorus."

"I'm surprised I didn't think about the furnace and look there in the beginning. I just thought you would have a clean filter. You should have turned the furnace off when you first smelled the odor."

"The odor that just came out of the filter smells like the same odor from the chemicals you brought in the house. Are you telling me this filter caused the odor?"

"No, I'm just telling you you need a clean filter. Seems to me a successful lawyer like you would have a clean filter in his furnace. They only cost a buck or two. No big deal. I'll get you one myself over at Sears."

"Hold it a minute! It's perfectly obvious the smell in the house came from the chemicals you used to kill the termites. Isn't that correct?"

"Well, I guess you could say that."

"I'm not just saying that. You're the one who said it originally to me. You said you solved the mystery weeks ago. You traced all these odor problems back to your employees who left the holes unplugged. Remember the unplugged holes in the foundation in the unvented crawlspace and the basement? And then you got a contractor to vent the crawlspace."

"Yeah."

"And aren't you the same guy who told me the fans would blow the bad air out of the crawlspace and the house and we could all get on with our lives?"

"Well, I didn't exactly say that."

"Well, Able, if you knew all that before you injected the chemicals into my wall, why did you put that shit into my foundation walls and fail to plug the holes?"

"That's just the way we do it. It's done everyday. How the hell did I know this odor would stay around here this long. You know, I've already lost money on your job. I've been out here a half dozen times. I tried to take care of your problem, and I don't know what else to do. I'll get you a new filter. You call Dow and see what they have to say."

"I'll do that, Able."

7

The Psychiatrist

I left the house and wandered the streets for a while. At one point Able came to the door and spoke to Eloise. He asked if I had returned and Eloise told him I had not. He suggested that this odor problem was something in my head and that perhaps I should see a psychiatrist.

I was familiar with a psychiatrist's office. I am a Type A personality with frequent bouts of depression and anxiety. I was told I had a chemical imbalance. The treatment was talking to the therapist and taking medication. I was fortunate to have an excellent therapist who was a researcher at the National Institutes of Health and an expert in depression. I had taken almost every antidepressant on the market with little success. If I took something for my depression, it gave me a stomachache. If I took something to calm my stomach, it gave me a headache. We never found the right prescription. There was always an unexpected side effect.

"You might as well be living in the 14th century," said Dr. Norman Rosenthal. "The last 600 years of pharmacology are of little help to you. The only prescription you tolerate is a mild dose of Lorazepan. Some patients require many times the dosage you take. You might as well take a placebo."

I sought therapy when I was under a lot of stress. As a trial lawyer, I felt this was a means of remaining functional and maintaining my stability. I needed to be able to think rationally and make decisions based upon merit, not emotion. I also knew I could not depend upon medications and that I would have to learn to control my emotions. I saw Dr. Rosenthal before and after the termite treatments. He concluded that there was a definite cause-and-effect relationship between the exposure to the Dursban termiticide and my symptoms. "That house is poisoning you," he said. "It's time to get out."

So I did.

8

The Nearest Relative

An elderly aunt lived alone nearby in a large home. Her husband, Father's brother, died several years before. Eloise and I loved her and spent a lot of time with her.

I told her what had happened at my home and asked if she would let me stay with her for a few days until the bad odor cleared out. She invited me to stay as long as I needed. She gave me an upstairs bedroom and a private bath. I slept for several nights with the windows wide open to clear my head and my lungs. I felt better than I had felt in my own house. I moved more of my clothes and personal effects to Aunt Ruth's and began to spend more time there. She asked what was going on. She pointed out that Eloise remained at home and seemed fine. She asked Eloise to join me. Eloise declined and said she was okay.

"Are you sure you and Eloise are not having domestic problems? You know I really like Eloise, and I don't understand why she doesn't come over here with you."

"No, Aunt Ruth. We're not having any problems. I am here strictly because I get sick in my house."

"Well, I just never heard of anything like that before."

"I never did either, but it's happening."

"Well, when are you going back?"

That question shook me up. I certainly did not want to put her under any stress, so I said, "Actually, Aunt Ruth, I think it best if I leave this afternoon. I regret if I have put you to any trouble."

"Well, I know it's a big house, but my sister is coming to visit me and then my grandchildren and other company. I'm sorry."

"That's quite all right, Aunt Ruth. I appreciate your hospitality. I'll be okay."

"I just never heard of anybody getting sick from a termite treatment of their house, and none of my friends have either."

I moved my clothes out that afternoon.

I thought that after a few days at Aunt Ruth's I would be strong enough to tolerate my own house. That was not what happened.

When I returned to my home, the problems also returned.

I had to get out once more.

The Early Moves
Homes - Motels - and Other Locations
Nausea - Headaches - and Disorientation

Some excerpts from my daily dairy:

Tuesday, April 26, 1988 — *Spent night at Venice Motel.*

Saturday, April 30, 1988 — *To Bedford, Pa. Nite at motel in Bedford.*

Sunday, May 1, 1988 — *11 p.m. check into Venice, Rm. 496.*

Tuesday, May 3, 1988 — *I woke up at the Venice in distress with nasal, eye, stomach problems. I decided to look for an apartment.*

Thursday, May 5, 1988 — *Biospherics, Inc., at house. Took air samples and history.*

I checked out of the Venice on May 7 and left for Virginia Beach, Va., to attend a Lions Club convention. I hoped the salt air would make it easier to breathe and give me relief. The beach and the sea air were part of my happiest and healthiest memories.

But the weather was cool and rainy and the motel was several miles from the beach. The beach was wet and empty. The motel windows didn't open and the indoor air was polluted.

I returned home on May 17 and was invited to stay at the home of a friend. I stayed there for several nights, but again because of something in the air that I was unable to pin down, I spent more time outside than inside. I had to leave.

Eloise arranged to have our wall-to-wall carpet steam cleaned and the drapes dry cleaned. We thought that cleaning the upholstered furniture, the drapes and carpet would make a difference in the air quality. It did not. It added a smell of dry cleaning to the already foul odor. We were advised to get an ozone machine and put it in the den to clear the air. Ozone machines are used to clear the air after a fire. After several days with the ozone machine, Eloise was coughing and hacking more than before and her eyes were tearing. The ozone machine did not work for us. We moved to the Luxury Budget Inn.

We traveled to a rustic resort in West Virginia, which we had visited many times with pleasure before the Dursban incident. But now I couldn't tolerate the place.

I became very ill at the Budget Inn. It was like I was drunk. I phoned my doctor and made no sense. I phoned Dr. Rosenthal and sounded like I was intoxicated. The doctors told me to get out of there.

The next day, one of my oldest friends, David Ginsberg, who had recently lost his lovely wife, invited me to spend some time at his house. I was given a private bedroom upstairs with a private bath and full use of the kitchen. Dave and his son Bob did their best to make me comfortable. I stayed a few weeks, but for some reason I was becoming disoriented and confused.

And so it went throughout April and May. Visits to doctors, calls, attempts to fix the house, wandering, spending nights in different places, investigating the air at my home and office—nothing could explain what was happening to me.

I carried my affliction wherever I went, wherever I slept. At the same time, I was certain all of this was going to clear up soon.

10

Dow Chemical U.S.A.

To find out what was happening to me and to the house, I contacted representatives of Dow Chemical, the manufacturer of Dursban. The people with whom I spoke were courteous, considerate and helpful.

I spoke first with Ann G. She put me in touch with Jim V., an industrial hygienist with a bachelor's degree in chemistry and an expert on Dursban. Later, Ken R. phoned and asked me to share my facts with him.

I explained to them what had happened. They questioned me at length about the way the Dursban was applied at my home. When I repeated what Able had told me about the unplugged holes, it was evident to the Dow people that Able had failed to follow instructions on the label and on other material. Failure to plug the holes was a misapplication and the obvious cause of the odor. The Dow people told me my physical complaints and symptoms were consistent with overexposure to Dursban and with organophosphate poisoning. They explained that Dursban was composed mostly of chlorpyrifos which was a cholinesterase inhibitor, and that overexposure would almost certainly result in symptoms such as mine, and that the odor in the house was to be expected if holes were not plugged. This was very enlightening. These people were not surprised. Obviously my story was not unique. For the first time I knew that I was not the only person who had ever been poisoned by exposure to Dursban. In fact, the people I spoke to at Dow were specifically assigned to help people like me, victims of misapplication.

"Well, what do we do now? I need help. My house is not livable and I'm sick." "Well, Mr. Berkson, we're going to send you information and send a representative from our Richmond office to install activated carbon filters in all of your vents. He'll be there in a few days. His name is Dave McC. and he'll be calling you shortly. One other thing, the odor is not from the chlorpyrifos but from xylene, the solvent in that termiticide. The xylene is what you are smelling. So there really isn't anything to worry about. We'll send you some papers on how to reduce the odor. In the meantime you ought to have some air samples taken in the house to determine the concentration of the Dursban in the air, and you ought to have some blood tests taken to find out the concentration of the Dursban or the xylene or other chemicals in your blood. Who is your toxicologist?"

"I have never seen a toxicologist."

"Well, we have toxicologists here at Dow but we believe you would be happier if you had your own toxicologist. Then have your toxicologist get in touch with our toxicologist. And stop worrying about this because as a last resort we can always deactivate the Dursban that was put in there. There's a way to deactivate it. So we can help at your house and we can also help you. Keep in touch."

The dark clouds hanging over me and my home were about to disappear.

11

The Tent and the "Y"

Early in June of 1988, it became clear that sleeping in other people's houses was not making me better. I was not recovering, and my health problems were making my hosts uncomfortable. I could not expect anyone to understand what was happening to me. They were not in any distress in their homes.

The problem was me. Something happened to me after the termite treatments. I never had any discomfort in the homes of any relatives or friends or in motels or hotels before March 23. I had slept all over the world.

It was real, not psychosomatic.

My first priority was to find a safe and healthy place to live until I could tolerate my house. I had no way of knowing what, when or where that might be.

I had lived aboard navy ships, in quonset huts overseas, camped as a scoutmaster and with my family on our farm along the Potomac River. The idea of camping again sounded like the right choice.

I bought a two-man tent and other camping supplies. I pitched the tent in my backyard some distance from the house. A large spruce tree that I had planted 40 years earlier provided shade. I used a picnic table for a desk and moved my telephone outdoors with a 100-foot extension cord. This was going to be an adventure, I thought.

I thought it would be safe to go back into the house whenever I needed to use the toilet or to shave or shower. But whenever I went inside, the stomach distress and nervousness would reappear in a matter of minutes. The odor in the house seemed to trigger various symptoms. I would become agitated and hyperactive and my mind raced. I had an urgent need to urinate and defecate, and while I was sitting on the john my eyes would start to tear, my nose would stop up, and my mouth would fill with saliva. I wanted to get the hell out of there as quickly as possible but I needed to stay on the john. The longer I sat, the more severe the symptoms became. But as soon as I got up and headed outside, I had the urgent need to return.

When I was outside, I had to go inside, and when I was inside, I had to go outside.

The nearest public building with bathroom facilities that I could use was the YMCA, about a mile from my house. I was a member of the "Y" and exercised there regularly. But it was not convenient to live in a tent in my backyard and have to drive downtown to use the facilities of the YMCA.

Each night I was optimistic that the next day would be better. Weeks had passed.

I used the men's locker room along with a lot of other fellows who lived at the "Y" or who worked out there. There was no carpet on the floor. These guys didn't use fancy fragrances and I never noticed any cleaning spray. Later on I decided to try out the fancier and more expensive quarters at the "Y" known as the Men's Athletic Club. It was carpeted wall to wall and had fragrances in the air. Some of these guys used fragrant soap, hair spray and after-shave lotions. An attendant sprayed the walls and mirrors with a chemical cleaner. Within a few minutes, my symptoms returned. I got out of there in a hurry. I was better off in the regular locker room without the carpet, than in the Athletic Club with carpet, sprays and air fresheners.

12

Father of the Bride

During all of this hullabaloo about the termites, I forgot that my daughter, Susan, was to be married in New Jersey on June 12. As the father of the bride, I was expected to give her away. I did not want to give away my only daughter, especially since she had selected as her groom a short writer from Brooklyn.

A few days before the most important event in her life, I called her from my tent. I explained what was going on and told her I might not be able to attend her wedding. We had a father-daughter talk.

"Dad, are you kidding or what?"

"No, Susan. I am not kidding."

"Are you telling me that you are not coming to Jerry's and my wedding because you have termites in your home? Are you out of your mind, Dad?"

"Some people think I am."

"Well, this is no time to play games. We will see you up here at the Marriott Motel Somerset in four days. Don't forget, Dad, you are paying for the wedding!"

That did it.

I decided to forget about the termites, rent a tux and make the effort.

Susan was living in Plainfield. Susan had a beautiful voice and was studying to be a Cantor. She was to be married at the Temple in Plainfield, where she then held the position of Cantor.

It took Eloise and me three days to travel from Maryland to

New Jersey, a distance of approximately 250 miles. The first day we stopped in Lionville, Pennsylvania. That was as far as I could go.

The second day we stopped at Valley Forge. I remember looking at the rough cabins and tents where the Revolutionary soldiers had spent a freezing winter under the command of General George Washington. I identified with the soldiers. These simple cabins and tents looked good to me. There was nothing in them to give off odors or make me sick. I offered a tour guide a premium to let me spend the night in one of the cabins.

"No one sleeps here but General Washington, buddy! Find yourself a nice motel," the tour guide said.

We found an inn at Lambertville, N.J. across the Delaware River from New Hope, Pennsylvania, which I tolerated well. The third day we traveled from Lambertville to Plainfield, where we ended up at the Marriott Motel Somerset. That Friday evening we attended the Temple service and heard Cantor Susan sing. She received many favorable comments and we were very proud of her.

The following day I visited Jack Garver, an old high school friend, at a hospital in New Brunswick. He was recuperating from operations on his knees. Jack and I grew up together in Hagerstown. He was an artist and head of the art department at Lawrenceville, a fashionable boys' prep school in New Jersey. We spent several hours reminiscing about high school and our experiences in World War II (Jack was severely wounded in a battle in France and was later an MP in Paris). Of course we discussed our sexual conquests, he with his bum knees—now new knees—and me with some kind of mysterious illness. That visit reinforced a friendship that exceeded a half century.

I was not in very good shape for the wedding, but my daughter was a beautiful bride. My memories of the wedding are very positive, and I had no illness or side effects that I can recall. Jerry, my new son-in-law, turned out to be a good husband and a good friend, despite his early years in Brooklyn.

We returned home from Plainfield on Monday, making the trip in one day. I went to the YMCA, showered, used the toilet, and went home to my backyard. I dreamed about serving under General Washington at Valley Forge. I awoke with New Hope.

13

The RV

The initial exhilaration of living outdoors began to wear off after a few weeks. Using a picnic table for a desk and conferences and sleeping outdoors was enjoyable. Running back and forth to the "Y" was not.

My friend, Rupe Cuneen, suggested an RV.

"What's an RV?"

"A recreational vehicle. They have everything you need in them. It is like a house trailer, except smaller and portable. You can bring one right up here in your backyard where your tent is and hook it up to the electricity and water already in your house. You will have a place right here to shave, shower, toilet, eat, sleep, and work. You don't have to run to the 'Y' every time your bladder gets full. That's the way to go till you can get back in your house. Why don't you give me a tough problem to solve."

Rupe was a genius and independent as hell. A former client and business associate, he farmed 1,500 acres by himself and could build anything. He was now a Realtor and a computer whiz. Rupe was a friend of mankind.

His formal education was interrupted by service in the Navy during World War II. He entered college at the age of 60, older than any of his professors. Upon graduation he was so elated that he wore his cap and gown for four weeks.

We shopped around for an RV. We had to get a permit from the City and approval from our adjoining neighbors. That done, Eloise and I purchased a 1983 Yellowstone 29-foot Camino travel trailer for $8,525.77. It was delivered the next day, June 15. Rupe helped us set up in my backyard. We connected the electricity and ran a hose from an outdoor spigot to the RV. All the necessities of life were there. No longer would I have to worry that my neighbors would see me slip out of my tent at night and water the flowers in the backyard.

14

The Visit to the Toxicologist

June 16 was a memorable day. It was on that day that I traveled
to Washington, D.C., for my appointment with Dr. L. W., a
toxicologist at George Washington University Medical Center. I
drove to Shady Grove and took the Metro to Foggy Bottom. I
walked around Foggy Bottom within spitting distance of this
hospital, asking people up and down the street how to find GW
Hospital. I was confused and disoriented. I had been a federal
attorney in Washington for more than five years, from 1970 to
1976, on the staff of the U. S. General Services Administration.
GSA offices were at 18th and F Street, N.W., a few blocks from
GW hospital. I often walked past the hospital during the lunch
hour. I knew exactly where it was, but on the day of my
appointment I had difficulty finding my way from the Metro stop
to the hospital which was practically across the street.

I told Dr. W. my history. She examined me. She asked, "What
was your cholinesterase level before you had your house treated
with Dursban?"

"Doctor, I never even heard the word 'cholinesterase' before I
had my house treated with Dursban. I'm still not sure what it is. I
don't have any idea what my cholinesterase level was before the
incident."

She explained that Dursban or its major ingredient, chlorpyrifos, is a cholinesterase inhibitor. Cholinesterase is some kind
of enzyme that is essential for the nervous system to work properly.
The Dursban poisons the nervous system of the termites and they
die. In some cases chlorpyrifos may also affect the nervous system

of people.

She seemed to be saying that termites and people are reliant upon the same—cholinesterase—for the health of the nervous system.

I was wondering if I heard her correctly.

Imagine, an insect less than an inch long and weighing less than an ounce has a nervous system that works like a person's. That may explain my nervousness, irritability, and confusion following my exposure to Dursban. Nevertheless, she was asking me what my cholinesterase level was before my house was treated with Dursban. I tell her I have no idea. She tells me, "Well, it would be helpful to know."

I had been to a number of doctors before I was examined by Dr. W. Not one of them had even mentioned the word "cholinesterase."

I recall asking one of these doctors to do this test after I read about it. He declined, saying it was outside of his field of practice. I went to the pathologist at a local hospital and asked that his laboratory technicians test me for cholinesterase. The technicians told me they didn't know what it was. They said they looked in their lab books and couldn't find anything about it.

"Don't you mean 'cholesterol?'" one said. "We can do that."

This question came up time and again, especially after I filed a lawsuit. This was an important test because it confirmed a diagnosis of organophosphate poisoning.

To now, my complaints were mostly about pain, and pain is subjective. Pain does not show up on a test. I do not know of any medical test to prove that one has a headache. Tests for gastrointestinal pain often come back negative. That doesn't mean there is no pain. It means the test didn't show any physical abnormality. They could see my eye was irritated or bloodshot or tearing or that my nasal passages were swollen or irritated or blocked. But what they saw did not prove the symptoms were caused by exposure to Dursban, an organophosphate.

The questions I wanted answered were: 1. What is causing my symptoms? 2. What is your diagnosis? 3. What is the treatment?

I needed treatment.

Treating the symptoms without treating the underlying cause is not effective. I knew there was a link between my exposure to the Dursban and my complaints.

Organophosphate poisoning can be diagnosed from one's history. It is confirmed by comparing the cholinesterase level in the blood before the exposure with the level after the exposure. A drop in the level confirms it has been inhibited. But how many people have ever heard of cholinesterase, or have it tested before they are poisoned?

You would think that a simple blood test, described on the label of Dursban, would be familiar to any experienced doctor in an emergency room, and certainly to the pathologist at an accredited hospital.

Dr. W. diagnosed me with organophosphate poisoning, based on my history and her exam. There was no need for a cholinesterase test. She suggested that I continue to ventilate my house.

"Make sure the holes in the crawlspace are plugged. It is probably a good idea to stay out of the house and use the RV as living quarters until such time as the house clears up."

She did not know when the odor would disappear but she felt that by fall I would be able to move back into the house. She said she knew Jim V. and the people at Dow. She said she would call them and tell them to speed up the carbon filter treatment in the house.

I had now been examined by a leading expert in the field of toxicology at an eminent national medical center. She gave me advice to follow and hope for recovery. I felt that she believed me and would help me get well.

15

A Similar Case

A woman, whose name I never knew, was also a patient of Dr. Rosenthal's. She had the Saturday morning therapy session before mine. When her session was over, she entered the waiting room where I was sitting. We would chat like long-lost friends for five or ten minutes, enough time for the doctor to clear his head and prepare for me.

I don't recall how it was that Beauty (not her name) and I started talking to each other. I imagine it had something to do with the fact that she was beautiful. I was curious about what it was that brought this bright-eyed, well-dressed and cheerful woman to a psychiatrist's office. She was equally curious about me and my conflicts. Psychiatry and our respect for Dr. Rosenthal was our common bond.

We were interested in how the other was getting along and how long it would be before we "graduated" from Dr. Rosenthal's program.

At an earlier session, I told her about the termites and what was happening to me and to my house. I was frustrated because my symptoms and the problems with the house persisted. I still had never met or read of anyone else who had developed an illness like mine following a pesticide application. Beauty was interested in my plight and promised to help. On June 18, she gave me a copy of *The New Yorker* magazine dated Jan. 4, 1988. She opened it to an article entitled, "Annals of Medicine, The Fumigation Chamber," by Berton Roueché. It was about two doctors from Philadelphia—specifically a woman doctor referred to as Betty

Page and her husband, Lewis. They owned a cottage on a lake in northern Pennsylvania, where they spent weekends. Betty Page became ill on a trip to the cottage in 1984. She had nausea, abdominal cramps and diarrhea. She didn't link it with anything.

The following week she returned and was stricken with similar symptoms, plus saliva filling her mouth. She went home and saw several doctors who found nothing wrong with her. She developed breathing problems and other symptoms and saw more doctors, but got no effective treatment. Doctors were unable to find anything wrong despite thorough exams and tests. She became ill each time she returned to the cottage. Even though she was a doctor, she made no connection between the cottage and what was happening to her. Apparently she did not notice any odor like I did. She finally discovered an invoice on the kitchen table from an exterminating company that sprayed the cottage regularly for carpenter ants.

She phoned the exterminator to find out what pesticide was used and told him of her symptoms. The exterminator said he saw no connection between the spray and her symptoms. He told her they used FICAM and DURSBAN.

She phoned her husband in Philadelphia and asked him to look up "insecticides" "organophosphates" in the standard text. Dursban is an organophosphate.

Suddenly it all came together.

What happened to Dr. Page was almost exactly what happened to me.

This article probably did more to validate my case in my own mind than anything that had happened before. It was almost as if Mr. Roueché had written the story to tell me I was not the only one who became ill following an exposure to Dursban. I made copies of this article and distributed it to my skeptical doctors. It was like finding authority and significant precedent for a legal case after months of unproductive research. We finally struck oil. Dr. Page was on leave from her academic duties as an assistant professor of clinical medicine at the University of Pennsylvania School of Medicine as a result of her exposure to Dursban. She was still on leave when the article was published in 1988.

"The Fumigation Chamber" ends on a wistful note:

"Dr. Page smiled her wide smile and shook her head. The smile faded away. 'I'm just beginning to realize that the world is a very dangerous place. It's something nobody really wants to think about. I mean the thousands and thousands of toxic chemicals that have become so much a part of modern living. I mean the people who use them without really knowing what they can do. I mean the where and how and why they use them. It's frightening. I think I'm pretty much recovered now. I haven't had any trouble for over a year. But you never know. The only thing I'm sure of is that I'm going to have to be very careful for the rest of my life.'" (From "The Fumigation Chamber" © 1988 Berton Roueché. Originally in *The New Yorker*.)

Beauty had furnished me an account of another human being who had a case history similar to mine, "a case on all fours," we used to say when I practiced law in those good old days B.C. (Before Contamination).

16

The Man from Dow

Dow Chemical U.S.A. sent David F. McCormick from Richmond, Va., to install activated charcoal filters in all of the heating and air conditioning vents in my home. He and a helper spent a day on the job. I watched them work from outside. Mr. McCormick gave me literature about odor reduction and deactivation of Dursban. This was proof that Dursban had an odor that sometimes had to be reduced and sometimes deactivated. I was impressed by Mr. McCormick and his work and his openness in answering the many questions I had about Dursban. This went a long way toward defusing my anger with the manufacturer of the chemical that I believe had poisoned me.

I received the following letter from McCormick:

DOW CHEMICAL U.S.A.

June 28, 1988   8002 DISCOVERY DRIVE-SUITE 415
                                           RICHMOND, VA 23288
                                           804   288-1601

Mr. Jacob Berkson

RE; ACTIVATED CARBON FILTERS

Dear Mr. Berkson:

As a follow-up to my visit, I wanted to remind you to remove the charcoal filter inside the heat return unit (in the basement) prior to turning the heating system on later in the year. The charcoal filter is very effective in removing organic vapors, but is not a substitute for the lint and dirt filter on your heater for the long term.

My advice is to turn your heater fan on and let it run to obtain maximum filtration of ambient air. I also suggest the same for the air conditioning unit. Both units will serve to constantly recirculate air through the double filtering system. All other filters can remain in your system as long as they are effective. I would expect them to last several months.

Mr. Berkson, it was a pleasure to be of service. Please telephone me if you have questions.

Sincerely,

David F. McCormick
Industrial Insecticide Sales

• • •

"Now we are getting somewhere," I thought to myself.

17

Results of Air Sampling for Chlorpyrifos (Dursban)

I received a written report from Biospherics Incorporated dated July 11, 1988, on the air sampling they performed on May 5, 1988.

The three-page report, supported by three pages of technical data, included a description of the sampling strategy and analyses for the detection of chlorpyrifos (Dursban).

The key findings as I understood them were:

"Two air tests (crawlspace and den) had detectable concentrations of Dursban…

"Two wipe samples had detectable concentrations of Dursban…

"…Both results were relatively low and are generally not considered to present a health hazard."

"Not considered to present a health hazard to whom?" I wondered.

Apparently in anticipation of that question, the report stated:

"Although Dursban levels were not detected in significant concentrations, by the time of the inspection, some individuals may react to trace amounts as well as to the standard solvents (typically standard petroleum distillates) used as a carrier for termiticide solutions (e.g. xylene)."

I was obviously one who did react. The concentrations on March 23, 1988, are unknown.

No opinion or data can tell what levels of Dursban were in the house on March 23, 1988, when the termiticide was applied, nor for the weeks before May 5.

The air samples were taken after the injection holes were plugged, the crawlspace was vented, fans had been running continually for six weeks and the windows and doors had been kept open most of the time. The report continued with recommendations:

"Some measures which *might* prove beneficial in further reducing trace termiticide constituents identified at this location include:

"1. Continue current measures being taken to ventilate the basement and crawlspace.

"2. Seal any cracks or openings in crawlspace cinderblocks with polyurethane foam.

"3. Install an activated charcoal filter in the ventilation system to control residual solvent vapors."

The bill from Biospherics totaled $2,132.50.

Able and I split the cost.

I mailed copies to my doctors for their information.

I was still unable to tolerate the house even though it now contained "trace amounts." It would be a long time before I understood how "trace amounts" could produce devastating reactions to nearly every system in my body.

The good news was that I now had a written report from scientific experts who had sampled the air and concluded that the house was safe.

18

News Reports of Other Victims
Trigger Request for Deactivation

During my quest for information about Dursban, I kept hearing that it took the place of chlordane as the pesticide of choice. It was said that chlordane was banned by the federal government because it has been proved to cause cancer in humans.

On July 15, 1988, a news article by Emilio Alvarado in *The Daily Mail*, Hagerstown, Maryland's afternoon newspaper, carried the headline

Lawn products with chlordane sold at auction
Area residents who bought banned chemical alerted

Pertinent parts of the article follow:

"The substance, chlordane, was banned by the federal government in April because it has been proven to cause cancer in humans...

(Wash. Co. Ag Extension agent Don) "Schwartz said the chemical is very dangerous and should be handled with great care.

"'Its first cousin is DDT. It should send up red flags,' he said.

"He said once the chemical is taken into the body by inhalation, through the skin or by ingestion, the body will not be able to rid itself of it." (Reprinted with permission.)

Some people I talked to suspected that the exterminator had used chlordane, but there was no evidence.

I heard many people speak highly of chlordane.

"We used it for years and it worked fine. No one here got cancer. You can't believe all that shit the government puts out," a farmer friend said.

This was echoed time and again. "What can you believe?" I wondered.

That article was soon followed by another of interest. "Orkin sentencing set" was the headline in the August 9, 1988, *The Daily Mail*. Because it was the first article to come to my attention on the subject, it made an indelible impression on me. The short article read as follows:

"ROANOKE, Va. (UPI) — Orkin Exterminating Co., the nation's largest exterminating firm, faces a fine of up to $500,000 after being convicted of a federal misdemeanor charge in the 1986 fumigation deaths of a couple.

"Sentencing is scheduled for Sept. 6 and is expected to be lengthy as government prosecutors try to prove that two workmen's failure to use a monitoring device after treating the home with chemicals led to the death of Hubert and Freida Watson of Galax. Orkin, with headquarters in Atlanta and offices nationwide, was convicted Monday of failing to use a device to detect the chemical Vikane in the Watson home before allowing them to return. In an agreement struck between the government and Orkin's Roanoke lawyer, U.S. District Judge James Turk dismissed four other misdemeanor charges against the company." (Reprinted with permission.)

A friend of mine who had heard about my plight sent me a similar article from *The New York Daily News* of Wednesday, August 10, 1988. The article reads:

"Exterminators guilty

"ROANOKE, Va. — An exterminating company has been convicted of failing to follow label instructions in using a pesticide on the home of a couple that died within a week of the spraying.

"Federal Judge James Turk convicted the Atlanta-based Orkin Exterminating Co. Inc. of violating federal pesticide law in the home of Hubert and Freida Watson, who were allowed to move back in before the house had been ventilated as called for on the label of the pesticide, Vikane.

"Orkin also was accused of removing warning signs before the home was aired out and failing to test the home to make sure it was safe. Watson, 73, died three days after the fumigation; Mrs. Watson, 65, four days after her husband. "Atlanta-based Orkin could be fined

$500,000 when a sentence is imposed Sept. 6."

From this point on I kept a scrapbook of articles about people who were poisoned, injured, damaged or killed by chemical pollution. It developed into A *Canary's Tale,* Volume II. Please refer to the Introduction to this book for a further explanation of Volume II.

On August 30, 1988 I wrote to Dave McCormick at Dow directing him to deactivate the Dursban.

19

Living in the RV

The RV, while not as spacious as any one room in my home, was adequate, and a mansion compared to my tent. The RV had a bedroom, lots of closet space, a bathroom, a small kitchen, and a living room. Everything was built-in to save space.

It was an office and a home. Jack Garver visited and occasionally stayed overnight. It was fun. The RV was alongside this large shady spruce tree. If the weather was not too hot or too humid, the air conditioner was effective. But when it was too hot, the air conditioner couldn't handle the job. It was a bit crowded in the bathroom for even one person.

The windows on all four sides opened. It was almost like sleeping outside.

I now conducted my legal work from the RV and in the backyard at a table beneath the awning. The extension to my office telephone was now in the camper.

"It all depends on the way you look at it," one of my friends said. "So what's wrong with living in your backyard, sleeping in a trailer, and practicing law beneath a towering spruce tree? You're closer to flora and fauna than you've ever been."

"I dated Flora in high school and Fauna in Japan, and you don't know how close I ever got to either of them."

The only physical reaction I got from living in the RV was from the smell of gas. This agitated my nervous system. I called the propane company several times and asked them to check for leaks. The serviceman always arrived promptly, checked out the rig and assured me that the smell was from a safe chemical designed to warn a person that the gas was on. It was not the gas I was smelling but a certain warning chemical. I later learned my immune system no longer distinguished between toxic and nontoxic.

I had never used propane gas before. Changing the gas tanks and hooking up the lines for the stove and the heater was another learning experience.

I later discovered that trailers and RV's are built with materials that contain a lot of formaldehyde. Formaldehyde is an element that is said to cause chemical sensitivity in many people. But whatever odors had originally been in the RV had dissipated by the time I bought it.

The weather and the trailer grew colder together. These temporary residences are not well insulated, and the heater is sometimes overwhelmed by the elements.

So in the fall I began to look for an apartment. I still could not tolerate the house.

20

The Apartment

After looking over a number of rental houses and apartments in the community, I found a two-bedroom, two-bath apartment at Hickory Hill (not the real name), a brick garden apartment project in the countryside about three miles north of my home. It had been built about 30 years ago and at that time was considered the most comfortable apartment complex in the area. My apartment, on the second floor, had a large living room/dining room combination, with sliding doors from the dining room onto a small porch. From the porch one had a sweeping view, first of horses grazing in a grassy meadow, then of cultivated farm fields bordered by a tree line, and beyond the trees rose the Blue Ridge Mountains some 10 miles to the east. The view was beautiful and had a calming effect on the nervous system. The apartment was clean. Waxed and polished hardwood floors glistened like midshipmen's shoes at a Saturday morning inspection. Plaster walls were freshly painted. The apartment was a good distance from the nearest main road. It was quiet and peaceful.

The apartment was unfurnished. Eloise and I decided to furnish it slowly and sparsely. This was still a temporary place of refuge.

I signed the lease for a year beginning November 1, 1988, and moved in. I slept on an air mattress the first night. The air escaped. It did not matter. I was feeling okay.

On November 8, 1988, while I was screwing around with a defective air mattress in a rented apartment, George Bush was elected President of the United States and preparing to move into the White House. Some guys get all the breaks. My lease required me to carpet the floors since I was on the second floor and there were neighbors in the apartment below. A good friend and client of many years installed the pad and the carpeting. I did not know the carpet would give me trouble.

We furnished the bedrooms, living room, dining room and kitchen with as little furniture as necessary. I had my desk, one file cabinet, an EZ chair, a bed, and a TV.

During all of 1988 I continued to go to the YMCA three days a week to exercise and to swim. That always made me feel better.

We worked with architect Norm Morin on plans for a new home.

We sold the RV and, with mixed emotions, watched the buyer and his children happily haul it away.

We were doing pretty well until something happened to the right side of my neck.

21

The Salivary Gland and Its Excision
Overcoming Skepticism

The year was coming to a close. Since the 23rd of March I had been searching for ways to live in my house and regain my health. Nothing seemed to work. My symptoms continued. I could not live in my house or work in my office for any extended period. Nothing seemed to work. It is true that I hadn't lost an arm, a leg, or an eye, and I was not confined to a bed or a wheelchair. I was able to function. I generally felt better outside than inside, no matter whose building it was or where it was located. The climate and weather did not permit me to live outside all the time. I had to go inside, and when I did, my symptoms returned.

Toward the end of the year, the right side of my neck began to hurt. Soon something seemed to pop out like a bump on an inner tube. It was visible and the size of a small chicken egg or a ping-pong ball. I went to Drs. Slasman and Bandy, ear, nose and throat doctors. They examined me and diagnosed an obstructed salivary gland. I was sent to my family doctor and internist, Dino J. Delaportas, M.D., for a pre- operative exam to determine my fitness for surgery.

Dr. Delaportas' notes of that visit accurately describe my physical condition and his impression 47 years after Pearl Harbor Day:

12/7/88

Mr. Berkson is still having symptoms referrable to being exposed to items from his house secondary to Dursban exposure. He was seen by Dr. Slasman for right salivary gland problem, probably secondary to obstruction from stone. He will need surgical excision. Hypertension is being managed with HCTZ 25 mg daily and one quarter of a 5 mg Vasotec tablet daily. He is taking Lorazepam 3 mg daily. Tylenol occasionally for headaches.

PHYSICAL EXAMINATION: Blood pressure 130/80.
CHEST: Clear.
HEART: Unchanged.
ABDOMEN: Benign.
HEART RATE: 60

IMPRESSION: Hypertension controlled. Abdominal problem controlled. It seems that the patient's main problems are ferrable to this exposure to Dursban earlier this year. On entering home or upon being around items taken from home, he experiences extreme nausea and watery eyes. He apparently was seen by so called expert at GW, who does not seem to be able to help him. He does not want to manage this case any further. The exterminator, Dow Chemical, who makes Dursban, and Biospherics Incorporated did not seem to help this situation at the present time. Patient is living in an apartment away from home. He is naturally concerned about personal effects in the house.

PLAN: Patient will continue taking the same medication. Case was discussed with Dr. Newby regarding possible blood work for chlorpyrifos.

Before I describe my salivary gland surgery, I want to interject this anecdote.

Dr. Delaportas is a caring and competent physician. I respect him and he is still my primary physician.

When I first visited him after the chemical treatment of my house, he looked at me with skepticism. He shook his head. He had never heard of this happening before. He had not had one patient complain after exposure to chemicals, and had apparently never smelled the odor from chlorpyrifos and xylene.

Several weeks later, he phoned to tell me that he understood what I was talking about. He had had his home and office treated for termites. The odor was so strong that he and his patients began to exhibit eye and nose irritation and breathing problems. He remembered me and feared for the health and safety of the patients in his waiting room. He told them to leave and canceled the rest of his office appointments for that day and the next day. The odor soon moved from the basement to the second floor where he lived. He closed his office and moved his family from their living quarters over the office into a motel. He said he immediately thought of what had happened to me. He was smart enough to get the hell out of his office and his home. He was also fortunate in that the applicator did not inject any holes or chemicals into the foundation block or into any part of the building. The injection holes were confined to the ground outside. In a few days the odor disappeared. His initial skepticism of the causal connection between my exposure and my illness also disappeared. He became a believer after he smelled that odor and reacted to it.

Excerpts from the hospital records bring us back to the tale of the salivary gland.

WASHINGTON COUNTY HOSPITAL
251 EAST ANTIETAM STREET
HAGERSTOWN, MARYLAND 21740-5771

Berkson, Jacob B.
A:12/14/88

CHIEF COMPLAINT: Obstructed salivary gland.

HISTORY OF PRESENT ILLNESS: This 63-year-old white male developed a sudden painful swelling of the right submandibular area while eating on 11/19/88. No antecedent trauma, infection or other causative factors can be recalled. From that time until the present, the patient has continued to experience persistent post-prandial swelling and tenderness of the same salivary gland with no significant change up to the present time. X-rays have confirmed the presence of a large obstructing calculus in the substance of the right submandibular gland close the origin of its duct. Because of the intractability of patient's discomfort, he is now being admitted for an elective excision of the right submandibular gland.

PERSONAL HABITS: He does not smoke. He drinks one cup of coffee per day. He does not hardly ever use alcoholic beverage. Occupation: He is an attorney. He has had exposure to dust and fumes in the past, most recently being exposed to a toxic chemical known as termidicide in March 1988. He is still being evaluated for possible toxicity from this exposure. He has not had any significant exposure to excessively loud noise.

On December 14, 1988, Dr. Bibhas Bandy removed the right submandibular salivary gland.

The doctor did an excellent job and I recovered quickly.

I wondered after the operation whether there was a link between this obstructed salivary gland and the earlier chemical exposure to the Dursban and/or xylene. The surgeon did not know. Perhaps no one knew or would ever know. Another mystery.

Several years later, while reading *Chemical Exposures—Low Levels and High Stakes* (Ashford and Miller [New York: Van Nostrand Reinhold, 1991]) I found this in the Appendix: "Health Effects Associated with Chemicals or Foods under Eye, Ear, Nose, and Throat Disorders - 'Salivary Gland Disorders. See Eye, Ear, Nose, and Throat Disorders' on page 172."

Perhaps there was no connection in my case. But perhaps there was. I suppose we will never know. It remains a mystery.

Gerald Kloth in "CIIN Member Profiled," *Our Toxic Times*, September 1994 publication at p. 8 reported that Jason Anderson, a 16 year old star athlete living in Illinois, "pointed out to his mom and dad that his glands were swollen. There was a lump on his neck the size of a golf ball." He had started spring baseball practice and it was learned that the ball field had been chemically sprayed. Other players had flu like symptoms.

The Athletic Director said he had treated the field with the same thing he used at home and he noticed that his dog had gotten sick after the home treatment. (Reprinted with permission.)

My guess is that Jason's problem was a result of chemical exposure.

22

House for Sale

In late November of 1988, after moving into Hickory Hill, I reflected upon my health and my home. A new year was approaching.

Eight months had passed since my house was treated with an EPA-registered chemical to exterminate a swarm of subterranean termites. I was assured that the chemical was safe. All we had to do was ventilate, the foul odor would disappear in a matter of hours and I could move back. But the time frame kept changing from hours to days to weeks to months to seasons. I wondered whether any future predictions would have merit or validity.

I had spent the year moving from place to place, from motels to the homes of friends and relatives, to a tent in my backyard and then to an RV, and now I was a renter in an apartment.

Before moving from one place to another, I always returned to my home, hoping that I could move back in and that my wandering was at an end. Each time I was disappointed.

The symptoms were usually the same. My eyes would tear or burn, then my nose would stop up and burn. My sinus hurt. My head hurt. And if I stayed too long I started getting pains in my stomach, followed by nervousness, agitation, salivation, urination, and defecation. I couldn't live in my home.

All of this time we were ventilating the house. Fans in the basement and the crawlspace had been running continuously. We had ventilated the crawlspace and Dow representative McCormick had placed activated charcoal filters in all of the heating and air conditioning vents and in the furnace.

In addition, I had been assured by everyone—the pest control operator, Dow Chemical U.S.A., the county health officer—that Dursban was safe, that the odor would dissipate in a short time, and that an air sampling of the house found traces of Dursban well below acceptable limits.

Dow had furnished me a technical report dated March 1988 entitled "Airborne Chlorpyrifos Concentrations Measured During and Following Applications of DURSBAN TC Insecticide to Residential Dwellings" by J. Vaccaro and others of Dow Chemical Company. The report indicated that of 32 dwellings recently measured across the United States, none came close to exceeding National Academy of Science guidelines for airborne concentration of chlorpyrifos. As a trial lawyer with many years of experience, I had to concede that if I were to sue the manufacturer, the only evidence I had to rebut all of the scientific and technical literature was my account of what was happening to me, supported by my medical and hospital records.

I telephoned a friend of mine, Bob Bohman, a real estate broker, and told him what had happened to me and the house. I asked him if he would inspect my house and if he would be interested in handling the sale of my house.

After walking through the house and inspecting it from top to bottom, Bob told me he detected no odor, found nothing unusual and thought the house was in excellent condition. He would be happy to list it for sale.

We agreed on the terms of sale and signed a contract. Bob then brought members of his staff to the house for their inspection and comments and to familiarize them with his new listing. All of the comments were positive. There was no hesitation to show the house.

Early in December Bob put a "For Sale" sign in the front yard. I looked at that sign with mixed emotions. I had never expected to sell my home. I had emotional attachments to it, memories of my parents living here and of entertaining friends and relatives.

Memories of this home and of my parents sustained me often when I was overseas during the Korean War. We had a wonderful party on the patio the day before I left for Korea. Close friends came to say goodbye. My best friend and fellow naval officer, Len Bjorklund, was there. He was traveling with me across the Pacific. Photos of my friends at that party including Bill and Sherry Hamilton and Tom and Jean Kaylor traveled with me around the world.

Years later, I was there when my father suffered a heart attack. An ambulance crew carefully carried him out of the house and into a waiting ambulance for the short trip to the hospital. He never returned to the house he built and loved. My mother lived there as a widow for nearly 20 years after Father died, cooking and baking and giving delicious delicacies to everyone who came to the kitchen door. I also had memories of my children coming to visit their grandparents and of all the happy times we had together.

When my mother died she left the house to me. It was not just a house. It was the family home—all of the photographs, the diplomas, the scrapbooks, the sheet music, the library, the endless files of family activities were there. It had meant love and safety and security and comfort and family. It was our place, safe from the rest of the world, a place to come to when there was no place else to go. It had been a part of our lives for nearly 40 years. When Bob hammered that "For Sale" sign post into the ground, it was as if someone had hammered a spike through my heart.

My home was now for sale.

Year Two
1989
A.D.

"Can anyone believe it is possible to lay down such a barrage of poisons on the surface of the earth without making it unfit for all life?"

1

Odors in the Apartment

I got along fine in the apartment while it was unfurnished, unheated and without carpet. I was never affected by exposure to carpets prior to being poisoned in March of '88.

The air in the apartment changed after the carpet was installed. It smelled different. My eyes, nasal passages, and sinuses became irritated. I began to have difficulty breathing. My stomach became upset. There was a distinct odor to the carpet. It seemed obvious to me that there was a link between the new carpet and my health problems. I telephoned the carpet people. They denied that the carpet was causing my problems. They said they had never heard of such a thing. They ran a reputable business and were friends. I had no evidence to prove they were mistaken, but I knew what was happening to me was real. I continued traveling from one medical specialist to another. Not one doctor saw any connection between my problems and the new carpet. They were doctors and I was just a layman, and I had no scientific literature to support my theory. They gave me medication for my symptoms and I returned to the apartment, where I opened the doors and windows to bring in fresh air.

The heat caused more trouble. At first my apartment was being heated by the apartment below and by the adjoining units on each side, so for several weeks I did not need to turn on the heat. Then it got cold.

The heat was generated by a gas furnace which was located on the porch outside the living room. The furnace emitted a distinctive smell that I associated with gas stoves, gas appliances, and gas company servicemen. The smell permeated my apartment. I became mildly nauseated and my head began to ache. I opened the windows and doors, but when I closed them the smell remained. I thought there was a gas leak. I phoned the gas company and reported what was happening to me and in the apartment. A serviceman promptly arrived, inspected the furnace and hookup and assured me there was no leak. Like the RV gas serviceman, this gentleman told me I was smelling a certain warning chemical in the gas. He told me it was normal and safe and there was nothing to worry about. He left and the odor remained. I continued to ventilate the place. Prior to my poisoning I was never affected by gas heaters.

The odors began to proliferate. Eloise put curtains over the windows for privacy, but mostly to control the heat and glare from the sun. When I got close to the curtains I detected a sickening, somewhat sweet odor. It's hard to describe, but I became nervous and agitated. Again I would ventilate the apartment to bring in fresh air. My agitation would be followed by urgent and frequent dashes to the toilet. I saw a connection between the carpet, the gas, the curtains and my health. But I had no proof or literature or medical opinion to support my intuition. Never in my life before the poisoning in March of '88 had I become ill from the smell of carpet, curtains or gas.

I often left the apartment to go outside in the fresh air. I would walk for miles and sometimes for hours to clear my head. On the way in and out I passed through a hallway which had a strong smell of cigarette smoke. The odors of cigarettes and infrequent pesticide sprays combined with strong cooking odors, invaded our apartment. They were as welcome as the bastard son at a family picnic. The odors were not merely annoying. I was becoming ill, physically and emotionally. Frustration led to anger. Anger led to irritability. Irritability to stress. And stress plays havoc with the body systems.

This was particularly difficult for me because prior to the

chemical treatment of my home I never became sick from the smell of carpets or curtains or gas appliances or even cigarette smoke. I was not sensitive to chemicals before March of '88.

When I went to college in the '40s most students and professors smoked. In fact, classrooms at the University of Virginia were filled not only with students and professors but also with cigarette smoke. There was no air conditioning in our classrooms in the summer of '43. Movie Theaters and some restaurants were air conditioned, but not classrooms.

I didn't smoke but I was in the minority. I didn't like the smell but it didn't make me sick. I accepted it. It was part of life.

I had similar experiences in the Navy during World War II and the Korean War. Most of my fellow officers smoked. A pack of cigarettes was practically a part of the uniform. There was hardly a soldier, sailor, marine, or coastguardsman who was not smoking a great deal of the time. The Red Cross pointed with pride to the fact that they gave away millions of cigarettes to servicemen. The first thing medics gave a wounded soldier was a cigarette. Take a look at any of the movies about World War II or any of the wars since. You'll see servicemen smoking, and the odors from cigarettes, cigars, and pipes permeated the ships, offices, mess halls and hospitals of all of the armed services.

None of these odors made me ill or caused me to lose one hour's work.

Once, aboard a Navy destroyer on my way back to the States from Japan and Korea, I experienced what every destroyer sailor experiences: the smell of stack gas throughout the ship. Gas from the smokestacks completely envelops everyone aboard. Herman Wouk describes it brilliantly in *The Caine Mutiny: A Novel of World War II* (New York: Doubleday & Company, Inc. [now Bantam Doubleday Dell], 1952).

"22   THE WATER FAMINE

"In the days of sail, a following wind was a blessing; not so in the days of steam.

"En route to Funafuti, two hundred miles out of Kwajalein, the Caine was wallowing along at ten knots under masses of clouds like vast dirty pillows. It was enveloped in its own miasma, from which it could not escape. The breeze blew from astern at about ten knots. Relative to the ship there was no movement of air at all. The minesweeper seemed to be traveling in a nightmare calm. The stack gas swirled and rolled on the main deck, sluggish, oily, almost visible. It stank; it coated tongues and throats with an itchy, foul-tasting film; it stung the eyes. The air was hot and damp. The smell of the crated cabbages on the after deckhouse made a singularly sickening marriage with the stack fumes. The sailors and officers of the *Caine,* sweating, dirty, unable to obtain the relief of a shower, looked at each other with lolling tongues and dulled sad eyes, and worked with their hands to their noses." (Reprinted with permission.)

Diesel fumes, vapors and exhaust aboard ship and ashore did not make me ill. The odors at my home and at the apartment did after the termite treatment of '88.

Before March 23, 1988, I breathed a thousand other noxious odors from naval bases, industrial plants, railroad locomotives, airplanes, autos and trucks. None made me ill. I lived and worked and played with no restrictions until after March 23, 1988. Since then, these normal everyday odors have affected my life, and restricted my activities.

I was frustrated and angry. And I did not know what to do about it.

Then the phone rang.

"Hey, Jack. This is Ralph Ruben. Turn on your TV. Ralph Nader is on the Donahue show. He is talking about people getting sick from chemicals. It sounds like what you have, buddy. There is also some Doctor from UVA hospital on the show. Take care."

The program was almost over before I got to my TV.

Sometime later I phoned the UVA hospital and asked to speak to the toxicologist. I was connected to the toxicology department. The person who answered the phone identified himself as a technician. He told me there was no toxicologist there at the time. After hearing my story, he advised me to see an allergist, either there or back home.

I promptly placed a call to the Allergy Center for the Antietam Valley. (Antietam is a big name in my county. About 23,100 soldiers died in a single day in the Civil War at the Battle of Antietam, about 12 miles from my home.)

"This is Jack Berkson. I want an appointment with Dr. Snyder as soon as possible."

"The doctor will see you on Monday, February 13, at 1:30 p.m."

I thanked the Deity and relaxed. Help was on its way.

2

The Traditional Allergist

The sign on the door at 106-108 North Potomac Street, Hagerstown, read:

ALLERGY CENTER FOR THE ANTIETAM VALLEY
Clovis M. Snyder, M.D., F.A.C.A., P.A.

The historic building was across the street from the Antietam Fire Hall. City Hall was down the street, a block above the town square. The large waiting room was a comfortable place for patients with allergies and asthma and other respiratory problems. It was not carpeted, nor was it cluttered. File cabinets filled with patients' charts stood side by side against the north and east walls. Plain metal chairs (no synthetics) outnumbered the patients. A variety of up-to-date magazines and health literature was available for patients to read.

The air quality was good. There was nothing in the room to irritate the eyes, nose, or bodily systems.

I was directed into the doctor's office right on time. I furnished him my medical history and answered his questions and he gave me a thorough examination. He explained the procedure he would follow to arrive at a diagnosis.

Excerpts from his summary of evaluation and treatment follow.

PRESENTING SYMPTOMS: This 63-year-old man complained of the following symptoms: headaches; itchy eyes; sneezing; nasal stuffiness and drainage; cough; nausea; and abdominal cramps...

ALLERGEN EXPOSURE AT HOME, AND IN AVOCATION: The patient presently lives in an apartment after his home was treated with petrochemicals (termite extermination)...

DIAGNOSES: (1) Allergic rhinitis 477.0

(2) Irritable Colon

Plan of TREATMENT/MANAGEMENT: IA. Environmental control instructions were given...

III. HYPOSENSITIZATION, using appropriate F.D.A.- approved antigens to which the patient is clinically sensitive, was recommended...

Intradermal or skin tests are given to determine if one is sensitive or allergic to the injected substance. Swelling and redness are evidence of sensitivity. I tested positive for a number of these antigens, and Dr. Snyder recommended a course of hyposensitization.

The treatment was designed to reduce the allergies to a level that I could tolerate.

Dr. Snyder furnished me a chart titled, "Guide to 'desensitizing' a room." In summary, to desensitize a room means:

1. Avoiding ornate furniture. 2. Keeping all clothes in closets. No mothballs, insect sprays, tar paper, or camphor. 3. No fabric upholstery. 4. Wood or linoleum flooring. No rugs of any kind. 5. Avoiding toys or stuffed animals. 6. Painting or papering walls with washable wallpaper. 7. Installing roll-up washable cotton or synthetic window shades. No venetian blinds. 8. Using washable cotton or fiberglass curtains. No draperies. 9. Installing window unit or central air conditioning. 10. No smoking by anyone in the house. 11. Using dacron or other synthetics for pillows, not kapok, feather, or foam rubber, which grows mold.

The guide included cleaning tips and instructions for reducing mold in and around the home.

Dr. Snyder and his instructions and this guide served as my authority to get rid of the carpet in the apartment, the curtains, and some furniture we brought from home. Upholstered furniture is a reservoir for pesticides.

We put cheesecloth over the heat vents. It helped with dust but was ineffective against chemical odors. We turned off the gas furnace and brought in portable electric heaters, one for each room. This first chart was followed by numerous other charts, articles and books about how to furnish your home, especially your bedroom, where you spend perhaps one-third of your life. See Volume II for additional references.

I took Dr. Snyder's advice and began a course of allergy shots. I returned to his office at weekly or bi-weekly intervals to receive the shots. They were effective in controlling my allergies to such things as house dust, mildew, ragweed, trees, grasses—the sort of things that allergists have researched, studied, and practiced for many years. But the shots did not reduce my sensitivity to chemical vapors. And in today's society, there is no practical way to avoid all chemicals. Chemicals are found in the water we drink, the air we breathe, the soil in which we grow our food, the food we eat. Our homes, our workplaces, our automobiles, our public buildings, our schools, our parks contain numerous petro-chemicals. Many construction and furniture materials give off vapors, a process known as "outgassing." Some of these chemicals are toxic to the human body, depending upon the concentration, the amount and length of exposure and individual tolerance. Some people become ill with the kinds of symptoms I have described.

The point is that the classical allergist does not have effective treatment for the toxic or chemical load on the body.

This is no criticism of Dr. Snyder. He proved to be a caring, competent, conscientious physician as well as a friend. Time and again, he worked above and beyond the call of duty in helping me survive.

He took time to visit both the apartment and the home I had left to inspect the premises, to see with his own eyes, smell with his own nose and put his expertise to work in an effort to solve the housing problem.

In the meantime, he suggested that I purchase a face mask, sometimes known as a respirator, with cartridges that filter out certain pollutants. I took his advice and bought a twin-cartridge respirator from Mine & Safety International Company, which has offices and representatives in principal cities worldwide.

I find the mask, which looks like a gas mask, to be very helpful when I travel. I usually carry it with me because I never know when I will be confronted with car or truck exhaust, pesticide spray, or other chemicals that could cause a severe reaction and send me to the emergency room. I find the mask indispensable in airports and aboard airplanes waiting for takeoff.

3

Severe Pansinusitis, Pig Shit, and the Class Reunion

During the first half of 1989, my sinuses became more aggravated. I was treated with medicine, spray and antibiotics, none of which were effective. They merely delayed the inevitable.

Dr. Bandy sent me to the hospital for a CT scan of the sinuses in April. The final impression:

"There is markedly severe pansinusitis, with nearly all the sinuses involved. The findings on the left are worse than those on the right."

Dr. Bandy phoned me on May 2 and informed me that the CAT scan X-ray indicated that my sinuses were "terrible."

"You need an operation. Go on Ceftin, an antibiotic, two times a day. Begin Ceftin after supper."

There was now a smell in my nose so horrible that the only odor I can compare it to is pig shit. To use a less offensive term or descriptive phrase would be an injustice to the terrible odor that accompanied me day and night wherever I went. If you have ever been downwind from a pig farm, especially in the summer, you will not soon forget the smell.

I went to Johns Hopkins Hospital in Baltimore, where I was examined by Dr. Leonard Proctor, an otolaryngologist.

Prior to the sinus surgery I attended the 40th reunion of my law school class at the University of Virginia. What should have been a happy occasion was marred by my health problems and especially the sinus situation. The most shocking non-event to all of us was the list of peers who had died before the reunion. Fully half of my law school class of 1949 was dead. We looked at our graduation pictures and remembered our colleagues in their youth—healthy, handsome, intelligent, ambitious, talented. Of the 76 who graduated, 39 were gone to their eternal reward. We who survived were shocked. Most of us had been in our mid-20s when we graduated. Now we were in our 60s. How come so many of our classmates were no longer with us?

"Stress. Goddamn stress. Practicing law is exciting but it's a goddamn killer."

That was the consensus of those who survived.

"It's time to smell the roses, fellows," said the president of our class.

Tears rolled down my cheeks. I turned my head. Roses, hell. All I could smell was pig shit.

4

More Pesticide Cases
and an ALR Citation

On April 6, 1989, an article appeared in The Washington Post under the headline:

Pesticide Fears Leave Pair
A House That's Not Home
Virginia Couple Stay in Backyard Trailer

The article by D'Vera Cohn, Washington Post staff writer, told the story of Blanche and Ward Weaver, who had to abandon their modest white house in Mount Vernon, Va., to sleep in a mobile home in their backyard.

> "...The reason, Blanche Weaver said, is that her house is making her sick. The cause, she believes, is chlordane, a termite-killing chemical applied more than four years ago and now banned by the federal government...

> "The Weavers—she is 59, he is 62—are among a growing number of people complaining that pesticides caused them more problems than they eliminated.

> "This year, spurred by the 1986 deaths of a Galax couple who were killed after a botched pest extermination, Virginia's legislature enacted tougher laws on home, agricultural and forest pesticides..."
> (© 1995, *The Washington Post.* Reprinted with permission.)

A Fairfax County investigator who took air samples at their house in 1987 testified that there were no significant levels of chlordane, possibly because it had been three years since the house was exterminated. The county concluded there was no problem.

The Weavers hired a private lab that found there was enough

chlordane on surfaces in the house to pose a threat for absorption through the skin. The lab's director advised the Weavers to leave the house.

Seventeen days later, *The Herald Mail*, Hagerstown, Md., published a similar story about a family in Georgia:

Family has home hauled to toxic waste dump

"ATLANTA (UPI) — A jury awarded a suburban Atlanta couple $400,000 to build a new home and have their old house hauled off to a toxic waste dump.

"Donald and Linda Radtke of Stone Mountain east of Atlanta won the damage award Friday against Arrow Exterminators Inc. in Fulton County Superior Court.

"The Radtkes hired the exterminators in early 1984 to help get rid of termites in their new $125,000 home.

"The company used the chemicals chlordane and heptachlor, now off the market ...

"The Radtkes contended that long-lasting toxic vapor contamination made the house unliveable, causing them to suffer headaches and sore throats.

"Mrs. Radtke said the chemicals also caused her to contract a disease that affects her stomach and liver.

"A chemist hired by the family testified during the 10-day trial said he would not live in the house. Two scientists testifying for Arrow said they would have no trouble staying there.

"The family has been living in a rented home since 1987 and said it will use the lawsuit money to build a new house..." (Reprinted with permission.)

Sometime later I went to the Washington County Bar Association library and did some research on this subject. I found a 1980 Alabama Supreme Court case dealing with an exterminator's liability for personal injury or death. The victim had sued a pest control applicator for injuries following a pesticide application in his home.

The victim lost, but the case was a reference point for further research.

5

Shifting the Burden of Proof

After 11 months of suffering, countless hours of research and out-of-pocket losses of more than $30,000 with no end in sight, I filed a complaint with the Maryland Department of Agriculture, Pesticide Division. I asked that the agency investigate what had occurred at my home on March 23, 1988.

Two gentlemen from the pesticide division came to my home, interviewed me and Eloise and inspected the house. Then they went to see Able.

The chief of the Pesticide Regulation Section, Department of Agriculture, sent Able a Notice of Warning, and sent me a copy.

It read in part:

"Upon concluding our investigation it appears that your firm may have violated the Regulations Pertaining to the Pesticide Applicators Law. This section states that 'A pesticide shall be used in strict accordance with manufacturers' labeling directions except as provided by State and federal laws and regulations.' Our investigation revealed that your firm failed to plug holes that were drilled in the walls of the crawl space and basement of Mr. Berkson's residence. It is our understanding that the holes in question were not plugged until several weeks after the application...In addition, it appears that you have violated the regulations, regarding record keeping..."

The letter went on to say that since this was the first complaint, the department did not find it necessary to conduct a formal hearing.

The firm did not contest the decision.

The purpose of the investigation was to determine whether a

violation of the Maryland Pesticide Applicator's Law and Regulations occurred.

"May have" was the determination.

I was satisfied. By not appealing, the exterminator was, in my mind, admitting fault. In the event of a lawsuit, it would no longer be my word against Able's.

Violation of the regulation is evidence of negligence.

Negligence caused the indoor air pollution would be the argument.

The link between the indoor air pollution and the subsequent illness had yet to be proved.

6

Sinus Endoscopy

The results of Dr. Proctor's sinus endoscopy were remarkable. The terrible odor disappeared. I am eternally grateful to Dr. Proctor and his staff at the Johns Hopkins Hospital. Excerpts from Dr. Proctor's subsequent medical report follow:

October 25, 1989

Dear Mr. Berkson,

I am enclosing copies of my notes from your case. In my opinion, the nasal condition from which you have suffered was significantly aggravated by exposure to chemicals, as you have described to me. At the present time your situation is improved, but I believe it will be necessary for you to be under treatment and observation indefinitely. I base this opinion on my experience with rhinitis and nasal polyps, and the tendency for swelling to return, even to the point of redeveloping polyps, and certainly the possibility of recrudescence of chronic sinusitis problems.

If you have any questions or require any further information please do not hesitate to contact me.

Sincerely,

Leonard R. Proctor
Ear, Nose, and Throat Surgery

Dr. Proctor was correct. I have returned to him for follow up and observation, most recently in October 1995, where examination revealed redeveloping polyps.

7

♪♪ *A bright note* ♪♪
Daughter, Susan, becomes a Cantor

Eloise and I had the pleasure of attending the graduation ceremony of my daughter Susan from the School of Sacred Music, Hebrew Union College, in New York City.

The ceremony was held at Temple Emmanuel on Fifth Avenue. Susan was one of 10 to complete the rigorous four-year graduate course in Hebrew and Sacred Music. She won her Master's Degree and was invested as a Cantor along with her talented colleagues. She was then one of few women in the cantorial field.

The father of the bride became the proud father of the Cantor.

8

House — Off the Market

Despite all efforts to sell the house in 1989, the house did not sell. I thought it was because of the termite treatment in March of '88. The real estate agent assured me that the residential market was off and offered to continue the listing.

When the listing period expired, we took it off the market.

9

The Electrical Contractor

After the sinus endoscopy at Johns Hopkins Hospital in Baltimore, I returned to my apartment to recuperate. The June heat was excessive. The temperature rose high into the 90s outside as well as inside the apartment. The air-conditioning unit was not adequate, and to make matters worse roofers were putting a new roof on the apartment. Tar and asphalt vapors were unwelcome guests. I began to react to both the excessive heat and the roofing odors. The indoor air became intolerable, and the noise and dust and dirt from the construction jangled my nerves. This was not the place to recuperate from surgery. I had to get out of there. The question then became, "Where do I go to find a place I can tolerate?"

I tossed this question to Dr. Snyder. He was now my primary care physician, but he was treating allergies, not chemical toxins.

Dr. Snyder agreed that the apartment was no place for me to be. He suggested I gradually try to return to my home. He had been treating me for several months and thought that I might be able to tolerate my home again.

The air conditioning at home was working very well, and the odor from the Dursban or the xylene had dissipated. I could not smell it anymore.

In July I terminated my lease and returned home.

These were bad days for me. I was going from one doctor to another seeking treatment for my reactions. Bloody nasal discharges, nausea, nervousness, urinary frequency and urgency and depression sent me to the allergist, the internist, the urologist and the psychiatrist. All of them were caring, capable and competent. Each did his best to help. But my health problems did not respond to treatment.

Dr. Snyder came to my house, inspected it and suggested that we consider sealing off part of the crawlspace and basement. He added that with the proper heating, ventilation and air-conditioning system and filters, I should be able to tolerate the house as well as before the chemical exposure.

Dr. Snyder suggested that I speak to one of his patients, an electrical contractor who had severe allergies and who claimed to be knowledgeable about air quality.

I contacted this gentleman, made an appointment with him and laid out the history of my case. He toured my house, inspected it and assured me that he and his company could clear up this whole mess. He presented me with a contract to install two complete heating, ventilation and air-conditioning systems, one for the house and one for the office.

The contractor said he was an expert in the design and installation of heat pump systems. In addition to the heat pumps, he would install filters and an air-to-air heat exchanger to suck in fresh air and blow out the stale air. He convinced me that he had the expertise, ability and knowledge to fix the system.

I added an addendum consisting of five items to his contract, the most important of which was:

"5. All to improve the quality of the indoor air so that it is as pollutant-free and allergen-free as possible."

We signed the contract on Aug. 11, 1989. The price was $9,800.00.

I thought that was my lucky day. As it turned out, it was as FDR described Dec. 7, 1941:

"A date which will live in infamy."

10

L.A. Law

While waiting for the work to begin, I received literature from the California Bar about a convention in San Diego. Included in the agenda was a seminar entitled, "Toxic Torts." Two of the principal speakers were Don Howarth and Suzelle M. Smith, attorneys in Los Angeles. They had conducted a seminar on toxic torts at Newport Beach, Ca., on Aug. 26 and 27, 1989 and had furnished me a brief they had prepared.

I found the legal brief to be excellent and right on point for my case. This was important reference material. I contacted Mr. Howarth and made arrangements to meet him in San Diego.

I had passed the California Bar in 1975 when I was a Federal attorney. I made it a point to attend as many California Bar conventions as I could because the bar was usually on the leading edge of most of the subjects in which I had an interest. This certainly was the case with environmental matters.

I was amazed at the number of booths at the convention that dealt with environmental matters. I met folks who had literature and charts and exhibits that seemed light years ahead of anything I had seen.

They dealt with environmental health services, epidemiology, risk assessment and toxicology, corporate medical consultation, industrial hygiene, litigation support and health data systems.

The highlight was the seminar by Mr. Howarth and Ms. Smith.

After his seminar, Mr. Howarth and I reviewed the facts of my case. He said my case was an excellent one, but he was too busy handling cases in California to take mine. I left San Diego with a suitcase full of legal documents, briefs, articles and brochures.

The only adverse reaction I had at the convention occurred during a reception. A judge from Marin County glanced at my name tag and offered me a beer. His wife's maiden name was Berkson and he thought we might be related.

I took a swig of beer and within seconds felt as if I had been stabbed with a pitchfork. I doubled up in pain on the patio of the Town & Country motel. That had never happened before. I was never a heavy drinker. One or two beers was usually my limit for an evening. But I had barely managed a large gulp when this piercing pain hit me. That was my last beer. I can no longer tolerate alcohol, even wine on the Sabbath.

11

Notes from Medical Diary

September 18 — *11 p.m. Returned home from San Diego. Smell carpet and react. Stuffy nose, eyes puffy.*

September 19 — *2 p.m. Return to home. Workers fixing HVAC. Went to basement. Reaction like last year. Stomach, head, irritable, nervous, vision smokey. Phoned Dr. Snyder.*

September 21 — *Odor chlorine in and out house. 11 p.m.Stomach cramps. Left house for Venice Motel.*

September 22 — *10 p.m.Stomach cramps. Doubled up. 12 midnight Phoned Dr. Snyder. Go to emergency room, Washington County Hospital. Acute G.I. attack.*

September 23 — *5 a.m.Released from hospital. Diagnosis: gall bladder. 8 a.m. To Bethesda.*

September 24 — *Stay at Howard Johnson Motel. Notice odor at door to home. Believe heat exchanger or air exchanger under dining room pulling pollution into house.*

September 25 — *2 p.m. Follow-up emergency room. Gall bladder test negative.*

DINO J. DELAPORTAS, M.D.

9/26/89

Mr. Berkson is still having trouble with his home. Apparently with the air exchange system that was being installed and the cleaning of the ducts, old fumes were agitated and dispersed throughout the house and he again had episodes of abdominal pain requiring a trip to the emergency room and a visit here today. He takes an occasional dose of Bentyl for abdominal spasms.

PHYSICAL EXAMINATION: There is hyperactive bowel sounds, mild epigastric tenderness, no other abnormalities, no peritoneal sinus.

IMPRESSION: Abdominal spasms secondary to fumes in house. Patient has been having problems with this since exposure to Dursban TC, March 23, 1988. He will continue with his other medication as prescribed.

October 7 — 11 p.m. Stomach cramps severe. To Washington County Hospital till 4:30 a.m.

November 7 — 9 a.m. Washington County Hospital lab. Blood re calcium. 3 p.m. Abdominal cramp attack. 3:30 p.m. To Urology. Rx Hytrin.

November 27 — 2 p.m. Phone call from Dr. Malawer. Findings: biopsy indicates campylobacter pylori. Diagnosis: campylobacter pylori, a gastro intestinal disorder. Treatment: Pepto Bismol 4 times a day, 6 to 8 weeks, then 2 antibiotics — Flagel. 8 p.m.Begin Pepto Bismol. Continue for 6 to 8 weeks.

November 29 — 6 p.m. Ringing and buzzing in ears.

December 13 — 5 p.m. Dr. Malawer called. Said consensus of pathologists: Not campylobacter, so no penicillin or prescription. Get off Pepto for a week. See if side effects dissipate and clear up. After week start again. Call him in 2 or 3 weeks.

December 15 — 4 p.m. Outside frigid. 20°. Snowstorm. Eloise is depressed and tired. Look after Eloise. Uncomfortable.

December 18 — 2:30 p.m. Dr. Jones, Urology. Tests OK. Call in 3 months.

December 21 — 9 a.m. Temperature in office 55°. Basement 55°. Pipe bringing in cold air. Electrician here.

December 22 — 7 a.m. Dr. Rosenthal called re conference, consultation with Dr. Malawer. Consensus: No infection therefore no antibiotics. Sensitivity fully investigated. Either being poisoned in home and/or chronic, irritable colon. Try Klonopin for anxiety. ½ Klonopin. "Stay out of home."

In summary, since my return to Hagerstown in September, I had been seen, examined, tested, treated and instructed by no less than six eminent specialists, not including radiologists and technicians and assistants in hospitals. My team of doctors included an allergist, an internist, a gastroenterologist, a psychiatrist, several urologists, an otolaryngologist and a partridge in a pear tree. I expected to be sued any day by a firm of veterinarians charging me with discrimination because I had failed to consult with them, as well.

12

Campylobacter and Other Afflictions

I got the surprise of my life when I looked up "campylobacter" in a medical dictionary. The first thing I read was "bovine genital c., a venereal disease of cattle caused by *Campylobacter (Vibrio) fetus* subspecies *fetus;* characterized by infertility and early embryonic death…ovine genital c., an infectious disease of sheep …characterized by abortion, and transmitted orally."

I knew damn well I had not been having sex with any goddamn sheep or cow. Either that dictionary definition was screwed up or the diagnosis was way off base.

I finally got myself calmed down and looked at that dictionary again. They used to have a saying about somebody being in the right church but the wrong pew. My eyes had focused on the word "campylobacteriosis." Above it in bold letters was "Campylobacter …C. pyloris, a species that causes gastritis and pyloric ulcers in humans."

That was more like it.

This series of gastrointestinal pains and cramps seemed to have been triggered by something the electricians did when they installed the new HVAC system, filters, air-to-air heat exchanger and ductwork. I had been getting along okay at home before the electricians started their work. Then all hell broke loose.

As I look back over all these records and notes and diaries, I am convinced I should have stayed out of my home instead of continuing to return, expecting everything to be okay. What was happening to me was real. Exactly what was causing the symptoms was still a mystery. But the biggest mystery of all is why I kept returning home.

13

The Wall Street Journal Sounds Alarm
EPA Finds Bad Air

A s 1989 drew to a close, I was finding mounting evidence of a
link between chemical exposure and illness.

Four significant items were brought to my attention:

1. "In Some Workplaces, Ill Winds Blow," subtitled "Indoor
Pollution Spurs Lawsuits, Taxes Economy," by Amy Dockser
Marcus, Staff Reporter of *The Wall Street Journal* reported on litigation arising from a new phenomenon known as "sick-building
syndrome." Employees refused to work in a company's new office
building because of headaches, dizziness and bleeding.

A box in the article read:

"The EPA estimates that the economic cost of indoor air pollution
totals tens of billions of dollars annually in lost productivity, direct
medical care, lost earnings and employee sick days. Sick-building
suits could rival those that have proliferated over asbestos."
(Reprinted by permission of *The Wall Street Journal*, © 1989 Dow
Jones & Company, Inc. All Rights Reserved Worldwide.)

2. The bold headline in the *Daily Mail* read, "EPA finds bad air
at own headquarters."

"WASHINGTON (AP) — The Environmental Protection Agency,
which monitors and regulates the nation's air quality, doesn't have
to go far in the search for sick air—only to its own headquarters.

"The EPA acknowledged Tuesday it has major indoor air pollution
problems after a survey of employees at its headquarters found as
many as 40 percent complain of headaches, dizziness and other
ailments they blame on the air at the office...

"Many of the EPA health problems have been blamed on poor air circulation and chemicals alleged to come from carpeting at the agency's maze of offices over a southwest Washington shopping mall..." (Reprinted with permission.)

3. A letter written by the Director of Education, Chemical Sensitivity Disorders Association, furnished to me by Dr. Snyder. It reads in part:

April 3, 1989

Dear Physician:

The lawn care industry has done a brilliant job of convincing the average American that lawn care pesticides are safe. But EPA considers the safety claims false and misleading. "Pesticides are not safe. They are produced specifically because they are toxic to something." Many pesticides were derived from nerve gases. Research on their toxicity is shockingly incomplete. Exceedingly little is known about the chronic health effects of single pesticide ingredients and almost nothing about the long- term consequences of the mixes that are the rule. While certain organ systems tend to be evaluated in pesticide research, there is relatively little data about the effects of pesticides on reproduction, the nervous and immune systems, and on vulnerable people such as the young, the elderly, and the chronically ill. (Reprinted with permission.)

4. Howarth and Smith, in their legal brief presented at the Toxic Torts seminar in California described earlier, point out an interesting phenomenon which remains a mystery.

"Human beings vary widely in their individual response to foreign chemicals as measured by their differing chemical allergy reactions or the degree to which a particular foreign molecule upsets their metabolism (consider Penicillin). Similarly, the reader has probably noted the widely divergent response of individuals to doses of alcohol or caffeine." (Reprinted with permission.)

14

The Hospitable Helen Sayler

In October of '89, I placed a classified ad in the local paper seeking a place to live temporarily. Mrs. Helen Sayler invited me to inspect her home. It was a small but comfortable home outside Hagerstown. Mrs. Sayler was very kind and helpful. She had a chronic illness herself and had empathy for others who needed help. She was a widow and the mother of several grown children, grandchildren and great-grandchildren. She had worked hard all her life, and her greatest satisfaction came from helping others, many of whom were better off than she in many respects. We became close friends during the months I stayed at her home. She had a great deal of common sense and sensitivity. She helped me retain my sanity in those dark days of confusion, chaos, disorientation and frustration. I was living there when the year ended.

15

The Drivers

When I was too ill to drive to the "Big City" to keep doctor and hospital appointments, four life-long friends volunteered and took turns driving my car. They endured excessive heat and humidity in hot weather and freezing cold in winter as I could not tolerate forced hot or cold air from the auto heater or air conditioner. To Harold "Curly" Custer, L. Victor Crist, Jr., Thomas C. Cochrane, and Ralph E. Wallace, my "Mini Olympic Race Drivers," go my eternal thanks. To their gracious wives, Ruth, Louise, Dotty, and Dottie thanks again for your help and for never complaining. Curly, Vic, Tom, and Ralph always "got me to the church on time."

16

To California—In Search of Clean Air

American Express came to the rescue. No, AE didn't fix my home or heal me, but they sent me a free airline ticket to anyplace in the U.S. provided it was used in December '89.

I spent my 64th birthday with my son Dan and his wife Julie in their home in Mt. View, Ca., south of San Francisco, where the climate and air quality is good.

Dan is the second-born of my three children. He earned a law degree and an MBA at Santa Clara after four years at UC Santa Barbara. He was working as a financial analyst for a nationwide trucking company, Consolidated Freightways, Inc., and its subsidiary, CF Air Freight. Julie was working for a pharmaceutical company in Silicon Valley.

They were hospitable as always. The indoor air and the outdoor air were tolerable. I took long walks during the day while they worked. We rode the train into my favorite city, San Francisco, and visited with my good friend from Navy days, Len Bjorklund, a prominent trial attorney who lives in Marin County with his son, Peter, and daughter, Amy.

I carried my respirator in the event I ran into polluted air. It came in handy on occasion. I had to use it in the airport and aboard the plane while waiting to take off. The air quality in airplanes on the tarmac is very poor. They suck in their own exhaust and the exhaust from planes nearby. Without a respirator I would have been at risk.

It was a good trip. I felt better.

As the plane lifted off the runway, so, too, did my spirits.

17

Norman Cousins and Psychoneuroimmunology
A Blueprint for Proving MCS Is Real

HEAD FIRST: the Biology of Hope by Norman Cousins was first published in 1989 by E. P. Dutton, New York. I write about this not only because of the effect it has had on me and others, but because this book offers a method by which doctors and scientists may prove or disprove the reality or unreality of a link between pollution and illness, between chemical exposure and disease.

Norman Cousins is the author of 20 other books, including *Anatomy of an Illness*. He had been editor of the *Saturday Review* from 1940 to 1971. At the age of 62, he was offered a new career as a faculty member in the UCLA Department of Psychiatry and Biobehavioral Sciences. He was not a doctor or a scientist, but his personal experience and his writings had captured the imagination of the American public and of many medical professors and writers.

Cousins' theory was that emotions and attitudes can affect the body's chemistry.

(From HEAD FIRST: the Biology of Hope by Norman Cousins. Copyright © 1989 by Norman Cousins. Reprinted by permission of Dutton Signet, a division of Penguin Books USA Inc.) Cousins points out on page 2—

"There was abundant medical research to show that the brain, under circumstances of the negative emotions—hate, fear, panic, rage, despair, depression, exasperation, frustration—could produce powerful changes in the body's chemistry, even set the stage for intensified illness. But there was no comparable evidence to show that the positive emotions—purpose, determination, love, hope, faith, will to live, festivity—could also affect biological states."

Cousins goes on—

"It is well known that we have the ability to make ourselves ill. What about the ability to make ourselves well?"

This book is about the study, planning, organization, research, problems, medical and scientific tests, findings and recognition of Psychoneuroimmunology, a new branch of medicine based on the interaction of the brain, the endocrine system and the immune system.

This 368-page book describes how the obsession of Norman Cousins was studied, researched, tested, discussed and critiqued by supporters and opponents and how, in the end, the obsession and belief was accepted as accurate, true, valid and real. My goal is to prod the medical establishment into researching, testing, discussing and critiquing MCS so that in the end MCS will be recognized and accepted as a real disease and acceptable treatment will be effective.

Cousins and the task force had to bridge the gap between "anecdotes" and scientific proof. Victims of chemical exposure have the same task. Cousins relates that—

"In referring to an individual case, I did so as illustrative of a principle and not necessarily as proof of a principle." This was after a learned doctor had explained to him the dangers of "anecdotes."

"The quickest and surest way for a doctor to discredit or disparage an account of a single experience is to label it an anecdote."

After completing 10 years at the UCLA School of Medicine, Cousins made a written report to the dean. It is a 14-page report set forth in Chapter 22 of the book. It is an excellent synopsis of the relationship between emotions and health.

So persuasive were his writings that he was invited to join the faculty of a great medical institution, and that faculty of great minds gave him and his theories all of their support in his effort to produce scientific evidence linking emotions and health. Further, this program was financially supported by a multi-million dollar grant from the Kroc family. Joan Kroc, the widow of Ray Kroc, the founder of McDonald's, generously contributed an initial grant of $2 million to fund the study.

We who have been poisoned are well aware of the link between chemical exposure and disease. There is no doubt in our minds. But when we go to our doctors for diagnosis and treatment, many of us are dismissed because the AMA does not recognize MCS as "real." What we say is considered an anecdote. We, as patients, do not have the resources to prove cause and effect. The medical and scientific establishment has the resources.

The similarity is inescapable. Norman Cousins had personal experiences that gave rise to what he termed an obsession or belief. His belief went against the grain of traditional medicine. The majority of the medical establishment dismissed his writings as fantasy, just as the majority of doctors dismiss our accounts of illness following a chemical exposure as "anecdotal." But just because the doctor has not studied the relationship between chemical exposure and disease does not mean it does not exist. It merely means that the doctor has not studied it and the medical establishment has not come up with an effective treatment.

One of the goals of A Canary's Tale is to find and recruit individuals as important and influential as Norman Cousins and Joan Kroc, and some great medical institution such as UCLA or The Johns Hopkins, free from influence by the chemical and pharmaceutical industries, unbiased and unprejudiced and with an open mind, to begin research with scientific methods to confirm the link between chemical exposure and cancer, chemical sensitivity and other medical breakdowns. Many researchers have been working on this for years. Their work should be reviewed and tested. It is not necessary to reinvent the wheel. Sooner or later this link will be confirmed and recognized by the mainstream medical profession.

Year Three
1990
A.D.

VENTILATING
SYSTEMS
INSTALLED
BY
CO.

"In the final analysis, our most basic common link is that we all inhabit this small planet. We all breathe the same air. We all cherish our children's future. And we are all mortal."

President John F. Kennedy, American University, 10 June 1963

1

Medicals

The multiple symptoms continued off and on, requiring me to spend a great deal of time in doctors' offices, hospitals and laboratories.

I knew there was a link between my exposure to the Dursban in March of '88 and all or some of these health problems. But my belief did not constitute medical or scientific proof.

A significant event occurred in Dr. Norman Rosenthal's office in Bethesda, Md., on March 3, 1990. There was no one in the waiting room when I arrived for my appointment. I took a seat and picked up a magazine while waiting for the doctor to call me. Within minutes, my eyes became irritated as if there was sand or dust in them and they began to tear. That was followed by a sneezing spell. I went into the bathroom for some tissue and immediately had the urge to urinate, followed by the need to defecate.

By this time, my nasal passages were clogged and I was having difficulty breathing. I became nervous and agitated and walked around the waiting room. All of this took place within five to ten minutes, before the doctor called me into his office.

I do not recall who spoke first, but I distinctly recall asking the doctor if there was something in his waiting room or bathroom that may have triggered my reaction. I was very agitated and told him what had happened since I entered his building.

He took one look at me and immediately said, "Let's go outside now." We left his office and went into the yard. We then walked down the street. "I have something to tell you, Mr. Berkson," he said. "I had an infestation of insects in my waiting room and office the other day, and I had to call an exterminator to spray and get rid of them. At first I was going to call you and tell you about this so that you might be prepared for what you would find here. But I thought it over, and on second thought since what you are suffering from is so controversial among the medical establishment, I wanted to see with my own eyes what would happen to you or how you would react in my office if you did not know the office had been sprayed. I want you to know that I have always believed what you have told me, but as you know, many doctors are skeptical of these reports about numerous symptoms attributable to pesticides. This was in effect a deliberate challenge to you. If you had no reaction after being in that sprayed office, that would have told me one thing. But since you were completely unaware of the fact that my office and waiting room had been sprayed and you came down with all of the symptoms you have been telling us about for nearly two years, I believe this completely validates your complaints. I apologize to you for not warning you, but I am certain you were not in there long enough to do yourself any harm. We got you out of there within a matter of minutes. How do you feel now?"

"I am okay out here in the fresh air," I said.

We had walked several blocks from his office in the fresh air with no traffic on the road, and I was certain that my head would clear up shortly and it did. This was a defining moment.

Even before that incident Dr. Rosenthal was on record supporting my position. He was the first doctor to recognize that there was a link between my chemical exposure and my illness, and he was the first to tell me, "You are being poisoned. Get out of your house!" But this clinched the deal. He saw what happened to me when I was exposed to a pesticide at a level so low that he could not even smell it.

That same month I had some painful problems with my eyes. They were itchy, irritated and red. I was examined, treated and given medication by Drs. Sachs and Beckner in Hagerstown. The medication was not effective. They referred me to Dr. John D. Gottsch at The Wilmer Institute of Johns Hopkins Hospital.

The Wilmer Institute is a leading center for the treatment of eyes. After a thorough exam and testing, the doctor's impression was that I had an apparent allergic conjunctivitis and my symptoms seemed to be related to inhabiting my house. He suggested that I move out. So I went back to Helen Sayler's. I began using eye drops several times a day and was looking again for a place to live.

During all of this time we were trying to fix our home's heating, ventilating and air-conditioning system. The electricians were in and out of the house. The intake and the exhaust to the air-to-air heat exchanger were installed too close to each other. The intake was sucking in the exhaust. It was moved a number of times. The exhaust was left in the front of the house but the intake was moved to the rear through the attic and out onto the patio—a distance of nearly 100 feet. This effort failed and when the manufacturer was contacted, it became clear that the motor on the exchanger was not adequate to draw in air more than 50 feet away. All of this time, trouble and expense was for nothing. The air quality became worse and so did my symptoms.

A friend and fellow member of the Hagerstown Lions Club, the Rev. Clark Hayes, told me that he and his wife each had similar symptoms that seemed to be triggered by some of the things that triggered my symptoms. They had been treated at Johns Hopkins Hospital Asthma and Allergy Center by Dr. Richard Summers. He suggested that I make an appointment to see Dr. Summers.

I spoke with Dr. Clovis Snyder, who had become a close friend. I did not know whether he would be receptive to a second opinion from an allergist at Hopkins. To his credit, Dr. Snyder thought it was an excellent idea and wrote to Hopkins on my behalf.

My first visit to the Allergy and Asthma Center at Hopkins to meet with Dr. Summers was on June 11, 1990. Dr. Summers was a cheerful, personable, confident and competent physician who reminded me of Dr. Hawkeye Pierce on MASH, a TV sitcom. The doctors at Hopkins know how to listen. They do not rush a patient. Though the waiting rooms and reception rooms are generally full I have never felt rushed by a doctor. I always had ample time to explain my problem and to ask questions, and the doctor never appeared to be in a hurry to get me out.

After taking a history, tests and examination, Dr. Summers reviewed my case with me and explained that it was complicated. He could not guarantee a cure, but he did believe he could help relieve my symptoms. He prescribed certain medications and told me how to use them. I was told to keep in touch and to call back for an appointment whenever I felt the need to do so.

Dr. Summers seemed sincerely interested in my case and in helping me. He invited me to bring him any information I picked up along the way. I was now collecting newspaper articles, magazine articles and books on subjects that I thought were relevant to my case. On return visits I would show Dr. Summers an entire notebook. Each time Dr. Summers took the time to review each article.

Of all the articles and books I had read, none could answer this question: "How long is this pesticide, Dursban, going to affect my health?"

Literature from Dow Chemical U.S.A. indicated that at least the odor would dissipate within days. However, the pesticide itself would have to remain effective for many years to keep the termites out of the house.

A significant item appeared in *The Washington Post*, Saturday, Feb. 10, 1990, at page A2, entitled "Hypersensitivity to Chemicals Called Rising Health Problem." This article by Washington Post staff writer Michael Weisskopf reported on a study by Nicholas A. Ashford, associate professor of technology and policy at the Massachusetts Institute of Technology, and Claudia S. Miller of the University of Texas Health Science Center. While all of the material in that article is important, several relevant excerpts are set forth below.

> "Hypersensitivity to low levels of toxic chemicals is a serious and growing medical problem, threatening to cause "significant economic consequences" by disabling large numbers of otherwise healthy people, according to the most comprehensive study yet of the condition.

> "The nature and extent of 'chemical sensitivity' has been debated by medical experts for years. A National Academy of Sciences workshop in 1987 estimated that 15 percent of the population may suffer such wide- ranging symptoms as headaches, breathing problems, irregular heart beat and disorientation as a result of exposure to chemicals. And an emerging group of physicians called clinical ecologists treat patients as chemically sensitive.

> "But the established medical community has dismissed the problems as psychosomatic or undiagnosed allergies, complicating efforts by patients to claim health insurance and disability payments or persuade employers to improve working conditions.

> "Seeking to clarify the issue and remove victims from the 'cross-fire' of legal and medical debate, the report, prepared for the New Jersey Department of Health, concludes that scientific data are 'highly suggestive' that chemical sensitivity is a real medical problem and cast 'serious doubts on the detractions offered by many critics.'..." (© 1990, The Washington Post. Reprinted with permission.)

While this article by Weisskopf is more than six years old, it is still true and accurate today.

I obtained and reviewed a copy of the "New Jersey Report." It became the basis for Ashford and Miller's *Chemical Exposures: Low Levels, High Stakes* (New York: Van Nostrand Reinhold, 1991).

2

Is Your Office Making You Sick?

The April 1990 issue of REDBOOK magazine contained an excellent article beginning at page 114 entitled, "Is Your Office Making You Sick?" by Charles Piller, a medical writer at the University of California's San Francisco Medical Center, and Michael Castleman, editor of *Medical SelfCare* magazine in Pt. Reyes, Ca.

In bold letters next to the title is this synopsis:

"The symptoms include constant fatigue, coughing fits, headaches, burning eyes, breathing difficulties and dizziness. Millions of Americans who work in modern offices may be victims of the sick-building syndrome without knowing it. Are you one of them?" (Reprinted with Mr. Castleman's permission. This article was originally published in REDBOOK.)

The symptoms described in this article correspond to the symptoms I have had since March 23, 1988. The conclusion of the authors is: "Too little fresh air".

This magazine was furnished to me by Dr. Delaportas.

We were educating each other about the link between chemical exposure and illness.

3

Introduction to Rev. Charles and Paula Orr,
John and Lynn Bower,
and Allan Lieberman, M.D.

In 1990 we installed a new electric baseboard heating unit in place of the heat pump system. We also installed a radon mitigation system, removed carpets, upgraded the electrical system and installed vents in the laundry room and the bath.

Dr. Delaportas told me in June of 1990 that he had met another patient with chemical sensitivity. Her name was Paula Orr, wife of the Rev. Charles Orr, the minister at Harvest Baptist Church in Hagerstown.

I phoned Rev. Orr and made an appointment with him.

Rev. Orr was a young man—I would estimate in his mid 30s—with a great deal of enthusiasm. He introduced himself with a southern accent and, smiling, asked what he could do to help me.

I told him what had happened more than two years ago and what had been happening since. My story was not unfamiliar to him. He recounted how he and his wife Paula had been exposed to chemicals while living in Florida in a mobile home. Paula became very ill, which they later attributed to formaldehyde in the trailer and pesticides right outside. They left their home in Florida and came to Hagerstown for a better environment. Paula was a musician, composer and singer and the choir director, of the church but she was unable to mingle with the congregation or even the choir. She had to stay in a glass-enclosed contraption next to the choir. It was like a big box, only made out of glass so that she could see the choir and they could see her. She could also see the congregation and they could see her through the glass. This was like living in a bubble. Rev. Orr was an outstanding minister, and the congregation liked this young couple so much that they built them what was called a "safe home" on Fairview Mountain west of Hagerstown and north of Clear Spring, Md.

Rev. Orr invited me to inspect his home and to stay there while he and his family were on vacation. They were going to the beach, where, he said, the salt air was very healing for Paula.

He also came to my home with a crew of parishioners. They removed everything from my bedroom and used nontoxic material to seal it off from the rest of the house.

He made a number of helpful suggestions about coping with chemicals in the household and left me a tape cassette of beautiful songs composed and sung by Paula.

He gave me a copy of a newspaper clipping entitled "Hoosier creates 'safe' homes." This article was written by Kitty Unthank, a special correspondent for the newspaper in Bloomington, Ind. The story was about John and Lynn Bower. Bower designed and built a "safe" house for his wife Lynn, who is described as having an "eco-logical illness."

This was the first I had ever heard of John Bower, but I would hear much more about him later. And in 1996 I met him at the NCAMP Conference. He is the author of *The Healthy House* and other books and reports listed in Volume II.

Rev. Orr took me to his home in the mountains and gave me a tour. It was a pleasant, two-story frame and brick home with spacious rooms and bath. He had built with as many nontoxic building materials as he could afford. The HVAC system was designed to provide fresh and clean air. They also had an air fil-tration system that could be moved from room to room. It looked like a silver set of trays or shelves that filtered the air through activated carbon. I had a number of delightful meetings with Rev. Orr and attended several of his Sunday morning church services.

I thought it was wonderful of him to devote so much of his time and energy to helping me with my problem, considering I was Jewish and he was a Baptist. I found him to be a most tolerant person. He showed me great respect and courtesy and never tried to persuade me on religious matters.

He was called to another church in the south a year or two later, and he told me he intended to visit Israel and then go on a worldwide mission.

Paula had been suffering from chemical sensitivity for several years before my exposure, and they were both several years ahead of me in their knowledge of the affliction and how to cope with it.

Rev. Orr was a devoted husband who was always searching for ways to help his wife. He was from the south, and somehow he heard of a Dr. Lieberman who had a clinic for treatment of environmentally ill people. It was located in N. Charleston, S.C. He took Paula there for examination and treatment. When they returned to Hagerstown, he was enthusiastic about Dr. Lieberman and his work. They found it very helpful for Paula and her condition, and he recommended that I travel to Dr. Lieberman's clinic.

I took his advice. I was glad I did.

4

Radon Mitigation

Because the indoor air quality at my home was still not tolerable for me but was for others, in June 1990 I was referred to an outfit in Virginia called Infiltec that tested and treated homes for radon.

The gentlemen from Infiltec advised me in June 1990 that they were very interested in my problem because it may tie in with their radon mitigation research. Many people have theorized that the techniques used to mitigate the entry of soil gas containing radon may also work to prevent other pollutants such as termiticides from entering the house. Unfortunately there was little experimental data on this subject.

They were interested in working on my house with the objective of solving my problem and collecting data to write a research paper. They were trying to interest the EPA in providing funding for the research side of the work. They proposed to charge me their commercial rates for the basic work.

They made it clear that they would not be able to guarantee that my symptoms would be relieved since the procedures that they would use were experimental, and my symptoms may be due to hypersensitivity induced by initial high exposures.

At that point I had heard the word "radon" many times, but didn't know anything about it other than that I didn't want it in my home.

I met the gentlemen from Infiltec. They were experts and professionals. They were interested in my problem. And while they could not guarantee success, it was an exciting prospect. They were candid and honest and knowledgeable about chemicals and hypersensitivity. I accepted their offer.

They were able to interest the EPA. The EPA hired a contractor from Research Triangle Park, N. C., to do air testing during the summer of '90.

The EPA hoped to use a successful experiment as a basis to clean up the contaminated homes in Love Canal.

Radon mitigation has been proven to be effective. The theory and hope was that the system to clear the radon would also clear the pesticide or whatever was polluting the air.

James White, an EPA expert on indoor air quality, took charge of this project. He, his staff and the executives from Infiltec knew about indoor air quality in spacecraft and in submarines. I was in awe of their technical expertise.

If the project was successful, the benefit to the public would be enormous.

5

Concern About Chemicals and Cancer

In July, while all this other stuff was going on, I was advised to put my home back on the market. I turned it over to Frank Shank, a Realtor and fellow member of the Hagerstown Lions Club. He suggested a number of ways to spruce up the property and make it more marketable. He recommended a carpenter and jack-of-all-trades named Robert Muritz to do a little fixing up. Mr. Muritz was an older man who did things right. He took his time and did a lot. Frank Shank helped with landscaping and clipping shrubbery and made suggestions to Mr. Muritz.

The house was on the market while we were sampling the air, testing for radon and doing fix-up work.

I was sleeping outdoors on the patio on an army cot that summer.

There was no way I could forget about the illness. The illness was a part of me and it restricted my activities. I could go anywhere, but if I went to the wrong place, I paid the price in poor health.

In addition to the everyday symptoms, I was concerned about the development of chemical sensitivity and cancer.

Cancer was something I did not want to think about, but it was a threat hanging out there, like a sword of Damocles always hanging over my head.

It took the government years to ban chlordane. Meanwhile, innocent victims developed cancer and suffered and died from it. And other pesticides were reported to be carcinogenic. Dursban, or chlorpyrifos, was reported non-carcinogenic by Dow Chemical

Co. Every once in a while an article would appear in a newspaper or magazine linking cancer to different chemicals.

Such an article appeared in *The Daily Mail*, Hagerstown, Md., Thursday, July 26, 1990. The article was entitled "DDT linked to cancer in workers." As usual the report had supporters and skeptics.

The Healthy Home

In August 1990 I purchased a copy of *The Healthy Home: An Attic to Basement Guide to Toxin-Free Living*, by Linda Mason Hunter, published by Pocket Books, 1990. This was an important book for me because it defined the healthy home, gave advice on how to rid your house of hazards, how to create a healthy emotional atmosphere, how to make your house safe and secure and how to maintain the healthy home.

I did not have to read many pages to discover that the author knew about people like me. On page 5 I read the following:

"Medical problems caused by environmental hazards in the home are far-reaching. They range from respiratory irritations—stuffy nose, itchy throat, wheezing, shortness of breath—to more serious complaints of ear infection, asthma, and bronchitis. Such subtle symptoms as fatigue, headaches, inattentiveness, and dermatitis are possible reactions to an unhealthy environment.

"Some people react more quickly to contaminants than others do...But the people who have the most difficulty living in the 20th century are the chemically sensitive. For them, such ubiquitous phenomena as car exhaust, smog, formaldehyde in carpeting and building materials, hydrocarbons in vinyl furniture, perfumes, detergents, and fabric softeners cause severe problems.

"Some extremely sensitive people have to struggle to change their lifestyle to reduce exposure to debilitating chemicals.

This was a clear summation of what had been happening to me.

"One theory about hypersensitivity is that the chemicals that irritate hypersensitive people are poisonous to everyone—but most people never know it. There is growing evidence that the levels of chemicals we used to consider safe are really not...." (Reprinted with permission of the author.)

Precisely.

7

Chemicals Are Everywhere

When life is toxic, one must learn to cope.

I learned a great deal by trial and error during my quest for clean air and an environment that I could tolerate.

From my doctors, from reference books, from magazine and newspaper articles and from fellow sufferers, I gradually absorbed some of the rules of the game.

The medical treatment was alleviating some of my symptoms at times, but I hadn't found a cure. The best treatment is avoidance of the materials that trigger one's illness.

At this stage of my illness, more than two years after the onset, I was reading books about health and about houses and about healthy houses and about pollution and what could be done to clean up the environment.

Dursban, the chemical that made me sick, is one of thousands of pollutants we live with every day. We live with them not only in our home and other buildings, but in our cars and our trucks and our planes and our trains and in the places we visit, from hotels to shopping malls, from street corners to our great national parks. Chemicals are in the air, they are in our soil, in our water, in our food. They are everywhere.

The classical medical advice is avoidance, but if any place on this planet is chemical- and pollutant-free, I haven't found it.

8

Searching for a "Safe" House

Eloise and I spent a great deal of time looking for a new house. We searched Hagerstown and Washington County. And because Hagerstown is only seven miles from Pennsylvania and West Virginia, we looked at houses in all three states.

We read the classified ads and the real estate section of the newspapers. We met with real estate brokers who gave us tremendous amounts of time and took us to dozens of homes and properties in urban and agricultural areas within 50 miles of home.

We learned that if a house was new or newly remodeled, the indoor air quality was not tolerable.

So we finally decided to avoid going into new housing units.

We put the following ad in several newspapers:

"RETIRED professional couple desire to lease or lease w/option to buy a chemical-free & allergen-free 3-bdrm. 1-story residence in good residential neighborhood w/electric baseboard heat, central air, hardwood floors (no carpet), plaster walls, natural materials only..."

The ads were run in several papers over a period of several weeks, but there was no response. Not one.

We thought this simple ad boiled down all of the books and reference materials to a few simple criteria.

Forty or fifty years ago, what we were asking for was considered state-of-the-art and normal. There was nothing unusual about a home in a residential neighborhood with hardwood floors and no carpeting, plaster walls and natural materials. Electric baseboard heat came a little later, but it has been around for 30 or 40 years.

But most homes today are being built from synthetic, petro-chemical-based material and these give off toxic vapors. Some people become ill from the exposure.

Unable to find a new home that we could tolerate and afford, we looked at homes from 10 to 60 years old. Many had bare hardwood floors. Many had plaster walls, not drywall. Many had windows that opened. But unfortunately we found that the older the home, the more run down its condition. In certain communities the basements were wet and moldy and the heating systems were fueled by oil or coal or wood, which give off powerful odors and chemicals from combustion that I cannot tolerate. Lead and asbestos were also found in older homes.

We never found the right combination, though we looked almost daily for many months. A simple cabin in the woods, a residence with a magnificent view, a home on a golf course in a most desirable location—each had a significant defect. By then, I was so ill or sensitive to pollutants that I could not find a home where I felt any better than I did at my home.

We knew what we had at home. We did not know what other problems we would be getting into, assuming we would be able to take care of the obvious defects we found on our tours. New homes, old homes, city homes, or country homes, all seemed to be too great a risk. This was terribly stressful and frustrating. One had to maintain a sense of humor to avoid depression. We decided to take the home off the market and keep trying to try to fix it.

Chapter 9

"When Life is Toxic"

The most definitive and comprehensive magazine article on multiple chemical sensitivity that I found in 1990 was by Robert Reinhold in *The New York Times* magazine section, Sept. 16, 1990, beginning at page 50 entitled: "When Life Is Toxic: They Suffer Agonizing Reactions From Contact With Almost Anything Chemical, Forcing Them Into Protective Cocoons. They Call It a Disease, But Is It? Not All Doctors Are Convinced." (Copyright © 1990 by The New York Times Co. Reprinted by Permission.)

Reinhold presents case histories of a number of MCS victims, descriptions of the people while he was interviewing them and the ways they have adapted to their illness.

He discusses the relationships between the victims and medical doctors, studies about whether MCS is real or imaginary, the controversy among doctors and allergists and clinical ecologists, the variety of treatments used by clinical ecologists and the alleged results, and differing philosophies among physicians about how to treat the patients.

But the fact remains that every individual is endangered by the continued irresponsible use of thousands of toxic chemicals. What happened to me and thousands of other victims of chemical exposure can happen to you the reader. No one is safe. The public's health must be protected and given priority over the profits of special interests who are polluting our planet and devastating the lives of an unknown number of formerly healthy and productive citizens, most of whom are ignorant of the fact that their illness is caused or aggravated by pollution of the environment in which they live. Articles and books are not enough. We need a march on Washington and state capitals.

Year Four
1991
A.D.

"We are at a critical crossroads. We have at this time a small window of opportunity that may close if we do not take action to address the problems of the chemically sensitive individual in a caring and equitable way."

Nicholas A. Ashford and Claudia S. Miller, Chemical Exposures: Low Levels and High Stakes, *(New York: Van Nostrand Reinhold, 1991). Reprinted with permission.*

1

EPA: Your Home is Not a "Sick Building"
Ashford and Miller on "Chemical Sensitivity"

Significant excerpts from an EPA letter follow:

UNITED STATES ENVIRONMENTAL PROTECTION AGENCY
AIR AND ENERGY ENGINEERING RESEARCH LABORATORY
RESEARCH TRIANGLE PARK
NORTH CAROLINA 27711

January 30, 1991

Mr. Jacob Berkson

Dear Mr. Berkson:

I am wrapping up the work that we did at your home and desire to provide some information for your files to cover that work. First off, I want to thank you for your participation in the study and for the time and effort that you contributed. I realize that it was an inconvenience for you in several respects. However, the positive side is that nothing in our survey indicates that your house merits the label of a "sick building."...

In summary, as best as can be determined from both the contractor and in-house analysis of the data, there is nothing in your home that would merit labeling it as a "sick building." Your home has only "typical" concentrations of everyday vapor phase organics, none of which are directly attributable to soil gases and which could be used as an indicator of removal efficiency for further work...

Subsequent discussions of our data with health researchers have led me to conclude that it is possible for you to have become so sensitized as a result of your initial exposure that you might be responding to residual Dursban concentrations present at concentrations below our analytical ability to detect. However, there are no analytical reasons to believe that a "normal" (i.e., non-sensitized) person exposed to the indoor environment of your home would suffer the same adverse effects...

Finally, I have enclosed a copy of a recent New Jersey report on chemical sensitivity. There are references in the report that may help you locate a physician or other professional who can be of further assistance to you."

I was pleased to have this official letter assuring me that my home was not a sick building. This supported the position of the real estate agents and others who had visited and detected no problem.

It was now time to focus on the subject of chemical sensitivity.

The New Jersey Report on Chemical Sensitivity was written by Nicholas A. Ashford, Ph.D., Associate Professor of Technology and Policy, Massachusetts Institute of Technology, and Claudia S. Miller, Fellow in Allergy and Immunology, University of Texas Health Science Center, San Antonio.

At the time, this report was the most definitive on chemical sensitivity to come my way.

In the preface the authors point out:

"Sufficient 'proof' is not available to satisfy the most skeptical critic that chemical sensitivity exists as a physical entity; nor is there convincing proof that it does not. We, however, are persuaded that the collective evidence, in part anecdotal and in part based on good scientific studies, does present a sufficiently compelling case to warrant further study."

Among the groups prone to chemical sensitivity, according to the study, are industrial workers, "tight building" occupants, residents whose air or water is contaminated by chemicals and individuals who have had personal and unique exposure to chemicals in indoor air, pesticides, drugs, consumer products and so forth.

Under "Magnitude and Nature of the Problem" the authors state:

"Just how large a problem exists is not known at this time. The

National Academy of Sciences has suggested, without providing documentation, that approximately 15% of the population may experience 'increased allergic sensitivity' to chemicals [National Research Council 1987].

"To circumvent this problem, we propose the following *operational* definition of multiple chemical sensitivity, a definition that is based upon environmental testing:

> "The patient with multiple chemical sensitivities can be dis-covered by removal from the suspected offending agents and by re-challenge, after an appropriate interval, under strictly controlled environmental conditions. Causality is inferred by the clearing of symptoms with removal from the offending environment and recurrence of symptoms with specific challenge." [page v]

I heard Professor Ashford speak at the National Coalition Against the Misuse of Pesticides Conference in Alexandria, Va., in March 1991. I met him afterward and described my situation. He suggested that I write a book to help educate the public on this subject.

Ashford and Miller followed the New Jersey report with a book entitled *Chemical Exposures: Low Levels and High Stakes* (New York: Van Nostrand Reinhold, 1991). I got a copy in April of '91 and highly recommend it. A few pertinent excerpts follow:

> "Chemical exposures are endemic to our modern industrial society. Patients who believe they are chemically sensitive are caught up in an acrimonious cross fire among several different groups of physicians—traditional allergists; clinical ecologists; and in some cases, ear, nose and throat specialists; occupational physicians; and others."...

> "Science is not served by continuing to deny the probable existence of the problem in the face of massive and growing cir-cumstantial evidence, although admittedly subjective in many respects. A better approach would be to acknowledge that something appears to be going on, that low levels of chemicals can affect the body in subtle ways that currently escape our under-standing, and that individual susceptibility to environmental agents may vary by several orders of magnitude...

"...criticisms of therapies should not be used to foster a denial of the existence of chemical sensitivity altogether." (Reprinted with permission.)

Their recommendations include research, information, health care, alternative employment and housing, medical insurance, compensation, social and legal services, regulation of chemicals and resolution of conflicts among medical practitioners and their patients.

When I first read *Chemical Exposures: Low Levels and High Stakes*, I felt as if I were an undersea explorer who had just discovered a sunken Spanish galleon but had not yet learned the value or significance of its cargo. It would be a long time before I found the key to unlock the hold in which the cargo had been stored.

Moving to a Cabin in the Mountains of West Virginia

Unable to find safe housing after many months of searching, I accompanied Eloise to a rustic cabin she owned in Shannondale, a community that initially was developed for second homes and recreation in Jefferson County, W.Va. It consists of several hundred homes on several thousand acres from the foot to the peak of a ridge of the Blue Ridge Mountains. The focal point is a beautiful freshwater lake surrounded by nice homes, many of which are used year round. Eloise's log cabin was in the woods. It had a large living room, dining room, kitchen, two bedrooms, a complete bath and a large front porch. An annex building was beside it.

The cabin had not been opened for a long time and had a musty odor on that first visit. As I looked at the site and the location, the architecture, and the building material, it seemed close to what the books on healthy homes recommended.

"You had this cabin in the woods all this time and we never really thought about it," I remarked to Eloise. She had it beautifully furnished and used it often before her husband died. Her nieces and nephews loved to visit and play in the sand beach along the lake or hike in the woods.

Everything I read indicated that simple and less were better. I asked Eloise if she would consider moving most of the furniture from the cabin into the annex. She agreed and with helpers cleaned the cabin from top to bottom with water and baking soda. The solid wood furniture was left in place and the overstuffed furniture was removed. I converted the living room into a writing room by moving a large desk and my office chairs to where the sofas had stood. The floors, walls and ceiling were all wood. There was no carpet, drywall, particle board, or other synthetic material. The heating system was electric, so there were no odors from fuel oil or gas. All of the windows opened, permitting fresh mountain air to ventilate the living spaces. The cabin was less than a half-hour from Harpers Ferry.

I established my residence there in West Virginia. Eloise wanted to stay in Hagerstown. So we both got to spend some time alone. I was difficult to live with. The constant problems with my eyes, nose, head and stomach made me frustrated, angry and irritable. Eloise, on the other hand, was calm, cool and stoic. She put up with me and my complaints and I was grateful for her understanding and her loyalty. It is difficult for one to live with a spouse or a friend who has a chronic illness for which there appears to be no cure. All parties to the relationship are victims. Their lives are not normal. They are restricted in many ways. Each must do his best to be considerate of the other. This is easy to say but hard to accomplish.

3

"Exaggerated Sensitivity to an Organophosphate Pesticide"

A letter written by Norman E. Rosenthal, M.D., and Christine L. Cameron, B.S., was published in the February 1991 issue of the *American Journal of Psychiatry*.

Dr. Rosenthal and Cameron sent me a copy of the letter along with this note:

Dear Mr. Berkson:

Enclosed is a copy of "Exaggerated Sensitivity to an Organophosphate Pesticide" as it appears in the American Journal of Psychiatry. Once again we would like to thank you for sharing your experiences and helping us to further expose the problems associated with pesticides.

Sincerely,

Norman E. Rosenthal, M.D.
Christine L. Cameron

The letter to the editor reads:

Sir: Although it has been reported that organophosphate pesticides induce psychiatric symptoms—most notably, depression, psychosis, and anxiety—in chemical workers (1) or after intentional overdose, little has been written about the toxic effects of "routine" exposure in vulnerable individuals. Roueché (2), in a magazine article, reported on a woman whose idiosyncratic sensitivity went unrecognized by physicians, heightening her sense of isolation and despair. We present a case report of a patient with a long history of recurrent depressions.

Mr. A, a 64-year-old retired attorney, had been treated with a variety of mood-altering medications with limited success, due largely to his intolerance of side effects, even at low doses. Nevertheless, he had maintained reasonable mood control through psychotherapy, stress management, and regular exercise.

Following termite treatment of his house with the organophosphate chlorpyrifos, Mr. A noted a foul smell and shortly thereafter complained of severe abdominal pains, nausea, headaches, difficulty breathing, fatigue, and irritation of the eyes, nose, and throat, accompanied by anxiety and irritability. These symptoms have continued to plague Mr. A for the 2 years since the termite treatment whenever he is in his home and for many hours thereafter, and the irritation of his mucous membranes over the years has been validated by examination. His search for alternative lodgings whenever possible has created considerable stress but does help relieve the toxic symptoms.

Anticholinergic antidotes have offered minor relief. He is currently taking 2 mg of lorazepam at night to help him sleep and has tolerated this medication reasonably well. He has met with considerable skepticism about the authenticity of his symptoms both inside and outside the medical profession.

The symptoms reported by Mr. A are well-documented effects of organophosphate intoxication (3). However, they have been unusually severe and long-lived in his case. He has shown evidence of sensitivity to other environmental chemicals, for example, those emanating from new furniture and carpets, as well as to a variety of psychotropic medications.

Patients with extreme chemical sensitivity such as Mr. A offer the following lessons for psychiatrists. 1) We may be in the best position to detect and validate symptoms of intoxication from "safe" chemicals that do not appear to affect most people. 2) Like the oxygen-sensitive canaries that miners used to detect dangerously low levels of oxygen, these hypersensitive individuals might be signaling to us toxic effects experienced by far larger numbers, although to a lesser degree. The psychiatrist can act as a sentinel to alert public health officials of such cases and dangers. 3) Environmental toxins should be considered as potential triggers of apparently "idiopathic" exacerbations. Patients who are intolerant of psychotropic drugs and other chemicals may be prime candidates for such consideration. These patients should be encouraged to avoid the harmful chemicals, and in some cases antidotes may be available, for example, anticholinergic drugs for organophosphate intoxication. 4) For the researcher, this abnormal sensitivity raises the question of mechanism. It has been hypothesized that patients with depression are hypersensitive to the effects of acetylcholine (4), the very chemical whose breakdown is retarded by organophosphate pesticides. Such vulnerability to the effects of acetylcholine might account for both environmental hypersensitivity and the endogenous tendency to become depressed.

NORMAN E. ROSENTHAL, M.D.
CHRISTINE L. CAMERON, B.S.
Bethesda, Md.

American Journal of Psychiatriy, 148.2: 270 (1991), Copyright 1991 the American Psychiatric Association. Reprinted by permission.

Several readers commented on the Rosenthal-Cameron letter. One doctor who did not believe the illness as real criticized the writers for not recognizing a simple case of depression. On the other hand, Dr. Claudia Miller praised Dr. Rosenthal for his understanding of the problem and sent him a copy of her book.

Although my name was not mentioned, I received telephone calls from a number of people who knew me and knew my problem, wanting to confirm that "Mr. A" was really me. They were elated that a renowned psychiatrist recognized that the link between the chemical exposure and subsequent symptoms was real and not imaginary.

4

NCAMP and Dursban

I do not recall when I first heard the acronym "NCAMP," but as time went by, I heard of NCAMP more and more. I first contacted NCAMP in 1990 and received the following letter, dated Oct. 10, 1990.

> Dear Mr. Berkson;
>
> Thank-you for contacting the National Coalition Against the Misuse of Pesticides (NCAMP). I am sorry to hear of your problem resulting from the use of Dursban. The plethora of phone calls and letters we receive regarding this pesticide signify it as a particularly "bad actor." I am increasingly becoming aware of adverse incidents occurring and the pursuit of personal injury lawsuits. As such, I am considering undertaking a litigation clearinghouse project for this chemical as we have in the past for chlordane...
>
> For your information, I am enclosing a selection of materials regarding Dursban and some of the adverse human health incidents that have resulted from its use....
>
> I hope these materials are helpful to you. Let us know if we can be of further assistance.
>
> Sincerely,
>
> Catherine Karr, MS
> Staff Toxicologist

The enclosures were helpful and provided much valuable information.

The literature described NCAMP as "a national, nonprofit membership organization of groups and individuals seeking to better protect the public and workers from the dangers of toxic pesticides through improved chemical controls and the promotion of alternative pest management strategies…"

I joined NCAMP in February 1991 and in March I attended their 10th Anniversary Pesticide Forum at Alexandria, Va., four days of workshops, seminars, lectures and meeting new friends, culminating in a trip to meet with congressmen on Capitol Hill.

It was an exciting and educational forum. I met Janette D. Sherman, M.D., of Alexandria, Va., and Mel Reuber, M.D., staff toxicologist for NCAMP in Washington at the workshop on Toxicology and Human Health.

Dr. Sherman, an internist and toxicologist, compared the ingredients in pesticides to those in war gasses developed by the Nazis and used in World War II. She specifically mentioned chlorpyrifos, exposure to which sometimes resulted in headaches, confusion and seizures. She stated in no uncertain terms that Dursban constitutes a major public health threat and that we must take Dursban off the market.

I asked her what the acceptable treatment is for one poisoned by Dursban.

"No effective treatment is known. We don't know what works. Prevention is the only answer," she replied.

"Where does one go for relief while suffering from Dursban poisoning?" I asked.

"There is no safe place."

I was impressed with Dr. Sherman and her presentation. I had the privilege of meeting her after the workshop, and she offered to help in any way she could.

5

Chemical Exposure and Disease: Diagnostic and Investigative Techniques, By *Janette D. Sherman, M.D.*

I ordered a copy of Dr. Sherman's book. The revised edition is published by Princeton Scientific Publishing Co., Inc., P.O. Box 2155, Princeton, New Jersey 08543, Tel. 609-683-4750, Fax 609-683-0838, 1994. When it arrived, I could not put it down.

Dr. Sherman devoted an entire chapter to pesticidal chemicals. She points out that if you want to buy certain medications, you must have a prescription from a doctor trained in the effects of that medication; but under the Federal Insecticide, Fungicide and Rodenticide Act (FIFRA), those hired by the holder of the pesticide license, the people who perform the actual application, might have little or no understanding of the toxicology of these products and may indeed be illiterate. There is no provision under FIFRA for the consumer to receive advance information about a product intended for use in the home or workplace. Dr. Sherman wrote at p. 139:

> "Pesticides are biocides ('bio' meaning life and 'cide' meaning kill)— chemicals that kill life. Any prudent person must learn about and understand the toxicology of these products before their use. The products registered and controlled under this EPA regulation kill insects, fungi, and rodents, as its name indicates..."

> "There is no federal record-keeping repository to track the health status of persons living in homes treated with any of the various pesticidal chemicals approved for home use..."

This is what she has to say about Dursban at p. 144 specifically.

"The structure of Dursban[R], an organophosphate, is responsible for anticholinesterase effects, in addition to the properties conferred upon it by its organochlorine structure. This pesticide, Dursban[R], is promoted by its manufacturer, Dow Chemical Co., as a substitute for chlordane. Despite an EPA finding of omissions and inadequacies in the company's studies, it continues to be used both inside and outside of buildings. Like data submitted by many other manufacturers to EPA for registration of pesticides, many of the data submitted for DursbanR are unpublished, and access to the data is limited, negating a prime precept of science, that is, open critical review of research efforts. One might argue, if a product is claimed to be safe, why can't the public have access to the data on which the opinion is based?..."

To the pesticide applicator and the consumer goes this advice:

"...before you use *any* pesticidal product be sure you obtain information about, and understand its potential for adverse effects. These are products designed to kill, and their harm may extend to non-target species."

At page 150 Dr. Sherman warns us that:

"Cancer is a major cause of illness and death, and various pesticides have wide-ranging effects that include cancer, neurological disorders, and birth defects; so it is imperative that a registration and monitoring system be put in place to track the use of these chemicals." (Reprinted with permission.)

If this were monitored on a national level, such as by the Centers for Disease Control, we may learn of thousands of our fellow citizens who were in the wrong place at the wrong time and were poisoned by Dursban.

Rachel Carson warned the public about DDT, but it took many years before public pressure forced the government to remove it from the market. Cancer-causing chlordane remained on the market for 20 years after the first documented cases of cancer caused by chlordane were in the public domain. Unknown numbers of innocent people developed cancer or died from exposure to chlordane long after it was known to be a carcinogen.

Dr. Sherman picked up the torch carried by Rachel Carson in *Silent Spring* and, in my opinion, someday will be as honored and recognized for her work as Rachel Carson was for hers. Her work is in the public interest, and people will be healthier if they and the government pay attention to what Dr. Sherman has to say and take appropriate action.

6

Pesticides and Cancer

Pesticides are a major health threat. No one is safe. Everyone knows what a "risk" is, but what is the definition of risk in terms of exposure to pesticides? That subject was discussed by experts with respect to cancer risk assessment at the NCAMP forum.

Dr. Samuel S. Epstein, professor of Occupational and Environmental Health at the University of Illinois Chicago, and William Lijinski, director of the Chemical Carcinogenesis Unit, NCI Frederick Cancer Research Facility, Frederick, Md., spoke at the forum. Dr. Epstein told us that we are in the midst of a cancer epidemic. One in three people are getting cancer, and one in four are dying from it. There has been a big increase in cancer cases over the years. In the same time that 300,000 people are alleged to have died from AIDS, more than 5 million died of cancer.

There were only a few synthetic chemicals before 1940. By 1950, 50 billion pounds of synthetic chemicals were on the market and few were tested adequately.

Epstein is a pathologist. He gave a chronology of the Delaney risk assessment. He said we are dealing with scam and rubber numbers when we listen to the EPA and industry. In 1954 the Miller amendments established that pesticides can be used if the benefit is greater than the risk. In 1958 Congressman Delaney sponsored legislation to prohibit use of carcinogens in food.

Epstein pointed out that no one knows how to find a safe level of a carcinogen, and that the FDA has plotted to overturn the Delaney amendment. It speaks of "safe levels" and "negligible levels," but there really is no such thing. Epstein wants us to keep the Delaney amendment.

Epstein is a powerful speaker and advocate for public health. He does not contend that pesticides or chemicals are the sole cause of cancer, but it is his opinion that these toxic chemicals, including pesticides, are a factor and that there are alternatives to their use.

Unfortunately, Dr. Samuel Epstein and Dr. Janette Sherman are in the minority among those who speak about cancer and its causes. We need at least a hundred more Dr. Epsteins and Dr. Shermans—two or three for each state. Perhaps the legislators won't agree with them, but at least they will be heard. One Dr. Epstein or one Dr. Sherman cannot appear before every legislative body in the United States. We need people like them to educate not only the Congress, but also the state legislatures, county commissioners and local mayors and councilmen. Each has constituents dying or dead of cancer. Many have relatives or friends afflicted with cancer or other diseases caused or aggravated by chemical exposure in the home, in the workplace, in the school and public buildings and on our highways.

Everyone is at risk. Like the canaries in the coal mine who warned that the air was poisoned, we the victims of toxic chemical exposure are warning you, the reader, that what happened to us might eventually happen to you or to someone you love unless this misuse of toxic chemicals is halted.

7

Diet for a Poisoned Planet

David Steinman, author of *Diet for a Poisoned Planet: How to Choose Safe Foods for You and Your Family* (New York: Harmony Books, a division of Crown Publishers, Inc. 1990, Copyright © 1990 by David Steinman) was the featured speaker at the NCAMP Conference. As a journalist and a fisherman in Los Angeles, he found in 1985 that Santa Monica Bay was a large reservoir of DDT. Thirty people who ate fish caught in Santa Monica Bay were found to have high levels of DDT, DDT-metabolites and PCB's in their blood.

DDT causes cancer. Steinman was told not to write about that. He went to interview California health officials and came to the conclusion that they were public relations people, not public health officials. When he looked into other foods including meat, dairy, raisins, strawberries, he found that they were as bad or worse. He published stories on food groups and reported on safe fish for the National Academy of Sciences.

His book furnishes evidence that the foods we eat and the water we drink are no longer pure sources of nourishment and pleasure. Modern methods of farming and food processing, including heavy reliance on pesticides and other dangerous chemicals, have brought poisons into the food chain.

In the Foreword to the book, William Marcus, Ph.D., Senior Science Advisor, U.S. Environmental Protection Agency, writes:

"This book will change how you approach the food you eat every day. It may even change the methods used by our farm community to produce our food. Written in the tradition of Upton Sinclair's *The Jungle* and Rachel Carson's *Silent Spring*, *Diet for a Poisoned*

Planet overturns the idea that our food supply is free of contamination from toxic chemicals. With great insight and clarity, David Steinman explains which foods promote good health and which foods are so burdened with poisons that they adversely affect your health...

"I heartily recommend this book as required reading both because it can help you cut down your exposure to carcinogens and because by following the steps outlined here you can immediately and dramatically improve your health." (Reprinted with permission.)

In an appendix to the book, Mr. Steinman provides a safe foods shopping list that he calls "green light" foods, a personal action guide and a glossary of pesticides and toxic chemicals. Certain foods are given the yellow light, signifying caution, and other foods are given a red light. The red light foods are hazardous to your health, according to Mr. Steinman, based on EPA and FDA data.

This book is a warning that what we eat may be hazardous to our health.

When I told David Steinman briefly what had happened to me following exposure to Dursban, he suggested that I write a book. I told him I did not know how to write a book. He took me into a nearby room and wrote an outline, off the top of his head of what he thought the book should contain. He got me started writing *A Canary's Tale*.

I had been wandering in the woods for the past three years trying to find out what was happening to me and to my house, and at this seminar I met leading experts who were helpful, considerate and encouraging.

8

Environmental Activist Diane Heminway

Besides meeting some of the leading authorities on pesticides, I met with many environmental activists and victims of exposure to pesticides, including Dursban. For the first time since my traumatic exposure I met other people who had similar experiences in their own homes, in schools, public buildings, the workplace and on farms. There were people much worse than I: people wearing oxygen masks and people with nervous tics and sickly looking people who were no longer able to work or function in society. Some came to tell their stories, others came to listen. Some came for help, others came to give help and advice. I met people from many walks of life who were disabled after exposure to pesticides.

One young woman who greatly impressed me was Diane Heminway. We were in several of the workshops together. Her children were exposed to methyl isocyanate while attending school close to a chemical company.

"How are the children now?" I asked.

"They're okay but vulnerable. We have to be very careful."

She gave me an article which I did not read until I returned to my new home in West Virginia.

"The Great Big FMC Corporation and a Schoolyard" by Diane Heminway was a four-page piece published in the Spring 1989 *Journal of Pesticide Reform*. In it Diane explained what happened in November 1984.

"On that 1984 autumn day, while attending school, my five-year- old daughter and seven-year-old son were exposed to methyl isocyanate (MIC), the same chemical which, 18 days later, destroyed the lives and health of thousands of people in Bhopal, India. The exposure was caused when 50 gallons of the chemical was accidentally spilled at the FMC plant.

"Methyl isocyanate, used in the production of the pesticide carbofuran, is not only extremely reactive, it is also very volatile. Within minutes the fumes were being drawn into the elementary school classrooms through the ventilation system... Nine children and two adults were taken to a nearby hospital and were examined by FMC's plant doctor...

"As it was, our children received an estimated exposure of two to four parts per million—100 to 200 times the federal exposure limit for an adult's eight-hour work day.

"Not unlike those studied in Bhopal, my son Aaron experienced a severe asthma attack five months after his exposure to MIC. Since then, on numerous occasions, he has been rushed to the hospital or a doctor's office for emergency treatments. I have watched my son's health deteriorate to the point of requiring an air filter in his bedroom, a breathing machine at his bedside, a pocket bronchodilator for use in school and during severe bouts, and prescriptions of prednisone....

"Despite documented *groundwater* contamination and recommendations in 1975 to test private wells, little was done over the next decade to investigate the possibility that people were *drinking* contaminated water or being exposed to contaminated *soils.*

"...As expected, elevated levels of arsenic, lead, and pesticides were revealed in the schoolyard...

"The New York State Department of Health acknowledged the presence of contamination and in fact stated that the children were 'at an increased risk of exposure.'..." (Reprinted with permission.)

I was shocked. I had not absorbed what she told me when we were together. I had no idea that this young lady, probably as young as or younger than my daughter Susan, had faced such a tragedy and had led a battle against a giant corporation without the support or assistance of the state or other authorities until they were dragged by the neck to face the consequences of their adverse effects on the environment and human beings.

I wrote her a letter commending her. I soon heard from Diane and she assured me that she and her husband and children had moved from that contaminated community to a much cleaner place next to a federal wildlife refuge in upstate New York. I was relieved to hear that they had moved. Diane was several years ahead of me in environmental activism, and she gave me a lot of information about chemical exposure and illness. Networking and support groups are important.

The work that Diane did inspired others to investigate similar incidents and ask questions, to learn to write and expose the polluters to public humiliation and finally to force the governmental authorities to enforce the law, which they should have been doing in the first place.

Center for Environmental Medicine
North Charleston, South Carolina

In May 1991 I traveled to N. Charleston, S.C., for examination and treatment at the Center for Environmental Medicine.

Upon my arrival I saw cars with license plates from many states parked in the Center's parking lot. On the front door the following instruction:

REMINDER...PLEASE READ

CENTER FOR ENVIRONMENTAL MEDICINE
7510 Northforest Drive
North Charleston, SC 29420

PLEASE READ BEFORE ENTERING OFFICE

We absolutely cannot allow you in the office if you are wearing perfume, cologne, aftershave, or have the scent of tobacco smoke, fabric softener or perfume in your clothing!

Many of our patients are triggered by these odors and the scents dramatically interfere with testing. If you are wearing any scented product or are in the habit of wearing scented products, please RING THE BELL to the right of the entrance door. Do not enter the lobby!

We must have your cooperation and appreciate your consideration for our chemically sensitive patients.

PLEASE REMEMBER...
NO PERFUMESNO SCENTED BATH POWDERS
NO COLOGNESNO SCENTED HAIR SPRAYS
NO AFTERSHAVESNO FABRIC SOFTENERS
and NO TOBACCO!

(Reprinted with permission.)

The medical director is Dr. Allan D. Lieberman, a distinguished specialist in environmental and occupational medicine, respected here and abroad. Dr. Lieberman reviewed my records and gave me a thorough physical examination. He explained to me the concept of environmental medicine.

> "Our approach is wholistic," as explained in a brochure cited in Volume II Section V, A. "We focus on every part of your body, including the brain which controls thinking, perception, mood and behavior.
>
> "Your body is subjected to many stresses such as infection, weather, emotion, allergy, addiction and toxic chemicals. In time, such stresses may lead to chronic illness and disease. We are interested in reducing your total stress load and in particular, reducing your total allergic and toxic chemical load. This load encompasses the total environment—the air we breathe, the food we eat, the water we drink and the chemicals which pollute them."

That afternoon he utilized a procedure known as provocation-neutralization to determine if I was sensitive to petrochemicals.

I was amazed that this technique brought out or provoked all of my symptoms. A small dose of a chemical was placed under my tongue and I was given a clipboard with an alarm clock on it, usually set for about 10 minutes. After the drop was put under my tongue, the clock was set and I sat on a chair beside a number of other patients who also were being tested. When the alarm clock went off I would return to the technician who had administered the dose and tell her what my symptoms were to that point. She would then squirt another dose under my tongue and repeat the process. Symptoms included irritation of the eyes and nose, headache, odors in the nose and, lastly, severe abdominal pain which doubled me up. I said I did not want to continue the test because it was too painful. They reduced the dose and after a while, all of the symptoms disappeared. It was like magic. When I left the office late that afternoon, my head was clear, the aches and pains were gone and for the first time in many months I did not have a bad smell coming from my nose and my sinus.

The doctor's summary described what I was exposed to, my symptoms and the development of the gland enlargement that signaled the onset of multiple chemical sensitivity.

After diagnosis, the doctor gave me a written plan involving nutritional support and use of Petro-Proteus drops and Atropine. He suggested that I consider the biodetoxification program and set forth instructions for follow-up.

The biodetoxification program was explained as a process by which the toxins could be sweated out of the fatty tissue through a rigorous program of aerobic exercises followed by time in a sauna. The plan was to begin with five to 10 minutes in the sauna and work up to 30 minutes. The temperature in the sauna was to be about 140°, somewhat lower than usual. The program was to run five and a half days a week for four to six weeks.

The doctor compared my body to a glass of water that was over-flowing, and suggested that through this detox program the body would be made less than full. In other words, decreasing the toxicity in the body would reduce my reactions when exposed to additional toxins.

I was taken to the clinic's detoxification area. It was a clean, hospital-like atmosphere with several saunas, separate locker rooms and shower rooms for men and women, a TV and VCR for exercise tapes and cots for resting and massages. There were, as I recall, six patients going through detox. I was introduced to each of them and given the opportunity to join them for a few days. I did, and noticed the patients all seemed to be cheerful. This surprised me. I thought people with this illness would be rather sad. But after exercising with them and hearing them joke with each other, I asked, "Why are you people laughing?" Julie (not her real name) answered, "We're going to get well. We have a doctor who believes us and who is helping us." Julie, a nurse, had been exposed to Dursban and became ill with symptoms similar to mine. She was no longer able to work as a nurse.

Sheila was a schoolteacher who had been poisoned from

Dursban sprayed in her school—her classroom and her cafeteria. She was no longer able to teach. She had seen several doctors without any kind of effective treatment. She was humiliated when a doctor told her to see a psychiatrist. She got no support from the board of education. She had saved her money for quite some time to enroll in this program. She was convinced that she was going to get well.

Linda, who had been a stockbroker, was poisoned by Dursban and no longer able to work. I have been in contact with Linda since meeting her at Charleston and visited her in the winter of 1992 at her new home in St. Augustine, Fl., which she and her husband built to be safe and nontoxic. It was built in a development that had environmental restrictions and would not permit pesticide spraying. I wrote to Linda in August '93 requesting permission to summarize her story She agreed. This is what she provided:

Poisoned by Dursban. Between 1985-87 monthly spraying in work place and occasional spraying at home.

Initial symptoms: excessive salivation, diarrhea, vomiting, joint pain, spacey, inability to concentrate, memory loss, hypoglycemic-like symptoms.

Initially approached traditional M.D.'s of various specialties like arthritis, gastroenterologist, urologist, cardiologist. All said they could find no problems. They did not help me. They did not recognize the link between my chemical exposure and my symptoms.

Treatment: Various medications, mostly antibiotic & heart meds.

Bloodwork for pesticides & VOC's showed 7 solvents. I reacted to everything. Was not chemically sensitive before the incident. Had no allergies before the incident.

Normal activities/career before exposure incident: Worked full time for 25 years as Secretary-Administrative Asst.

Age when poisoned: 36 to 38

Treatment that has been helpful: Sauna, provocation-neutralization, rotation diet, avoidance.

All exposures to all chemicals triggers my symptoms. Only through total isolation can these triggers be avoided.

Activities: Swimming at beach, TV, reading, writing, environmental education & activist.

Was in good health before this incident.

My life is entirely changed. I am unable to seek gainful employment. I am severely limited in social contacts and lead a life of isolation to avoid chemical exposures.

Before MCS I led a full & active life. I did choral & group singing, attended church & various social functions, attended college, worked full time, and raised a family. Since the poisoning I can barely care for myself & home, without hired help.

A typical day:
Rise 8:30 & dress.
Cook all meals for day before noon.
Go to beach to breathe for several hrs.
Rest in afternoon.
Bed rest from 7 PM to 11 PM or later.
Midnight to dawn - intermittent sleep.

How do I cope:

I long ago decided I could only cope with my own personal losses from this illness if I could help prevent someone else from facing the same suffering I have. I cope by peer counseling, educating on environmental issues, letter writing to legislators and linking up with like minded Activists. I also write articles about my experiences. All of this has given purpose to my illness.

Linda Wilson

(Reprinted with permission.)

John (not his real name) was a victim of Agent Orange in the Vietnam War. This was the first time he had been given effective treatment.

Another of the men had worked as a technician in a chemical laboratory in Pittsburgh and had been overcome by vapors and fumes from the chemicals he worked with. He was in bad shape and there was some question whether he would live, but Dr. Lieberman gave him hope and encouragement. His capable staff members were well- trained to help these patients.

I couldn't stay with the program because I couldn't tolerate the motels I stayed in. Dr. Lieberman suggested that I take a trip to one of the beaches. He felt the ocean air would help.

He was right. Daily walks on the beach, breezes off the Atlantic Ocean and ocean bathing cleared my head and relieved my symptoms. But I still had problems tolerating the condo, which was more or less a new building, fully carpeted and with upholstered furniture that one finds in a typical beach home. Fortunately, I could open windows. I could not tolerate the air-conditioning. The real saving grace was a large screened-in back porch which served as an extra room. I ate, slept and spent most of my inside time there.

I usually felt better outside, no matter where I went.

Following the trip to Kiawah Island, I checked out with Dr. Lieberman and flew back to West Virginia.

I talked with Dr. Lieberman several times after that and he was always very helpful. I met him again in the spring of '93 on my way back from Florida, and he was very encouraging about my book.

I returned to Charleston in October '93 to consult with Dr. Lieberman and to inspect a "safe house" that was remodeled by Jim Jackson, one of Dr. Lieberman's patients. I found the house to be well designed for chemically sensitive people and would recommend it to others. In summary, I found the Center for Environmental Medicine to be an appropriate and excellent place for education, examination, diagnosis and treatment of my illness. When I returned home I made copies of Dr. Lieberman's report for my other doctors, all of whom seemed to be impressed.

Unfortunately, the traditional medical establishment does not recognize multiple chemical sensitivity (MCS) as a real disease, does not recognize the concept of provocation-neutralization and does not accept detoxification as an appropriate treatment. They demand more scientific proof. The problem for the patient is that the patient is ill and needs help NOW. The established medical profession is not providing effective treatment. Patients go to environmental centers for treatment. Insurance companies do not pay for treatment that is not recognized. This is very sad, indeed. To my knowledge, there is no cure for MCS but there are treatments to relieve symptoms.

Environmental medicine offers no cure but does hold out hope. It offers the patient an education and methods to cope with the results of exposure to toxic chemicals. Dr. Lieberman also teaches avoidance and prevention. He is a very caring, competent, and knowledgeable medical doctor.

Avoidance is best, but avoidance of chemicals is difficult in a chemical society. That is why it is important to prevent pollution and prevent exposure in the first place, rather than accept pollution and attempt to clean it up after the fact. Prevention is the key, and education is the key to prevention.

10

Back in West Virginia

We did not have much rain that summer and the road system at Shannondale, W.Va., was not all hard-surfaced. Vehicles created a lot of dust on unpaved roads. I walked along these roads from the cabin to the lake. Every passing car kicked up dust. The air was not good. I carried my gas mask with me and covered my nose with it every time I saw a car approach. On occasion, smoke drifted from other cabins into mine and once in a while someone would throw chemicals on weeds and burn them, making this recreational resort unsafe for anyone, especially a chemically sensitive person.

The air conditioning ducts, as it turned out, were made of fiberboard, which contains formaldehyde. We took them out and put in metal ductwork. The forced air then had an oil smell. I telephoned the Allergy Relief Shop in Knoxville, Tenn., and asked one of the advisors there why the air smelled like oil. I put the contractor on the extension phone. The advisor asked, "Did you remove the oil from the metal before you made the ductwork?"

I had never heard of oil on ductwork and I looked at the contractor.

"There was oil on all of the metal," he admitted.

The counselor said, "Yes, the manufacturer puts oil on the metal to keep it from rusting. Before you take the flat metal and make ductwork out of it, the oil should be removed by steam cleaning or TSP."

The contractor had been focused on preventing insulation, dust or dirt from getting into the ductwork and had completely overlooked the oil on the metal. The contractor agreed to remove the ductwork and clean it up, but he never did.

• • •

In October I took a trip to Oregon, where my sons Dan and Jim were living. I saw my grandson Randy for the first time.

Both sons were living in apartments. I stayed in a separate apartment in a complex where Danny lived. Although it was carpeted and had overstuffed furniture, I was able to open the windows and tolerate it.

I was eager to test the air on the Oregon coast so Danny and his wife Julie drove me to Cannon Beach, some miles from Portland, where the air was clean. We drove through beautiful forests and along the Pacific Ocean.

In Portland, one smells smoke in the air. Some people use wood to heat their homes. Occasionally, the smoke makes it difficult to breathe. People with asthma, emphysema and other lung and respiratory problems are adversely affected by wood smoke.

Avoidance is one method of coping. Using a respirator is another. Prevention at the source would be welcomed by the victims, but is unlikely to occur unless the air quality becomes a problem for many more people and is recognized as a health hazard by the guardians of the public health, whoever they may be.

11

Prostate Surgery
Enlarged Salivary Gland

I had been having problems with frequency and urgency of my urinary system for some time following the chemical exposure. By July the urologist prepared me for prostate surgery, all other treatment having proved futile.

Prior to the surgery, the salivary gland in my neck on the left side had enlarged noticeably. I presented myself to Dr. Bandy, the surgeon who had removed the salivary gland on the right side of my neck following the exposure at my home in 1988. Dr. Bandy recommended surgical excision of this submandibular and there was some discussion as to whether it could be done at the same time as my prostate surgery. The urologist explained the prostate surgery would be under a local anesthetic, while Dr. Bandy's surgery required a general anesthetic. The matter became complicated. The urologist moved forward to make all arrangements for the prostate matter. It was not good practice to attempt to do both surgeries at the same time. After the trauma of the prostate, I decided to obtain a second opinion on the salivary gland matter and with Dr. Bandy's permission went to Johns Hopkins Hospital where Dr. Koch, an expert in that field, put me through tests and recommended that we not undergo surgery at this time but follow the gland. That is the procedure we have followed to date. It waxes and wanes depending upon the exposure.

At the hospital, my bed was separated from the other bed in the semi-private room by a large, heavy odoriferous plastic curtain. So smelly was the curtain that I pushed it as far as I could from my bed but had no way to take it down nor did I think that I had the authority to do that. I called the hospital housekeeping staff and told them that I was a chemically sensitive person and that the plastic curtain separating the room was irritating and making me ill. I was assured that someone would check into it. While I was undergoing prostate surgery housekeepers removed the offensive curtain and replaced it with a clean cotton one free of any fragrance. I found the hospital staff to be most cooperative in getting rid of the fragrances in the bathroom and at every request I made.

This was progress.

My third grandchild, Joel Isaac Slaff, was born to Susan and Jerry on November 7, 1991, while I was in the Washington County Hospital for the prostate surgery.

My excellent urologists were Dr. Lawrence A. Jones FACS, Dr. Hugh J. Talton FACS, Dr Wayne A. McWilliams FACS, and Dr Patrick J. Dennis FACS of the Urological Center PA of Hagerstown.

12

Your Home, Your Health, & Well-Being

Before the end of '91, I purchased the book, *Your Home, Your Health, & Well- Being* (Berkeley, California: Ten Speed Press, 1988) by David Rousseau, Dr. W. J. Rea and Jean Enwright.

Dr. W. J. Rea is one of the best-known clinical ecologists in the country and scarcely an article, either for or against chemical sensitivity, omits his name as a leading proponent of environmental medicine. Dr. Rea is a surgeon who became poisoned from chemicals used in the operating room and had to give up surgery a while. He was treated and became very knowledgeable about environmental illness. He is director of a well- known environmental health center in Dallas. I refer to the book as Dr. Rea's book although there are two other authors and many contributors.

The book tells you everything you need to know about how your home and your health are affected by the environment. The section on building materials tells you what to use from foundation to roof. The book can't be beat for readability and completeness, helpful not only to people who are chemically sensitive but to anyone who wants to live in a healthy home. I have referred to this book many times and bought copies for my children and some of my doctors. I highly recommend it.

The year ended with me living in West Virginia and visiting Eloise in Hagerstown. I was treated by 10 medical specialists that year. It was a year filled with learning, meeting other people and discovering that environmental pollution and environmental illness were mighty big subjects to study.

Year Five
1992
A.D.

"The global environmental crisis is, as we say in Tennessee, real as rain, and I cannot stand the thought of leaving my children with a degraded earth and a diminished future."

From EARTH IN THE BALANCE by Al Gore. Copyright © 1992 by Senator Al Gore. Reprinted by permission of Houghton Mifflin Company.

1

Medicals

My medical problems continued like a plague throughout 1992. The symptoms were the same, more or less, as in the prior years. During 1992 I was examined and treated by nearly 20 different medical specialists—in urology, dentistry, environmental medicine, the sinus, the salivary gland, gastroenterology, allergy, psychiatry, dermatology, ophthalmology, podiatry, internal medicine, allergy and asthma, diagnostics and taste and smell.

The most unusual was the taste and smell clinic on MacArthur Boulevard in Washington, D.C. The director, Dr. Robert Henkin, took a thorough history and put me through multiple testing. The conclusion was that my taste was normal but my sense of smell was dysfunctional. His clinical tests confirmed my complaints. I was looking for treatment.

The doctor explained that my cholesterol was too high and that I should cut down on fats, meats, dairy and eggs (all of the things I did not eat to any extent) and eat more vegetables and fiber, which was exactly what I had been eating for many years.

My diet was low in cholesterol and saturated fats, but it did not seem to reduce my cholesterol, which generally tested a little below or a little above 300.

Dr. Henkin suggested I use Puritan vegetable oil in place of margarine and butter.

The most significant treatment he prescribed was to irrigate my nasal passages by schnuffeling salt water through the nose. You fill an eight-ounce cup with lukewarm water and stir in 1/4 teaspoon of salt. You then pour the solution into the left hand, put that hand under the left nostril and suck up the solution. You do that twice then change hands and repeat.

At first I thought this was hilarious. I had read about this taste and smell clinic, waited weeks for an appointment, written page after page of my medical history, suffered through hours of testing, had kept a log of what I had eaten—everything that had gone into my stomach over a period of a week or 10 days, all of which was put into computers—and I end up with a prescription my grandmother used before there were computers and before there were doctors who specialized in the field of taste and smell.

You do this after you get up and again before you go to bed, and sometimes in between. It clears the nose, aids breathing, and seems to prevent infections.

To my surprise, this simple prescription turned out to be half of the most effective treatment I received during my years of searching for medical treatment. When I reported this to my other doctors, they usually smiled, nodded and said that their grand-mothers, too, used this as a treatment.

Dr. Snyder had given me the same prescription on several occasions. It consisted of boiling 8 ounces of salted water, pouring some into a smaller bottle and putting 10-15 drops in each nostril up to four times a day to wash out encrusted mucous. Dr. Summers at the Johns Hopkins Asthma and Allergy Center suggested that I follow this up by using a nasal spray containing Intal or Cromolyn solution.

Eloise followed Dr. Snyder's instructions faithfully and made a new solution each week with two bottles of the simple saline solution and one bottle mixed with Intal. It was more effective schnuffeling the saline up the nostril than using a dropper. This was further refined when I met Natalie Golos, co-author of *Coping With Your Allergies*. New York: Simon and Schuster, Inc., 1986.

"When you pour that saltwater into your hand, doesn't it leak out and you find yourself schnuffeling air instead of water?" she asked.

"Yeah, that has always been a problem. Some of the water always leaks out."

"Well, here is a saucer. Try pouring the saline solution from your cup into this saucer and then hold the saucer under your nostril and schnuffel it from the saucer."

I tried it. It worked. I use it two or three times a day. Thanks, Natalie!

I use a combination of the saline nasal irrigation, followed by the Intal-Cromolyn solution, followed at times by Vancenase AQ nasal solution. These nasal solutions contain no preservatives or additives.

Each person has to experiment with these medications to find out which are most helpful. I found that each doctor had something to offer.

Near the end of the year I was fed up with my lack of improvement. I was tired of going from doctor to doctor to have my symptoms treated without curing the underlying disease or condition. I could not avoid chemical exposures.

I decided I needed a diagnostician who could put my whole medical history together and come up with a diagnosis and prescribe some effective treatment that would put me on the road to recovery and robust health. I was sick of being sick. I was okay sometimes, but then something would break down. I was referred to Dr. Norman Anderson of Johns Hopkins, a distinguished and brilliant diagnostician.

After taking my history, Dr. Anderson advised me that multiple chemical sensitivity was not recognized as a disease. "There is no scientific evidence to support it," he said.

I told him I was not there to defend or debate the issue of chemical sensitivity. "I have genuine medical problems that are devastating my life, and I came here for a diagnosis and treatment." The scariest of my symptoms, I explained, were the severe gastrointestinal pains that double me up and have forced me to the emergency room on numerous occasions. "Hardly anything ever shows up on the testing. The last blood test showed my amylase elevated, my triglycerides elevated, and of course my cholesterol has been elevated for years. I recognize that there is a psychiatric factor in all of this and I have been treated for anxiety and depression over a period of many years."

He looked at me and said, "No one who sits in that chair is without some psychiatric factor."

"Well, I want you to give me a comprehensive and thorough examination and evaluation and see if you can do anything to help me."

He resembled a character in the TV sitcom "Northern Exposure" known as Maurice, a former astronaut.

Dr. Anderson initially suggested that I had been misdiagnosed for multiple chemical sensitivity. He was one of the vast majority of doctors who did not believe chemical sensitivity is real. At the same time he said, "I know you're not crazy. I believe you may have Sjögren's syndrome."

When he finished talking he sent me to an outer room, where his aides took several vials of blood.

He referred me to an ophthalmologist, a gastroenterologist and a dermatologist. I was given an MRI to rule out pancreatitis. The dermatologist took a biopsy of my lip. Dr. Francis D. Milligan, the gastroenterologist did a colonoscopy, an upper Gastrointestinal endoscopy and something known as an ERCP, an endoscopic retrograde cholgangio-pancreatography. This ERCP test involves the use of a flexible endoscope to inject dye into the bile duct and pancreatic duct to get X-ray pictures.

As the gastroenterologist worked, I found myself in a hospital gown lying on a gurney. While I waited for the procedure to begin, a male nurse or technician approached. I smelled a fragrance, like an aftershave lotion. I began to have a reaction. Something from the fragrance triggered my nasal congestion, making it difficult for me to breathe, and my eyes became irritated.

"What's that fragrance I smell?" I asked him.

"That's my aftershave lotion. Really great, isn't it?"

"I am allergic to what you are wearing. Please get away from me."

"You must be kidding," he said, smiling. "This stuff's about $15 a bottle."

"I don't care what it costs. Get away from me. I'm having trouble breathing!"

He stood there as if I had tossed a bedpan full of cold water on his face.

"Go talk to the doctor. He knows I'm chemically sensitive."

The technician ran to talk to the nurse. The nurse walked over to talk to me.

"Do you want someone to substitute for him?" the nurse asked me sternly.

"Yes. I am sensitive or allergic to whatever fragrance that chap is wearing. I can't help it. My system is out of control when I am exposed to certain products. I want to avoid an asthmatic attack."

The nurse appeared not to understand what I was saying. She began to defend the technician and his $15 aftershave lotion, which she thought smelled delightful. I called for the doctor. He came over and apologized and assured me the technician would be replaced by someone without a fragrance.

But as I was wheeled into the operating room, this same fragrant fellow came up to me, put his fragrant face right next to mine and told me he would be in the next room operating certain instruments. It was all I could do to control myself. I was embarrassed and becoming angry. I was surprised and disappointed that these nurses did not know that some fragrances are hazardous to the health of certain patients entrusted to their care.

I had never heard of Sjögren's syndrome. Dr. Snyder furnished me a medical Report by Elaine L. Alexander, M.D., Ph.D. My symptoms did sound like Sjögren's:

"Sjögren's syndrome is a common autoimmune connective tissue disorder, which conservatively affects 2 percent of the adult population (more than 4 million Americans), the majority of whom are women (9:1). The disorder is often unrecognized or misdiagnosed by unsuspecting patients and physicians because of the characteristic insidious, slowly progressive, and subtle symptoms.

"...Patients with Sjögren's syndrome should be under constant surveillance for the development of lymphoma, for they have a 43-fold increased risk of developing lymphoma compared to normal individuals..." (Elaine L. Alexander, M.D., Ph.D., "Sjögren's Syndrome," in Dr. Lawrence M. Lichtenstein and Dr. Anthony S. Fauci, ed., *Current Therapy in Allergy, Immunology, and Rheumatology—3* [Toronto: B.C. Decker, Inc., 1988], pp. 125-130.) Reprinted by permission Mosby - Year Book Inc. St. Louis, Mo.

To make a long story short, after all these examinations and tests Dr. Anderson told me the conclusion was that I did not have Sjögren's. That was good news. Dr. Anderson told me the tests indicated my cholesterol was too high and that I should go on a low cholesterol diet.

I was given the following instructions:

- No decaf or coffee;
- Not more than one cup of tea per day;
- No eggs;
- Meat - 3 out of 21 meals and only lean meat;
- Skim milk is okay - No cheese, no pizza, no margarine, no butter;
- Get more fiber - Take Metamucil before breakfast and before dinner.

The good news was that they found no tumors and no cancer. I followed these instructions. The severe cramping came under control, but I still have multiple complaints when I am exposed to toxic chemicals.

2

The Toxic Tort Litigation

He who represents himself has a fool for a client."
This adage is taught in law schools and repeated orally and in legal literature as a truism. One who has an interest in his own case may be too emotionally involved to be objective and realistic and may be too prejudiced to understand that there are at least two sides to every case.

I had been a trial lawyer for many years before I became ill following the termite treatment. I had represented plaintiffs in personal injury cases since my graduation from law school in 1949. And for many years I represented insurance companies defending personal injury lawsuits. I had years of experience in the preparation, negotiation and trial and appeal of civil suits.

I did not consider filing a lawsuit until more than a year after the extermination. My physical complaints became more aggravated and my financial losses became a great burden. There appeared to be no end in sight.

I took a friend's advice and hired a big city law firm, Echo and Foxtrot (not their real names), to represent me in my claim for personal injuries and damages. They would advance the costs and expenses and I would ultimately reimburse them. I turned over to them several notebooks that Eloise and I had prepared setting forth a clear explanation of the case.

A civil suit in negligence or a toxic tort or personal injury case is divided into several parts.

First, we listed the facts of the case. Then based upon those facts, I prepared a form for pleading, known as the complaint. I, as plaintiff, set forth the facts, what the defendant exterminator, Able, and his employees did or did not do that constituted negligence or a failure to meet the standard of care required in the industry, what happened to me and the house as a result of the negligence, the personal injuries and damages that flowed from the negligence, the absence of contributory negligence and a demand for damages to compensate me for my losses.

Following the pleading I set forth a written exposition and analysis of the law in point. In this case we had statutory law, regulatory law and case law.

Since I had suffered a number of the same symptoms such as headaches, sinus problems, allergies and gastrointestinal problems prior to the incident of 1988, but not caused by chemical posioning I included the law on aggravation of pre-existing injury. After the incident of 1988 I was no longer the same person. I could not function in the same way, and I was subject to many restrictions—where I lived, where I worked, where I visited. My entire life and everything I did was being controlled by the quality of the air, and I had not found effective medical treatment beyond temporary relief.

In a toxic tort case one must prove what is known as liability and causation, that is, that the alleged acts caused or aggravated the injuries. The plaintiff must link his injuries to the acts of negligence to prove the defendant liable.

The plaintiff must prove (usually by experts) what the standard was, what the label and regulations were, and evidence by eyewitnesses or admissions from the defendant admitting what he did or did not do, contrary to the standards or regulations.

In my case, we had standards set by Dow in its literature on Dursban. We had written instructions on the label. We had regulations being enforced by the Maryland Department of Agriculture, Pesticide Regulation Division. We had admissions from the defendant. Eloise and I and other witnesses were available. We saw that the injection holes were not plugged, that the crawlspace was not vented, that the basement of the house and crawlspace had odors of the chemical or solvent months after the treatment. We had the statements of the representatives of the manufacturer of Dursban as well as the inconsistency between the instructions on the Dursban label and the conduct of the exterminator. All of this was thoroughly documented and prepared before we hired attorneys. They were handed this case on a silver platter. In more than 40 years of practice I never had a client or clients, including some of the biggest insurance companies in the country, present me with a brief or briefs organized so comprehensively.

Unfortunately, my attorneys and I were not on the same wavelength. I know what it takes to prepare a case for trial. Thorough preparation is the key to success. I did not see evidence that they were preparing my case for trial. Instead, it appeared to me that the defense attorney, Not One Cent (not his real name), was in control. Echo and Foxtrot were reacting to whatever the defense attorney advanced. Some defense attorneys delay, hoping that the plaintiff will die or go broke before the case gets to trial and that the witnesses will also disappear or no longer be available or will forget what they saw or heard or did. Other defense attorneys plaster the plaintiff's attorney with so much paperwork that it is difficult to keep abreast or stay afloat. In this case, Not One Cent used both strategies. Both sides delayed confrontation almost until the case was set for trial, and then the defense began filing motions and setting down depositions, all of which could have been done months before. My attorneys took two depositions, one from Able and one from one of his employees. They never interviewed Eloise or deposed any of my doctors or experts. Not One Cent took only two depositions, those of my two Realtors. According to my attorney the second Realtor's deposition took nearly six hours. My attorney was angry. That witness's testimony could have been completed in about 15 minutes. The witness, a busy Realtor, was also angry as hell. Defense counsel was paid by the hour.

Other depositions were now scheduled by the defense back to back for several weeks. The trial date was getting close.

Echo called and demanded that I pay them $25,000 if I wanted them to remain as my attorneys. I could not believe my ears. We had a written contingent fee agreement. I had never heard of such a demand from ethical lawyers in all my years of practice. I refused. They told me they would be filing a motion to withdraw from the case.

"Your case is shit, you are shit, and we are getting out of this case," said Echo and Foxtrot, my loyal and faithful attorneys.

They hung up on me. This was approximately six weeks before the scheduled trial date. I had mixed emotions. I felt these guys were not prepared to try the case. They had failed to interview and prepare my expert medical witnesses and failed to obtain an expert on the standard of care. They told me none of that was necessary. I knew better. I was angry about their forthcoming withdrawal, but relieved that they were getting out of a case they obviously were not prepared to try.

I filed a motion asking the court to block their withdrawal. They filed a motion to withdraw admitting they had requested $25,000 but explaining that the money was to be used for case expenses, not as a fee for themselves.

A close friend, Oscar S. Gray, a law professor at the University of Maryland, represented me at the hearing on their motion to withdraw. Oscar did not believe any court would permit attorneys with a written contingent fee agreement to withdraw after making a demand for $25,000. It was unheard of. Professor Gray made a brilliant argument on my behalf. It fell on deaf ears.

The court stated that if my attorneys did not want to represent me, they would obviously not do a very good job, and this would not be fair to me. Therefore he would permit them to withdraw. He added that he had signed an order postponing the trial to the following year, and therefore I had plenty of time to obtain other counsel and no harm had been done. I did not know about or consent to this delay. I did not want the trial postponed.

The judge would not let me speak, but he permitted a brief recess for me to consult with my counsel. I smelled a skunk in the woodpile. I anticipated that Echo and Foxtrot would hold onto my files and probably demand a percentage of any future recovery. I requested my counsel to ask the judge for an order requiring Echo and Foxtrot to return my files promptly and to further order that they not be permitted to seek any compensation or fee.

After the recess Prof. Gray stated these matters to the Court. Before Gray completed his remarks, Foxtrot leaped to his feet demanding justice. Red-faced and angry, he claimed that his firm had put in a tremendous amount of time, energy and expense and that "under the rules" they were entitled to a pro rata share of any future recovery. That is exactly what I expected. I leaped to my feet and while I was still in the air the judge ordered me to sit down. The law of gravity prevailed or I would still be in the air.

"You have counsel, Mr. Berkson. The Court will not entertain any remarks from you."

The judge then stated that he thought it was only fair that if Echo and Foxtrot withdrew from the case they would forfeit any right to attorneys fees that might be recovered in the future. E&F demanded that I pay the costs and expenses they had advanced and disbursed on my account. The judge asked them how much they had paid out. They produced a figure of less than $2500, which was a far cry from the $25,000 they had demanded. The judge stated that I would be required to pay the costs and expenses as set forth in the contingent fee contract.

The Court later issued a written order which made it sound like there was an amicable agreement between us: First, that I agreed that E&F would be permitted to withdraw in consideration for which E&F gave up their right to attorneys fees, but that I was responsible for the costs and expenses already disbursed.

Foxtrot returned my files by messenger collect. I then looked for new counsel. I contacted attorneys who had won toxic tort cases, but was unable to find any willing to take on my case at this late date. I had known and been friends with some of them, and they were very sympathetic, but were not willing to take on a complicated, complex toxic tort case. One attorney who had been successful in a prior case said he never wanted to go through that procedure again. It was too long and burdensome. And even when he won in trial court, the other side appealed. Very few had ever recovered a nickel despite headlines about huge verdicts.

Obtaining a verdict is one thing; getting paid is another.

I spent several months seeking counsel. During this time, Not One Cent was harassing me with demands to complete work. My position was that I was entitled to be represented by counsel.

Not One Cent went to court and got an order requiring me to do all of the things my former counsel had not done. The judge stated that I had ample time to obtain counsel, and that if I did not comply with this order, judgment would be granted to the defendant.

It became crystal clear to me that further efforts to obtain experienced trial counsel were a waste of time. Every judicial ruling in my case had gone against me. I was concerned about getting a fair and unbiased hearing.

I decided to represent myself from this point on. I went to work answering the interrogatories, furnishing the information demanded by the defense and plastering the defense with as much paperwork as they heaped on me. I knew how to play the game. I was not stupid. I was just sick. I was tired, exhausted, disoriented, found it difficult to concentrate, impatient, nervous and forgetful, but somehow I was able to pound the defense as it had been pounding me.

Finally, Not One Cent began to reel and I felt it appropriate to suggest that perhaps we should stop the bullshit and talk settlement. I had been trying to get this case into a settlement posture for many months but did not want to negotiate from a position of weakness. I was not surprised when Not One Cent agreed to hold a settlement conference.

The meeting was scheduled promptly. I was told I could prepare a brief or any informal paper explaining my case, what I wanted and why.

I put together a packet similar to the original papers I had turned over to E&F. The facts were the same. The law was the same. The liability was the same. The causal connection was the same. The damages were much greater, as it seemed my disability would be permanent and not merely temporary.

The magistrate before whom we appeared had the proper Judicial temperment and demeanor that commanded respect. My impression of this man was that he would be fair and honorable. I respected him immediately.

"Tell me about your case, Mr. Berkson," said the magistrate.

I spoke without notes for about 45 minutes, handing the magistrate documents and photographs and diagrams. Forty-five minutes may seem like a long time, but I had four years of experiences to talk about. To boil down four years into 45 minutes and remain effective requires years of training. It was like the closing statement or summation after a lengthy trial. Defense counsel then made an excellent statement on behalf of his client and placed an offer on the table. The magistrate asked me for my demand, and I pulled a figure out of the air and placed it on the table. I was then asked to leave the room and the magistrate reviewed the case with defense counsel. After some time, defense counsel came out of the chambers and I was called in by the magistrate. He made it clear that he felt my case had merit and that I was entitled to some compensation, but not as much as I had requested. He said he had instructed the defense counsel to call his insurer and get authority to raise his offer to a more acceptable level. A few minutes later defense counsel came in with a higher figure. I reduced my demand and we met somewhere in the middle. The offer and settlement was made on the condition that I not be permitted to disclose the amount. I did not like that but I was unwilling to give up the settlement offer for the privilege of discussing the amount. However, when defense counsel added a condition prohibiting me from discussing the case, I refused. I stated that I was an environmentalist and a conservationist and that I intended to write a book on the subject and that I was not willing to make any settlement that would prohibit me from writing or lecturing on the subject. The magistrate agreed and so did defense counsel. After a few weeks Not One Cent handed me my check. Case closed.

That was a happy ending to a difficult matter. It was a great relief to put this case behind me but no amount of money can adequately compensate the victim of a chemical exposure that devastates his life. Nor is there adequate compensation for the anxiety and stress of civil litigation, which is harsh and oppressive and unduly burdensome and expensive. But it is only through the efforts of victims willing to undertake the task that our society will become more just and lawful.

Carved into the stone atop the portals to my beloved law school at the University of Virginia are these words:

"THAT THOSE ALONE MAY BE SERVANTS OF THE LAW WHO LABOR WITH LEARNING, COURAGE AND DEVOTION TO PRESERVE LIBERTY AND PROMOTE JUSTICE."

It was my fantasy that Thomas Jefferson, president of the United States, author of the Declaration of Independence and the founder of the University of Virginia, to whom I am greatly indebted, may have looked down from his heavenly repose upon those scenes of legal practice and smiled, knowing that another who benefitted from his foresight and his academic village had persevered and struck another blow for justice.

Silent Spring

Some say that the environmental movement in the United States began with the publication of *Silent Spring* by Rachel Carson in 1962. A 25th anniversary edition published by Houghton Mifflin Co., was highlighted and offered for sale by the New York Coalition for Alternatives to Pesticides at the NCAMP Conference in 1992. I read it after it first came out but did not appreciate the significance of it. But on my odyssey of discovery, nearly every book I read about the environment refers to *Silent Spring*. I thought it was about time I reread the book. I found the writing to be beautiful and the substance prophetic. *Silent Spring* is dedicated to Albert Schweitzer, who said,

"Man has lost the capacity to foresee and to forestall. He will end by destroying the earth."

"This book is the most important chronicle of this century for the human race," wrote U.S. Supreme Court Justice William O. Douglas in a review for the Book-of-the- Month Club News. Each sentence is a jewel, and she offers evidence many of our medical and scientific so-called experts have not yet discovered.

Remember, our local public health officer had never heard of pesticides making someone sick. And perhaps he had not. But Rachel Carson had. These hazards were well-documented years before her book was published. Many people give lip service to Rachel Carson, but not one out of a hundred I talk to has read her book.

Rachel Carson was 50 years old when she started writing *Silent*

Spring in 1958. She had been a marine biologist and writer with the U.S. Fish and Wildlife Service and was alarmed by the widespread use of DDT and other long-lasting poisons in so called agricultural control programs.

Rachel Carson began writing *Silent Spring* in 1958—thirty years before my home and office were treated with a toxic chemical formulation registered with the EPA for the extermination of subterranean termites. What happened to me and to my house and what I learned after 1988 was foreseen by Rachel Carson in *Silent Spring*. For example, in Chapter 12, The Human Price, she writes:

"As the tide of chemicals born of the Industrial Age has arisen to engulf our environment, a drastic change has come about in the nature of the most serious public health problems...

"The new environmental health problems are multiple—created by radiation in all its forms, born of the never-ending stream of chemicals of which pesticides are a part, chemicals now pervading the world in which we live, acting upon us directly and indirectly, separately and collectively. Their presence casts a shadow that is no less ominous because it is formless and obscure, no less frightening because it is simply impossible to predict the effects of lifetime exposure to chemical and physical agents that are not part of the biological experience of man."

Rachel Carson asks the same question we hear today:

"Why does not everyone handling and using insecticides develop the same symptoms? Here the matter of individual sensitivity enters in... What makes one person allergic to dust or pollen, sensitive to a poison, or susceptible to an infection whereas another is not is a medical mystery for which there is at present no explanation. The problem nevertheless exists and it affects significant numbers of the population." (From SILENT SPRING. Copyright © 1962 by Rachel L. Carson. Copyright © renewed 1990 by Roger Christie. Reprinted by permission of Houghton Mifflin Company. All rights reserved.)

Silent Spring should be in every household. Some organization should distribute it as the Gideons do the Bible. *Silent Spring* is a warning that we are destroying our planet, and it is a call to action to change our lifestyle for the survival of humanity.

My dear friend and mentor, Supreme Court Justice William O. Douglas, has said it best in his report for the Book-of-the-Month Club News:

"Rachel Carson, the author-biologist who wrote *The Sea Around Us* and *The Edge of the Sea,* now adds another illustrious book to her list. The title sets the mood of the text: man's power of destruction is now so great that, some coming spring, the birds and the bees may be extinct and there may be no fish to cause a swirl on the smooth waters of our lakes. Poisons are in all the menus; the insolubles that make up many insecticides are eventually stored in human tissues. Disease mysteriously appears in man. The alarming story is calmly told, with no theatrics and in a sober, factual way. This book is the most important chronicle of this century for the human race."

"We need a Bill of Rights against the 20th-century poisoners of the human race. The book is a call for immediate action and for effective control of all merchants of poison." (From Justice William O. Douglas in his review of *Silent Spring, Book of the Month Club News.* Copyright © 1962 by Book-of-the-Month Club, Inc. Reprinted by permission.)

• • •

"The [Rachel Carson] Council, [Inc.]...was founded by friends and colleagues of Rachel Carson, at her behest, to respond to the flood of pesticide information requests from the public following the publication of *Silent Spring.* In its thirty years of existence its role has come to include more proactive educational efforts such as alternatives booklets, a periodical newsletter, single-issue pamphlets, and a major scientific reference (*Basic Guide to Pesticides*) on all pesticides in use or persisting in the environment as of its publication in 1992."

The Mission of the Council is "Rachel Carson Council is devoted to fostering a sense of wonder and respect toward nature and to helping society realize Rachel Carson's vision of a healthy and diverse environment."

• • •

To become a member of this environmental organization and

carry on the work of Rachel Carson write to the Council at 8940 Jones Mill Road, Chevy Chase, Maryland 20815. Telephone: 301-652-1877.

• • •

The author assisted Justice Douglas in preserving the C&O Canal and the ultimate establishment of the C&O Canal National Historical Park. He also serves as a member of the Board of Directors of the Rachel Carson Council, Inc.

4

Earth in the Balance

The campaign for President of the United States, one-third of the U.S. Senate and the entire House of Representatives was probably the most significant event to take place in this country in 1992. The Republicans, led by Ronald Reagan and George Bush, had occupied the White House since 1980. The environment did not have a high priority during those years. Agencies responsible for enforcing environmental regulations were headed by conservative politicians who appeared to be more interested in protecting the polluters than protecting the health, safety and welfare of the public. Despite mounting evidence of environmental pollution of all types—air, water, soil, food—Reagan and Bush and their staffs were perceived as being opposed to significant environmental safeguards. Calls to action by scientists who wrote and spoke about the environmental crisis, especially the depletion of the ozone layer, the greenhouse effect and the ecology movement as a whole fell on deaf ears. The polluters and the special interests had the Reagan and Bush administrations in their vest pockets.

As expected, George Bush won the Republican primary. Bill Clinton won the Democratic primary. And H. Ross Perot led a third-party movement that captured the votes of millions of Americans fed up with the greed and corruption of both major parties.

Bush will long be remembered for his reluctance to attend the environmental conference in Rio prior to the election. His negative attitude nearly destroyed the entire conference. The United States is the only superpower left in the world, and without the enthusiastic support of the United States, no global environmental conference could be successful.

A very significant book about the environment was published during the campaign.

Earth in the Balance: Ecology and the Human Spirit (New York: Houghton Mifflin Company, 1992) by Sen. Al Gore hit the bookshelves with brilliant timing in terms of the environmental movement.

Gore was Clinton's vice presidential running mate. Gore had the best environmental record of any candidate.

Earth in the Balance hit *The New York Times* best-seller list almost as soon as it was published and remained there for nearly a year. I bought it and read it with great interest. Gore was years ahead of me in his knowledge and experience and in word and deed.

The 408-page book includes a very personal introduction by Gore, three main parts, acknowledgements, notes, bibliography, an index and credits.

In Chapter 15, Gore offers A Global Marshall Plan, action that he says must be taken to ensure the survival of our civilization.

Reagan and Bush and their supporters ridiculed the book and constantly made fun of Sen. Gore, attempting to paint him as a far-out extremist.

Whether or not one agrees with Gore's plans to solve the crisis, the denial of the crises are irresponsible and not worthy of belief. This is a well-written and readable book, and it is so comprehensive and thorough in its coverage of the environmental crisis that I believe *Earth in the Balance* should be mandatory reading for every high school, college and graduate school teacher and student. The subject is worthy of debate.

As one of millions of Americans who have made a commitment to work for a healthier environment, I commend the vice president for *Earth in the Balance* and stand ready to help in any way. At the same time I look to him to provide the leadership, integrity, sincerity, devotion, courage, wisdom, fortitude, diplomacy and political expertise that is needed to bring the earth back into balance.

During the 1992 campaign I listened carefully to all of the candidates. I heard very little, if anything, about the environment, or any mention of any environmental crisis.

Theodore Roosevelt spoke of the presidency as a bully pulpit. In the first three years of the Clinton presidency, very little progress, if any, was made either in calling attention to environmental crises, recognizing them or offering any solution to save humanity and the planet. It is as if *Earth in the Balance* was never written.

1996 has arrived. Earth remains in the balance. It is my hope and my prayer that *Silent Spring, Earth in the Balance, A Canary's Tale,* and hundreds of other books that call attention to the link between environmental pollution and health will educate, influence and persuade the public and our political leaders to act before it is too late.

5

League of Conservation Voters

While I was studying *Earth in the Balance*, I received a letter from Bruce Babbitt, then president of the League of Conservation Voters in Washington, D.C. Mr. Babbitt, a former governor of Arizona and former presidential aspirant who had been out of the headlines for some years, stated that he intended to devote the rest of his life to environmental issues and that the League of Conservation Voters was an important organization dedicated to helping elect public officials who were sensitive to environmental matters. It was a letter that struck a responsive chord. What he said in his letter was practically identical to an article I had written the day before about the need to elect public officials who understood environmental crises and would work to protect mankind and the planet from polluters.

I dashed off a note to Mr. Babbitt and a few days later received an invitation to attend a meeting with him and representatives of many environmental organizations at the National Press Club in Washington, D.C. This was in August '92, three months before the election. I first met Mr. Babbitt's personal secretary, Claudia Schechter, who introduced me to the executive director, Jim Maddy. Within a short time they introduced me to Bruce Babbitt. Even though I am in my late 60s and have been in politics since my early 20s, it is still exciting to shake hands with a public figure, especially one who has run for president. Babbitt is a tall man, big-boned, with large eyes, chocolate brown hair and the look of a country feller. He was very cordial and thanked me for coming. I showed him a copy of my book proposal and assured him of my support for his organization. I did not realize at the time that this was actually a meeting to support the Clinton-Gore ticket and several other candidates for public office. The highlight was Sen. Gore's appearance on a huge TV screen. He gave an excellent speech.

Another speaker was John Javna of The Earth Works Group, author of *50 Simple Things You Can Do To Save The Earth* (Berkeley: The Earth Works Press, 1989), which was on the bestseller list for more than a year. He later wrote a sequel, *The Next Step: 50 More Things You Can Do To Save The Earth*. This too was a huge success. I met him after his speech and showed him my book proposal. He did not have time to go through it but suggested I send him a copy. He told me he had so much difficulty finding a publisher for his initial book that he decided to print it himself. He and a couple of friends rented a small shop and printed 10,000 copies. He ended up selling over 3½ million copies and becoming a millionaire as well as a leading environmental activist.

He distributed copies of *Vote for the Earth: The League of Conservation Voters' Election Guide*, a special pre-publication edition of *Vote for the Earth*.

I offered my services to the league to help elect officials who would vote to protect the planet, who would vote for safe food and clean air and clean water, to save our ancient forests and endangered species, for wetlands and to control toxic wastes, to stop global warming and to stop ozone depletion.

Clinton and Gore won the election, but not a majority of the votes. Perot's presence held Clinton and Gore to 43% of the votes cast. Babbitt was appointed Secretary of the Interior.

With Gore elected as vice president, and Babbitt Secretary of Interior environmental activists felt more secure. Gore was expected to use his influence to help bring the earth back into balance Unfortunately, during the first three years of the Clinton administration, there was very little evidence of progress in environmental matters. Skeptics say this administration is no better than the last two, and that Clinton makes environmental decisions against the public interest based upon the amount of campaign money received from special interests who profit from pollution. The President can overcome this criticism by making his deeds consistent with his speeches. Actions speak louder than words. Profits and pollution will prevail over the public health until the political leadership can no longer breathe the air, drink the water, eat the food or tolerate the pollution in their own homes and workplaces, or until a fed up public rises up and votes the enemies of the environment and human health out of office.

• • •

"The League of Conservation Voters (LCV) has published a National Environmental Scorecard every year since 1970, the year it was founded by leaders of the environmental movement following the first Earth Day...

"This [February 1996] edition of the National Environmental Scorecard provides objective, factual information about the records of the members of the first session of the 104th Congress. Experts from 27 mainstream environmental groups volunteered their time to identify and research crucial votes...

"For copies or information about joining, please contact LCV, 1707 L Street NW, Suite 750, Washington, DC, 20036. Phone (202) 785-8683." (From: The Scorecard, League of Conservation Voters, National Environmental Scorecard, February 1996, 104th Congress, First Session.)

6

Trips in Search of Clean Air
Santa Fe, New Mexico, and
Casey Key, Florida

Santa Fe, N.M.—
My younger brother Barry invited me to visit him before he sold the home he built outside Santa Fe, N.M. Barry had recently retired after many years as an attorney with the Department of the Interior. He spent much of his career working on Indian affairs, from the huge Navajo reservation outside Gallup, N.M., to the mountains and plains and deserts of the far west.

I followed his career and visited him in a number of interesting and colorful western towns. His favorite place was Santa Fe, and he bought a highly desirable residential lot outside town where the owners of a several-thousand-acre estate had subdivided portions for residential usage. This was a low-density, highly restricted community 6,000 to 7,000 feet above sea level.

Barry lived in a one-story Spanish-style adobe in the tradition of the southwest. The back side faced the sun from sunrise until sunset, and he could see the sun making its rounds from east to west, rising in its highest arc at noon, from any spot in the rear of their house which featured glass, windows, doors and sliding doors. From the rear patio one could see Los Alamos to the northwest, the Rio Grande to the west and the Sandia Mountains and Albuquerque some 60 miles to the southwest. The San Juan Mountains were to the north. The Sangre de Cristo Mountains were to the north at elevations of more than 13,000 feet and were snow covered most of the year. The scenery was magnificent in every direction and the air was clean. It was easy to breathe and I had no trouble there with my health. The interior had wood and tile floors with very little carpet. The walls were natural adobe, so there was no outgassing. The huge beams in the ceiling gave off no odors. The house was a healthy one for me.

Barry explained that the climate and the air quality and the way of life in the Santa Fe area is considered so superior to the smog, congestion, crime and pollution in other western cities, especially Los Angeles, that some people who can afford it are moving from Los Angeles to the Santa Fe area. They continue to work in L.A. during the week but live in Santa Fe on weekends. Some of them commute by plane daily. He knew this not only from what he read in the papers but from personal experience. Prospective buyers who came to look at his home were mostly from the L.A. area.

I ask myself if it would not be better to prevent the pollution in the first place, so that all of these people do not have to move hundreds to thousands of miles away and commute to work. Unfortunately, history has shown that many of these people who leave a contaminated or polluted area end up polluting their new community with their cars, their trucks, their shrubs, and their material possessions. Instead of living with nature, they destroy the natural environment either by clear-cutting trees and destroying forests or attempting to convert a desert into a series of green lawns that require extensive watering. They not only create a water shortage but begin to use chemical lawn sprays. The lawn sprays run off and end up in the ground water, where they pollute the aquifers, contaminate the wells and harm the health of the inhabitants. They pollute the air, water and soil, and then look for another community that is clean.

Communities that used to be considered heavenly and healthful, such as San Diego, Denver and numerous ski resorts in Colorado, are paying the price for permitting profits of the developers to take priority over public health. Thousands of

Californians have migrated to Oregon, where the air is cleaner and the quality of life superior. Oregon is one of the last environmentally safe states. Not perfect, of course. There is no perfect or safe place, especially for the chemically sensitive. But the leadership there seems to realize that what attracts the visitors, the tourists and future residents is the environment.

Here in the East, we have thousands of workers commuting from western Maryland, Pennsylvania, W.Va. and Virginia into the Washington, D.C., area, some 70 to 100 miles away. Americans who commute accept it as part of life.

Santa Fe itself is a historic, colorful, busy town with a population of about 50,000, has an elevation of some 6,000 feet and no huge polluters or smokestack industries. Nevertheless, as in any town, especially those which cater to tourists, the traffic is congested with automobiles, trucks, buses and RV's, which pollute the air in the central district. Perhaps 80 percent of the air pollution is caused by vehicle exhaust. Some years ago the people there blocked plans for a large airport, which would have changed the environment of this community completely.

Santa Fe is blessed with colleges and an educated populace greatly interested in music and the arts and humanities.

There are health food stores, and many of the people living there are attempting to heal from exposure to toxic chemicals. I spoke with several of them by phone but did not meet with any of them. I also had heard of a number of ill people residing in Albuquerque, and I spent a day at the home of Nancy Noren meeting with other sick people and discussing our common problems, challenges and coping methods. Nancy had "rehabbed" an adobe home to make it less toxic. She had earlier tried to buy a large tract of land to build an environmentally safe community, but could not get the money to support this much-needed project. The people I met at her home were from different walks of life, from different areas, from different ages and backgrounds, but with a common bond. Each had been poisoned by exposure to toxic chemicals and subsequently became ill. They were unable to get effective medical treatment, became worse, lost their jobs, their homes, their families, their confidence, their self-esteem, but were still fighting to survive. One, John Schwindt, had been a professor at a university in Florida for many years. At his college the authorities sprayed chemicals from machines. They polluted the air as well as the soil and damaged the lungs and respiratory systems of vulnerable individuals. John did not realize the sprays he was breathing were going to make him ill and eventually disable him. He discovered that he could no longer concentrate, remember, distinguish and articulate as he had before. He now becomes confused, disoriented, frustrated, angry, irritable and depressed. He finds himself with nowhere to turn except to other individuals in similar circumstances. John moved to Gila, N.Mex. but was forced to sell his house because of smelter smoke and forest fire smoke that emanated from prescribed burning. He had lived in a home without heat and was in the process of moving to Rio Rancho, N.Mex.

Diane Canfield of Corrales, N.Mex., worked in a laboratory and became ill from the chemicals to which she was exposed.

In summary, the community of Santa Fe and its suburbs was a delightful place to visit. I hope the leadership of Santa Fe will continue to preserve it as a model for the rest of the nation and the world. A clean environment is a healthy environment. And a healthy environment ensures a healthier population. And a healthier population is a more productive and happier population. And good health is more important than the bottom line of either a corporation or an individual's financial statement.

Casey Key, Fla.—

Casey Key is a narrow spit of land a few miles long just off the west coast of Florida, north of Venice Beach and south of Sarasota. A little community on that key is known as Nokomis, which is the same name as the mother of "Hiawatha."

I was referred to Iris Ingram, who I was told was chemically sensitive and had a "safe house" with a room she sometime rented to others who had been poisoned.

I phoned Iris in November '92 to find out if she could accommodate me for a week or so while I checked out the area for air quality. She said she could put me up in a guest room and that she was on her way to Maryland and a little town near Gettysburg, Pa., to spend Thanksgiving with her family. She invited me to join her for Thanksgiving dinner. I accepted her gracious invitation and spent a wonderful day meeting Iris, her two daughters and their husbands, her grandchildren and great- grandchildren, all in a colonial farmhouse surrounded by apple orchards in the rolling hills north of Gettysburg. The family had a lot of spirit and a lot of tradition, and the scene at the table, with Iris as the senior family member joined by four generations down to infant twins, could have been painted by Norman Rockwell.

It was hard to believe Iris was a great-grandmother and the head of such a large family. She was a small lady who did not look her age. She was a cheerful and gracious hostess, and we got along very well.

I had wanted to visit Florida for some years but just could not get up the energy. I had never been to the west coast of Florida, where Iris lived.

I first headed for St. Augustine on the east coast to meet with Linda Wilson and her husband Lester.

They had purchased a lot in a subdivision that was highly restricted for environmental preservation. One of the restrictions was a prohibition against toxic chemical lawn sprays. Linda and her husband had built a charming home with less toxic materials, based upon the information they had after a number of years of studying healthy homes.

She took me to the beach, where I breathed Atlantic Ocean air for several hours. To me, the ocean air has healing powers, and it clears up my congestion.

Linda and Lester insisted that I spend the night in their new home, which I seemed to tolerate very well. There was no carpet. The floors were tile or marble, as were the window sills. The walls were plaster. There were many windows. The home was spacious. The HVAC system was a Thurmond unit with 60 or 80 pounds of activated charcoal filter through which all of the air was forced before it entered the house. The materials for the most part were natural, not plastic or synthetic, and so too were the interior furnishings.

But the forced hot air at night began to irritate my eyes and congest my nose. I was and still am sensitive to forced-hot-air heat, so I had to turn off the heating unit and plug in an electric heater as an alternate source. Electric heat is most tolerable for me, and I now have electric baseboard hot water heat in my home. It is clean heat but it has a downside. It is extremely dry, so I need a humidifier. The downside to a humidifier is that one must clean it often to ensure that the humidity does not nourish toxic bacteria. My reason for going to Florida in December '92 was to see if I could find a tolerable place to rent for a month or so during the winter.

An old friend of the family, Bill Bearinger, who now lived in Tampa, had been in touch with me and suggested I visit a new development on the west coast of Florida. I drove from St. Augustine on the east coast to this new development Bearinger recommended.

It was a beautiful place but unfortunately it was too new—new carpet, paint, insulation, blacktop and roofing, all of which were normal building materials but not recommended for a chemically sensitive person.

I drove from there to St. Petersburg, where I had reserved a room at a fine motel with instructions not to clean my room with chemicals, not to use fragrances in the room and to please ventilate and open the balcony doors to the room prior to my arrival.

The lobby of the hotel was perfumed and fragrant. So, too, was the room clerk, the elevator, the hallway and the room to which I was escorted.

Since I was exhausted and unable to look for other quarters, I opened the doors to the balcony, turned off the air-conditioning system and walked outside. I sat under a beach umbrella in the rain to clear my head. When I returned to my room, a good deal of the fragrance had dissipated, and I headed to a restaurant for supper. I went to four restaurants before I found one that had tolerable air quality. By then I was almost too exhausted to eat, but I managed. Then it was back to the hotel. I wore my gas mask through the lobby and the hallway to my room. But I slept okay and was happy to leave the next morning for my visit with Iris Ingram.

Iris' house was about as safe as any I have found, and Iris was a delightful hostess. I spent a glorious week walking on the beach from one end to the other. I found a suitable home in Venice Beach, which I rented for the month of January 1993. It was several blocks from the beach in a middle-class, working neighborhood.

A big problem in Florida for the environmentally ill (EI's) is the constant and continuous spraying of pesticides. Before I signed the lease, I knocked on neighbors' doors and asked if they sprayed their lawns. I was pleased to find that not one of them used pesticides. I found that it was in the wealthier neighborhoods that the homeowners insisted upon using chemical lawn pesticides.

It is my custom on Friday nights to attend Sabbath services. I phoned the office of a Reform Temple in Sarasota to find out whether they sprayed their temple with pesticides. I was told they had not done it lately and that there was no smell in the temple. So I invited Iris to accompany me to services.

Within minutes after our arrival at the temple, my eyes began to water, my nose began to get stuffy and I began to have difficulty breathing. I looked at Iris and her eyes were tearing and she was having a difficult time breathing. She said she could put up with it. I tried to convince myself that I could tough it out and remain for the service. I walked outside for some fresh air and returned before the service began. Iris appeared to be in distress so I took her outside. We left. Had we remained we may have been overcome by the vapors from the pesticide. We drove back to Casey Key, parked at the public beach, got out of the car and breathed in the clean air from the Gulf to recuperate.

I later learned that a number of Florida friends quit going to church and Sunday school because the churches were regularly sprayed with toxic chemical pesticides that made them sick. The fresh sea air was healing, the Ingram home was safe, the hospitality was excellent and the weather was beautiful, but restaurants with acceptable air quality levels were hard to find.

As long as I could spend my time outdoors on the beach, I was okay.

I flew back to Maryland to pick up Eloise, and on Jan. 2, 1993, we left home, headed for Florida.

7

The Johns Hopkins Medical Handbook

T*he Johns Hopkins Medical Handbook* is intended to provide a compendium of the 100 major medical disorders of people over the age of 50 - along with a directory to the American medical care system. It has been prepared with the cooperation of some of the leading medical societies and health information organizations in the United States.

The book contains numerous illnesses that are caused or aggravated by exposure to pollution and toxic chemicals.

The book warns the reader of the effect chemical exposure can have on people with conditions such as asthma, cancer, dementia and lung disease, as well the connection between chemical exposure and headaches and sore throat.

For example, an information box on asthma at page 327 warns that an attack can be precipitated by, among other things, "Air pollution: cigarette smoke, ozone, sulfur dioxide, auto exhaust," and "Household products: paint, cleaners, spray."

A passage on emphysema prevention at page 331 advises people with symptoms of the disease to "reduce your exposure to air pollution, which may aggravate symptoms of emphysema...when pollution levels are dangerous, remain indoors..."

The link between chemical exposure and certain types of cancer is well-established but worth repeating. We know now that cigarette smoke and asbestos fibers can destroy the lungs, but consider this advice for people over 50 at page 22: "Being exposed to large amounts of household solvent cleaners, cleaning fluids, and paint thinners should be avoided...In addition, inhaling or swallowing lawn and garden chemicals increases cancer risk...Such chemicals should not come in contact with toys or other household items."

The book also warns at page 99 that poisoning by lead, mercury or exposure to carbon monoxide, some pesticides and industrial pollutants are potentially reversible dementias. Isn't that nice? All the physical problems and dementia, to boot.

Other symptoms of chemical exposure are less severe but still painful and annoying. Repeated exposure to nitrate compounds can result in a dull, pounding headache and flushed face, the Hopkins manual reports. Under the heading of "Chemical culprits" on page 126 we find: "Vascular headache can also result from exposure to poisons, even common household varieties like insecticides, carbon tetrachloride, and lead. Anyone who has contact with lead batteries or lead-glazed pottery may develop headaches.

"Painters, printmakers and other artists may experience headaches after exposure to art materials that contain chemicals called solvents. Solvents, like benzene, are found in turpentine, spray adhesives, rubber cement and inks." Selections quoted are reprinted with permission of the *Johns Hopkins Medical Handbook* © Medletter Associates, 1992. To order copies of the book, please call 1-904-446-4675.

Stop and think for a moment. What do the examples mentioned above have in common? The answer is that each of these conditions are either a direct result of or aggravated by exposure to common, everyday household chemicals, air pollution or cigarette smoke.

Now consider this: Does it not stand to reason that if these chemicals can aggravate already-diagnosed medical conditions, they can also mount an attack on an otherwise healthy individual?

The bottom line is that we're talking about toxins, which, by definition, are capable of harming creatures large and small.

Unfortunately, the evidence we now have is considered strictly anecdotal when the subject is environmental illness or multiple chemical sensitivity (MCS). In the absence of empirical data, the mainstream medical community will continue to keep discussion of such maladies at arm's length. Only by pushing MCS closer to the top of the medical agenda will we begin to see effective treatment and prevention. Only then will the tunnel turn toward the light.

"The public should have the right to know the health and safety data for all components of a product.

"The contest between the proponents of health and environment and those intent on more use of toxic chemical pesticides will go on. It has been a sometimes dramatic, often tedious and frustrating business for both sides. More public attention to the process can improve the quality of the debate."

Shirley A. Briggs and the staff of Rachel Carson Council, Basic Guide to Pesticides: Their Characteristics and Hazards, *Washington, D.C.: Taylor & Francis, 1992. (Reprinted with permission.)*

Year Six
1993
A.D.

"Is humanity suicidal? If Homo Sapiens goes the way of the dinosaur, we have only ourselves to blame."

1

Florida in January

Saddle up!" I said to Eloise early on Jan. 2. "The meter is running on our Florida house."

Before we left I went to the AAA and explained my sensitivity problem to Coleen Thompson. I explained that I needed motels that were fragrant and odor free and had windows that opened. She spoke with reservation clerks at various motels. We finaly settled on a Radisson high-rise at Charlotte, N.C. for the first night and the Marriott Courtyard in Savannah, Ga. the second. The staffs there followed AAA instructions and provided us with clean, comfortable rooms and bath with no odors and no fragrances.

It was a beautiful trip. We achieved our goal of traveling from home where the temperature was freezing to Venice where the temperature was in the 80s. We picked up the key to our rental house from the Realtor and arrived at our new home before sunset. I showed Eloise through the house, pointing out the tile floors without carpet, the large living room, extra large sun porch, the abundance of doors and windows to let in the breeze off the gulf.

Eloise seemed pleased with what she saw and that made me very happy. We walked over to the beach and sat on one of the many benches overlooking the calm blue water. The Gulf was smooth as glass. We watched the sun setting like a big red ball into the void beyond the horizon. I thought of Juan Ponce de León looking for the Fountain of Youth in 1513. This was our quiet time. The breeze from the gulf, which I often call the ocean air, was clean and cool. We walked back to the house, did a little unpacking, had a light supper, watched some TV and turned in for the night.

I was awakened from a lovely dream by what sounded like a cannon being shot from a Spanish galleon outside my window, followed by the stinking smell and sight of gray and black smoke permeating my bedroom. I leaped from my bed, slammed the windows shut, strapped on my gas mask and ran outside to see what was going on.

I saw a speedboat in the driveway of the house next door with its engine going full speed. The boat was on a trailer that was hitched to a pickup truck, just sitting in the driveway. I walked over to that boat in my pajamas and my gas mask. I stood upwind of the exhaust and yelled at the guy in the boat.

"What are you doing?" I hollered.

He cut the engine and looked at me as if I had just leaped out of a UFO.

"I am cleaning the motors on my boat. I am getting rid of all this black soot. I am getting ready to put my boat in the water. Who in the hell are you, and why are you in your pajamas and wearing a gas mask?" he replied.

"I have just traveled twelve hundred miles to come to this place for a nice, quiet, peaceful vacation. I did not travel all this distance to be awakened at 6 a.m. by boat engines and polluted air."

"Well, this is where I clean my engines, and I don't see where a little bit of black smoke ever hurt anyone."

"I am allergic to that exhaust. It makes me sick. It gets in my lungs and I have trouble breathing. It might get so bad that I have an asthmatic attack and you may have to call an ambulance for me or take me to an emergency room at a hospital. So I am asking you very courteously, please do not clean your boat engines in this driveway and please stop polluting the air. Your boat exhaust is a hazard to my health and the health of everyone in this neighborhood."

"Well, this is my driveway and this is my boat and this is the only place I can clean my boat motor," he said, punctuating each point with a thrust of his forefinger.

I handed him my card which identified me as an attorney. He read it. It seemed to have a calming influence on him. I did not have to say anything more. He looked at me and said nothing.

"Hi, I'm your new next-door neighbor," I said with a smile after removing my gas mask.

"Yeah, well, glad to meet you," he replied. "How long you here for?"

"Here for my health. Sooner my lungs heal, the sooner I leave."

I returned to the house and waited for the other shoe to drop.

Believe it or not, the rest of my stay was without incident—no more motors, no more exhaust, no more smoke, no more noise.

I took no pleasure in that confrontation with my new neighbor. I had no idea what the consequences would be. I wish that the incident had never taken place. The exposure to that exhaust was, to me, a life-threatening situation that called for extreme measures. The psychiatrists call it a "fight or flight" situation. I chose to fight, or at least confront, rather than to accept the situation. In this instance it worked. But it could have ended in disaster. The neighbor could have laughed at me, told me to go screw myself, gotten angry and beaten me or continued to run his boat engines every day. There was really nothing I could do about it if he had not been a reasonable man. I would like to be the kind of person who is calm, cool and diplomatic on such occasions, but I'm not. When I am threatened with poison gas, I recall pictures of endless lines of acquiescent Jews walking peacefully like sheep to certain death in the gas chambers during the Holocaust. I grieve for them and realize they had little choice—they would have been killed one way or another. I also recall the Jews who fought the final battle in the Warsaw Ghetto and those who fought the battle and the war to create the State of Israel.

Some things are worth fighting for. Freedom to breathe clean air is one of them.

Florida has a registry for chemically sensitive people. The state requires pesticide applicators to notify these people before they spray adjoining properties and requires them to put little signs on lawns that have been sprayed. I was invited to a public hearing in Sarasota held by the Florida Division of Agricultural Environmental Services. The subject was "Especially Sensitive Persons: Pesticide Chapter 120." That hearing, attended by perhaps 10 or 15 exterminators and 25 or 30 chemically sensitive people, crystalized the dynamics of the controversy about pesticides. It was an emotional confrontation between two groups with entirely different interests. On one side were the exterminators, most of whom despised the chemically sensitive EI's (canaries). They saw no health problem connected with the use of pesticide. It was their jobs, and they were not about to agree to any restrictions or regulations to accommodate a couple of complainers. And on the other side were the canaries whose lives had been devastated by these very exterminators and the poison chemicals they use and continue to use. The drift of the pesticide from one lawn to another, the air pollution, the inhalation and ingestion was too much for these victims to bear. People on both sides could have killed the opposing group, so strong were the emotions. The pesticide issue was escalating into thoughts of homicide.

"Our livelihood is at stake!" screamed the exterminators. "You are trying to keep us from earning a living."

"You are killing us with your pesticide!" cried the canaries. "Each time you spray we are poisoned and sometimes we become sick for weeks. This is a matter of life and death and you are killing us. We are unable to work. We are unable to earn a living. We have lost our homes. There is no medical treatment that is effective."

I tried to mediate. My message to the hearing officer was:

"Do not water down this law. You're dealing with a controversial subject. Resolve the controversy in favor of the public
health. There are over 100 research papers which link pesticides
to cancer and other diseases. You are not dealing with only 40 or
50 people here. You're dealing with everyone. Do not water down
the restriction. We must try to prevent pollution and prevent the
exposure to these dangerous pesticides."

I spoke to people on both sides and after the hearing to a staff
member of this Florida agency. He thanked me for coming to the
meeting and for attempting to bring some reason into this chaos.
He agreed that the subject was very controversial but felt that
there was no scientific evidence to prove any causal connection
between the pesticide spraying and the illness of all of these
people.

"We have to spray," he said. "People cannot live in this area
unless they spray. The insects will take over everything."

I looked at him with amazement and said, "Are there no alternatives to toxic chemicals that make people ill?"

"None that are effective, " he replied and walked away. So
there you have it. I wondered if there would ever be peace and
understanding.

Later in the year, two other groups that had been fighting and
killing each other for years finally tossed in the towel and signed a
peace treaty. The Israelis and the Arabs began the long road to
peace. Yitzhak Rabin and Yassar Arafat signed a treaty and shook
hands. But peace has not come to the Middle East. Rabin was
assassinated in 1995 by a Jewish extremist or lunatic. Hope for
understanding between the pesticide applicators and the pesticide
victims is not high. The victims, the canaries, pray that the
president of the United States and all government officials will
use their good offices and all of the energy and power at their
command to control the irresponsible use of toxic chemicals and
prevent continued pollution of our air, soil, water and food.

The rest of the trip was without incident. The upside was the weather, sunny days, ocean breezes, beach, collecting sea shells, observing sea gulls, hunting for sharks teeth, eating seafood, taking long walks, meeting new friends—on balance, a good vacation.

2

HEALING AND THE MIND
by Bill Moyers
Recognition of the Environmental Factor

From *HEALING AND THE MIND* by Bill Moyers (Copyright © 1993 by Public Affairs Television and David Grubin Productions Inc. Reprinted by permission of Doubleday, a division of Bantam Doubleday Dell Publishing Group, Inc.), we read wonderful interviews between Moyers and prominent medical doctors or Ph.Ds. about the work they are doing on what is considered the frontier of healing. They discuss the research they are doing with patients, support groups and science dealing with what is referred to as the mind/body connection.

In the introduction to *HEALING AND THE MIND*, Moyers describes and explains the influence Norman Cousins had on him to bring this information to the public by means of television. *HEALING AND THE MIND* is an outgrowth of that 1993 television series.

And it is interesting, if not amusing, to note that a number of these famous doctors in their interviews cite Norman Cousins and his work as their reference point, though Cousins was not a medical doctor or a scientist. He was a famous editor and author who had overcome several medical crises, which he wrote about in his best-selling book *Anatomy of an Illness* and others, including *Head First*.

Two important questions shaped the series: How do thoughts and feelings influence health? How is healing related to the mind?

In Part I, The Art of Healing, Moyers interviews Dr. Thomas Delbanco, director of the Division of General Medicine and Primary Care at Beth Israel Hospital in Boston.

DELBANCO [page 17]: "I have trouble seeing patients in isolation. We learn more from people when we see them in context. We don't make home visits much anymore, although the best place to learn about people is in their homes..."

He points out that one of the reasons doctors don't make house calls anymore is that "time is expensive."

Two more outstanding doctors, Ron Anderson, of Parkland Hospital in Dallas and David Smith, Texas Department of Health, are interviewed under Part I The Art of Healing. While all of the scientific and technical evidence is not yet in, they base their opinions upon experience. At page 29—

MOYERS: "So mind/body is the art of caring."

ANDERSON: "I think it's the art of understanding the whole person and not just the physiological system. In medical schools we deal with diseases and tissues and organs and body systems. But when you put the art in medicine, you deal with persons and with their families and communities. You have to have that connectedness. You deal with the spirit."

Dr. Anderson understands that the environment is a factor in public health.

MOYERS [page 39]: "You keep coming back to the impact of environment on health."

ANDERSON: "You know how the environment of Eastern Europe has been devastating to the health of the people..."

In a tribute to Native Americans, with whom he has had a close relationship—

MOYERS [page 42]: "What do medicine men know that we don't know?"

ANDERSON: "They know about the spirit of man. They don't know the technologies and even the disease theories that we know. But they know about wholeness and try to deal with that... They also have a sacred bond with their environment..."

Anderson then gives another example, on page 43, of Americans on the cutting edge who suddenly become aware of the importance of the environment.

"We have an astronaut cardiologist at the medical school who says that what impressed him most in his NASA flight was the thinness of the atmosphere around the earth. He said it looked like it was a few millimeters thick. And he realized how fragile things were. The Indians knew that too. They didn't kill all the buffalo for their tongues and their hides. They had reverence for those things that they had to take for food. They saw that their spirit extended into other animals, and they had a bond with those animals."

Education and Prevention are the keys to cleaning up the environment. Trying to clean up hazardous waste sites is like locking the barn door after the horse has been stolen. There is not enough money in the world to clean up all the present hazardous waste sites, even if all pollution were to stop immediately. The adage, "an ounce of prevention is worth a pound of cure," makes good sense, both for solving the environmental crisis and in the practice of medicine.

Dr. Anderson makes that same point on page 44.

"When patients come in, literally at death's doorstep, and you're trying to pull them out of the jaws of death, you're practicing resurrection medicine. It's exciting. We spend a lot of money on resurrection medicine, and we write a lot of articles about it... But the question is, why do we have to practice resurrection medicine when we can practice preventive medicine?"

Dr. Anderson closes at the bottom of page 45 with:

"I think we need to humble ourselves a little bit and realize that we don't need many more transplant surgeons, we need people who deal with fundamental things..."

Dr. David Smith, on page 55, says:

"...In this society we take care of our cars at the front end by changing the oil filter and doing other preventive maintenance. But our health care system offers no incentives for the preventive things, or for getting you to understand how you can avoid coming to our emergency room. We don't reimburse for prevention, and we also don't train people to do it... There are rising rates of asthma deaths in communities like this..."

Dr. Smith gives another example on page 57:

"...If we can prevent a stroke that's going to come to $100,000 in intensive care costs, doesn't it make sense to invest $200 a year in health maintenance? One way or the other, you're going to pay."

Moyers then raises the question:

MOYERS: "But then why doesn't the health care system recognize the need for the kind of preventive care offered by people like nutritionists, psychologists, social workers, and translators?"

SMITH: "I wish I had an answer to that question. I don't know, because prevention is just common sense. It's just common sense to embrace strategies that save money and save lives and help people be more functional and enjoy life. One of the things we know is that seventy-five percent of these people work. Who is going to be our labor force in the year 2015?..."

People who have been poisoned by toxic chemicals and who get sick from subsequent exposure to those chemicals, or to synthetic materials made and derived from those chemicals, are told that the only effective treatment is avoidance. But avoidance of chemicals in a chemical society is well nigh impossible.

Dr. Anderson recognizes this when he says at page 60:

"You know, you can cure people, but if they're still dealing with the environment that contributed to the problem, the stress will continue, and the problem will return. We see that often with asthmatics. We improve them to the point that they can go back home, but if we don't deal with what's going on at home, they're going to be back. So we haven't made any real difference, we've just created a dangerous cycle of sickness and temporary relief."

That is what has happened to me and to people I know, have interviewed and spoken with. We cannot control the environment as individuals, but we can do a better job as communities and regions and states and on a federal governmental level. It is not a battle between jobs and the environment. If the environment is a mess, sooner or later there will be no healthy work force. Industry must be concerned about the health of its workers and the health of its neighbors as much as, if not more than, the health of its bottom line.

The interview with Dr. Smith closes with remarks that can be understood by the least intelligent of us.

SMITH [page 64]: "...It doesn't make good business sense to keep paying for making sick people well when we could have prevented the illness in the first place."

MOYERS: "Change the oil now for ten bucks and save a thousand-dollar ring job."

SMITH: "Absolutely. We're paying for the thousand-dollar ring jobs every day in our large hospitals. What we aren't doing is changing the oil filters."

While Moyers in HEALING AND THE MIND did not focus on environmental matters or the environment as a factor in causing illness, a number of those interviewed volunteered that information. For instance, in his interview with Dr. David Felten, Felten volunteers this, which is really not responsive to Moyers' question:

FELTEN [page 233]: "...We have to start looking at the impact of the environment on how a patient recovers."

MOYERS: "If you really believe that there's something to this mind/body thing, what difference does it make to you in how you practice your profession, or your calling?"

FELTEN: "I think it means that we have to pay attention to the patient directly. We have to care about how that patient perceives what is going on. It also means that we have to ask whether there are adverse circumstances, like lousy housing conditions, or poor nutrition, that may be stressing them. If we really believe the patient is the center of the healing process, then we have to go after whatever circumstances contribute to a bad outcome. And if that means taking social action, fine, then let's take social action to change some of those factors that have an adverse impact on a patient's ability to recover from disease."

And now we come to the nugget that links HEALING AND THE MIND, to A Canary's Tale.

MOYERS: "What do you mean?"

FELTEN: "Well, think about the early days of industrialization, when ten-year-old children were developing pneumonia from working in dark, dank factories eighteen hours a day. The solution is not to come up with better antibiotics for treating pulmonary diseases in children, but to pass child labor laws so that children are not exploited. We may have more subtle aspects of that, where poor living conditions may contribute to a patient's poor health. Isn't it the job of society to try to go after those factors and eliminate them so that the general population can have the best health status possible?"

MOYERS: "That's politics, not medicine."

FELTEN: "Sure, it's politics—but politics inevitably get involved in the practice of medicine. Are we treating geriatric patients, or aren't we? Are we going to use fetal tissue, or aren't we? Politics is so heavily imbedded in all of medicine and research that it can't be extracted."

MOYERS: "So you're talking about changes that go beyond meditation and other techniques for altering our inner perceptions. You're talking about the environment in which we live."

FELTEN: "Yes. Maybe changing the living environment helps people recover from autoimmune disease, for example, or helps people have a better immune response in old age."

Felten is a professor of Neurobiology and Anatomy at the University of Rochester School of Medicine. He and his wife Suzanne have discovered nerve fibers that physically link the nervous system and the immune system. Dr. Felten was the recipient of a MacArthur Foundation Prize Fellowship in 1983 and is associate editor of the journal *Brain, Behavior and Immunity*.

Felten provides a glimpse of the link between environmental cause and the autoimmune effect, which we believe to exist as a result of our experiences but which the traditional medical establishment labels mere anecdotes.

Each succeeding interview was better than the one before it. *HEALING AND THE MIND* is an important and exciting book, especially to people who are interested in solving the "mystery" of MCS.

3

Does Anybody Care?

Five years had passed since my home and office had been treated with a chemical termiticide known as Dursban. I became ill and was diagnosed as having been poisoned by an organophosphate. I had spent five years of my life learning about pesticides, illness, and the link between the two. The truth of the matter was that in March '93, I was still vulnerable to chemical exposures. No matter what steps I took to improve my health and my environment, the reality was that I had little or no control of the air quality outside of my home.

In March '93 I attended the annual NCAMP conference in Alexandria, Va. The theme of the forum was, "Safe Food and Sustainable Agriculture." Experts on organic farming, farming without the use of pesticides spoke to us on topics such as pesticides in schools and foods and lawn care.

Before the conference began a group of us went to dinner. Shelly Hawks and Margaret Hue of Kennewick, Wash., were two beautiful young mothers who lived on farms polluted by the drift of pesticide sprays from airplanes that sprayed nearby and adjoining farms. Their young children were exposed, became ill and suffered severe and debilitating symptoms.

Barbara (not her real name), from Nashville, became ill when her workplace was sprayed with pesticides. She was exposed to the toxic chemicals each day. She got so sick that she had to give up her job. She lived for some time in a tent, nursed by friends and family, went to Dallas to be treated by Dr. Rea and then moved to a community on the Atlantic Coast north of Boston, where she enrolled at Tufts to qualify for a new career. Barbara had a friend with her also from Nashville. The friend had also been poisoned by chemical exposure, but looked healthy and had a constant smile.

Frank Fuzzel of Leesburg, Fla., was a farmer whose entire crop of nursery stock was destroyed by the chemical benlate. He and his family became ill after exposure to the benlate.

Rex Stewart was from West Virginia and a former employee of DuPont. Most of us had never met, but we knew instinctively that there was a common bond. Everyone sitting around that table in that restaurant in Alexandria was a victim of toxic poisoning from exposure to chemicals. But not one spoke of his or her illness or appeared sad or depressed. There were no tears. It was only when we returned to the hotel that I heard what happened to my dinner companions. Frank Fuzzel told how the chemical benlate destroyed his family's health. He was fearful for the lives of his wife and children.

After Frank left the lobby, Rex Stewart and I took a walk down toward the river. Rex told me what happened to him and his family. We had checked into the hotel at about the same time and my first impression was that he was a well-dressed business executive. Rex told me privately what he told the Conference the next day when he was a featured speaker. It was the first time he ever spoke publicly about the working conditions in the DuPont plant. This was his story: Until Nov. 11, 1992, he was a devoted employee of DuPont in a socially deprived area of West Virginia. DuPont provided people with an alternative to the coal mines. In the plant, exposed to toxic chemicals, workers did their tasks without gloves, without masks, without respirators and without goggles. Rex was with DuPont 14 years before he ever heard of a material safety data sheet (MSDS). Six mechanics serviced the plant, which was one mile long and three-quarters of a mile wide. He related tales of accidents in the plant. On one occasion a forklift truck driver dropped a large box of toxic powder, which was blown all over the building and breathed in by the workers.

Once there was a chemical spill and four people, including Rex, were assigned to clean up. They cleaned without goggles, rubber gloves or boots. When Rex was unable to breathe, he was given oxygen and instructed not to go to the hospital. Of the four workers who did the cleanup, Rex is the only survivor, and he is ill with multiple symptoms including cancer. He lost his job, his home, his family and his car. I knew nothing of this the night before when I had dinner with him. Some poison victims look healthy, despite their suffering. Rex had never before gone public with his case. Like many, he feared harassment, intimidation and even bodily injury for speaking out about what had happened.

Rex tried to warn his father and his family, his neighbors and his fellow employees about the hazards of the workplace. But he was unable to persuade them that there was a relationship between the chemicals in the plant and the disabilities and premature deaths of numerous plant employees. That industry was regarded as the salvation of the community. Residents ignored arguments about pollution and sickness. Rex was like the canary in the coal mine, but in his case nobody in his community paid heed. They were like the millions of tobacco smokers who have heard all the arguments about cigarette smoke and cancer but who continue smoking. This is truly the mystery illness: the willingness of man to ignore evidence and choose to self destruct.

• • •

David Lyons, Herald Staff Writer, reported on a jury verdict awarding $4 million to Juan, Donna, and John Castillo in a lawsuit against DuPont Co. alleging John was born without eyes, after Donna, a pregnant woman, was exposed to a spray of Benlate 50 DF while strolling with her baby daughter in South Dade, Florida in 1989.

Lyons, David, "Benlate Blamed for Birth Defects" Dade Jury Awards Couple $4 million, The Herald, The Broward Edition of the Miami Herald of 8 June 1996:1.

4

NAFTA (No Aid for Toxic Americans)

On April 1, the television program "Prime Time," aired a story about babies born in Texas without brains. About the same time I read a magnificent book by William Greider—*Who Will Tell the People, The Betrayal of American Democracy*, New York, New York, Simon and Schuster, 1992. Greider writes "A gripping portrait of American economic civilization..." according to the *Wall Street Journal*. A chapter called "The Closet Dictator" describes economic conditions in Mexico along the U.S. border in the "maquiladora" zone in 1992. This is a brief resumé of what is happening there.

In the past few years, more than a thousand American corporations have closed plants in the United States and moved operations to Mexico. There they have the advantage of exploiting cheap Mexican labor and ignoring environmental regulations designed to protect the public health. They can make their product for less and increase their profits. These same corporations pollute the air that drifts across the Rio Grande into the U.S. They have also dumped hazardous wastes onto the soil beside their plants. These wastes contain carcinogens that have seeped into the groundwater and into the Rio Grande itself, which is now too polluted to sustain normal sea life. These 20th century captains of industry have not only polluted the air, the soil and the water in Mexico, but have watched the pollution cross the border into the United States. They are immune to any prosecution. Unfortunately, the poor people living in these border towns, many of whom are Hispanic, have become ill and the women have had an extraordinary number of babies born with genetic defects, including the absence of brains. Epidemiological studies have been conducted and the results are not surprising. One does not have to be a Ph.D. from M.I.T. to conclude that something has gone wrong along the Mexican border. This is not a secret. It has been written about time and again. These are poor people. They cannot afford to contribute a thousand dollars a plate to their congressman and to the president. Consequently, they have no influence in the government. The polluters, on the other hand, do make their contributions to politicians in both parties in both governments, and have plenty of influence. They continue to pollute and poison people with impunity.

The Congress passed the North American Free Trade Agreement (NAFTA), and the president hailed it as a triumph of his administration. The public was assured the environment would be protected. Anyone who is aware of the sad record of the enforcing agencies responsible for protecting the environment in our own country simply does not believe NAFTA will improve the environment in Mexico or anywhere else. The speakers are shoveling smoke. And the smoke is toxic.

Many Americans believe the only problem along the Mexican border is illegal immigration. The media have published a hundred articles on that subject to every one on the subject of the Mexican pollution, which will result in long-term suffering and death for both Americans and Mexicans.

5

A Letter to Hillary

In April I was invited to meet with a group of chemically poisoned victims at the home of Natalie Golos in Montgomery County, Maryland. The purpose of the meeting was to prepare letters to be sent to Hillary Clinton and Tipper Gore who were heading President Clinton's Task Force on Health Care Reform.

We wanted to inform them about environmental pollution and the medical needs of the many victims poisoned as a result of exposure to so-called "safe chemicals."

I did write a letter to Hillary Clinton as my contribution to the Task Force on Health Care Reform. It summed up what I had learned over the past five years, where I stood, and what I thought government should be doing about the problem of pollution and the victims of that pollution. The predicate of that letter became the Preface to this book, each concluding with a Call to Action.

The task force later announced that they had received more than 700,000 letters from citizens and organizations eager to express their views on health care reform.

I was pleased to be a part of that movement and especially pleased to receive a card of thanks signed by Hillary and letters from Tipper and other cabinet secretaries.

Health Care Reform Legislation died in 1994, but I am hopeful that my letter had some lasting influence on those who read it.

6

"Waging One Final Battle"

Bill Callen, staff writer (now Sports editor) for *The Herald-Mail*, interviewed me for a feature story. I had been out of the public eye for a long time, and apparently someone was curious about what I was doing. I thought the story was going to be about my political opinions, or important legal cases I lost, or why I had not lived up to my potential.

Callen became very interested in what I had to say about environmental pollution. I was surprised to find my picture on the front page of the Sunday April 18 paper under the following quote:

"We are fouling our own nest. We have a right to know what is going on in our environment, and we're not being protected by government, we're not being protected by industry."

The article was titled:

Waging one final battle
Berkson writing book on chemical pollution

(Reprinted with permission.)

Callen's article greatly exceeded my expectations and set the stage for a multitude of letters and phone calls from people all over the tri-state area who had become ill or knew of people who became ill following exposure to toxic chemicals. The Associated Press picked up the story and versions of it appeared in other newspapers around the state and in adjoining states. I received calls from the Midwest and from California from people wanting help. My experience was similar to that of author Roueché after publication of "The Contamination Chamber" in *The New Yorker* back in 1988. He later wrote that he had received numerous letters from readers who had similar experiences but who had been told their experience was unique. That was in 1988. Here it was five years later, 1993, and despite all of the work and research over the last five years most of the people suffering from chemical poisoning who contacted me had been told by their doctors they were unique and should see a psychiatrist. I spent the next several months sharing my information with fellow victims from around the country. I was not a doctor or a scientist or any kind of expert, and I had not discovered a cure for MCS or chemical sensitivity. But by listening and caring I helped them to understand that what was happening was real, not imaginary. By helping them validate their illness I paid back those who had earlier helped me. Counseling others gave meaning and satisfaction to my life.

It was obvious from all the discussions that there was a great need for education, understanding, tolerance, research, recognition, competent medical diagnosis, and effective medical treatment.

It was time for me to start writing *A Canary's Tale*.

Johns Hopkins Allergy and Asthma Center
Baltimore, Maryland

N. Franklin Adkinson, Jr., M.D., Professor of Medicine at Johns Hopkins Asthma and Allergy Center at the Francis Scott Key Medical Center, Baltimore, Maryland, examined and evaluated me for intolerance to multiple irritants/chemicals on November 4, 1993.

My chief complaint was multiple chemical sensitivity. Upon conclusion of the exam a comprehensive five page single spaced report was dictated by Amir A. Bajoghli—clinical clerk—and signed by him and Dr. Adkinson and distributed to Dr. Snyder, Dr. Wayne Koch, and Dr. Leonard Proctor. The report included my Complaint, Allergic Profile, Environmental History, Allergic Family History, Previous Allergic Evaluation, Past Surgical History, Past Medical History, Current Medication, Non-Allergic Family History, Social History, Review of Systems, Physical Examination, Impression, Treatment/Plan.

The Impression:
#1 Irritability/intolerance to multiple chemicals/irritants.
#2 Chronic sinusitis.
#3 Nasal polyposis (right nostril).
#4 Seasonal allergic rhinitis.

The Treatment advised was:
#1 Continue saline nasal drainage.
#2 Continue using Intal.
#3 Start Vancenase again.
#4 Discontinue using Atrovent.

#5 Follow up in 4 to 6 months.

This was a most thorough medical examination, evaluation, and treatment plan and Report by a distinguished Professor of Medicine and his staff. The #1 Impression stated above validated my chemical intolerance as well as my sinusitis and seasonal allergies.

I followed Dr. Adkinson's plan, continued to practice avoidance, and am pleased to report that I improved steadily following his advice.

8

Carpets, Pollution, Illness, and Politics

H i, Lois, how is everything?" I said to one of my former high school classmates as we were passing each other in front of the Peoples Drug Store at the Longmeadow Shopping Center on a sunny December day in 1993.

"Well, I'm doing just fine and Jack is too, but we do have a rather unusual situation over at our house. We recently installed brand-new wall-to-wall carpet in several of our rooms, and you would not believe how terrible the air smells in those newly carpeted rooms. It is unbelievable."

"I believe you. I know exactly what you are talking about. I had the same experience almost five years ago to this very day, back in 1988 when I had brand-new carpet installed in my apartment when I had to move out of my home," I replied.

"Well, I never knew carpet gave off such foul odors, and it is just making us sick."

"This has been going on for years, Lois. It is happening all over the country. People are buying carpet, the carpet is polluting the indoor air with toxic chemicals, people are breathing that polluted air and becoming ill, the carpet dealers and manufacturers are denying that there is any link between their carpet and the illness people are complaining about, and the Environmental Protection Agency, which is supposed to protect the environment and the public health, has been playing politics for years protecting the carpet industry all to the detriment and harm of the American public, including you and me."

"Do you mean the EPA is promoting pollution?"

"Were you given any warning or disclosure that the carpet you purchased contained chemicals hazardous to your health or would outgas foul and noxious odors and pollute the indoor air in your very home?"

"No, we certainly did not receive any disclosures or any warnings."

"Would you have purchased and installed that carpet if you had known that you were undertaking a risk of danger to your health and the health of your family?"

"Of course not. I thought the government was there to protect us from pollution. What you are telling me is very hard for me to believe."

"Well, I found myself in the same situation five years ago that you seem to be finding yourself in now, and I know what you are going through. For a long time I thought I was the only person in the world who was affected by vapors and fumes from wall-to-wall carpet. The merchant who sold me the carpet and whom I trusted gave me no warning although he knew I had been poisoned and was suffering from respiratory problems, and when I reported to him that I had come down with headaches, irritated eyes, nasal and sinus problems after they installed the carpet in my apartment, he told me he had never had a complaint from any customer about the carpets he sold, that he had never heard of such a complaint, and he utterly denied that there could be a link between the carpet he installed and my complaints. I sought advice from numerous people including doctors, and each one looked at me as if I were reporting that I had sighted a UFO and little aliens with antennae sticking out their heads like you see in cartoons. I thought they thought I was off my rocker. I was beginning to question my own sanity. Things were happening to me that seemed obvious, but I did not know anyone who had a similar experience and I had nothing in writing to back me up. I did not give a thought to research. I did not think I needed to hire a Ph.D. from M.I.T. to support my thesis. Before the carpet was installed the air quality was fine. After the carpet was installed the air quality was bad. No other factors entered into the equation. It was obvious to me that there was a link between the carpet and the foul odor in the apartment, and subsequently a link between the odor and my illness."

"Well, this is all very interesting, but I have to go home and fix lunch. I wish I had known about all this before I bought that carpet."

"I will make copies of a few articles I have about carpets and pollution and I will drop them by your house and you can read about this at your leisure. Take care."

As she walked to her car, I felt very sorry that one of my friends had to suffer and risk possible serious health problems because of the perfidy and greed of the carpet industry and the incompetence, if not criminal negligence, of high government officials who made decisions not in the public interest as they had sworn to do but made decisions protecting polluters responsible for causing devastating health problems to thousands, if not millions, of our citizens.

I went back home and began putting together a file composed of articles I had collected over the past few years about carpets and the part they were playing in indoor air pollution. I could picture the headlines—they were inscribed on my brain forever.

Further material on carpets is set forth in Volume II of *A Canary's Tale* under Topic Heading I—Indoor Air Pollution.

Year Seven
1994
A.D.

"INTRODUCTION Human beings and the natural world are on a collision course. Human activities inflict harsh and often irreversible damage on the environment and on critical resources. If not checked, many of our current practices put at serious risk the future that we wish for human society and the plant and animal kingdoms, and may so alter the living world that it will be unable to sustain life in the manner that we know. Fundamental changes are urgent if we are to avoid the collision our present course will bring about.

"THE ENVIRONMENT The environment is suffering critical stress."

"Over 1670 scientists, including 104 Nobel laureates—a majority of the living recipients of the Prize in the sciences—have signed the Warning so far. These men and women represent 71 countries, including all of the 19 largest economic powers, all of the 12 most populous nations, 12 countries in Africa, 14 in Asia, 19 in Europe, and 12 in Latin America."

From "World Scientists' Warning to Humanity," sponsored by the Union of Concerned Scientists, Cambridge, MA, 1993. Reprinted with permission.

1

Bjorklund-Romeu Wedding
Key Biscayne, Florida

Len Bjorklund invited me to be best man at his wedding in Key
Biscayne, Florida, on Saturday, January 29. This was to be a
happy time for Len and Pat, his wife-to-be. I was pleased to be
included in these festivities. Len, Jim Wilber, and I first met in
1945 on the island of Saipan in the Mariana Islands, Pacific
Ocean area at the close of World War II. When we returned to
the States in 1946, Len went to Harvard, Jim Wilber went to
Syracuse, and I went to Virginia. We all graduated from law
school and passed the Bar.

In 1952, Len and I were recalled to serve a two year tour of
duty in Korea and Japan. Afterwards, Len moved to California
and established a successful law practice in Sausalito and Jim
practiced in upstate New York and later in Boca Raton, Florida.

I flew to Key Biscayne on January 27th.

The air quality on the airplane (USAir) was fine. I had my respirator with me in the event of an emergency, especially during
landings and take offs when the exhaust permeates the cabin. I
was vulnerable but coping.

Key Biscayne is an island just outside of Miami connected by
the Rickenbacker Causeway. I caught a cab at the airport and rode
to the Key. There I was met by Len and Pat, who were holding
hands and gazing at each other like young lovers.

They drove me to a beautiful high rise complex on the ocean
front. The complex was known as Key Colony and it was a
sumptuous place, all marble and tile and glass with modern fur-

nishings. Len and I shared one bedroom and Pat's sister, Suzanne, and her daughter, Alex, shared another which they kept locked, bolted, and chained. The kitchen, living room, and dining room were for common use but we spent most of our time outdoors.

The air quality at the condo was excellent.

The beach was wide and clean. It was wonderful to breathe the clean ocean air, to walk in the warm sand, and to feel well again.

We visited Pat's daughter, Molly, and her husband, Dr. Eddie Alfonso, who had a magnificent "healthy" home. I took photos of the interior and the exterior of that home as it seemed to have everything that a healthy home should have and nothing to make it unhealthy. The building materials and furnishings were natural and not synthetic.

We had a wedding rehearsal Friday evening at Saint Agnes Catholic Church and everyone there on both sides was Catholic except me. However, I had visited Catholic churches from Saint Mary's in Hagerstown to Notre Dame in Paris, and Saint Peter's and Saint Paul's in Rome. I felt comfortable in the Catholic church. However, when it was discovered that the wedding party was missing an altar boy, the Catholic priest, Father Ruy, naively assuming I was "one of his," asked me if I would assist him with the Communion. I agreed to help out despite Len's negative body language and hand wringing. The wedding ceremony was as beautiful as the bride.

Following the ceremony, Pat's children had a reception at Molly and Eddie's healthy home. It was a joyous occasion. Everyone was happy and everyone was blessed. They called on me, the best man, for a toast. Without any authority, I invited all the guests present to visit with the bride and groom at their new home in San Rafael, California. I urged them to bring their children and stay as long as they were having a happy time in the California sunshine.

Before they left for their honeymoon Len and Pat told me that I could use Pat's apartment in Ocean Village, another large complex just off the beach near Key Colony. This was a wonderful treat as the apartment was in a building that was also constructed of natural materials and had windows that opened and doors that opened to a balcony. The large building itself had an atrium with palm trees and ferns and waterfalls in various courtyards. The light yellow stucco building was set off by a red tile roof and surrounded by palms and flowering trees of every description.

I thought back to my days of affliction, all of which were stressful and left me angry, upset, and ill. But now I was in a different world, a world of joy and peace and friendship. Len and Pat and their families made me feel wanted and glad I had travelled the distance to join in this joyous occasion.

What was happening to me was written a long time ago in Ecclesiastes, "Chapter III:

"1 To every thing there is a season, and a time to every purpose under the heaven...

"4 A time to weep, and a time to laugh; a time to mourn, and a time to dance;..."

Within a few days I had wept and I had laughed, I had mourned and I had danced, and now I was healing.

2

James E. Wilber, Esquire, and Boca Raton, Florida

I kept in touch with Jim Wilber and he kept in touch with me over the years since our days on Saipan. Later we met in Washington when he was inducted into the American Academy of Trial Lawyers. Jim was a highly successful trial attorney, a senior partner in a large New York law firm.

These days Jim was retired making his home in Boca Raton, Florida about an hour's drive from Key Biscayne. After the wedding he invited me to move up to Boca Raton for a few days while his wife, Florence, was in the hospital. Jim picked me up and took me to his home. It was in a beautiful section near the Boca West Country Club.

Jim and I had a great time reminiscing about our days on Saipan and then about what had happened to each of us since we had gotten out of law school. Jim had funny stories about the lawyers he worked with and the Judges he appeared before in New York State. He kept me in stitches. Laughter is a healing therapy as Norman Cousins taught us in his books. But as Ecclesiastes explains it there is "a time to every purpose under the heaven" and while there was great joy in my reunion with Jim, there was an unexpected downside.

The development in which Jim lived was as beautiful as any landscaped area I have ever seen, the most gorgeous palm trees, ferns, flowers, lakes, lawns, golf courses, country clubs, all being manicured and maintained by a large and industrious work force. The only problem for me was the work force all used toxic chemicals on the lawns in the community.

While I was at Jim's home, two exciting events occurred. First I received an invitation from the United States Public Health Service, Agency for Toxic Substances and Diseases Registry (ATSDR) to speak at a conference on chemical sensitivity to take place in Baltimore in April. This was to be an official conference with some 30 doctors and neuroscientists and I was one of three patients invited to speak. I was asked to submit a paper which related my story of exposure to Dursban and the consequent health effects.

I was told that these proceedings would be published by the government. This was a tremendous event. It meant that chemical sensitivity was being recognized and the government was beginning to take seriously what had happened to me and to others.

The other exciting event that occurred while I was a guest at Jim's home was a phone call I received from Dr. Norman Rosenthal. The doctor told me that he had decided to write a book on the subject of multiple chemical sensitivity. He said he wanted me to hear it first hand from him rather than from someone else, so that I would not think that he was stealing my thunder. He did not need my permission to write a book on that subject or on anything else. He had already written numerous scientific papers and had written and published several books on seasonal affective disorder (SAD). He was a recognized authority in the field of psychiatry. I was very happy to hear this news and I told him so.

He told me that as a result of the article he had written in the *American Journal of Psychiatry* about my case he had been invited by the United States Public Health Service ATSDR to speak at the same conference in Baltimore, in which I was to speak. He said he was very excited about this project and that he wanted to get together with me when I returned to my home. I offered to make all of my reference material available to him and promised to call him when I got settled back home. I thanked the good doctor for his interest in my case and in MCS and I was happy that I had another ally working on a book to get the word out to the public that certain chemicals are hazardous to your health.

I was really amazed to receive that long distance phone call from Dr. Rosenthal. The doctor sounded more excited than I. I thought that the two of us together, with one book by a patient and another book by a doctor, might very well make a most valuable contribution to medical science. It might serve to heighten the public awareness of the link between environmental pollution and the illnesses that pollution causes or aggravates.

The experiences I had in Florida clearly proved to me, as a canary very sensitive to air quality, that where man had not degraded the environment as along the beach at Key Biscayne the air quality was excellent. But a few miles away from the Atlantic Ocean where man had turned a natural environment into a country club development maintained by thousands of gallons of toxic chemicals in the air, the soil, and the water, that polluted environment, though beautiful to the eye, free of all dandelions, but with an altered ecology, was to me, a canary,—unhealthy— and I was forced to leave that synthetic and seductive "shangri la." If I had remained there, my health, like that of the canary in the mine shaft, may have been further damaged.

3

Twelfth National Pesticide Forum

In March 1994, NCAMP held its 12th national pesticide forum in Virginia.

The conference was entitled "Freedom From Pesticides Is Every Body's Right: Preventing the Poisoning." It was a forum to discuss policy and strategy regarding protection from pesticides.

The call to action was given by Dr. Samuel Epstein, professor of Occupational and Environmental Medicine at the University of Illinois. His report, "Environmental and Occupational Pollutants are Avoidable Causes of Breast Cancer," was distributed. He found:

"For over three decades, evidence has accumulated relating avoidable exposures to environmental and occupational carcinogens to the escalating incidence of breast cancer in the United States and other major industrialized nations. This evidence has until very recently been totally ignored by the cancer establishment, the National Cancer Institute, and the American Cancer Society, despite expenditures of over $1 billion on breast cancer research. Recognition of these environmental and occupational risk factors should lead to the belated development of public health policies directed to the primary prevention of breast cancer. Their recognition should also lend urgency to the need for radical reforms in the priorities and leadership of the cancer establishment." (International Journal of Health Services 24.1 [1994]: 145-150. © 1994, Baywood Publishing Co., Inc. Reprinted with permission.)

Many articles and papers were distributed about cancer and the likely link between chemicals and breast cancer. In light of all the scientific evidence, it is a mystery to me why doctors and scientists continue to ignore environmental factors and pollution as a probable cause. If the evidence is correct, many cancer deaths are preventable.

Michael Gregory, Director of Arizona Toxics Information, submitted two papers and, in an emotional talk, compared risk assessment (RA) to a computer game. "The so-called experts are now playing with figures and they can come out with anything they want. They are unreliable protectors of the status quo. Risk assessment gives polluters the right to continue to pollute. That should be balanced against the right of the public not to be poisoned and the right to know by whom the public is being poisoned and disclosure which gives the public the right to say 'No.' The first step would be to ban the materials we know about that are carcinogens. Prevention and prudence is the key."

Some of the other subjects at the conference included food safety laws, insecticides injuring farm workers, and airline insecticide spraying.

As a former staff attorney I was extremely interested in hearing about the work General Services Administration is doing to protect workers in federal buildings. I was pleased to hear Mr. Albert Greene, regional entomologist with GSA, talk about how GSA, the largest manager of public buildings in the United States, continues to reduce pesticide application, a move that will enhance the health and well-being of more than one million federal workers.

More than 100 people and organizations participated in the forum. It was an exciting and educational experience. It was an opportunity not only to learn, but to socialize with old friends and new acquaintances. And as if that was not enough, participants were invited to spend an evening dancing, talking and eating.

I had a great time that evening watching the younger activists dance much the way I had seen modern dancers on TV programs. This was no two-step, or jitterbug, or waltz, but some kind of a cross between the gyrations of Elvis Presley and my YMCA aerobic exercise class. I joined in the fun and had the time of my life, putting to use almost every limb, muscle, ligament and joint in my body.

On Monday many of the participants went to Capitol Hill to meet with their representatives and staff members. Others went to the federal agencies to discuss the implications of the conference.

Before I left, Will Snodgrass, a member of Missoulans for a Clean Environment of Missoula, Mont., met with me during an open lunch hour and videotaped a half hour interview for his TV program back in Montana.

Mr. Snodgrass was poisoned some years ago and developed chemical sensitivity. He now devotes as much time as he can to the cause of environmental protection.

Year after year NCAMP under the direction of Jay Feldman continues to lead the battle and to produce speakers on the cutting edge of medicine, science, politics and strategy.

4

ATSDR Conference

Following the NCAMP conference I turned my attention to an April conference sponsored by the Department of Health and Human Services' Public Health Service, Agency for Toxic Substances and Disease Registry (ATSDR). The conference was to have a number of panels discussing various aspects of low-level exposure to chemicals and neurobiologic sensitivity.

The patient panel consisted of Helen Keplinger of Bethesda, Md., an attorney for the Environmental Protection Agency; Cynthia Wilson, Editor of *Our Toxic Times*, a monthly publication of the Chemical Injury Information Network; and me.

I met Helen Keplinger for the first time at this conference. She is a beautiful and intelligent woman who developed MCS after being poisoned at EPA Headquarters several years ago.

I am a subscriber to *Our Toxic Times* and a great admirer of the work Cynthia Wilson does in disseminating information to victims of MCS.

Dr. Patricia Price of ATSDR advised me to tell my own story and to confine it to the chemical exposure, the adverse health effects, the institutional responses and the sociological outcome. I was not to attempt to prove my case. I was not to discuss specific medical treatments and not to produce medical or hospital records. The focus was to be on neurobiologic sensitivity and my talk was to be limited to 10 minutes.

This assignment reminded me of a story Judge Dobie, one of my former law professors, used to tell about Woodrow Wilson. Whenever Wilson was asked to speak at an important occasion, he would ask, "How much time do I have to speak?" "What difference does it make?" he was asked.

"If I only have 10 minutes to speak, it may take me weeks to prepare my talk. In other words the shorter the speech the longer it takes to prepare," Wilson replied.

I have found his remarks both valid and astute. I had spent six years on my odyssey of learning about environmental pollution and illnesses, reviewed hundreds of books, magazines, newspapers, medical, scientific and technical papers and completed more than 400 pages of this manuscript. Yet I found that this assignment of preparing a 10-minute talk to a group of some 30 neuroscientists one of the most difficult tasks of my career.

Like Woodrow Wilson, I could speak for an hour or two without much preparation, but it took me three weeks of hard work to boil down my material. In addition, I was working under the handicap of continuing symptoms of MCS, such as difficulty with concentration, short-term memory loss, lethargy and sometimes confusion. These symptoms waxed and waned according to my exposure to chemicals.

Helen Keplinger described the debilitating effects that the air in EPA Headquarters had on her respiratory system, her memory and her energy level. She went from being a person who jogged regularly, who traveled for the EPA frequently and who had a bright future to someone who must now work out of her home, who is extremely sensitive to any chemical exposure and who must adjust to a restricted lifestyle.

Cynthia Wilson couldn't attend because of her extreme MCS, but she spoke via videotape from her home in Montana.

Cynthia said that before she was poisoned, she had an I.Q. of 187. After the poisoning her I.Q. tested at 117, 93 and 143 on three different tests. She was confused, disoriented and suffered numerous system breakdowns. She was forced to give up her successful career in construction and other businesses. She is the author of *Chemical Exposure and Human Health* and coauthor with

Cindy Duehring of *The Human Consequences of the Chemical Problem*. She is devoting her life to helping victims of MCS learn how to cope. The work she does as editor of *Our Toxic Times* is outstanding and deserving of recognition.

In all, more than 30 leading authorities, in diverse medical and scientific fields, participated in the two day event.

Dr. Claudia S. Miller, assistant professor of Environmental and Occupational Medicine at the University of Texas Health Science Center at San Antonio, presented an outstanding paper entitled "Chemical Sensitivity: History and Phenomenology." Her conclusion was right on:

> "Understanding MCS is pivotal to establishing sound environmental policy. If there is a subset of the population that is especially sensitive to low level chemical exposures, a strategy for protecting this subset must be found. If it were to be determined that certain chemical exposures can lead to MCS, then perhaps these [sensitizing] exposures could be avoided. Perhaps by preventing chemical accidents, forbidding occupancy of buildings prior to finish-out or completion, avoiding use of cholinesterase-inhibiting pesticides indoors, etc., society could protect more vulnerable individuals from becoming sensitized in the first place. It would make little sense to regulate chemicals at the parts per billion level or lower if what was required was to keep people from becoming sensitized in the first place. Indeed, by understanding the true nature of MCS and who is at risk, we may prevent unnecessary and costly overregulation of environmental exposures in the years to come... In not understanding MCS, we take an immense gamble." (Later published by Princeton Scientific Publishing Co., Inc. in *Toxicology and Industrial Health* 10.4/5 [1994]: 253-276. Reprinted with permission.)

In other words education, understanding and prevention are the keys to the solution.

"Neuropsychiatric Aspects of Sensitivity to Low Level Chemicals: A Neural Sensitization Model" presented by Iris R. Bell, M.D., Ph.D., Department of Psychiatry, University of Arizona Health Sciences Center and Tucson Veterans Affairs Medical Center, Tucson, Arizona, was the focus of discussion by the participants.

> The...paper summarizes the proposed time-dependent sensitization (TDS) and partial limbic kindling model for illness from low level chemicals; reviews and critiques prior studies on CNS aspects of multiple chemical sensitivity (MCS); and outlines possible experimental approaches to future studies...

> The focus of the paper is the controversial claim of altered sense of smell and illness from low levels of environmental chemicals (i.e., "cacosmia"), levels that should not have any biologically harmful effects by the rules of classical neurotoxicology...(Later published by Princeton Scientific Publishing Co., Inc. in Toxicology and Industrial Health 10[4/5] [July- October 1994]: 277:312. Reprinted with permission.)

Dr. Norman Rosenthal, my psychiatrist and friend, was one of the most respected speakers at the conference. He told of his research in the field of Seasonal Affective Disorders (SAD) and suggested a variation of his methods and experience with SAD might eventually prove the mechanism that links chemical exposure and chemical sensitivity.

Dr. Theron G. Randolph, of Illinois, the father of environmental medicine, was present. It was a great thrill to meet this pioneer. Someday he will be given the recognition he deserves for his contributions to medical science.

Numerous patients—canaries—participated in question-and-answer periods. Mary Lamielle of Voorhees, N.J., editor of *The Delicate Balance* spoke. She is president of the National Center for Environmental Health Strategies (NCEHS) and one of the nations most influential and prolific environmental activists. Both Mary and *The Delicate Balance* are playing an important role in education, research and recognition for MCS.

This was a momentous occasion, especially for the MCS patients. We were grateful to those who recognized our illness and were working to discover the mechanism to prove the scientific link.

I felt that my participation was the culmination of six years of studying, learning and working in this controversial field.

In retrospect I felt I had come a long way from the incident of March 23, 1988, and the days, months, and years following, when I seemed to be wandering in the desert for 40 years, like my ancestors several thousand years ago in their exodus from Egypt.

Sooner or later medical science will accept and recognize chemical sensitivity as a real disease, and effective treatment will be recognized and prescribed. All of the canaries, victims, patients and their families can be encouraged by this ATSDR conference. These proceedings are now published (by Princeton Scientific Publishing Co., Inc., in *Toxicology and Industrial Health* 10.4/5 [July-Oct., 1994]). More researchers will enter the field, more papers will be written and more books will be published. And some day, those of us who have been wandering in the wilderness will reach the promised land.

5

Clean Air and Great Hope

In July I travelled to Oregon in search of good air quality and to visit my sons Dan and Jim and my grandchildren, Torrey and Randy. Dan is EMCON 2000 Project Coordinator for Emery Worldwide Global Logistics Services. Jim is a Quantitative Fishery Scientist with the Columbia River Inter-Tribal Fish Commission. He works with the Yakima, Nez Perce, Warm Springs, and Umatilla Indian Tribes. The weather was perfect in Portland and I felt healthy again. Norma Grier, a friend and director of NCAMP and director of the Northwest Coalition for Alternatives to Pesticides in Eugene, put me in touch with EI's in Portland who could help in event of an emergency. Rosalind Hamilton, a knowledgeable and considerate EI, invited me to a meeting of EI's at the Easter Seal Office. Deborah Cohen showed us a video she had written and produced on MCS. She made a copy of it for me. Dan and Julie and Jim and Ginger took me to some of the many parks and natural attractions in the Portland area. Many people choose to live in Oregon because of the natural beauty and progressive environmental policies established there.

My next stop was San Francisco, one of the most exciting cities in the world. I stayed with my friends Len and Pat Bjorklund in their elegant mountain-view home in San Rafael. Pat took me to Point Reyes National Seashore on the Pacific Coast north of San Francisco. I fell in love with the beauty of the beach, the flora and fauna and the air quality at Point Reyes. I felt alive and healthy there.

I enjoyed the ferry ride from Larkspur Landing across the Bay to

San Francisco several times. In San Francisco I had the pleasure of meeting with Joan Clayburgh, director of Pesticide Watch and a director of NCAMP, and her staff. I was impressed with the number of college students working in her offices as volunteers, helping on a number of important projects. I took photos of these enthusiastic activists and felt elated that we had young people working to inform the public about the hazards of pesticides.

Monica Moore, director of Pesticide Action Network (PAN) North America Regional Center, another friend from NCAMP, gave me an overview of the history and work of PAN. She has a wonderful library with all books catalogued, indexed and retrievable. Students from around the world work there. Monica is another outstanding and helpful environmentalist. My hopes for a healthier environment were raised after I met with Joan and Monica. They are working in the public interest.

I have three cousins who are medical doctors practicing in the San Francisco and Bay Area. Dr. Jerold Lowenstein is chief of Nuclear Medicine at Pacific Medical Center. We had lunch together and he provided me with some papers for my book. Dr. Ken Passamaneck is a psychiatrist who was then working with victims of a California disaster. Dr. Ron Berman was very interested in my book because he had been exposed to the drift of a toxic acid cloud accidentally released by General Chemical Corp. in Richmond, Calif. The toxic spill occurred on July 26, 1993, and bold headlines on the front page of the *San Francisco Examiner* the next day read: "HUGE FINES FOR TOXIC WASTES: Safety woes at chemical firm. Thousands flock to clinics for treatment after acid cloud from Richmond company chokes area."

A paragraph from the article reads:

"General Chemical Corp. is under investigation again after 9,500 gallons of a potent form of sulfuric acid called oleum leaked out of a rail tank car Monday and spewed a noxious cloud that spread 15 miles."

Ron described what happened to him: "My own exposure to the disulfuric acid (oleum) cloud caused 2 months of wheezing, cough, infection of lung and sinuses, sloughing off of the pulmonary endothelium and sinusitis with similar sloughing." Several thousand victims of this chemical spill have joined in a class action lawsuit. We don't have to convince them or their families that there is a link between chemical pollution and adverse health effects.

One person I had read about and heard described as the ultimate activist was Susan Molloy. She has been written about in numerous articles, including "When Life Is Toxic" in the *New York Times*. I wanted to meet her. She is the editor of "The New Reactor," The Newsletter of the Environmental Health Network, P.O. Box 1155, Larkspur, CA 94977. Susan met me at a health food store and we spent a glorious day together.

We went to Point Reyes Seashore. On the way we stopped at the home of Richard Conrad, a biochemist. Dr. Conrad is a housing consultant and another famous EI. He remembered meeting me at the ATSDR Conference and welcomed me to his "less toxic" home. He was receiving calls from victims around the country who sought help in fixing and building healthy homes. The three of us drove to Point Reyes and had a great time breathing clean air. I took photos of them on the beach and treasure them along with the memories of the day.

Finding a place with excellent air quality is to an EI a thrill comparable to an Olympic athlete winning a gold medal. Breathing unpolluted air is like finding diamonds. We smile and laugh and joke and act like kids at a school recess. We then thank the Good Lord for this blessed clean air.

Susan had fought for environmental causes all over the country and was preparing to move to Arizona to compile 10 years of Newsletters, a "Best of the Reactor" project. She had found what seemed to be a healthier place to live. The next day she introduced me to friends from Environmental Health Network, including Chris Sabey and Carol Kuczora, victims of chemical poisoning. They were cheerful people who lifted my spirits. I returned to Maryland with renewed hope. With the help and leadership of these remarkable folks in Oregon, California, and Arizona, we are going to succeed in our battle to prevent future pollution and aid the victims of the present polluted planet.

Year Eight
1995
A.D.

"I strongly urge that your committee cause Congress to enact by statute a requirement that future membership of the Science Advisory Board contain no scientists whose research or livelihood, in main or in part, is dependent upon financial support from corporations. We have learned that such scientists can be less than objective. The result is that Vietnam veterans have been denied for over 20 years the benefits which the law would have provided had scientific truth prevailed over pseudo-scientific manipulation."

Admiral E. R. Zumwalt, Jr., USN (Ret.), Chairman, Agent Orange Coordinating Council, statement before the House Subcommittee on Energy and Environment, 13 Dec. 1995. Reprinted with permission.

1

Justice William O. Douglas and the C&O Canal

I hiked along the Potomac River and the C&O Canal towpath
with the late Supreme Court Justice William O. Douglas and
others for more than 15 years in an effort to gain recognition for
our movement to preserve and protect the natural beauty and
environment and to convert this long narrow stretch of public
land into a national park. The Canal, which ran along the
Potomac from Georgetown in the District of Columbia to
Cumberland, Md., was approximately 185 miles long, and in 1954
plans were revealed to bulldoze and blast the Canal and towpath
into a highway.

The canal's operation is a rich part of American history. It was
originally the dream of George Washington to have this waterway
built through the Potomac Valley. It was to run "along the
established Potomac and trans-Allegheny trade route to the Ohio
River." Construction began in 1828. President John Quincy
Adams turned the first spade of dirt. For nearly 75 years the canal
served to carry raw materials from the "Western frontier" to the
Nation's capital, and back again with finished products. Later, the
superior efficiency of the B&O Railroad, whose construction
ironically began on the same day as the Canal's, made the Canal
obsolete even before the flood of 1924 finally closed it down. The
B & O RR bought the bonds of the C&O Canal Co. The US
Dept. of the Interior bought the land from the B & O RR in 1938
for $2,000,000. Canal and towpath became public land.

In 1954 a group of politicians decided that the Canal and its towpath should be turned into a superhighway from Washington D.C. to Cumberland. Mr. Justice Douglas, an avid conservationist and hiker long familiar with the natural beauty along the towpath, opposed this highway project. He was soon joined by other conservationists. *The Washington Post*, however, supported the highway. Douglas, realizing the influence on public opinion of this newspaper's stand, challenged its editors and publishers to join him on a 185 mile hike from Cumberland to Georgetown. Editors of *The Post*, including Bob Estabrook, accepted the challenge, and in the spring of '54, 14 hearty hikers joined in the adventure. When the hike was over *The Post* reversed its position and supported Douglas.

Justice Douglas was one of my heroes. I followed his career on the Court and read the books he wrote each year. His cause became my cause. He became my mentor on conservation and the environment.

The Canal, towpath and river stretch many miles through my county. I had hiked and camped along the Potomac as a boy scout and later as a scoutmaster. I understood the value of this land for recreation and I treasured it as a part of the nation's history.

Though I had missed the original hike because of my Naval commitment in Japan and Korea, I signed on with Justice Douglas and the Douglas hikers in the fight to preserve the Canal and towpath and environs, and then to establish it as a national park.

But the idea of turning the abandoned C&O Canal into a national park became very controversial in Maryland, especially in the counties that bordered the Potomac. Many of the landowners who had properties adjacent to the Potomac were violently opposed to the federal government exercising any control over these canal lands.

Despite receiving personal threats and hate mail from opponents of the national park plan, I spoke to clubs and organizations up and down the river describing the benefits of having a national park in this section of the country. To further assist in disseminating information and developing strategies to gain public support, I helped organize and establish canal clubs in Williamsport, Hancock and Sharpsburg, three Washington County river towns. John Frye of Gapland, Ralph and Adele Donnelly of Hancock, Mel Kaplan, Adam Harsh, Hooper Wolfe, Clarence "Bub" Baker, Charles Myers, W. W. Teach of Williamsport, Mayor Tom Conlon of Cumberland, Thomas F. Hahn of Shepherdstown and many others led the way.

Later that year I was elected a director of the C&O Canal Association of Washington, D.C., which had among its directors nationally known environmentalists, including Mr. Justice Douglas.

In 1954 I was elected to the Maryland House of Delegates. Our local delegation was divided on the issue of the Canal becoming a national park. I led the battle in the Legislature to gain state support for the project and defeated a resolution that opposed the national park. Delegates William G. Porter, Jr., and Howard "Buffalo" Ankeny of Washington County, Noel Cook and George Hughes of Allegheny County, and my colleagues from the Judiciary Committee, Joe Tydings (later U.S. Senator) of Harford County, Dan Brewster (later U.S. Senator) and A. Gordon Boone of Baltimore County (Speaker of the House), Lloyd "Hot Dog" Simpkins (later Judge) of Somerset County, Lanny Sasscer and Carlton Sickles (later Congressman) of Prince Georges County, Blair Lee (later Governor) and Gilbert Gude (Later Congressman) from Montgomery County and Harry Hughes of Caroline County (later Governor) are just a few of the great guys who supported me in that battle. This battle led me to Washington, where I spoke before the U.S. Congress Subcommittee on Interior and Insular Affairs in support of the C&O Canal National Historical Park.

The fight dragged on for years. Each spring the Justice Douglas Reunion hike drew more and more people, topping out in the late '60's, when there were close to 1,000 participants. It became a well-publicized event covered annually by *The New York Times*, *The Washington Post* and many other newspapers across the country. These were exciting occasions, made even more so when Justice Douglas would invite famous personalities from the nation's capital. Sens. Paul Douglas of Illinois, Richard L. Neuberger of Oregon and Daniel Brewster of Maryland, Rep. DeWitt S. Hyde and Rep. and later Senator Charles Mathias of Maryland and Cabinet secretaries Orville Freeman and Stewart Udall joined the hikes along with members of the Kennedy family.

In 1961 President Eisenhower signed a bill designating the C&O Canal and its towpath as a national monument. We fought the battle for another decade in and out of Congress until finally President Richard Nixon signed legislation establishing the Chesapeake & Ohio Canal National Historical Park in 1972.

The park was dedicated to Justice Douglas, who died in 1980. I attended his funeral along with hundreds of other mourners. He was our leader and our inspiration. His death was a great loss for the environmental movement and for all of mankind.

We had spent more than 15 years working together to preserve a piece of American history in an environment of natural beauty. We had overcome apathy, ridicule and personal threats in the battle to establish this national park. And in what I consider the ultimate satisfaction for a hard-fought victory, more than 4 million visitors hiked and biked the C&O Canal National Historical Park in 1995.

This was not a battle for life or death—but it was fought with the same passion. On one side were forces led by Justice Douglas that were fighting to preserve the environment in the public interest. On the other side were strong forces fighting for their private and special interests.

This chapter was included in *A Canary's Tale* to illustrate how long and difficult it is to win any battle in the public interest even with substantial and exhaustive work by dedicated volunteers committed to overcome every challenge.

Silent Spring was a call to action in 1962. Thirty-four years have passed. It is time for action. The Final Battle is one for a better quality of life rather than a slow or speedy painful death.

2

CSDA Meeting at Woodburn on the Potomac

The following announcement appeared in *The Chemical Sensitivity Connection*, P.O. Box 24061, Arbutus, Maryland 21227, July 1995

"SATURDAY, SEPTEMBER 9: Enjoy Jack Berkson's scenic property on the Potomac River near Hagerstown. Wooded trails, cliffs, a dock, a large screened pavilion, a stream with waterfalls, meadows, and the C&O Canal towpath are some of the amenities…Bring food, water, blankets, lawn chairs, hiking shoes, and Frisbees. Bring a nontoxic close friend or family member…Jack says to feel free to camp out Friday night or Saturday night if you like."

A number of friendly folks who had been poisoned from exposure to toxic chemicals and later developed MCS came to Woodburn on the Potomac from their homes in Maryland, Virginia, West Virginia, the District of Columbia, and Pennsylvania. It was a beautiful end of Summer day. The air was clean. The fields and trees were green. The trails were cleared and shaded. The never failing springs and stream were running swiftly, the Potomac was clear and calm enough so that one could see fish swimming from the waterfall to the side of the dock. The weather, temperature, humidity, and visibility were perfect for me. The guests enjoyed the outdoor recreation and held their meeting half in and half out of the picnic pavilion. Dr. Larry Plumlee, President, presided. Nancy Gorman, Ann Gariazzo, Natalie Golos, Jack Jacobs, Carol Beauregard and other officers and directors led the discussion. Marilyn McVicker and Ellen Kinnear gave the guests a tour of their customized van which was a beauty.

New friendships were made and old ones were renewed. Plans were made for future activities.

To satisfy the guests curiosity about Woodburn and how I came to own it this is what I told them: I recall the day I first inquired about the land which would later become "Woodburn on the Potomac." It was 1960 and I was hiking a stretch of the canal when I came upon these lovely waterfalls almost hidden by ferns and trees, set back from the towpath. The water in the stream was clear and cold below the falls. I dropped my backpack, drank deeply from the water and climbed the rocks beside the falls until I came to a level stretch of ground. I hiked through the woods along a rushing stream until the woods gave way to a meadow. I saw a stone farmhouse and a wooden barn in the distance. I hiked across the field to the farmhouse and looked around for someone who might be the owner or a tenant. As I approached the barn, a giant of a man looked down upon me from the hayloft.

"What do you want?" he asked, in a gruff and angry voice.

"Are you the owner of this farm?" I replied.

"Yeah, what do you want?"

"I was just hiking along the towpath and I spied a waterfall and I followed the stream through the woods and the fields to your spring house. I just wanted to meet the owner and see if he might be interested in selling me a few acres of land in the woods on top of the cliffs overlooking the river."

"I'm the owner and I'm not interested in selling anything."

He did not want to discuss the matter further and suggested that I leave.

I retraced my steps back to the waterfalls, retrieved my backpack and continued the hike.

Later I checked the tax maps at the courthouse and learned the name of the owner. I decided that if the opportunity ever presented itself, I would buy this property. A few months later the local newspaper carried a notice of the farm's public sale. The farmer's wife had divorced him and had forced the sale to obtain her share of the marital property. Three weeks later I was the successful bidder at the auction.

From that day forward I have had the pleasure and privilege of being the steward of this beautiful piece of land. I have shared it with family, friends and colleagues. It has been used by YMCA day campers, boy scout troops, church organizations, C&O Canal hikers and bikers, fishermen, bird watchers, wild flower enthusiasts, foresters, deer, game birds, wild turkeys, turtles, squirrels and woodpeckers.

It has been a place of sanctuary, a place where people can go and unwind—a place where the beauty of nature surrounds you and the worries of the world disappear. In a grassy knoll surrounded by giant cedar trees I hope to build a safe house, a less toxic house, one in which I will read and write in comfort and live out a useful life. And if the home I build turns out to be a safe and healthy one, perhaps others will use it as a state of the art model to build healthy homes for themselves and their families.

3

Environmental Publications

In the Book of Genesis at 22:15:

"...[T]he angel of the LORD called to Abraham from the heavens,

"'I swear by myself'—it is the oracle of the LORD—...'I will indeed bless you, and will surely make your descendants as numerous as the stars of the sky, or the sands that are on the seashore, so that your descendants shall take possession of the cities of their enemies, and through your descendants all the nations of the earth shall invoke blessings on one another—just because you heeded my injunction.'"

Each day when the mail lady makes her rounds and empties what must be a substantial portion of her heavy leather bag into my mailbox, I hear her breathe a sigh of relief. And as she lifts her beautiful head to the heavens, I have heard another voice say:

"I swear by myself—it is the law of the land—that since you have joined one environmental organization, I will indeed bless you and will surely share your name with every other environmental and conservation organization in the land, so that your mail and your reading material will greatly increase and your third-class mail and your environmental publications and your solicitations shall be as numerous as the stars of the sky, or the sands that are on the seashore, and your descendants in all the nations of the earth shall marvel at your ability to read and absorb and retain all of the information that is delivered to you."

At last count there were approximately 1,500 environmental organizations with offices in the nation's capital and a goodly number in every state capital, college and university in the country. Each one is worthwhile and has a special purpose, from saving aardvarks and alligators to bald eagles, condors, dolphins, elephants, the owl, the penguin, the peregrine falcon, the porpoise, the seal, the whale, the zebra. Each animal, bird, fish, flower, tree, mammal, reptile, insect and disease has its supporters, protectors, admirers, organizers and spokespersons.

I do not mean to imply that these organizations should reduce their activities or eliminate any of their goals. I actually read everything they send me and save a great deal of it for reference material. There are a lot of wonderful people out there working very hard to preserve and protect life on this planet.

Unfortunately it is difficult, if not impossible, to process and retain all of the information delivered to us. I suppose that is why people select their favorite causes and become expert in one or two fields. But in attempting to understand pollution and the link between pollution, illness and disease, you must do exhaustive research to try to find answers to your questions. It is like looking for a needle in the haystack, except the haystack keeps getting bigger, and the needle becomes smaller and farther away.

The environmental movement is good news because it demonstrates that millions of public-spirited citizens are working hard to warn us and our elected officials that we are living in a polluted world, that the pollution is harmful to all God's creatures and time is running out.

For names, addresses, and telephone numbers of some Environmental Organizations/Publications see Volume II Section XI.

4

Politics

Lobbyists for the chemical industry have substantial resources and can buy tickets to a senator's campaign dinner at $15,000 a table or $1,000 a plate. In return they get the ear of the senator and can explain why pesticides are essential and the benefits they provide. Most pesticide victims cannot afford to pay $1,000 for a seat at the table. We are then written off because we can't come up with the price. Money, in the form of campaign contributions and other perks and benefits, is the mother's milk of politics. A politician believes his first obligation is not to the public but to get himself elected. These days that requires a tremendous amount of money. Contributors call the shots. Little guys get to hear the speeches on TV. It makes no difference which party wins the election, the Washington insiders—the influence peddlers, the lobbyists—are there forever. They change color, like a chameleon, and continue to represent the same interests before a different set of officials. Sometimes those officials want to be wooed and dined by other lobbyists, so industry and the special interests hire those lobbyists and law firms and insiders and influence peddlers preferred and designated by the officials. Industry and special interest money buys the lobbyists and the lobbyist buys the official and the general public gets screwed.

They don't tell you that, of course. They issue press releases from the White House, the Congress and the federal agencies that tell you exactly the opposite of what is happening. We have had a government by press release for many years. We now have career officials designated as "spin doctors" who are no more nor less than excellent liars whose job is to mislead the public. For

example, Congress passes the Clean Air Act only after the air in
some cities is so polluted that it is brown and people are getting
sick. Headlines proclaim this great step forward. The public is led
to believe the problem has been solved, but it is only the
beginning. Regulations have to be written, legislation has to be
implemented, bureaucracy is established. People are hired,
buildings are rented, furnishings and computers are purchased. For
years, all the money appropriated for cleaning the air is spent on
administrative and bureaucratic costs. In the meantime, industry
has done its best to weaken the bill, to weaken the legislation.
And, if anything positive remains, there is never enough staff to
enforce the regulations. And on that rare occasion when a low
level staff member acts responsibly and attempts to enforce a regulation, he had better make sure he is not challenging an industry
that is owned by big political campaign contributors. Government
invariably protects the polluter, and if there is a penalty, it is
generally a slap on the wrist. It's more profitable to pollute than to
comply with the law.

William Greider has related a number of these stories in his
excellent book *Who Will Tell The People: The Betrayal of American
Democracy*, New York: Simon & Schuster, 1992. He gives
example after example of the cozy relationship between industry
and government and the revolving door between the two. Three
of four successive EPA administrators took jobs with the industries
they were supposed to regulate when they left government service.
And when vacancies occur in the regulatory agencies, they are
routinely filled by employees of the industries the agency is
supposed to regulate. Industry writes the legislation and the regulations, and then provides staff to enforce the regulations. It is
only when the public becomes educated, knowledgeable, aroused
and the evidence is overwhelming that great harm has occurred
that prosecution goes forward and heavy fines are levied against
big corporations. It is usually the small businessman who is driven
crazy by harassment from OSHA investigators. And the executive
officers of these polluters nearly always walk away unscathed.

They have no responsibility to the public health. The corporation pays the fine. There is no personal responsibility for the president or the directors who ordered, directed, supervised and supported the pollution. Future legislation must carry with it a deterrent to prevent pollution. One deterrent is to hold the executive officers of the corporation as responsible as a ship captain for the pollution and violation of the law. We will never know the true cost to society of the Prince William Sound oil spill. A penalty that looks large to the average person is a drop in the bucket to a huge corporation. The public has lost confidence in the government because it sees examples every day where the government has failed to protect the health, safety and welfare of its citizens and has gone out of its way to take care of its political campaign contributors.

Year Nine
1996
A.D.

"...WARNING We the undersigned, senior members of the world's scientific community, hereby warn all humanity of what lies ahead. A great change in our stewardship of the earth and the life on it is required, if vast human misery is to be avoided and our global home on this planet is not to be irretrievably mutilated."

"Over 1670 scientists, including 104 Nobel laureates—a majority of the living recipients of the Prize in the sciences—have signed the Warning so far. These men and women represent 71 countries, including all of the 19 largest economic powers, all of the 12 most populous nations, 12 countries in Africa, 14 in Asia, 19 in Europe, and 12 in Latin America."

From "World Scientists' Warning to Humanity," sponsored by the Union of Concerned Scientists, Cambridge, MA, 1993. Reprinted with permission.

1

Environmental Politics 1996

In the spring of '96 a flood of letters arrived at my home from different environmental organizations to which I belong. The messages were similar—"We need your help!" Each organization called attention to the battles going on in the Congress between the forces of ignorance (anti-environment) who were determined to destroy the Clean Air Act, the Clean Water Act and all of the gains of the environmental movement over the past 25 years.

Here is a representative sample.

RALPH NADER

Dear Public Citizen Member,

When a city official takes cash from a local contractor and gives him preferential treatment, *it's called bribery.* If they're caught, both the official and the briber are usually shipped off to jail.

But they do things differently in Washington, D.C.

When a member of Congress takes money from the PAC of a managed health care company, then pays back the favor by wrecking Medicare and herding America's seniors into corporate HMOs—it's simply called a campaign contribution.

Business PAC contributions are nothing more than sugar-coated Washington doublespeak for the unpleasant truth—*it's legalized bribery...*

Sincerely,

Ralph Nader
Public Citizen
1600 20th Street, N.W.
Washington, D.C. 20009

Reprinted with Permission

● ● ●

OFFICE OF THE EXECUTIVE DIRECTOR

Dear Friend,

As I write you, anti-environmental forces in Congress are escalating their all-out *war on America's environment.*

If they succeed, *they will rob us of our natural heritage*—pollute our air and water...cut down our forests...close some of our beloved national parks...and threaten the health and quality of life of thousands of American families.

What is turning out to be the *most anti-environmental congress in history* will—if we let them—literally wipe out some of the most vital protections environmentalists have fought for over the last 100 years! Ardent anti-conservationists are taking full advantage of their powerful positions in congress—from which they are mounting a *devastating assault* on our nation's air, water, forests, parks and wilderness.

Behind them are powerful special interests—big timber, oil, mining and others—who have succeeded in *buying* their way into the halls of congress. And now, *they* are the ones calling the shots on the fate of America's precious natural resources!

America's environment belongs to YOU. so now is the time for you to *exercise your environmental rights by standing up for the things you care about*—BEFORE they are taken away from you!

And the very best way you can do that is to *become a valued Member of the Sierra Club*—joining us as we fight against the forces threatening America's environment on every front...

Sincerely,

Carl Pope
Executive Director
Sierra Club
730 Polk Street
San Francisco, California 94109

Reprinted with Permission

• • •

MESSAGE FROM THE PRESIDENT

The 1994 congressional elections led to an environmental train wreck in the House and Senate. The 1996 elections present an opportunity to get on track.

The polls and our instincts tell us that Americans do not want to roll back the environmental gains of the past 25 years. Nevertheless, this past year, when people tried to persuade Congress of the need to keep environmental protections, they met with only meager success.

In truth, all of the public's efforts to persuade the 104th Congress can accomplish only so much. To stop the assaults, we need to change the members of Congress. This November we need to elect the best, defeat the worst, and make the others think twice before they vote against the environment. Only a new election—the 1996 election—can turn the tide...

Deb Callahan, President
League of Conservation Voters
1707 L Street, NW, Suite 750
Washington, DC 20036

Reprinted with Permission

• • •

To join LCV and obtain a copy of "The Scorecard," League of Conservation Voters National Environmental Scorecard, February 1996, 104th Congress, First Session, write to the above address.

• • •

This is a battle—perhaps The Final Battle to save our environment and the Public Health. We do not have the money to match special interest money, but we have the votes to elect responsible public officials and to throw the rascals out. We need to educate the public and get out the vote.

2

The Blond Nurse

I first met Juliet (not her real name) at Dr. Lieberman's Center for Environmental Health in Charleston, S.C., when I first visited there in 1991. She was a beautiful blond nurse being treated for organophosphate poisoning in the detox program. She had been poisoned by pesticides in Florida while living in a rental house owned by a pesticide applicator. She was very athletic, conscientious, knowledgeable and confident that the detox program in conjunction with her lifestyle changes would reduce her toxic load and restore her to the robust health she had enjoyed prior to being poisoned. She and her husband Mike (not his real name) visited me in Florida in December 1992 when I was staying with Iris and again in January 1993. We took long walks on the beach at Venice and talked for hours in the clean fresh air. We shared personal experiences, compared notes on adverse health effects and linked them to various pollutants that triggered our symptoms. We talked about ways to cope that worked for us at times, and tried to figure out how to improve our treatment. Mike had not been poisoned, nor was he sensitive. He was tall, well built and very strong. He was a builder attempting to steer his business into healthy homes. Before Juliet was poisoned, they were very active outdoors people. They were hikers and backpackers. They had backpacked down the Grand Canyon and back up. These were healthy, hard-working people, not malingerers or psycho cases. When they moved from the Midwest to Florida in 1987 they did not know that daily exposure to multiple pesticides stored in the yard and the house they rented would harm either of them. But after some period of time and exposure to the pes-

ticides, Juliet became very ill and subsequently developed many of
the symptoms attributed to MCS. She was forced to reduce her
working hours and was unable to tolerate the air in the offices of
the health care company that employed her. She was relegated to
treating patients in their homes.

Before she began her daily home care visits, she called the
mosquito control board in various locations to find out where the
helicopters were spraying that day. She had to avoid the chemical
spray from those helicopters. Exposure to the spray would do her
in. When she made house calls, many of the houses had polluted
air from cigarette smoke, outgassing from formaldehyde products,
odors from fresh paint or new carpet—normal items found in most
homes. She drove with her car windows closed, used her air conditioner and an air filter and carried an oxygen tank, a respirator
and a "gas mask." She wanted to work to help support the family.
She did not give up easily. She was in a constant state of flight
from triggers which she called "terminators." She was sensitive to
normal odors on the beach such as cigarette smoke, suntan lotion,
and fragrances such as Downey. These odors had never bothered
her before she was exposed to the pesticide. After exposure she
developed MCS. Once when we were walking on an uncrowded
beach, she quickly strapped on her respirator and raced for her car.
I did not know what was happening. A few moments later, I heard
a helicopter approaching. I thought about "Radar" a character on
the sitcom "M•A•S•H." He could hear a helicopter before
anyone else. Juliet had become so conditioned to helicopters and
the chemical poisons they sprayed that she took no chances.
When she heard a helicopter approach, she raced for a safe place.
She had spent too much time recuperating from exposure to pesticides. Mike had fixed their home to the best of his ability to
make it less toxic and safe for Juliet, but there was no way they
could control the activities of the city, the county, the state,
industry and their neighbors. I watched their attempts to cope
with environmental pollution with shock, sorrow and anger. No
one seemed to be able to help. "This is no way to live," I said. "No

one should have to live like this!"

They were both convinced that Dr. Lieberman's detox program had been effective in reducing the toxic load. Before treatment she could not work. After treatment she was able to return to work. However she returned to the same old environment where she continued to be exposed to pollutants. This played havoc with her health. When I talked to her in 1994 she told me that she had to give up her job. She restricted herself most of the time to her less toxic home. She was safer at home than anywhere else she could find. Pesticide spraying in Florida is ubiquitous. I suggested that she and Mike move out of that polluted environment or move close to the beach where they could breathe the clean gulf air. She told me that when she went to the beach she was subjected to so many exposures on the highway that the benefit of the trip was negated by the pollution. I tried to cheer her up, but that is easier said than done.

Early in 1996 a letter arrived from Arizona. It was from Juliet. She could no longer tolerate the pesticide pollution in Florida and decided the only way to survive was to move to a place where the air was reputed to be clean. She and Mike divorced and she moved to Arizona to regain her health. She survived a cold winter alone in a trailer high in the mountains of Arizona. We keep in touch by mail and phone. She bolsters my spirits with her courage, cheerful demeanor and insistence that I finish A Canary's Tale promptly. I can tell by her voice that she is getting stronger each day. Clean air, exercise, proper nutrition, organic food, and calls to Dr. Lieberman are all playing a role in the healing process.

3

Admiral E. R. Zumwalt, Jr., and the Agent Orange Controversy

In March of '96 I wrote to E. R. Zumwalt, Jr., Admiral USN (Ret.), Chairman, Agent Orange Coordinating Council, Arlington, Virginia, to request a copy of the 1990 Report by the Committee on Government Operations, 101st Congress, 2nd Session, House Report 101-672 entitled "The Agent Orange Coverup: A Case of Flawed Science and Political Manipulation," U.S. Government Printing Office, Washington, D.C., 1990. I advised him of my interest in his work and enclosed some of my writings.

A few days later the Admiral sent me a gracious letter with the report I requested and also a more recent statement he made before the House Subcommittee on Energy and Environment, December 13, 1995. In my opinion Admiral Zumwalt's statement of December 13, 1995, is important and relevant to not only the cause for which he is fighting but further evidence of the cover ups, deceit, fraud and pseudo science we have encountered in our battle to obtain research funds, recognition and effective medical treatment for the victims of chemical poisoning and MCS. I feel compelled to print it in its entirety to share it with you. When you read Admiral Zumwalt's Statement I believe you will be shocked and dismayed at the battle he was invited to lead to obtain for the disabled American veterans of the Vietnam War what they were entitled to as American citizens. You can see the similarity to the battle we are fighting against the merchants of poison and their political supporters. His letter and statement follow.

E. R. ZUMWALT, JR.
ADMIRAL, U.S. NAVY (RET.)

April 1, 1996

Jacob B. Berkson, Esq.

Dear Mr. Berkson:

Many thanks for your gracious comments in your letter of March 25. I attach the documents to which you refer.

Under separate cover, I am sending you an inscribed copy of my book, On Watch.

Sincerely,

E. R. Zumwalt, Jr.
Admiral, USN (Ret.)
Chairman, Agent Orange Coordinating Council

(Reprinted with permission.)

• • •

E. R. ZUMWALT, JR.
ADMIRAL, U.S. NAVY (RET.)

STATEMENT BY

Admiral E. R. Zumwalt, Jr., USN (Ret.)
Chairman, Agent Orange Coordinating Council

before the

House Subcommittee on Energy and Environment

December 13, 1995

I am here in my capacity as Chairman of the Agent Orange Coordinating Council whose membership consists of most of the veterans and veteran-related organizations. I became involved in great detail in the Agent Orange issue in the following manner.

I commanded U.S. Naval Forces, Vietnam, from 1968 until 1970 and had further responsibilities for forces fighting in Vietnam while I served [as] a member of the Joint Chiefs of Staff from 1970 to 1974.

In 1989 the Secretary of Veterans Affairs, The Honorable Edward Derwinski, asked to me to serve as an unpaid special assistant to do an analysis for him of the Agent Orange issue. I spent seven months, in conjunction with respected scientists, reviewing the studies on dioxin. In May 1990, I submitted a report which listed numerous health effects which, in my judgement and that of my scientific advisors, were as likely as not to result from exposure of Vietnam veterans to Agent Orange and its dioxin contaminant.

This report, among other things, commented on the flawed nature of the scientific analyses done by the statutory committee advising the Secretary of Veterans Affairs, the Committee on Environmental Health Hazards, whose deliberations had, in my opinion, been heavily weighted by those of its members who had associations with corporations whose products generated dioxin.

In addition, I was able to establish that it had been the policy of the U.S. Government in the early '80s to instruct government agencies involved in Agent Orange studies that it would be most unfortunate if a correlation between Agent Orange and health effects were to be found.

A copy of my report to Secretary Derwinski is attached.

Soon thereafter, the House Committee on Government Operations on August 9, 1990, submitted its 12th report entitled *The Agent Orange Coverup: A Case of Flawed Science and Political Manipulation,* copy attached, which, in my judgement, constituted a devastating indictment of the U.S. Government's interference with science.

I quote two of the findings of that report:

> "The White House compromised the independence of the CDC and undermined the study by controlling crucial decisions and guiding the course of research at the same time it had secretly taken a legal position to resist demands to compensate victims of Agent Orange exposure and industrial accidents.

> "The Federal Government has suppressed or minimized findings of ill health effects among Vietnam veterans that could be linked to Agent Orange exposure."

I should note that industry weighed in by insuring that a minority of the committee took issue with the findings concerning the interference of the government with science.

My report stated that based on my review with respected scientists of all available studies, there were 28 diseases which met the statutory test that it was 'as likely as not' that exposure to Agent Orange caused them. At about the same time, the Agent Orange Scientific Task Force, commissioned by veterans organizations to study the issue, found that a large number of diseases were as likely as not a result of exposure to Agent Orange.

To his credit, President Bush on being apprised of the foregoing overruled the Bureau of the Budget and accepted Secretary Derwinski's recommendations, as a result of which three diseases: chloracne, soft tissue sarcoma, and non-Hodgkin lymphoma were approved as diseases for which Vietnam veterans or their families should receive compensation.

Soon after the foregoing events, Congress disestablished the Committee on Environmental Health Hazards and assigned the responsibility for Agent Orange studies to the National Academy of Sciences which contracted with the Institute of Medicine (IOM) to produce such studies.

Dr. Kenneth Shine, President of the Institute of Medicine, agreed to establish the policy that no scientists would be on the panel who had taken a position pro or con on the correlation between exposure to Agent Orange and health effects. Highly credible scientists who had not previously taken such positions were named to a panel which reviewed all the literature. In July of 1993, the IOM panel issued its first report as a result of which seven more diseases have been authorized for compensation.

Thus in the case of the study of dioxin done by IOM to get to objective conclusions for veterans exposed to Agent Orange, the elimination of scientists who had corporate conflicts has led to a total of ten diseases being found, as likely as not, associated with such exposure.

It is a source of deep concern that the Science Advisory Board reviewing EPA's draft reassessment of dioxin has not been selected on the same basis as the IOM panel, but rather contains as members and consultants scientists who have accepted in one form or another financial support from corporations who have a strong interest in finding negative correlation between dioxin and health effects.

In my judgement, based on consultation with scientists for whom I have great respect, the Science Advisory Board review of EPA dioxin reassessment, is, like the work of the flawed Committee on Environmental Health Hazards, tilted in some respects away from proper scientific conclusions, for the purpose of making the findings of EPA less than objective in places, for the benefit of interested corporations.

I regret that the practice of inviting scientists with obvious conflicts of interest to testify is being continued by this committee.

I strongly urge that your committee cause Congress to enact by statute a requirement that future membership of the Science Advisory Board contain no scientists whose research or livelihood, in main or in part, is dependent upon financial support from corporations. We have learned that such scientists can be less than objective. The result is that Vietnam veterans have been denied for over 20 years the benefits which the law would have provided had scientific truth prevailed over pseudo- scientific manipulation.

With regard to the present hearing, surely it is not too much to ask that the financial conflicts of interest of the members and consultants of the Scientific Advisory Board be published within the final record of the hearing.

With regard to the substantive outcome of these hearings, I am aware of the great pressures brought to bear by lobbyists for the corporations who produce dioxin as a by-product of the operations. As a representative of the major veterans groups by virtue of my chairmanship of their Agent Orange Coordinating Council, I am also aware that thousands of Vietnam veterans and their families are equally convinced that corporate and government manipulation of science has delayed for years their obtaining appropriate compensation for the diseases resulting from exposure to Agent Orange. By and large such veterans have supported the efforts that I have made to initiate joint research of Agent Orange using the heavily exposed Vietnamese people to obtain further evidence of health effects. The veterans, by and large, have recognized that the time has come to put the war behind us with the restoration of diplomatic relations with the former enemy regime. They clamor for the final step in such closure to take place. That final step is to establish the scientific truth with regard to their exposure to Agent Orange.

This hearing, if it does not interfere with the objective scientific analysis carried out by EPA in its draft dioxin risk reassessment, will have contributed to the achievement of that final step.

Sincerely,

E. R. Zumwalt, Jr.
Admiral, USN (Ret.)
Chairman, Agent Orange Coordinating Council

(Reprinted with permission.)

• • •

(Attachment, cover sheet only)

Union Calendar No. 415
101st Congress, 2d Session   House Report 101-672

THE AGENT ORANGE COVERUP: A CASE OF FLAWED
SCIENCES AND POLITICAL MANIPULATION

TWELFTH REPORT

BY THE

COMMITTEE ON GOVERNMENT
OPERATIONS

together with

DISSENTING VIEWS

August 9, 1990.—Committed to the Committee of the Whole
House on the State of the Union and ordered to be printed

U.S. GOVERNMENT PRINTING OFFICE
WASHINGTON: 1990

32-392

• • •

As I was completing the manuscript to A *Canary's Tale* I thought of the tremendous burden shouldered by Admiral Zumwalt during his career in the Navy and after his retirement. He fought in World War II, the Korean War, the Vietnam War and rose to the highest position in the U.S. Navy—Chief of Naval Operations. At the same time he served as a member of the Joint Chiefs of Staff. After his well deserved retirement he wrote a magnificent book, *On Watch* (Admiral Zumwalt and Associates,

Inc., Arlington, Virginia, 1976). It is his personal story and includes his criticism of high policy and politics in the Nixon administration. He retired in 1974 with a bitter taste for the Nixon-Kissinger perversion of the policy-making process. He concludes his Preface with: "I think what I learned during four years in the thick of that miasma made it my duty to write a book." The key word was "duty." And what a book he wrote! *On Watch* records the exciting adventure of his entry into China at the close of World War II, his interview with Admiral Rickover which is as high drama as Herman Wouk's "Caine Mutiny Court Martial." *On Watch* records his life long romance with his beautiful White Russian bride. He reports on the military and political intrigues in which he participated with the leading figures of the day from the highest positions of authority. He retired with an unblemished record—a role model for any public official to emulate. *On Watch* is an exciting book to read. But that is another story. The point of all this is that following his retirement, instead of going fishing or hunting or playing golf or a life of self-indulgence which he had earned, he took up the cause of the American servicemen who were exposed in Vietnam to the toxic chemical mix known as Agent Orange. After the exposure thousands of veterans became ill with terrible diseases including Cancer. Some were never able to work or function again. And what we have seen throughout *A Canary's Tale*—Industry's and the Government's denial of responsibility for the poisoning and personal injuries of American citizens. The Agent Orange cover up is about American soldiers and sailors who went to war for their country in good health, were exposed to toxic chemicals in battles in Vietnam, became ill and were denied recognition of their illness and treated unfairly by their government for more than 20 years. And this tragedy continues today. The Government rests its case on the false pseudo-science reports of so called "experts" who say they are unable to find a link between the chemical exposure and the disease. Despite evidence to the contrary and all common sense, these merchants of poison and their experts have prevented the victims from obtaining the appropriations needed for medical research essential to establish that link and thereafter obtain medical treatment and compensation. The American people know that our soldiers and sailors went into Vietnam healthy, lived under horrible conditions, were sprayed with or exposed to Agent Orange, a toxic poison, and became ill. The American people do not want their brothers and sisters who fought that horrible war and were victimized by the enemy and the treachery and deceit of their own leaders (see Robert McNamara's Confessional *In Retrospect*) to be further victimized by their government. The victims have not been treated honorably. It is a stain upon our national honor. I believe the American people would vote overwhelmingly to recognize the sacrifice of these veterans and do what is honorable to provide medical care and compensation for their wounds in line of duty, their service connected disability. The American people will not accept industry and government denials much longer. Industry and Government no longer have much credibility with the American people. The people know that industry has corrupted the Congress and the White House with special interest money. The majority of Americans are sick of this bribery and deceit. It is a betrayal of our democracy. It is time for the nation to take action to support Admiral Zumwalt and the victims of Agent Orange. The Admiral has paid his dues and earned the gratitude of the American people. It is long past time to help the disabled veterans of Vietnam and put this disgraceful treatment of American servicemen and women behind us. In my opinion we should all write to President Clinton and our Senators and Congressmen and demand that they take prompt and effective action to settle this scandalous stain on our National Honor.

4

Gulf War Vets
Exposed to Environmental Pollutants in 1991
Still Sick in 1996

Gulf War vets hit with health problems" was the headline in *The Daily Mail* Sept. 28, 1994. That article went on to say:

"The federal government is investigating reports of 'Gulf War syndrome' but has not recognized the existence of such a disease...

"The Department of Veterans Affairs is investigating whether Gulf War service is linked to soldiers' illnesses.

"About 29,000 veterans have called government or military hot-line numbers to request medical examinations of symptoms which the troops believe are related. About 650,000 U.S. personnel were in the Middle East for the war."

I opened a file on this subject in 1991 beginning with an article in the Feb. 4 issue of *Time* by Richard Lacayo. It was titled, "Environment. A War Against the Earth. Torching Oil Wells and Disgorging Crude into the Gulf, Saddam Makes the Planet His Latest Victim." Reporter Eric Schmitt described the scene this way in *The New York Times:*

"RIYADH, Saudi Arabia, March 2—The Persian Gulf war has caused an ecological calamity affecting a large chunk of Asia, and experts say it might take years to clean up...

"Dense, dark smoke from more than 600 burning oil wells in Kuwait hangs in a stinking, soupy pall over cities and farmland from Turkey to Iran, with predictions that plumes could reach northern India. The fires have spewed tons of toxic chemicals into the air, prompting doctors to gear up for respiratory illnesses and farmers to fear for crops tainted by greasy rains washing cancer-causing particles from the sky.

"'The ecology of the Persian Gulf is hurting pretty badly right now,' said William R. Moomaw, director of the Center for Environmental Management at Tufts University. 'The level of air pollution from the burning oil wells exceeds by hundreds of times the most polluted areas of the world.'...

"A visitor to Kuwait City on Thursday was greeted with pitch-black skies at 2 P.M. Cars drove with headlights on and some residents carried flashlights to find the nearest celebration of the Iraqi defeat.

"Mr. Moomaw said the clouds contain large quantities of sulfur dioxide, hydrogen sulfide and other hydrocarbons. If the concentrations persisted, he said that infants, the elderly and people with respiratory problems could be harmed.

"Longterm Effects Unknown"

(Copyright ©1991 by The New York Times Co. Reprinted by Permission.)

Those articles were written in early 1991. On Aug. 10, 1992, *The Daily Mail* carried the following report:

"Military probes oil fire fumes

"RALEIGH, N.C. (AP)—The military is looking into the possibility that fumes from oil well fires in Kuwait caused the mysterious ailments plaguing some Gulf War veterans.

"Soldiers have complained of such symptoms as fatigue, aches and breathing problems, and an Army study of 79 Gulf veterans in Indiana last month said stress may be the cause.

"But last week, doctors found high levels of hydrocarbons in the blood of a Navy veteran in Texas, and military officials acknowledged more study is needed of the effects of inhaling fumes from burning oil wells." (Reprinted with permission.)

Ten months later, in June 1993, Dr. Claudia S. Miller, a pioneer and author in the field of MCS, whom we have written about earlier, testified for the Committee on Veterans' Affairs subcommittee on Oversight and Investigations.

She highlighted three issues:

1. Growing numbers of physicians are becoming concerned that we

may be seeing a new medical problem, one that is being called 'chemical sensitivity'.

2. The origin and nature of this problem is the subject of intense debate among physicians and researchers.

3. A specially-designed hospital facility, an Environmental Medical Unit, is needed in order to diagnose whether or not veterans' health complaints are the result of chemical exposures."

She reported:

"Physicians are seeing growing numbers of patients who report chronic and disabling symptoms following exposure to solvents, pesticides, combustion products and buildings with poor indoor air quality. These patients include industrial workers, office workers, schoolchildren, persons living near Superfund hazardous waste sites, and, most recently, Gulf War veterans."

Some Gulf War veterans report similar symptoms to those suffered by victims of MCS.

"Growing numbers are reporting fatigue, numbness, dizziness, headaches, and other symptoms, which they link to common chemical exposures.

"Urgently needed is a clinical tool for determining whether or not chemical sensitization is at the root of these patients' problems."

Dr. Miller, speaking about the Environmental Medical Unit, concluded:

"The National Institute of Environmental Health Sciences has described this concept as the 'single most important way to develop a reliable clinical approach to the diagnosis and evaluation of chemical sensitivities.' The approach has also been endorsed by physicians and researchers attending two national workshops on chemical sensitivity—one sponsored by the National Academy of Sciences and the other by the Agency for Toxic Substances and Disease Registry.

"Today, almost two years later, no such facility for scientific inquiry exists. Without it, there is little hope of finding a solution. Just as the invention of the microscope enabled physicians to identify bacteria and control infections, so an Environmental Medical Unit now is needed to enable us to diagnose and treat the health problems of the veterans and other Americans whose health may be at risk from environmental exposures." (Reprinted with permission.)

Nearly three years have passed since Dr. Miller called for action.

Instead of action we got the following five months later: "Pentagon: Chemicals not to blame. Mysterious health problems plague Gulf War vets," in *The Daily Mail* Nov. 11, 1993.

"WASHINGTON (AP)—The Pentagon acknowledges that traces of chemical agents apparently were found in northern Saudi Arabia during the Persian Gulf War, but it insists something else is to blame for sickening thousands of U.S. troops there.

"'I think we're dealing with a specific exposure of some kind of industrial chemical,' Dr. Ronald Blanck, commander of Walter Reed Army Medical Center, said Wednesday...

"Some veterans contend that the military has ignored the possibility of chemical contamination for their illnesses, just as it for years dismissed the claims of Vietnam War veterans over the health effects of Agent Orange.

"'I hurt so bad that just for days I would just lie in bed and be in pain,' Kimo Hollingsworth, a Marine with the syndrome, said in an interview Wednesday. 'There's a cover-up and they're not being truthful with the veterans nor with the American people.'" (Reprinted with permission.)

After I read that article in 1993 I spoke with Hollingsworth at the National Headquarters of the American Legion in Washington, D.C. He told me that 8,422 vets were listed as of Aug. 31, 1993, on the Persian Gulf Registry for illness and that 158 vets had died since Desert Storm. He hoped the government would respond and provide effective treatment for the veterans.

Hollingsworth, Steve Robertson and other representatives of the American Legion were effective. On Dec. 22, 1993, *The Daily Mail* reported:

"WASHINGTON—Gulf veterans to get treatments

"President Clinton has signed legislation to require the Veterans Affairs Department to treat Persian Gulf War veterans for diseases that may have resulted from exposure to toxic substances.

"'Over the past 2½ years, Persian Gulf veterans have experienced a wide range of health care problems that have eluded diagnosis and cure,' Clinton said in a statement on Tuesday, a day after he signed the bill.

"He said the veterans' symptoms include fatigue, painful muscles and joints, bleeding gums, skin rashes, short-term memory loss and hair loss.

"Possible chemical and biological contamination during the Gulf War has become an issue because of the thousands of veterans suffering from debilitating and undiagnosed illnesses that have come to be known as Persian Gulf syndrome." (Reprinted with permission.)

Six months later, on April 27-29, 1994 a workshop was held at National Institutes of Health in Bethesda, Md., on the Persian Gulf experience and health.

"The intent...was to examine the information...on...illness reports, to assess the types and extent of environmental exposures of troops...in the Persian Gulf, to determine the adequacy of information...and to attempt to develop working case definitions for those illnesses..."

A draft report dated May 4, 1994, acknowledged that troops were exposed to a variety of hazardous chemicals and other substances, and that many were indeed battling long-term illness:

"Many of the cases include combinations of nonspecific symptoms of fatigue, skin rash, muscle and joint pain, headache, loss of memory, shortness of breath, gastrointestinal and respiratory symptoms, and intolerance to environmental chemicals, which may not fit readily into a common diagnosis...Some veterans have reported illnesses in their spouses and birth defects in children conceived after the conflict and are concerned about the spread of disease as a public health issue."

Sound familiar?

Here is what the governmental did:

"A number of governmental responses have been initiated as a result of the Gulf War veterans' complaints. The Department of Defense and the Department of Veterans Affairs have begun registration of Persian Gulf veterans. Special referral centers for clinical

evaluation of complaints have been established by the Department
of Veterans Affairs, and research proposals have been solicited."

After hearing the speakers the Panel concluded, "It is
impossible at this time to establish a single case definition.
Furthermore, a premature attempt to establish a case definition for
this illness may be misleading and inaccurate. Eligibility for
medical care should not depend on case definition."

The Panel went on to say:

"The complex set of exposures and stressors make the Persian
Gulf tour unique. Individuals who were deployed had severe psychological stresses upon entering the area. All had vaccines and
medications administered during this period, worked long hours,
and lived in crowded and often unsanitary conditions among flies,
snakes, spiders, and scorpions. The chemical contaminants from oil
fires, burning dumps (feces and trash), fuels, and solvents were
ubiquitous. The climate exhibited temperature extremes in a
sand/dust environment. The threat of biological and chemical
warfare was omnipresent. In this report, no single or multiple
etiology or biological explanation for the reported symptoms was
identified from the data available to the panel."

The panel set forth a laundry list of possible causative or con-
tributing factors, including exposure to petroleum vapors and
solvents, sand dust, depleted uranium pesticides and pyridostigmine, a "pretreatment" for nerve poisoning in the event of
chemical warfare which sometimes caused nausea, vomiting and
other discomfort.

The proceedings and conclusions were summed up in the June
24, 1994 edition of *The Daily Mail.*

"Panel: no one answer to Gulf vets' ills
But V.A. promises medical care available

"WASHINGTON (AP)—A scientific panel says it can find no single
answer to the riddle of sick Persian Gulf War veterans, dealing
another setback to the many who are awaiting treatment for their
maladies.

"The Defense and Veterans Affairs departments tempered the bad
news with assurances that all veterans will have access to

medical care.

"'This administration does believe these veterans are sick. Their symptoms are real and they do need our care,' VA Deputy Secretary Hershel Gober said Thursday." (Reprinted with permission.)

Although the expert doctors and scientists on the panel were unable to link the chemical exposure to the symptoms, *The Herald-Mail*, Oct. 9, 1994, reported:

"Washington: Benefits ordered for ailing Gulf vets

"WASHINGTON (AP)—The Senate approved and sent to President Clinton legislation Saturday to compensate Persian Gulf war veterans who are found to suffer from undiagnosed and unknown illnesses.

"The law is aimed at ensuring 'that (these) veterans will receive the benefits they have earned,' said Sen. John D. Rockefeller, D-W.Va., chairman of the Senate Veterans Affairs Committee." (Reprinted with permission.)

I spoke to Dr. Janette Sherman, author of *Chemical Exposure and Disease*, about the Gulf War veterans. She furnished me copies of letters she wrote to government officials as far back as August of 1992, offering comments and outlining a program of investigation whereby the cause of these problems can be reasonably determined.

She stated in part—

"To dismiss this constellation of symptoms as being due to 'stress' is callously simplistic. Fighting personnel have always been under stress. This constellation does not match any previous constellation of symptoms suffered by military personnel...

"This constellation of symptoms points primarily to changes in the neurological and immunological function of these Veterans. Possible causes include emissions from the burning oil wells, a virus, but more likely to chemically-induced disease...

"Those of us working in the field of toxicology have seen comparable problems in civilians in the United States, which mirror the complaints of those Veterans who served in the Gulf War. These similar problems, displayed in civilians were almost always as a result of exposure to a number of solvents or pesticides, especially the organophosphate type pesticides."

Dr. Sherman obtained the list of pesticides procurred through the federal supply system during Desert Shield/Storm. It included Dursban (Chlorpyrifos), Ficam (Bendiocarb), Lindane, Malathion and various Pyrethroids.

In a letter dated April 11, 1994, to the Senate Committee on Veteran's Affairs, in regard to Gulf War Veterans, Dr. Sherman wrote,

"At your request I have reviewed the list of pesticides available for use in the Gulf War exercise. The list includes both carbamate and organophosphate pesticides, as well as pyrethrins/pyrethroids and organochlorine pesticides...

"Exposure to a combination of organophosphate and carbamate pesticides can be expected to produce profound adverse effects...

"As in our discussion of my research proposal of August 1992, the signs and symptoms of many of the Veterans are very much like those of civilians I see exposed to the same chemicals, and each group shares the experience of not regaining their previous state of health with removal of the pesticide exposure." (Reprinted with permission.)

Mary Lamielle, president of the National Center for Environmental Health Strategies, speaking before the Institute of Medicine Committee to Review Health Consequences of Service during the Persian Gulf War, said

"Our Center receives up to a thousand requests for information each month...

"Over two years ago we began receiving calls and correspondence from Gulf War veterans, their spouses, and family members. I was struck by the remarkable similarity of the patterns of illness that these individuals reported to me to those reporting hypersensitivity to chemicals in the civilian population."

"The obstacles to investigating and acting on MCS have been ever-present from industry, segments of the medical community, and insurance companies, among others." (Reprinted with permission.)

I again spoke to Kimo Hollingsworth at the National Headquarters of the American Legion, on Oct. 26, 1994. He told me that 29,000 vets had signed the Registry as of September 1994. Investigations were going on, but in the meantime vets were ill and no effective treatment was being given.

On March 25, 1996, I spoke with Matt Puglisi at the American Legion Headquarters in Washington, D.C. He advised me that as of about six weeks ago approximately 60,000 Gulf War Vets separated from active duty had signed the VA Registry and some 30,000 Gulf War Vets still on active duty had now signed the DOD Registry, making a total of 90,000. Most have been assigned a diagnosis, primarily psychological. The DOD has not recognized MCS in any vet, while the VA has diagnosed most with stress, depression, and a few with MCS.

• • •

An AP story originating from the Pentagon appeared in the Herald Mail, June 22, 1996, at A2, under the bold four column headline "U.S. troops exposed to poison gas?" A new wrinkle was added to the 5 year "mystery". Pentagon officials reported that American troops destroyed an Iraqi ammunition depot in March 1991 that may have contained chemical weapons.

The long story rehashed the same old bunkum of denials by government officials who are "unable" to discover the link between chemical exposure and disease.

5

General Colin Powell and
General H. Norman Schwarzkopf
Two American Heroes of the Persian Gulf War

As it took a Four Star Admiral many years to persuade the
Congress and the White House to recognize the link
between chemical exposure and ten kinds of Cancer in the case of
the Vietnam veterans, it will take someone of similar intellect and
national stature to speak for the Persian Gulf War veterans. We
know our sons and daughters who were sent to the Gulf War were
healthy American soldiers and sailors. They were exposed to toxic
chemicals in that war, became ill with multiple symptoms similar
to those of the Vietnam veterans, and the victims of Multiple
Chemical Sensitivity (MCS), all of which have been recorded in
earlier chapters of this book. Thousands of American veterans are
now disabled after battle in the Killing Fields of Kuwait. They are
true casualties of war. (See chapter here on the Gulf War and the
references in Vol. II.) The truth is that no one of national stature
or influence who sat in the highest circles of power and were our
military and civilian commanders in the Gulf War have done
anything effective to recognize these casualties of war or have
helped these disabled veterans get the medical treatment they
need or the compensation to which they are entitled.

I thought of two great and celebrated heroes of the Gulf War.
General H. Norman Schwarzkopf, Commanding General of all
U.N. forces in the Gulf. And I wondered what if anything he has
done for the men disabled under his command. And then I
thought of General Colin Powell, the brilliant Chairman of the

Joint Chiefs of Staff, the principal military advisor to President Bush, the Commander in Chief of American Forces. I am not critical of these great generals as they are genuine American heroes and they have paid their dues. They served their country with honor and covered themselves with glory. General Schwarzkopf won the confidence and affection of the American people when he led our troops to victory on the battlefield and when he spoke to us on TV during and after the war. He was the right man in the right place at the right time.

General Colin Powell is so charismatic that he has been urged by both major political parties to serve in high office. Many have urged him to run for President of the United States in 1996. He was offered the post of Vice President on the Republican ticket and may yet accept it. Both of them are my heroes too. And I wondered what they had done about helping the disabled casualties of the Gulf War, the war they had so admirably won.

So I read General Schwarzkopf's autobiography, *It Doesn't Take a Hero*, written with Peter Petre (LG Linda Grey Bantam Books, October 1992). It is a great book full of adventure, excitement, drama, challenges and victories. I thoroughly enjoyed reading it. However, I found nothing in the book about any of the thousands of veterans who became ill in the Killing Fields of Kuwait in the Gulf War and who have been denied effective medical treatment. *It Doesn't Take a Hero* covers the Gulf War in great detail and points out General Schwarzkopf's great concern about casualties and his magnificent efforts to save lives. But his conclusion is that less than 200 casualties occurred among American servicemen, and many of them were from "friendly fire." When his book was published in October of 1992 there were not 90,000 servicemen on the VA and DOD registries.

My American Journey, Colin L. Powell with Joseph E. Persico, Random House, Inc., New York, 1995, is another great book by a great American who fought two tours in the battlefields of Vietnam and Korea, and served in high command during the fighting in Grenada, Panama, and served as Chairman of the Joint Chiefs of Staff during the Gulf War. He later helped to avert bloodshed and casualties in Haiti. He has really seen war in all its horror on the battlefield and off as the principal military advisor to three Presidents. And he has probably saved thousands of lives by his steadfast policies of demanding a clear mission and the use of maximum force to avoid another Vietnam. He has captured the love and respect of the American people and may someday become President of the United States. Yet in his autobiography, My American Journey, although there are many pages devoted to the Gulf War I was unable to find a single reference to the thousands of casualties who returned to the States after exposure to multiple toxic chemicals in the Killing Fields of Kuwait. My American Journey is a 617 page book with many details of the General's life and his political and military battles. He points out the official record of 134 American casualties of the Gulf War. Yet we now have more than 30,000 veterans still on active duty from that war who have signed the DOD Registry and 60,000 others now out of service who are on the VA Registry to be examined and treated. The evidence indicates more than fifty thousand casualties from the Gulf War plus children of veterans born with genetic defects. I recognize that these Generals have retired and have no legal obligation to care for the wounded who fought under them. But would it not be a humanitarian contribution for them to speak up and say what needs to be said to help these casualties of the Gulf War. Generals Powell and Schwarzkopf have the influence to persuade the Congress and the President to do the right thing. The American people know these veterans of the Gulf War are disabled and want them taken care of. Failure to do so is a stain on our national honor and our national conscience. As Lincoln said in his Second Inaugural address which General Powell repeated at the Vietnam Memorial on Memorial Day, 1993:

> "With malice toward none, with charity for all, with firmness in the right as God gives us to see the right, let us strive on to finish the

work we are in, to bind up the nation's wounds, to care for him who shall have borne the battle and for his widow and his orphan, to do all which may achieve and cherish a just and lasting peace among ourselves and with all nations."

And to quote General Schwarzkopf—"It doesn't take a hero to order men into battle. It takes a hero to be one of those men who goes into battle." And devoted leadership extends beyond the battle. Commanders who lead troops into battle have a duty to see that the wounded and disabled receive proper medical care after the battle.

Duty, honor, and country demand no less.

And I would add that in my opinion General H. Norman Schwarzkopf and General Colin Powell have demonstrated throughout their lives that they are endowed with the character and the integrity to face this enormous challenge and conquer it as they did all the others in their blessed and honorable careers. And thus history will record their names as among the greatest of American Generals—those who answered the Trumpet's call when they heard the cries and saw the tears of their disabled troops.

My father, Meyer Berkson, was an American soldier who fought and was severely wounded in the final battle of the Meuse-Argonne, in France in World War I, four days before the Armistice in 1918. He taught me that "In a place where there are no men, you must be a man."

• • •

Requiem

On May 20, 1996, The Daily Mail reported at p. 3:

"UNITED NATIONS

Iraq accepts offer of oil for food

"Iraq has accepted a U.N. offer to let Saddam Hussein sell oil to buy food and medicine for its people, Iraq's U.N. ambassador said today.

"An agreement would let Iraq sell $1 billion of oil every 90 days—its

first oil exports since the United Nations imposed sanctions on
Baghdad to punish it for invading Kuwait in August 1990. The pact
would be expected to reduce gasoline prices worldwide..."

The following day similar articles appeared in major
newspapers. *The Washington Post* on p. 1 described the deal as "an
accord that will permit Iraq to sell $2 billion worth of oil over six
months..."

USA Today on p. 1 reported, "The White House called it 'an
important victory for Iraq's humanitarian needs.'"

As an American citizen I ask, "What about the humanitarian
needs of the American Gulf War Vets who are now disabled after
service in Kuwait and Iraq? They have been waiting for more than
five years for the American government to recognize their claims
and provide them with effective medical treatment and compensation. How many more flawed government investigations and
cover-ups must they endure?

A survivor of the Holocaust, now a distinguished American
citizen, and knowledgeable about world affairs described this UN
deal with Iraq as a "slick political move to make sure gas prices are
lower in the United States before the American elections."

The result of the deal with Iraq is that disabled American
veterans are now waiting in line for their needs to be met after
Saddam Hussein and the Iraqi people are provided for. Americans
are relegated to second place behind Iraqis and their Satanic
leader.

Is this how we provide for disabled American servicemen? This
is not right. This is not honorable. It must not stand.

Despite White House and UN assurances that Saddam and his
regime will get very little of the billions of our dollars paid for Iraqi
oil we know otherwise. That press release has about as much credibility as O.J. Simpson and the tooth fairy together. Remember,
the money the UN gets and spends comes mostly from United
States taxpayers. Anyone who has followed the sad performance
and history of the UN in the aftermath of the Gulf War and its

inability to enforce its own policies and edicts knows that UN assurances are not credible.

Saddam, a merciless tyrant and mortal enemy of the American people is responsible for the torched oil wells and the toxic air pollution from the chemicals in the black smoke in Kuwait. It was one of the world's worst environmental catastrophes. For that evil deed alone he should be indicted and prosecuted as a criminal against humanity and nature, and if convicted executed promptly. Instead, he remains in power by the grace of our compassionate leaders. Saddam will make every effort to use the billions to buy more arms, tanks, and replenish his chemical and nuclear weapons stockpile from the same merchants of death who built Iraq into an enemy war machine prior to his invasion of Kuwait. And some of his evil providers were American corporations just doing business as usual, always ready to make a buck regardless of who might get hurt. The money is the bottom line—not the health welfare or safety of the American public or a doctrine of world peace.

In 1775 Patrick Henry thundered at a convention in Richmond, Virginia,—

> "The war has actually begun. The next gale that sweeps from the North will bring to our ears the clash of resounding arms. Our brethren are already in the field. Why stand we here idle?...Is life so dear or peace so sweet as to be purchased at the price of chains and slavery? Forbid it, Almighty God! I know not what course others may take; but as for me, give me liberty or give me death!"

Today, America needs a cleansing and a rebirth of freedom and another Patrick Henry to say what needs to be said. Can you hear Patrick Henry saying the same words about the Final Battle in which we are now engaged.

All of the above and—Is our need for oil so great that we must kneel before a tyrant who we have defeated in battle and pay him homage and tribute and grovel before the world to beg to purchase the oil beneath his realm? Forbid it, Almighty God!

6

Summer on the Lawn
Earth, Wind, Rain, and Fire
The Changing Global Environment

The most exciting, objective, and stimulating discussion of global environmental issues I ever had the privilege of attending was held at the University of Virginia, Charlottesville, Virginia, June 16-20, 1996.

"The 1996 Summer on the Lawn program presented challenging, balanced, and timely discussion of global environmental issues led by outstanding University of Virginia faculty representing very different perspectives and disciplines. The program focused on a range of provocative issues including environmental conflict resolution, the effects of global atmospheric change, the impact of the American frontier on attitudes toward nature, and the quest for a sustainable environmental future."

The speakers were outstanding. I was enthralled at the new information, technology, and data they presented from their research and travels throughout the world.

As stated in the program:

"Environmental issues impact on every aspect of human existence and are often characterized by conflicting perceptions and contrasting scientific evidence. Environmental pressures on the systems in which we live call for the public to become more informed on issues which will touch them and the next generation."

Each speaker touched on one or more problems I have been studying and writing about in A Canary's Tale. I was exhilarated by the fact that these great men were aware of, and way ahead of me in everything I had learned about the environment in which we live. Time and space do not permit me to cover the tremendous amount of exciting material they presented. I suggested that these proceedings be published and that this program be made into a documentary for PBS Television. This program reminded me of what Bill Moyers did with *HEALING AND THE MIND* which we wrote about earlier. The UVA faculty speakers were equal in every respect to the brilliant and caring doctors and Ph.D.s interviewed by Moyers. When I was called upon to lead off a discussion about my Odyssey I was very moved to find out these distinguished professors were actively interested in what I had to say. They understood that there is a link between environmental pollution and adverse health effects, and they are all concerned about the health of their children and their grandchildren and future generations. I do not consider myself in the same league with those fellows. They are far superior to me. I am in awe of them and the work they are doing. But Professor John R. Redick of the Division of Continuing Education of the University who put this magnificent program together with the assistance and cooperation of all faculty members made me feel very special as did every speaker I met. They made me feel like we were all climbing to the mountaintop together, each of us with a unique talent and perspective, and by working together and listening, and caring there is hope and still time to educate the public to take effective action to do what man can do to change the global environment for the good of all mankind.

The Faculty speakers were:

Richard C. Collins, Lawrence Lewis Jr., Professor, School of Architecture and Director, Institute for Environmental Negotiations.

John E. Echeverri-Gent, Associate Professor, Woodrow Wilson Department of Government and Foreign Affairs.

R. Edward Freeman, Olsson Professor of Business Administration and Director, Olsson Center, The Darden Graduate School of Business Administration.

Daniel A. Westberg, Assistant Professor, Department of Religious Studies.

Michael Garstang, Professor, Department of Environmental Sciences.

Harold H. Kolb, Jr., Professor, Department of English Language and Literature and Director, Center for the Liberal Arts.

Saul Levmore, Professor, School of Law.

William A. McDonough, Elson Professor and Dean, School of Architecture.

George J. Moein, Director, Hazardous Waste Management Institute and Earth 20/20, Division of Continuing Education.

Herman H. Shugart, W.W. Corcoran Professor of Environmental Sciences.

• • •

The attendees were from different walks of life, including medical doctors, lawyers and law professors, chemical engineers, business executives, environmental activists, writers, house wives, present or retired government employees, nurses, and teachers. They came from north, south, east, and west to spend a week on the beautiful Lawn and participate in this exciting conference. The influence of Thomas Jefferson is still keenly felt at the University, especially by alumni who return year after year to revel in fantasies of the "good old days at UVA." Friendships sprang up like grass among the attendees after class. When it was time to say, "Goodbye," we felt we had known each other for years, and looked forward to returning for another Summer on the Lawn next year.

7

Call to Action
to Prevent Further Pollution
and to Abate Existing Pollution

"Every time a man stands up for an ideal, or acts to improve the lot
of others, or strikes out against injustice, he sends forth a tiny ripple
of hope...and crossing each other from a million different centers of
energy and daring those ripples build a current that can sweep
down the mightiest walls of oppression and resistance."

Sen. Robert F. Kennedy, Cape Town, South Africa 1966

• • •

Awareness

A Assuming *A Canary's Tale* has heightened your awareness to
the link between environmental pollution and environmental
illness and between chemical exposure, disease, disability and
death we have met our first goal—to get your attention.

It is now my hope that you will use your new awareness to
experience with your own senses of sight, smell, taste and sound
adverse health effects that are linked to chemical exposure in your
daily life and to make a commitment to do something about this
situation.

Education

First it will take education. We must continue to read and to
study the problems. We must investigate and get the facts. Use
your public library, join an environmental organization, subscribe
to environmental magazines, newsletters and other publications.
Use Volume II, the Appendix to this book, for references and

resources. This is part of the research I did to write this book. This will save you a few years of hard work.

Analyze and Evaluate the Information

Analyze and evaluate the information you receive. Use your common sense. Define your personal goals. Plan to convert your knowledge into action. Attend conferences and seminars on environmental subjects in which you have a great interest.

Take Action

For example, request your local Board of Education to include courses in ecology, and petition your college to provide environmental education courses. Prepare petitions. Write letters: to public officials to support clean air and clean water, and oppose pollution; to polluters complaining of adverse environmental effects; to editors to heighten public awareness. Enlarge our constituency. Write articles for newspapers, magazines and brochures for organizations to which you belong. Write an editorial or an opinion editorial. Speak out. Give an informal talk or participate in a debate. Use TV, radio, public meetings and forums. Advance new ideas. State the problem and propose remedies. For example: alternatives to toxic chemicals, organic farming vs toxic chemicals in food supply.

Work for Prevention/Avoidance of Pollution

Support legislation to reduce pollution and clean up the environment. Vote for public officials who support sound environmental principles. Attend conferences, seminars and public meetings in support of a healthy environment. Attend education courses in schools and colleges. Join the Religious Movement that is becoming aware of the dangers of pollution. Participate in Earth Day Designation Special Day activities.

Before you know it you will be making a great contribution to the public health, safety and welfare and to a better and healthy quality of life for yourself, your family and the whole human race.

You will meet new friends and learn a great deal. It is an

exciting prospect and a satisfying experience.

You will be proud of yourself. If not now, when? If not me, who?

Only by being willing to take it upon ourselves to shape the future can we begin to make strides away from our reliance on pollution-causing chemicals. It's a call I'm willing to answer, and I hope you are too. After all, to borrow a phrase, the life you save might be your own.

294

Epilogue

Dana Rudikoff, writing for *Solutions* 1.1 (Spring 1996): 6 under the headline, "DowElanco Complies with EPA Penalty" reported:

"In the spring of 1995, the US Environmental Protection Agency fined DowElanco a record $732,000 for the corporation's failure to report health problems associated with the use of the insecticide Dursban (chlorpyrifos). Federal regulations require that any claim received by the manufacturer that a pesticide has caused harm to humans or pets must be disclosed to the EPA within 30 days. The EPA contended that DowElanco failed to report 250 incidents involving Dursban-related injuries, and their negligence reflected a clear unwillingness to comply with the "disclosure" directive. DowElanco, a joint venture between Eli Lilly and Dow Corporation, was delinquent in responding to fines issued in the spring, so in August of 1995, the EPA increased the amount they owed to $890,000. According to an attorney in the EPA's Office of Enforcement and Compliance Assurance who worked on the case, a consent agreement was reached on August 21, 1995. DowElanco agreed to pay a fine of $876,000, and is currently providing the EPA with the relevant documentation pertaining to the Dursban-related claims. The case has since been closed."

Reprinted with permission of New York Coalition for Alternatives to Pesticides (NYCAP).

• • •

What goes around comes around.

• • •

"Physicians are seeing growing numbers of patients who report chronic and disabling symptoms following exposure to solvents, pesticides, combustion products and buildings with poor indoor air quality. These patients include industrial workers, office workers, schoolchildren, persons living near Superfund hazardous waste sites, and, most recently, Gulf War veterans...

"Just as the invention of the microscope enabled physicians to identify bacteria and control infections, so an Environmental Medical Unit now is needed to enable us to diagnose and treat the health problems of the veterans and other Americans whose health may be at risk from environmental exposures."

> *Claudia S. Miller, M.D., M.S.* Presentation Before Presidential Advisory Committee on Gulf War Veterans' Illnesses Meeting. *San Antonio, Texas, 27 Feb. 1996. Reprinted with permission.*

People who are poisoned after exposure to toxic chemicals and who subsequently develop adverse health effects such as MCS serve a function for the rest of mankind similar to that performed by the miner's canary. We are telling you that the environment is polluted. It is not safe for us, and everyone is at risk, especially your children and your grandchildren.

As President Kennedy said in 1963:

"In the final analysis, our most basic common link is that we all inhabit this small planet. We all breathe the same air. We all cherish our children's future. And we are all mortal."

May the Lord give us the strength, the will and the common sense to take effective action in what may very well be The Final Battle to preserve and protect the environment and the public health.

And May God Bless America!

Jacob B. Berkson

Permission Acknowledgements

Acknowledgments

I wish to thank and express my appreciation to all those wonderful people who encouraged, helped and supported me in my efforts to learn, understand, and write *A Canary's Tale*. Most of them are named in my Odyssey i.e. Volume I and listed in the 12 Major Topics of Volume II. They are the Doctors who care, listen, study and treat patients suffering from exposure to toxic chemicals. They give us hope for effective medical treatment, a reduction of our symptoms and a tolerable quality of life.

Secondly to all the brave victims of chemical poisoning and especially to those who have helped educate me as to how to cope and permitted me to write about their experiences or list them in Section II of Volume II. I am extremely proud of them for their courage and desire to help each other and make this a better world for all humanity. They are the Canaries who serve as sentinels, as the first line of defense in the Final Battle to preserve and protect human health and the environment. They are warning the rest of humanity as to the hazards of chemical poisons that are part of our everyday life.

To the medical and scientific researchers who perform their studies without huge grants, funds, or monetary support from industry, government, or private sources, and to the editors, writers, authors, and spokespersons in the press and the media who educate the public as to the dangers that exist from the irresponsible use of hazardous substances.

To the Officers, Directors, Trustees, and Members of Environmental Organizations who are the leaders and the backbone of the environmental movement.

To the public officials who care about human health and the environment and who legislate, enforce, and interpret the laws in the public interest rather than for special interests.

To Jack Garver, the artist, my friend of sixty years who agreed to take his valuable time to illustrate *A Canary's Tale*. Jack, his wife Shirley and I were Associate Editors of our high school yearbook more than fifty years ago.

To my most capable right arm Kathy Pepper who labored over a complex computer and a thousand tons of paper covered with nearly illegible notes, and transformed my hieroglyphics into remarkable printouts, revision after revision, till we agreed—No more, No more, This is it. And my thanks to Stewart and the little Peppers, Jeremy and Katrina, who sometimes saw me invade their home three times a day organizing, revising, proofing, and setting goals. And to Melanie Schlosser, my first typist, who typed for a year or so on the initial manuscript before she returned to a full career in industry. And to Roger, Jennifer and Jessica for their cooperation.

To Bill Callen, now Sports Editor of the *Herald Mail*, who took the time to cut and edit my manuscript and gave me time to recuperate when I began to drown in paper work and confusion.

To Sandy Warfield, Ann Marie Reed, and Gloria Urban of the Washington County Free Library who assisted in reviewing, proofreading, and organizing my reference files consistent with their placement in Volume II.

To Janette Sherman, M.D., David Steinman, M.A., Elaine Kidwell Freckleton, M.D., Ellen Uzelac, writer, Lorraine O'Neill, physical therapist, and many others who peer reviewed the manuscript and furnished valuable suggestions to improve it.

To Richard F. McGrory, attorney at law, former law partner who stood by me in some dark days despite the fact that he had undergone a liver transplant. His refusal to "hang up the gloves" is inspiring.

To Richard Shank and his capable, competent, and professional staff at Copy-Quik, Hagerstown, Maryland, for their valuable

302

assistance in the publication of A *Canary's Tale*.

And last but not least, to my family and Eloise, my fiancee and "caretaker," who was poisoned along with me and sustained permanent damage to her body system, but without a complaint or a whimper. I thank you all for your encouragement and inspiration.

It is now time to heal.

A Canary's Tale

Volume 11

A Canary's Tale

The Final Battle

Politics, Poisons, and Pollution

vs.

The Environment and the Public Health

Volume II

Research, References and Resources

(1988 - 1996)

by Jacob B. Berkson

(Library of Congress Cataloging in Publication Data)

Berkson, Jacob B.
A Canary's Tale

DISCLAIMER

The material in this book is for information only and is not to be construed as medical, legal, or other professional advice. Inclusion herein does not constitute endorsement of any product or service. The use of this book is not a substitute for medical, legal, or other professional services. Consult a competent professional for answers to your specific questions.

Printed with soy ink on recycled paper.

*To all the children and grandchildren on the planet Earth in
this last decade of the twentieth century, and to the future
generations who survive The Final Battle.*

*With special prayers for my kind and gentle
son, Daniel, who died on July 1, 1996, and his widow,
Julie, and my grandson Randy.*

Preface

This Volume II is not a comprehensive file on any or each topic but it is a beginning point for one to start to recognize the depth of the environmental problems and what is being done or not being done to resolve the crises. The reader may want to begin his or her own scrapbook or reference book based upon resources he or she discovers in the educational process. We do not have to reinvent the wheel. A lot of wonderful people have been working to preserve and protect the environment and human health for many years before I ever knew there was a problem. Whether you are a layman, a lawyer, a doctor, a builder, or schoolteacher, or from any other walk of life I hope you will discover one or more topics in which you are interested and with which you can identify. Remember it is just a beginning—but a journey of a thousand miles begins with a single step.

It is my hope that *A Canary's Tale* will challenge you to think, discuss, debate, and act in what may be The Final Battle to preserve and protect the environment for our children, grand-children, and future generations.

A CANARY'S TALE

Volume II

Research, References and Resources

OUTLINE

Page

Expanded Topical Outline

              (3) Formaldehyde
              (4) Tobacco Smoke
              (5) Some Carpets
                   (a) Some Problems
                   (b) Some Remedies
              (6) Perfumes and Fragrances
              (7) Air Fresheners and Deodorizers
              (8) Solvents—Benzene and Xylene
              (9) Wood Stove Smoke
              (10) Carbon Monoxide

    2.   Outdoor Air Pollution
        a.   Some Places
            (1) Global
            (2) National
            (3) Mexico City
            (4) Regional/Local
        b.   Some Pollutants
            (1) Pesticides/Spray/Drift
            (2) Vehicle Exhaust
            (3) Lawn Mower Exhaust
            (4) Incinerators
            (5) Stack Gas/Smoke
            (6) Landfill Air
            (7) Chlorofluorocarbons (CFC's)
            (8) Wood Stove Smoke
        c.   Some Remedies

B. Water Pollution
    1.   Oceans
    2.   Seas
    3.   Bays and Gulfs
    4.   Rivers, Creeks and Streams
    5.   Lakes
    6.   Wetlands
    7.   Groundwater
    8.   Wells

Research, References and Resources

I. Environmental Pollution
    A. Air Pollution
       1. Indoor Air Pollution
          a. Some Places
            (1) Home
               (a) Some Problems

Boccella, Kathy. "Toxins Bombarding Us in the Comfort of Our Homes. Air Fresheners, Spot Removers, Toilet Cleaners. The Inside Pollutants May Be More Hazardous Than the Outside Ones." *The Philadelphia Inquirer* 2 Apr. 1995, sec. A:1+.

Booth, Nan and Lucy High. "Residential Hazardous Products: Household Wastes." *Water Resources*. College Park, Maryland: The University of Maryland, 1987-88.

Bowie, Liz. "Prolonged Battle With Pesticide Costs Family Their Home: Misapplied Chlordane Contaminates Their House." *Baltimore Sun* 19 May 1991, sec. A:1+.

"Bug Bombs Blast House; Cockroaches Still Kicking." (Westminster, Calif.) *The Daily Mail* 25 Apr. 1995, sec. A:1.

"Carbon Monoxide Victims Thought Gas Was in Their Home. Doctor Told Family They Had the Flu. 'My Nephew, John Michael, Was Not in This World. He Was Delirious, Tired, Non-Functional. This Doctor Should Have Known by the Symptoms of John Michael Alone.'—Mark Reed." (Cleveland [AP].) *The Herald-Mail* 24 Dec. 1995, sec. A:8.

"Carpets: A Health Hazard?" *The Daily Mail* 19 Aug. 1992, sec. A:1.

Cohn, D'Vera. "Pesticide Fears Leave Pair a House That's Not Home: Virginia Couple Stay in Backyard Trailer." *The Washington Post* 6 Apr. 1989, sec. D:1+.

Davis, Patricia and D'Vera Cohn. "Va. Woman Wins Case, but Still Has Toxic House." *The Washington Post* 21 Feb. 1992, sec. B:1.

Duehring, Cindy. "The Hazards of Chemicals in House Dust." *Our Toxic Times* 1993: 4(9):5.

_____. "Trapped by Her Sensitivity: She Is Unable to Tolerate Chemicals All of Us Are Exposed to Every Day." *The Lutheran* 20 Feb. 1991: 10-13.

"Family Has Home Hauled to Toxic Waste Dump." *The Herald-Mail* 23 Apr. 1989, sec. A:8.

Gram, David. "Does Health Threat Lurk Underfoot?" *The Daily Mail* 20 June 1993, sec. B:6.

"Household Pollution Can Be Long-Term Health Threat." *The Herald Mail* 26 Feb. 1993, sec. E:10.

"Indoor Environments Creating New Illnesses, Physician Tells ASHRAE Indoor Air Conference." *The Building Official and Code Administrator* May/June 1986: 29.

New Jersey Department of Health. *Facts on Formaldehyde: Division of Occupational and Environmental Health.* Trenton, New Jersey: Mar. 1987.

Pegg, Judy. "Dream Home Turns into a Nightmare: Insecticide Contamination by a California Pest Control Operator." *Journal of Pesticide Reform*, vol. 12, no. 2, Summer 1992: 24.

Perl, Rebecca. "Cover Story—Cigarettes: Lethal Little Packages." *The Washington Post* 11 Jan. 1994.

"Radon: The Health Risk Indoors." *Air Pollution in Maryland Fact Sheet.* Timonium, Maryland: American Lung Association of Maryland, Aug. 1992.

Shaw, Terri. "How Healthy Is Your House?" *The Washington Post* 7 June 1990, Washington Home sec. 7+.

Stammer, Larry B. "Indoor Air—How Clean Is It?" *The Washington Post Health* 23 Jan. 1990, 17+.

Unhealthy House, The. Unionville, IN: The Healthy House Institute, 1993.

United States Environmental Protection Agency. *Hazardous Substances In Our Environment: A Citizen's Guide to Health Risks and Reducing Exposure*. Washington: September, 1990.

(b) Some Remedies

Appleby, Julie. "Built to Be Bare: In Marin County, a HUD- Backed Haven Is Designed for the Chemically Sensitive." *Washington Home* 2 Mar. 1995: 8-11.

Bower, John. *The Healthy House*. New York, New York: Carol Communications, 1989.

_____. *Healthy House Building: A Design & Construction Guide. The Book Every Homeowner, Buidler, and Designer Needs to Reduce Indoor Pollution and Improve Health*. Unionville, Ind.: The Healthy House Institute, 1993.

_____. *Understanding Ventilation. How to Design, Select, and Install Residential Ventilation Systems*. Bloomington, Ind.: The Healthy House Institute, 1995.

_____. *Your House, Your Health. A Non-Toxic Building Guide*. Video. Unionville, Ind.: The Healthy House Institute, 1992.

Bower, Lynn Marie. *The Healthy Household: A Complete Guide for Creating a Healthy Indoor Environment*. Bloomington, Indiana: The Healthy House Institute, 1995.

Dadd, Debra Lynn. *Nontoxic, Natural, & Earthwise: How to Protect Yourself and Your Family from Harmful Products and Live in Harmony with the Earth*. Los Angeles: Jeremy P. Tarcher, Inc., 1990.

"Dust Control in the Bedroom." *House Dust Allergy*. Ridgefield, Connecticut: Allergy Control Products, Inc., 1993.

EarthWorks Group, The. *50 Simple Things You Can Do to Save the Earth*. Berkeley: The EarthWorks Press, 1989.

Golos, Natalie, and William J. Rea, M.D. *Success in the Clean Bedroom: A Path to Optimal Health*. Rochester, New York: Pinnacle Publishers, 1992.

Good, Clint, and Dadd, Debra Lynn. *Healthful Houses: How to Design and Build Your Own*. Bethesda, Maryland: Guaranty Press, 1988.

Greenfield, Ellen J. *House Dangerous: Indoor Pollution in Your Home and Office—and What You Can Do About It!* New York: Interlink Books, 1991.

Henig, Robin Marantz. "The Enemy Within: How to Protect Yourself from Indoor Pollutants." *AARP Bulletin* Sept. 1990: 2+.

Home Book: A Guide to Safety, Security & Savings in the Home, The. Washington, D.C.: Center for Study of Responsive Law, 1989.

Hunter, Linda Mason. *The Healthy Home: An Attic-to-Basement Guide to Toxin-Free Living.* United States: Pocket Books, 1990.

Joy, Linda. "Chemical-Free Home." *The Herald Mail* 9 Nov. 1990, sec. C:6.

Lehman, H. Jane. "'Healthy Homes' Designed to Combat Pollutants: Couple One of Rising Number Who Find They're Allergic to Conventional Construction." *The Washington Post* 15 Feb. 1992, sec. E:1+.

"Mold Control in the Home." *Mold Spore Allergy.* Ridgefield, Connecticut: Allergy Control Products, Inc., 1993.

National Pesticide Telecommunications Network. Telephone: 1- 800-858-PEST (7378) (Toll Free). A 24-hour hotline in Texas Tech University, Lubbock Texas.

Needleman, Herbert L., and Philip J. Landrigan. *Raising Children Toxic Free.* Farrer, Straus and Giroux, 1994.

Post, Dr. Diana. *The Other Road to Flea Control: Mechanical, Biological and Chemical Methods of Least Toxic Pet Protection.* Chevy Chase, Maryland: Rachel Carson Council, Inc., 1994.

Rose, Judy. "How Health House Solved Pollution Issues With a Variety of Innovations." *The Herald-Mail* 21 Apr. 1995, sec. D:5.

Rousseau, David, W. J. Rea, M.D., and Jean Enwright. *Your Home, Your Health, & Well-Being.* Berkeley, California: Ten Speed Press, 1988.

Snyder, Clovis M., M.D., F.A.C.A. *Guide to "Desensitizing" a Room.* Richmond, Virginia: A. H. Robins Company, n.d.

U.S. Consumer Product Safety Commission. *Poison Lookout Checklist.* Washington, D.C.

United States Environmental Protection Agency. United States Consumer Product Safety Commission. *Inside Story: A Guide to Indoor Air Quality, The.* Washington, D.C.: Sept. 1993.

_____. American Lung Association. Consumer Product Safety Commission. American Medical Association. *Indoor Air Pollution: An Introduction for Health Professionals.* Washington, D.C.: 1994.

(2) Workplace
(a) Some Problems

"Ammonia Leak Shuts Down Plant." *The Herald-Mail* 10 Oct. 1992, sec. B:3.

Chepesiuk, Ron. "Warning: Your Workplace May Be Hazardous to Your Health." *The Elks Magazine* Apr. 1992: 40-42.

"EPA Finds Bad Air at Own Headquarters." *The Daily Mail* 24 Nov. 1989, sec. A:10.

Halbrook, David. "Life Is Killing Bethna Hareld." *American Legion Magazine* Jan. 1992: 35+.

Lambert, Wade. "More Claim Chemicals Made Them Ill." *Wall Street Journal* 18 Jan. 1995, sec. B:1+.

Marcus, Amy Dockser. "In Some Workplaces, Ill Winds Blow: Indoor Pollution Spurs Lawsuits, Taxes Economy." *The Wall Street Journal* 9 Oct. 1989, sec. B:1.

Morison, Rufus, Ph.D. Letter to Jacob B. Berkson. May 1994.

Phillips, Don. "DOT's Main Building Found 'Sick.' Summer Cleanup Will Affect 5,500 Workers." *The Washington Post* 3 Apr. 1996, sec. A:1+.

Piller, Charles and Michael Castleman. "Is Your Office Making You Sick?" *Redbook* Apr. 1990: 114, 115+.

Saltus, Richard. "Hospital Staffers Battle Mystery Malady: Airborne Irritants Are Targeted for Cleanup." *The Boston Sunday Globe* 21, Nov. 1993, sec. :37+.

Schwartz, Shelly. "Use Building? No Thanks, Says NOAA. Agency Wants to Cancel Lease for Structure Where Workers Became Ill." *Silver Spring Gazette* 27 Mar. 1996.

Thrasher, Jack D., Ph.D. "Adverse Consequences of Accidental Methyl Bromide Exposure." *Informed Consent* 1.6 (Nov./Dec. 1994): 16+.

"Union Says Workers, Students Exposed to Asbestos Dust." (College Park ([AP].) *The Daily Mail* 3 Mar. 1992, sec. C:10.

U.S. Department of Health and Human Services. Public Health Service. Centers for Disease Control and Prevention. *Environmental Tobacco Smoke in the Workplace: A Selective Bibliography.* Atlanta, Georgia: Centers for Disease Control and Prevention, Feb. 1994.

United States Environmental Protection Agency. *Environmental Backgrounder: Asbestos.* Washington, D.C.: Mar. 1989.

"Workers Say Air Is Sickening." (Woodlawn, Md. [AP].) *The Daily Mail* 3 Apr. 1995, sec. A:6.

"Workers Say They're Sick of Being in Sick Building." *The Daily Mail* 17 Feb. 1992, sec. D:8.

(b) Some Remedies

Federal Register: Part II—Department of Labor, Occupational Safety and Health Administration. 29 CFR Parts 1910, 1915, 1926, and 1928. Indoor Air Quality; Proposed Rule. 5 Apr. 1994.

Lieberman, Allan D., M.D. Letter to Mr. Charles F. Chester. Re: Nancy Gorman. 17 Apr. 1991.

_____. Letter to Ms. Barbara P. Lawrence. Re: Nancy Gorman. 15 May 1991.

Multiple Chemical Sensitivities at Work: A Training Workbook for Working People. New York: The Labor Institute, 1993.

(3) Schools
(a) Some Problems

Anderson, Liz. "W.Va. School Closed Due to Rash." *The Daily Mail* 3 May 1990, sec. B:2.

_____. "Fiberglass Caused Rash; School to Reopen Monday." *The Herald-Mail* 12 May 1990, sec. A:1+.

"Carbon Monoxide Poisoning Sends Team to Hospital." *The Daily Mail* 20 Jan. 1992, sec. A:1.

Carson, Larry. "Chemical Aversion Makes Boy Sue School." *The Evening Sun* 20 Dec. 1990, sec. B:8.

Dillon, Sam. "School Unit Is No Stranger to Scandals." *The New York Times* 15 Aug. 1993, 35+.

"EPA Warns of Classroom Air Pollution." *The Daily Mail* 19 Mar. 1993, sec. A:2.

Hedges, Chris. "Girls in Egypt Faint by Score in Classrooms." *The New York Times* 18 Apr. 1993, 9.

Hendrix, Sheila M. Letter to Jacob B. Berkson. 12 Sept. 1991.

Malhotra, Sharon A., R.N. "Pollution in Our Schools." *Good Housekeeping* June 1992: 12.

Money, Jennifer L. "'Stuffy' School Probed: Northern Middle Teachers File Numerous Complaints." *The Daily Mail* 26 Apr. 1993, sec. A:1+.

_____. "Teachers: Illness in the Air—Noises, Fumes From North High Construction Bring Complaints. *The Daily Mail* 19 Mar. 1992, sec. A:1+.

Raab, Selwyn. "School Asbestos Inquiry Is Focusing on Choice of Labs by Contractor." *The New York Times* 15 Aug. 1993, 39.

"Sickening Fumes Force Evacuation." *The Daily Mail* 12 Mar. 1993, sec. A:6.

Wilkenfeld, Irene. "Schools and Health. Part III: Outdoor Chemical Hazards." *Informed Consent* Mar./Apr. 1994: 8- 10+.

(b) Some Remedies

Couturier, Brian J. "Waynesboro Leaders Hire Firm to Probe Air." *The Daily Mail* 1 Feb. 1990, sec. B:4.

Forbes, William. "Jared's Story: Least Toxic Approaches to Managing Pests in Schools." *In* Norma L. Miller, Ed.D., ed. *The Healthy School Handbook. Conquering the Sick Building Syndrome and Other Environmental Hazards In and Around Your School.* Washington, D.C.: NEA Professional Library, June 1995, p. 243-254.

Get Set Presenting Real Integrated Pest Management. Get Set, Inc. 1-800-221-6188.

Grow: Grass Roots the Organic Way. 38 Llangollen Lane, Newtown Square, Pennsylvania 19073.

Miller, Norma L., Ed.D., ed. *The Healthy School Handbook. Conquering the Sick Building Syndrome and Other Environmental Hazards In and Around Your School.* Washington, D.C.: NEA Professional Library, June 1995.

New York State Department of Law. Robert Abrams, Attorney General. *Pesticides in Schools: Reducing the Risks.* New York: March 1993.

Penenberg, Adam L. "Parents Pressuring Schools for Alternatives to Pesticides." *The New York Times* 30 Jan. 1994:1+.

Ross, Ilona and Tracy Frisch. "NYCAP Launches Safe Schools Campaign to Cut Pesticides." *NYCAP News,* vol. 4, no. 1, Early Spring 1993: 1.

United States EPA. Office of Pesticide Programs. *Pest Control in the School Environment: Adopting Integrated Pest Management.* Washington, D.C.: Aug. 1993.

Von Mehren, Laurie. "Better Ways to Pest-Proof School Buildings." Cleveland *Plain Dealer* 22 Oct. 1992, sec. B:11.

_____. "Getting Pesticides Out of Schools." *The Earth Day Coalition News* 4.1 (Feb. 1993):1+.

(4) Other Public Buildings
(a) Some Problems

"A Failure to Protect: The Unnecessary Use of Hazardous Pesticides at Federal Facilities Threatens Human Health and the Environment." *Pesticides and You* 14.3&4 (Winter 1994-1995): Insert.

"Employee-Illness Has Judge Request 'Sick Building' Study." *The Daily Mail* 11 Apr. 1990, sec. D:8.

Ford, Clyde. "Chemical Leak at Valley Mall Forces Evacuation: Firefighters On Scene Until 2 a.m." *The Daily Mail* 7 May 1993, sec. B:1.

_____. "Freon Gas Leak Drives Patients From War Memorial Hospital." *The Daily Mail* 5 Dec. 1990, sec. B:3.

Gugliotta, Guy. "Anti-Pesticide Coalition Finds Toxic Atmosphere at Most Government Sites in Survey." *The Washington Post* 7 Mar. 1995, sec. A:15.

Miller, Bill. "Pesticide-Linked Death of U.S. Worker in Cairo Raises Issue of Who's Accountable." *The Washington Post* 22 May 1994, sec. B:1+.

"Pollutants Sucked Into Operating Rooms." *The Daily Mail* 18 May 1992, sec. C:4.

Riechmann, Deb. "Workers: Air at MVA Still Bad." *The Daily Mail* 10 July 1991, sec. B:3.

"'Sick' Building Still Mystery After 5 Years." *The Daily Mail* 22 Apr. 1991, sec. D:8.

(b) Some Remedies

Green, A. *The Six Steps of the IPM Process in Buildings.* U.S. General Services Administration, 15 Jan. 1993.

_____. *Recommended Standards for Pest Control Operation in Occupied Space.* NCR Regional Entomologist, 19 Aug. 1993.

_____. *The Termination of Extermination: Meeting the IPM Imperative in Public and Commercial Buildings.* U.S. General Services Administration, 15 Jan. 1991.

_____. *Contrasts Between Traditional Pest Control and IPM for Buildings.* U.S. General Services Administration, 1 July 1992.

(5) Churches

Committee on the Environment of the Diocese of Maryland, The. "'We must proclaim the power of the Gospel to those in power.' Presiding Bishop Edmond L. Browning." For information on the Episcopal Public Policy Network call 1-800-228-0515.

Mission Education and Cultivation Program Department, General Board of Global Ministries, The United Method Church. *Accessibility Audit for Churches: A United Methodist Resource Book About Accessibility.* Revised Dec. 1994. Stock #3810. Order from: Service Center, General Board of Global Ministries, 7820 Reaching Road, Caller No. 1800, Cincinnati, Ohio 45222-1800

_____. *Church-Related Health facilities and Indoor Air Quality*. Mar. 1992. Stock #5138.

_____. *Indoor Air Quality: A Guide for Local Churches*. Aug. 1992. Stock #5136.

Oficina de Recursos en Español del Departamento de Programa de Educación y Cultivo Misional, Junta General de Ministerios Globales, Iglesia Metodista Unida. *La Calidad del Aire en los Espacios Cerrados: Guía para las Iglesias Locales*. Nov. 1991. No. de orders: 5137. 475 Riverside Drive, New York, NY 10115.

To Build a Just Society. Episcopal Church Public Policy Network. New York: The Public Policy Network.

(6) Sick Buildings

Can Buildings Make You Sick? Mike Tomlinson, producer. Robin Brightwell, ed. NOVA, PBS, Boston, 26 Dec. 1995.

"Employee-Illness Has Judge Request 'Sick Building' Study." *The Daily Mail* 11 Apr. 1990, sec. D:8.

"Fresh Air Doesn't Revive 'Sick' Buildings." *The Washington Post* 25 Mar. 1993, sec. A:26.

Godish, Thad. *Sick Buildings: Definition, Diagnosis and Mitigation*. Boca Raton, Fla.: Lewis Publishers, 1994.

Kennedy, Joyce Lain. "Careers: Sick Buildings." *The Herald- Mail* 27 Nov. 1988, sec. E:12.

Kreiss, Kathleen, M.D. "The Sick Building Syndrome in Office Buildings—A Breath of Fresh Air." *The New England Journal of Medicine*, vol. 328, no. 12, 25 Mar. 1993: 877-878.

Menzies, Richard, M.D., M.Sc., et al. "The Effect of Varying Levels of Outdoor-Air Supply on the Symptoms of Sick Building Syndrome." *The New England Journal of Medicine*, vol. 328, no. 12, 25 Mar. 1993: 821-827.

Phillips, Don. "DOT's Main Building Found 'Sick.' Summer Cleanup Will Affect 5,500 Workers." *The Washington Post* 3 Apr. 1996, sec. A:1+.

Riechmann, Deb. "Workers: Air at MVA Still Bad." *The Daily Mail* 10 July 1991, sec. B:3.

United States Environmental Protection Agency. Research and Development. "Sick Building Syndrome." *Indoor Air Facts No. 4 (Revised)*. Washington: Apr. 1991.

(7) Airplanes

"Airplanes Cut Back on Air." *The Herald-Mail* 6 June 1993, sec. A:7.

Grossman, Laurie M. "The Smell of Chanel May Be No. 2 Issue After Cigarettes. Strong Odors of All Sorts Make People Sick or Merely Mad; Now: Aroma-Free Zones." *Wall Street Journal* 13 May 1993, eastern ed., sec. A:1+.

McKinnon, John D. "Flight Attendants' Secondhand Smoke Suit Gets Go-Ahead. A Florida Appeals Court Has Upheld a Class Action By Flight Attendants Who Say They Were Sickened By Secondhand Smoke." *ABA Journal* Mar. 1996: 39.

"Pena: Stop Spraying Passengers." (Washington.) *The Daily Mail* 20 Jan. 1995, sec. A:3.

Tolchin, Martin. "Air on Planes Questioned." *The New York Times* 11 July 1993, sec. xx:3.

_____. "End Is Sought to Spraying Foreign Jets: U.S. Says Insecticide Imperils Passengers." *The New York Times* 17 Apr. 1994, sec. 1:17.

_____. "Frequent Fliers Saying Fresh Air Is Awfully Thin at 30,000 Feet." *The New York Times* 6 June 1993, sec.1:1.

_____. "U.S. Pushes for a Smoking Ban on Flights Abroad." *The New York Times* 13 June 1993, sec. 1:28.

Wade, Betsy. "A Non-Smoker Vs. an Airline." *The New York Times* 29 May 1994, sec. xx:4.

Winegar, Karin. "Trouble in the Sky: Pesticide Use on Aircraft." *Informed Consent* Jan./Feb. 1994: 4-7+.

_____. "Which Flights Pesticide." *Informed Consent* Jan./Feb. 1994: 37.

b. Some Pollutants
(1) Pesticides/Termiticides
(a) Termite Problem

Austin, Gene. "Termite Inspection Is Not a Guarantee." *The Herald-Mail* 12 Sept. 1993, sec. E:3.

Bower, John. "Termites and Wood" in "Chapter: Wood and Wood Products" in *The Healthy House...How to Buy One...How to Cure a "Sick" One...How to Build One*. New York: Carol Communications, 1989.

Hodgson, Michael J., Geoffrey D. Block and David K. Parkinson. "Organophosphate Poisoning in Office Workers." *Journal of Occupational Medicine* 28 (June 1986): 434-437.

United States Environmental Protection Agency. *Citizen's Guide to Pesticides*. 4th ed. 22T-1002. Pesticides and Toxic Substances (H7506C). Washington, D.C.: Nov. 1991.

Vasvary, Louis. "Subterranean Termites." *Rutgers Cooperative Extension: New Jersey Agricultural Experiment Station*, FS338.

(b) Dursban TC

Breisch, Nancy. Letter to Sandy Scott from Cooperative Extension Service, Maryland Institute for Agriculture and Natural Resources, Department of Entomology. 20 Apr. 1993.

Cox, Caroline. "Chlorpyrifos, Part 1: Toxicology." *Journal of Pesticide Reform* 14.4 (Winter 1994): 15-20.

_____. "Chlorpyrifos, Part 2: Human Exposure." *Journal of Pesticide Reform* 15.1 (Spring 1995): 14-20.

Dow. "Specimen Label." *Dursban* TC*. 86-1473. U.S.A.: Jan. 1984. (Xylene listed as active ingredient.)

_____. "Specimen Label." *Dursban* TC*. (Furnished author in 1991. Fails to list Xylene as active ingredient.)

Dursban* TC: Termiticide Concentrate—Peace of Mind Termite Control. Dow Chemical U.S.A.

Dursban* TC: Termiticide Concentrate—Odor Reduction and Cleanup. Dow Chemical U.S.A.

Dursban* TC: Termiticide Concentrate—The Subterranean Termite: Problem & Solution. Dow Chemical U.S.A.

"Fact Sheet for Spray Solution of Dursban® Brand Insecticides Up to a 1% Dilution." *Health & Safety.* Form No. 135- 1270-88.

Material Safety Data Sheet: Dursban (R) TC Termiticide Concentrate. Dow Chemical U.S.A.

Straight Talk on Dursban TC. Dow Chemical Company. Form No. 135- 1222-87.

(c) Alternatives

Best, Don. "Safer Termite Control: The Hazards of Chlordane Can Be Avoided." *Rodale's Practical Homeowner* July/Aug. 1987. In *The Home Book: A Guide to Safety, Security and Savings in the Home.* Washington, D.C.: Center for Study of Responsive Law, 1989. p. 89+.

Brown, Amy E. "Insecticide Options for Termite Control." *Pesticide Information Leaflet* 3. College Park, Md.: Department of Entomology, Cooperative Extension Service, University of Maryland System, Mar. 1988.

"Chapter 23: Termites." *Common-Sense Pest Control: Least- Toxic Solutions for Your Home, Garden, Pets and Community.* Newtown, Conn.: The Taunton Press.

Controlling Termites. Bulletin 245. College Park: Cooperative Extension Service, The University of Maryland, revised 1987-88.

Currie, William E., and John B. Gingrich, Ph.D. "Termites and Their Management—PartII: Inspection and Monitoring." *Informed Consent* 1.5 (Sept./Oct. 1994): 40-43.

Least-Toxic Pest Management: Publications and Services Catalogue. Berkeley, Calif.: The Bio-Integral Resource Center, Feb. 1993.

Long, Becky. "Alternative Termite Management." *Journal of Pesticide Reform* 13.3 (Fall 1993): 38-39.

Moses, Marion, M.D. *Designer Posions: How to Protect Your Health and Home from Toxic Pesticides.* San Francisco: Pesticide Education Center, June 1995.

Olkowski, William, Helga Olkowski, and Sheila Daar. "Termites—New, Less Toxic Controls! *Least Toxic Pest Management for Termites and Other Wood Damaging Pests.* In *Common Sense Pest Control I (1)* Fall 1984: 7-19.

Quarles, William. "Least-Toxic Termite Control." *Common Sense Pest Control* IX (1) (Winter 1993): 5-13.

_____. "Borates Provide Least-Toxic Wood Protection." *The IPM Practitioner: Monitoring the Field of Pest Management* XIV (10) (Oct. 1992): 1-11.

Saf-T-Shield™: Non-Toxic Biological Termiticide—The Alternative to Chemical Termiticides. Bohemia, N.Y.: N- Viro Products Ltd. Phone: (516) 567-2628.

Thorne, Barbara L., Ph.D. "Alternative Approaches to Termite Detection and Control." *Pest Management* Feb. 1993: 8- 16.

(d) Prevention

Dadd, Debra Lynn. "Termite-Prevention Tips" in "Household Pest Control." *Nontoxic, Natural, & Earthwise: How to Protect Yourself and Your Family from Harmful Products and Live in Harmony with the Earth.* Los Angeles: Jeremy P. Tarcher, Inc., 1990. pp. 173+.

(2) Building Materials

Rousseau David, W. J. Rea, M.D., and Jean Enwright. "Building Materials" in "Chapter 22: Materials and Selection." *Your Home, Your Health, and Well-Being.* Berkeley, California: Ten Speed Press, 1988.

(3) Formaldehyde

Facts on formaldehyde. Trenton, N.J.: Division of Occupational and Environmental Health, New Jersey State Department of Health, Mar. 1987.

Formaldehyde: Everything You Wanted to Know But Were Afraid to Ask. Washington, D.C.: Consumer Federation of America.

Thrasher, Jack D., Ph.D., Alan Broughton, M.D., Ph.D., and Paul Micevich, Ph.D. "Antibodies and Immune Profiles of Individuals Occupationally Exposed to Formaldehyde: Six Case Reports." *American Journal of Industrial Medicine* 14 (1988): 479-488.

_____, et al. "Evidence for Formaldehyde Antibodies and Altered Cellular Immunity in Subjects Exposed to Formaldehyde in Mobile Homes." 42.6 (Nov./Dec. 1987): 347+.

(4) Tobacco Smoke

Perl, Rebecca. "Cover Story—Cigarettes: Lethal Little Packages." *The Washington Post* 11 Jan. 1994.

"Secondhand Smoke: Is It a Hazard? The Tobacco Merchants Claim There's Still a Controversy. We Don't Buy It." *Consumer Reports* Jan. 1995: 27-33.

U.S. Department of Health and Human Services. Public Health Service. Centers for Disease Control and Prevention. National Center for Chronic Disease Prevention and Health Promotion. *Chronic Disease and Health Promotion. Adapted from the MMWR: Tobacco Topics 1990-1993*. Atlanta, Georgia: Centers for Disease Control and Prevention.

_____. *Office on Smoking and Health Publications List*. Atlanta, Georgia: Centers for Disease Control and Prevention, Aug. 1994.

U.S. Environmental Protection Agency. Air and Radiation (6203J). *Secondhand Smoke: What You Can Do About Secondhand Smoke As Parents, Decisionmakers, and Building Occupants*. Washington, D.C.: July 1993.

(5) Some Carpets
(a) Some Problems

"Carpets: A Health Hazard? *The Daily Mail* 19 Aug. 1992, sec. A:1.

Dominguez, Alex. "Carpet Fumes Fuel Debate at Indoor Air Pollution Conference." *The Daily Mail* 23 Apr. 1993, sec. A:8.

Duehring, Cindy. "Carpet...Part One: EPA Stalls and Industry Hedges While Consumers Remain at Risk." *Informed Consent* Nov./Dec. 1993: 6-11+.

"EPA Finds Bad Air at Own Headquarters." *The Daily Mail* 24 Nov. 1989, sec. A:10.

Gram, David. "Does Health Threat Lurk Underfoot? Family Blames Carpet for Illness." *The Herald-Mail* 20 June 1993, sec. B:6.

Hirzy, J. William, and Rufus Morison. "Carpet/4- Phenylcyclohexene Toxicity: The EPA Headquarters Case." *Advances in Risk Analysis*. Vol. 9: *The Analysis, Communication, and Perception of Risk*. Ed. B. John Garrick and Willard C. Gekler. Society for Risk Analysis. New York: Plenum Press, 1991.

Marcus, Amy Dockser. "In Some Workplaces, Ill Winds Blow. Indoor Pollution Spurs Lawsuits, Taxes Economy." *The Wall Street Journal* 9 Oct. 1989, sec. B:1.

(b) Some Remedies

"Carpet Makers Agree to Use 'Information Labels'." *The Daily Mail* 17 Nov. 1993, sec. A:9.

Duehring, Cindy. "Carpet: Laying It Safe." *The Green Guide for Everyday Life* 19 (7 Jan. 1996): 1-3.

Understanding Carpets, Floors and Allergen Avoidance. Ridgefield, Conn.: Allergy Control Products, Inc., 1993.

(6) Perfumes and Fragrances

Center for Environmental Medicine. N. Charleston, S.C. "Please Read Before Entering Office" notice.

Crockett, Roger O. "Scents Become Workplace Issue. With the Increase in Multiple Chemical Sensitivity, Perfumes May Become the Cigarette Issue of the '90s." *The Oregonian* 18 Feb. 1995, sec. E:1+.

Environmental Health Network. "The Perfume You Are Wearing May Be Harmful to Your Health!" ad.

Grossman, Laurie M. "The Smell of Chanel May Be No. 2 Issue After Cigarettes. Strong Odors of All Sorts Make People Sick or Merely Mad; Now: Aroma-Free Zones." *The Wall Street Journal* 13 May 1993, eastern ed, sec. A:1+.

Kendall, Julia. "How to Use the 'Notice of Noncompliance.'" *The New Reactor* Mar./Apr. 1995: 12.

Landers, Ann. "People Have Sick Sense About Perfumed Goods." *The Plain Dealer* 14 Oct. 1993, sec. D:10.

"New Sense of Smell, The. A Nationwide Survey of Evolving American Attitudes on the Sense of Smell." Advertisement. *The New York Times Magazine* 22 Oct. 1995, sec. 6:20+.

"Notice of Noncompliance Under Title II or Title III of the Americans With Disabilities Act (ADA)" *The New Reactor* Mar./Apr. 1995: 13-16.

Souder, William. "A Fragrant Violation? You Won't Believe the Stink a Little Perfume Caused at this Midwestern School." *The Washington Post* 11 Dec. 1994, sec. F:1.

"There Is Trouble in the Air." ABC TV *20/20*. John Stossel, reporter. 22 Dec. 1995.

(7) Air Fresheners and Deodorizers

"Air Fresheners." *The Home Book: A Guide to Safety, Security & Savings in the Home*. Washington, D.C.: Center for Study of Responsive Law, 1989, p. 98.

Center for Environmental Medicine. N. Charleston, S.C. "Please Read Before Entering Office" notice.

Dadd, Debra Lynn. "Air Fresheners and Odor Removers." In *Nontoxic, Natural & Earthwise: How to Protect Yourself and Your Family From Harmful Products and Live in Harmony With the Earth*. Los Angeles: Jeremy P. Tarcher, Inc., 1990.

Hunter, Linda Mason. "Aerosol Sprays, Air Fresheners, and Disinfectants" in "Hazardous Household Products" in *The Healthy Home: An Attic-to-Basement Guide to Toxin-Free Living*. United States: St. Martin's Press, 1989.

Null, Gary. "Deodorizers." *No More Allergies: Identifying and Eliminating Allergies and Sensitivity Reactions to Everything in Your Environment*. New York: Villard Books, 1992, p. 81.

(8) Solvents—Benzene and Xylene

Varkonyi, Charlyne. "'Big Bad Three' Chemicals Leach Out of Products." *The Herald-Mail* 6 Aug. 1995, sec. E:4.

Greenfield, Ellen J. *House Dangerous: Indoor Pollution in Your Home and Office—and What You Can Do About It!* New York: Interlink Books, 1991, pp. 61, 156, 157.

(9) Wood Stove Smoke

Saul, Steven, and Karin Lazarus. "A Burning Issue: Wood Stoves Pollute and Aggravate Health Problems. So Why the 'Green' Image?" *E Magazine* VI.6 (Nov./Dec. 1995): 48-51.

(10) Carbon Monoxide

Brown, Ann, Chairman, U.S. Consumer Product Safety Commission. "Brochure Details Carbon Monoxide Dangers," *in* "Hints From Heloise." *The Herald-Mail* 27 Feb. 1996, sec. C:2.

"Pa. Man Dies in Garage Accident." (McConnellsburg, Pa.) "A 34-year-old Dublin Township man died of apparent carbon monoxide poisoning while working on a car at his home near Burnt Cabins Monday evening, according to Pennsylvania State Police.

"Police said Bruce Allan Snyder was overcome around 7 p.m. while working on a running car in a closed garage." *The Daily Mail* 6 Feb. 1996, sec. B:1.

United States Environmental Protection Agency. Office of Public Affairs (A-107). *Environmental Backgrounder: Ozone and Carbon Monoxide*. Washington, D.C.: Jan. 1989.

2. Outdoor Air Pollution
a. Some Places
(1) Global

"Air Pollution: Is the Air a Common resource or a Common Sewer?" *The 1992 Information Please Environmental Almanac*. Compiled by World Resources Institute. Ed. in chief Allen Hammond. Boston: Houghton Mifflin Company, 1992:147+.

"Chilean Towns Slowly Die of Toxic Gas and Ashes." *The Daily Mail* 13 July 1989, sec. A:10.

Egan, Timothy. "Dream Gone Sour: Pollution and High Costs." *The New York Times* 29 Dec. 1991, National sec.:20.

"Emissions From Nylon Damage Ozone." *The Herald-Mail* 23 Feb. 1991, sec.A:2

"Le Phew! Pollution Hits Paris." (Paris [AP].) *The Herald- Mail* 13 Aug. 1995, sec. A:7.

Suro, Roberto. "Pollution Tests Two Neighbors: El Paso and Juárez." *The New York Times* 22 Dec. 1991, National sec.:18.

"Third World Cities Dirtiest: Study." *The Daily Mail* 2 Dec. 1992, sec. A:2.

Wald, Matthew L. "Officials Try Many Routes to Goal of Cleaner Air." *The New York Times* 14 Nov. 1993, Metro Report sec.:37+.

Winerip, Michael. "On This Beat, Pollution Is the Enemy." *The New York Times* 11 Oct. 1992, Metro Report sec.:41.

WuDunn, Sheryl. "Chinese Suffer From Rising Pollution as Byproduct of the Industrial Boom." *The New York Times* 28 Feb. 1993, International sec.:20.

(2) National

"Air Flunks Health Tests in 43 Regions." *The Daily Mail* 20 Oct. 1994, sec. A:2.

Brown, Michael H. *The Toxic Cloud: The Poisoning of America's Air.* New York: Harper & Row, 1987.

"Group: 23 Million at Risk From Air." *The Herald-Mail* 30 Apr. 1994, sec. A:2.

"90 Million Americans Still Breathe Dirty Air." (Washington [AP].) *The Daily Mail* 7 Nov. 1995, sec. A:3.

Suro, Roberto. "NASA Aura Dims as City Fights Rocket Test." *The New York Times* 16 Dec. 1990, National sec.:1+.

"Worst Corporate Polluters Listed." *The Daily Mail* 17 Nov. 1994, sec. A:7.

"Yosemite Being Damaged by Urban-Spawned Ozone." *The Daily Mail* 20 Dec. 1990, sec. B:8.

(3) Mexico City

Gorman, Christine. "Mexico City's Menacing Air: The Shutdown of a Refinery Will Only Begin to Curb a Toxic Cloud." *Time* 1 Apr. 1991: 61.

"Growing Concern in Mexico Over Smog's Affect on Children." *The Daily Mail* 10 Oct. 1991, sec. B:4.

Preston, Julia. "Mexico's Political Inversion: The City That Can't Fix the Air. Political Stagnation Helps Perpetuate Mexico City's Air Pollution. During a Pollution Emergency Last Month, Construction Work Continued." *The New York Times* 4 Feb. 1996, sec. E:4.

"Smog Alert Prompts Fan Plan." Mexico City. *The Daily Mail* 20 Feb. 1992, sec. A:6.

Uhlig, Mark A. "Mexico City: the World's Foulest Air Grows Worse." *The New York Times* 12 May 1991, International sec.:1+.

(4) Regional/Local

Cohn, D'Vera. "7-Week Fire Extinguished at North Potomac Dump." *The Washington Post* 13 Dec. 1994, sec. D:1+.

Flinn, John, and Tanya Schevitz Wills. "Residents Say Warning System Is a Failure. Many in Richmond—Including Mayor—Say They Never Heard From County's Emergency Network." *San Francisco Examiner* 27 July 1993, sec. A:1+.

"Fresh Air? National Parks Suffer from an Increase in Pollution Problems." *The Daily Mail* 9 May 1994, sec. A:5.

Heminway, Diane. "The Great Big FMC Corporation and a Schoolyard." *Journal of Pesticide Reform* 9.1 (Spring 1989): 2+.

Kay, Jane, Don Martinez, and Charlotte-Anne Lucas. "Huge Fines for Toxic Wastes: Safety Woes at Chemical Firm. Thousands Flock to Clinics for Treatment After Acid Cloud From Richmond Company Chokes Area." *San Francisco Examiner* 27 July 1993, sec. A:1+.

"Los Angeles Air Kills 1,600 a Year." *The Herald-Mail* 22 Feb. 1992, sec. A:10.

b. Some Pollutants
(1) Pesticides/Spray/Drift

"Campaign to End Pesticide Drift: Neighbors Fight Pesticide Drift." *Pesticide Watch* 6.3 (Winter 1996): 4.

Duehring, Cindy. "Where There Is Spray, There Is Drift." *The Green Guide For Everyday Life* 11(1 June 1995): 1+.

Grier, Norma, with Alexandra Foote. "Beyond Herbicide Wars: Trees, Weeds, and the U.S. Forest Service in the Pacific Northwest." *Journal of Pesticide Reform* 12.2 (Summer 1992): 2-8.

Malakoff, David. "Clouds of Discontent Drift Over Washington State's Horse Heaven Hills. After Seven Years, the Region's Pesticide Drift Problem Is Getting National Attention. *Pesticides and You* 13.3 & 4 (Winter 1993- 1994): 26-30.

Thrupp, Lori Ann. "Exporting Risk Analyses to Developing Countries." *Global Pesticide Campaigner* 4.1 (Mar. 1994): 3-5.

(2) Vehicle Exhaust

Derr, Mark. "Beyond Efficiency: Even If Lighter, Durable, More Efficient Cars Eventually Replace Those Now in Use, a Long-Term Solution to Overcrowded Highways and an Auto-Centered Culture Will Require Imaginative Transportation and Urban-Planning Options. Several Are Already in Place, With More to Come." *The Atlantic Monthly* Jan. 1995:86+.

Lovins, Amory B., and L. Hunter Lovins. "Reinventing the Wheels." *The Atlantic Monthly* Jan. 1995: 75+.

McFadden, Robert D. "Changes Seen in Auto Tests for Pollution: Drivers May Pay More After Waiting Longer." *The New York Times* 8 Nov. 1992, Metro sec.:43+.

"New U.S. Emissions Test, Debuting in Maine, Is a Flop." *The New York Times* 2 Oct. 1994, National sec.:28.

Sager, Steven T., Mayor of Hagerstown, Maryland. Memorandum to Bruce E. Johnston, City Engineer. 21 Aug. 1991.

Salpukas, Agis. "Unique Joint Effort Is Seeking to Reduce Sulfur in Diesel Fuel." *The New York Times* 26 Sept. 1993, National sec.:1+.

Sikorsky, Bob. "Drive It Forever: Car Exhaust Ingredient of Planet Degradation." *The Herald-Mail* 27 Jan. 1991, sec. C:1.

Steinberg, Jacques. "Albany Pressured to Draw Plans to Reduce Pollution: Federal Transportation Funds in Jeopardy." *The New York Times* 13 June 1993, Metro sec.:41.

"Study Finds Covered Pickup Trucks Can Expose Kids to Deadly Fumes." *The Daily Mail* 22 Jan. 1992, sec. A:6.

United States EPA. Air and Radiation. *Your Car or Truck and the Environment.* Washington, D.C.: Sept. 1993.

_____. Office of Public Affairs (A-107). *Environmental Backgrounder: Ozone and Carbon Monoxide.* Washington, D.C.: Jan. 1989.

(3) Lawn Mower Exhaust

Johnson, Marguerite. "The Backyard Besieged: Environmentalists and Regulators Want to Stifle That Suburban Icon, the Noisy, Air-Fouling Lawn Mower." *Time* 4 July 1994: 62.

Swanson, Stevenson. "A Cut Below the Rest: Mower Emissions Eat Up the Ozone." *The Herald-Mail* 8 Aug. 1993, sec. A:1+.

(4) Incinerators

"Fight Over Incinerator at a Crossroad." (East Liverpool, Ohio [AP].) *The Herald-Mail* 24 Oct. 1992, sec. B:6.

Schneider, Keith. "Ohio Orders New Public Review of Hazardous-Waste Incinerator." *The New York Times* 4 July 1993, National sec.:1.

_____. "Unfazed, a Utah Town Prepares to Burn a Toxic Piece of the Past." (Toole, Utah.) *The New York Times* 23 Oct. 1994, National sec.:33.

_____. "Another Army Report Criticizes Work at Nerve Gas Incinerator." (Toole, Utah.) *The New York Times* 4 Dec. 1994, National sec.:29.

Smolowe, Jill. "Chemical Time Bombs. The Race Is On to Destroy Weapons Filled With Deadly Toxins—Before They Destroy Us." *Time* 12 Feb. 1996: 42.

Swearingen, Terri. "Environmental Activist." *Time* 5 Dec. 1994: 64.

United States General Accounting Office. *Report to Congressional Requesters: Hazardous Waste—Issues Pertaining to an Incinerator in East Liverpool, Ohio.* Washington, D.C.: Sept. 1994.

(5) Stack Gas/Smoke

Wouk, Herman. *The Caine Mutiny: A Novel of World War II.* Garden City, N.Y.: Doubleday & Company, Inc., 1952. pp. 251+.

(6) Landfill Air

"Goo Surfaces in Refinery Town; Attention Turns to Old Oil Pit."
    (Baytown, Tex., Sept. 9 [AP].) *The New York Times* 10 Sept. 1995,
    National sec.:39.

Schneider, Michael. "Landfill Air Pollution 'Dangerous.'" (Baltimore
    [AP].) *The Daily Mail* 14 Apr. 1995, sec. A:6.

(7) Chlorofluorocarbons (CFC's)

Stevens, William K. "Keeping the Ozone Whole." *The New York Times*
    15 Oct. 1995, sec. E:4.

(8) Wood Stove Smoke

Saul, Steven, and Karin Lazarus. "A Burning Issue: Wood Stoves
    Pollute and Aggravate Health Problems. So Why the 'Green'
    Image?" *E Magazine* VI.6 (Nov./Dec. 1995): 48- 51.

c. Some Remedies

Beach, Charles, et al. *Recommendations for a Revised Federal Pest
    Management Regulatory System.* Final report of the Pesticide
    Registration Review Team. Canada: Minister of Supply and
    Services, 1990.

Comfo Elite™ *Respirators.* MSA. P.O. Box 426, Pittsburgh, PA 15230
    USA. In U.S. call nearest stocking location toll free at 1-800-
    MSA-2222. To reach MSA International, call (412) 967-3249 or
    Telex 812453.

Cushman, John H., Jr. "White House Considers Toughening Its Anti-
    Emissions Program." *The New York Times* 24 Sept. 1995, National
    sec.:31.

Holusha, John. "Hutchinson No Longer Holds Its Nose. At 3M,
    Cleaning Up Pollution Has Become the Corporate Ethic. It's
    Paying Off." *The New York Times* 3 Feb. 1991, sec. 3:1+.

Kennedy, Robert F., Jr. "Editorial: Freedom to Breathe." *The Herald-
    Mail* 4 Feb. 1996, sec. E:2.

"Scientific Sleuths Hope to Track Pollutants to Their Sources." (Boston,
    Feb. 3 [AP].) *The New York Times* 4 Feb. 1996, sec. 1:18.

Stevens, William K. "100 Nations Move to Save Ozone Shield." *The New York Times* 10 Dec. 1995, sec. 1:20.

United States EPA. Air and Radiation. *What You Can Do to Reduce Air Pollution.* Washington: Oct. 1992.

————. *Recognition and Management of Pesticide Poisonings.* 4th ed. Donald P. Morgan, M.D., Ph.D. Washington: Mar. 1989.

B. Water Pollution
1. Oceans

Broad, William J. "A—Waste Dangers Described as Low. Scientists' Group Says Ocean Dumping Seems to Pose Only Local Threats." *The New York Times* 13 June 1993, International sec. 1:6.

Easton, Robert. *Black Tide: The Santa Barbara Oil Spill and Its Consequences.*New York: Delacorte Press, 1972.

NOAA. *Our Water Planet Is Becoming Polluted with Plastic Debris...*Newport, Oregon: National Marine Fisheries Service Marine Refuse Disposal Project. Marine Debris Information Offices: Atlantic Coast and Gulf of Mexico Office—1725 DeSales Street, NW, #500, Washington, DC 20036.

Pitt, David E. "Pentagon Fights Wider Ocean-Dumping Ban." *The New York Times* 26 Sept. 1993, International sec.:8.

"Rape of the Oceans: America's Last Frontier Is Seriously Overfished, Badly Polluted, Poorly Managed and in Deepening Trouble, The." *U.S. New & World Report* 22 June 1992: 64+.

"Report Says Oceans Fished to Limit." *The Herald-Mail* 24 July 1994, sec. A:4.

Specter, Michael. "A Damage Report: The World's Oceans Are Sending an S.O.S.—Early Warning Signs Around the Globe." *The New York Times* 3 May 1992, sec. E:5.

2. Seas

Simons, Marlise. "The Black Sea Under Attack by Pollution." *The New York Times* 24 Nov. 1991, International sec.:1+.

————. "Dead Mediterranean Dolphins Give Nations Pause." *The New York Times* 2 Feb. 1992, International sec. 1:12.

3. Bays and Gulfs

Carvajal, Doreen. "Old-Style Drudgery in a Modern Cleanup: Workers Use Scoops and Scrapers to Get the Lead Out of Oyster Bay." *The New York Times* 3 Sept. 1995, Metro Report sec.:29+.

Cohn, Meredith. "Bay Watch: DNR Meeting Here to Discuss Tributaries' Impact on Chesapeake." *The Daily Mail* 19 Apr. 1993, sec. B:1.

"Former Gunboat Takes Aim at Bay Pollution." (Baltimore [AP].) *The Daily Mail* 24 Aug. 1995, sec. A:6.

Lacayo, Richard. "Environment. A War Against the Earth. Torching Oil Wells and Disgorging Crude into the Gulf, Saddam Makes the Planet His Latest Victim." *Time* 4 Feb. 1991: 32.

Wheeler, Timothy B. "Coastal Bays in Md., Del. Endangered. Expansion, Farming Pollute Waters Along Beaches, Study Shows. Growth Control Sought. Conference Considers Protection, Restoration Techniques for Shores." (Ocean City.) *The Sun* 10 Mar 1996, sec. B:1+.

4. Rivers, Creeks and Streams

"Chemical Leak Kills Off Fish." *The Daily Mail* 1 Sept. 1994, sec. A:8.

"Contaminated Sites Reported." *The Daily Mail* 8 Apr. 1992, sec. A:2.

"Diverted, Danube Fades, and the Rage Rises." *The New York Times* 8 Nov. 1992, International sec.:14.

"Endangered Rivers Announced." *The Daily Mail* 8 Apr. 1992, sec. A:7.

"Environmentalists Focus on Maryland's Streams." *The Daily Mail* 5 Nov. 1992, sec. A:7.

Exodus 7:15-28. *The Twenty-Four Books of the Old Testament*. New York: Hebrew Publishing Company, 1917.

Ford, Clyde. "Md. Officials Can't Explain Why Stream Ran Blood Red." *The Daily Mail* 19 May 1992, sec. B:2.

"Fuel Spill Reaches Potomac: D.C. Water Supplies Threatened by Spill." *The Daily Mail* 29 Mar. 1993, sec. A:1.

"Huge Cyanide Spill Poisons Area. (Omai, Guyana.) *The Daily Mail* 25 Aug. 1995, sec. A:3.

"Northwest Salmon Disappearing." *The Daily Mail* 8 Apr. 1992, sec. A:10.

Riechmann, Deb. "Potomac River Pollution: Study Finds Pesticides, Metals and Chemicals." *The Daily Mail* 10 June 1993, sec. B:8.

Rowland, Tim. "Pesticide Traces Found in Creek, Soil." *The Daily Mail* 24 Sept. 1992, sec. A:1+.

Rutledge, Archibald. "The Birthright and the Pottage." Fireworks in the Peafield Corner." Ed. Judge Irvine H. Rutledge. Clinton, New Jersey: The Amwell Press, 1986.

Simons, Marlise. "The Meuse, With Its Waters Growing More Polluted, Keeps Rolling Along." *The New York Times* 8 Dec. 1991, International sec.:18.

Suro, Roberto. "Border Boom's Dirty Residue Imperils U.S.- Mexico Trade." *The New York Times* 31 Mar. 1991, National sec.:1+.

"Toxin Killing Fish in River." *The Herald-Mail* 13 June 1993, sec. C:2.

5. Lakes

Erlanger, Steven. "U.S. Aid for Huge Russian Lake Is in Jeopardy." *The New York Times* 3 Sept. 1995, International sec.:3.

"Great Lakes Fish Said Risky." *The Daily Mail* 8 Apr. 1992, sec. A:2.

Mydans, Seth. "Questions Linger as Spill Sits in a California Lake." *The New York Times* 21 July 1991, National sec.:14.

6. Wetlands

Elmer-Dewitt, Philip. "Environment: Facing a Deadline to Save the Everglades. The Fate of Florida's Famous Wetlands Could Be Decided This Week." *Time* 21 June 1993: 56-57.

"Wetlands May Be Drained: Plan Negates Protection Rule." *The Herald Mail* 23 May 1993, sec. A:2.

7. Groundwater

Ansel, Shauna. "Central Chemical." *Washington County Network* Nov. - Dec. 1992: 2.

Jaffe, Susan, Special Assistant, et al. *Toxic Fairways: Risking Groundwater Contamination From Pesticides on Long Island Golf Courses*. New York: New York State Environment Protection Bureau, Robert Abrams, Attorney General, July 1991.

Magette, William L. "Ground Water Protection: An Introduction." *Water Resources*. College Park, Maryland: Cooperative Extension Service, The University of Maryland, 1987-1988.

Mosher, Jim. "Washington County Groundwater Study: A Ten Year Comparison. *Washington County Network* July - Aug. 1992: 5.

Riechmann, Deb. "Soil, Water to Be Tested at Central." *The Daily Mail* 27 Apr. 1993, sec. A:1.

8. Wells

"Bacteria in Jefferson Co. Water Above EPA Standard." *The Herald-Mail* 29 Aug. 1992, sec. B:2.

"Detrick Forum to Cover Well Contamination." *The Daily Mail* 28 Oct. 1993, sec. A:11.

Dorsey, George. "Trans-Tech Polluted Wells in Adamstown, Jury Rules." *The Frederick Post* 9 Apr. 1991, sec. A:1+.

"Nitrate Contamination From Farms Poses Well Water Health Risk: Study. (Washington [AP].) *The Daily Mail* 31 Aug. 1995, sec. A:10.

"Toxins Found in Wells That Supply Harford Residents With Water." *The Daily Mail* 21 May 1992, sec. B:4.

9. Tap Drinking Water

Berkson, Jacob B. Letter to Hagerstown Water Department. 22 Aug. 1991.

Easterbrook, Gregg. "Toxic Business: The Story of a Polluted Water Supply, an Outbreak of Leukemia and a Lawsuit That Dragged on and on." *The New York Times Book Review* 10 Sept. 1995, sec. 7:13.

Lee, Gary. "Public Seen as Uninformed About Tap Water Problems. Study: Contamination May Kill 900 Each Year." *The Washington Post* 27 Sept. 1993.

Lemonick, Michael D. "Environment: Toxins on Tap." *Time* 15 Nov. 1993: 85-87.

Milwaukee's Water Supply Contaminated by Parasite. City Officials Suspect Widespread Illness Caused by Livestock Runoff; Residents Learn to Cope." (AP.) *The Herald-Mail* 10 Apr. 1993, sec. A:3.

Nye, Peter. "Clean Drinking Water Becomes a National Problem." *Public Citizen* July/Aug. 1993: 10-13.

Parrish, William F., Jr., Program Administrator, Water Supply Program, State of Maryland Department of the Environment. Letter to Hagerstown Water Department. 7 Jan. 1991.

Reed, Dan. "Oakley Subdivision's Weird Water: Contra Costa Area's Residents Say It Gives Them Stomach Problems. *San Francisco Chronicle* sec. A:12.

Reidinger, Paul. "Don't Drink the Water: Mixed Results on Environment." *ABA Journal* Mar. 1990: 98+.

"Tap Water" in "Making News." *The Green Guide for Everyday Life* 14 (1 Sept. 1995): 1.

Terry, Sara. "Drinking Water Comes to a Boil." *The New York Times Magazine* 26 Sept. 1993: 42+.

United States EPA. Office of Water (WH-550). *Home Water Treatment Units. Filtering Fact from Fiction.* EPA570/9- 90-HHH. Washington, D.C.: Sept. 1990.

Wald, Matthew L. "Don't Worry But Be Wary: A Fine Line in Water Scare. Yes, You Should Boil Your Water Before Drinking. No, You Are Not in Danger. Get the Message?" *The New York Times* 1 Aug. 1993, Metro sec.:39.

10. Rainwater

"Herbicides Found in Maryland Rainwater." *The Daily Mail* 24 Apr. 1991, sec. B:5.

"Herbicides Rain Across the Nation." *Pesticides and You* Dec. 1991: 3.

11. Bottled Water

"Bottling Nature's Beverage." (Letter to the Editor.) *Time* 17 May 1993: 12.

McCarroll, Thomas. "Testing the Waters. As States and the FDA Crack Down, Bottlers of 'Nature's Beverages' Are Awash in Controversy." *Time* 26 Apr. 1993: 54.

United States EPA. *Bottled Water Fact Sheet.* EPA 570/F-91- 053. Washington, D.C.: Mar. 1991.

12. Wastewater

Banik, Sharmi. "State Explains Plant OK: Sandy Hook System Experimental Method." *The Daily Mail* 25 Aug. 1994, home ed, sec. A:1+.

————. "Sandy Hook Waste Water Raises Alarm. Delegate Wants Environmental Experts to Determine Soon Whether It's Safe." *The Daily Mail* 26 Aug 1994, home ed, sec. A:1+.

United States Environmental Protection Agency. Office of Public Affairs (A-107). *Environmental Backgrounder: Sewage Treatment Improvements.* Washington, D.C.: Oct. 1988.

13. Harbors and Beaches

Fried, Joseph P. "Closed Beach Tied to Man on Barge. Authorities Say Crew Member Takes Pain-Killer for Back." *The New York Times* 19 Jan. 1992, Metro sec.:31.

"Report: Local Pockets of Pollution Persist. High Contamination Levels Found in Baltimore Harbor." *The Daily Mail* 30 Jan. 1991, sec. C:4.

United States EPA. National Oceanic and Atmospheric Administration. Army Corps of Engineers. U.S. Coast Guard. Department of the Interior. *Enforcement for Coastal Protection: Closed Beaches...Polluted Waters...Unsafe Seafood...Destroyed Habitats.* Washington, D.C.: Oct. 1991.

————. Office of Public Affairs (A-107). *Environmental Backgrounder: Medical Waste.* Washington, D.C.: Mar. 1989.

14. Polluters

Bishop, Katherine. "Spill's Poisonous Legacy in a Once- Pristine Town." *The New York Times* 29 Dec. 1991, National sec.:12.

Chivers, Chris. "Currents: Troubled Waters. Despite a Wakeup Call Named *Exxon Valdez*, Oil Tankers Continue to Foul the World's Waterways." *E Magazine* VII.3 (May/June 1996): 14-15.

Mason, Jim. "Fowling the Waters." *E Magazine* VI.5 (Oct. 1995): 33.

"Polluters Say They're Cleaning Up Their Act." *The Daily Mail* 22 June 1993, sec. A:1+.

Possehl, Suzzanne René. "Keeper of the Green. Just as His Father Went After Organized Crime, Robert Kennedy Jr. Is Waging War on Polluters...and Winning." *ABA Journal* Jan. 1996: 56+.

Young, Rick, and Dan Noyes. "The Road to Summitville, a Gold Mining Debacle: How Promises of Riches Turned Into an Environmental Disaster. *The New York Times* 14 Aug. 1994, sec. F:5.

15. Criteria & Programs

Campaign for the Chesapeake Rivers: The Nature Conservancy of Maryland Accepts a Bold, New Challenge—A Special Report from Maryland Magazine. n.d.

Cushman, John H., Jr. "Clinton backing Vast Effort to Restore Florida Swamps." *The New York Times* 18 Feb. 1996, sec. 1:1+.

Nature Conservancy of Maryland, The. *Campaign for the Chesapeake Rivers: Preserving Maryland's Natural Heritage.* 2 Wisconsin Circle, Suite 600, Chevy Chase, Maryland 20815-7065. Phone: 301-656-8673. International Headquarters: Arlington, Virginia. Phone: 703-841-5300. Brochure Dec. 1993.

Revkin, Andrew C. "In Unusual Partnership, Farmers Help Safeguard New York Water." *The New York Times* 13 Aug. 1995, sec. 1:1+.

United States EPA. Office of Water. *Developing Criteria to Protect Our Nation's Waters.* Washington: Sept. 1990.

_____. Office of Wetlands, Oceans, and Watersheds. *National Estuary Program: Bringing Our Estuaries New Life.* EPA 842-F-93-002. Washington.

C. Soil Pollution
1. Agricultural Pesticides and Sprays

Carson, Rachel. *Silent Spring.* 25th anniv. ed. Boston: Houghton Mifflin Company, 1962, 1987.

Davis, Mark. "Deadly Insecticide Injures Farmworkers." *The Tampa Tribune* 16 Nov. 1989, sec. A:1+.

"Excess Cancers Among Farmers." *NYCAP News* Early Spring 1993: 5.

Gips, Terry. "'SOS' for Agriculture and Society." *Manna* Winter 1991/1992: 2.

Levesque, William R. "Benlate: Phantom on the Farm. A Special Report. 'A Tragic Mess': The Story of the Fungicide Benlate Is a Tale Without Equal in Modern Agriculture, Leaving Florida Farmers With Little to Do Other Than Watch As Their Crops Wither and Die." Lakeland, Florida *The Ledger* 15-19 Nov. 1992. Copies of this reprint are available at *The Ledger*'s main office, 401 S. Missouri Ave., Lakeland, Fla. 33801. Phone: (813) 687-7062.

Pierce, Emmet. "Action by Residents Pays Off in Pesticide Curbs." *The San Diego Union-Tribune* 21 Feb. 1994.

Rowland, Tim. "Limits Sought on Sludge Dumping on Farmland." *The Daily Mail* 26 Feb. 1993, sec. B:3.

Schwartz, Don. "Pesticides Safe, If Used Wisely." *The Herald-Mail* 23 May 1995, sec. A:7.

Toufexis, Anastasia. "Coming a Cropper: DuPont Faces Charges It Sold a Tainted Pesticide." *Time* 9 Aug. 1993: 51.

2. Toxic Sites, Dumps, Cleanup

Ansel, Shauna. "Central Chemical." *Washington County Network* Nov. - Dec. 1992: 2.

Belisle, Richard F. "Property Owners File $6 Million Lawsuit. Plaintiffs Complain About Leak From Berkeley County Landfill." *The Daily Mail* 17 Oct. 1990, sec. B:1.

Berger, Joseph. "A Long Battle Against Lead Contaminants: Complex Standards Slow Revere Cleanup." (Wallkill, N.Y.) *The New York Times* 27 Nov. 1994, Metro sec.:58.

Callen, Bill. "From CSX Property: EPA Regulation Change Could Complicate Creosote Removal." *The Herald-Mail* 26 July 1992, sec. F:1+

Cohen, Sharon. "'It'll Never Be Over': Dioxin Cleanup Ready to Begin After 10 Years." *The Herald-Mail* 14 Apr. 1991, sec. C:6

"Environmental Death in Eastern Germany: Ecological Cleanup Moves Slowly in Bitterfeld." *The Daily Mail* 20 May 1992, sec. A:8.

Epstein, Samuel S., M.D., Lester O. Brown, and Carl Pope. *Hazardous Waste in America: From Source to Solution—the First Comprehensive Study of Our Number One Environmental Crisis.* San Francisco: Sierra Club Books, 1982.

"Hazardous Waste." *Our Toxic Times* 93 4(8):4.

Hernandez, Raymond. "Underneath Cul-de-Sacs, Sludge Pits." *The New York Times* 9 July 1995, Metro sec.: 25+.

"Indiana Town Left with 16 Million-Gallon Petroleum Leak." *The Daily Mail* 15 Apr. 1991, sec. A:10.

"Irradiated Sand Imperils Pennsylvania Houses." *The New York Times* 15 Dec. 1991, National sec.:39.

"Lead Contamination Closes 2 Ballfields." *The New York Times* 13 June 1993, Metro sec.:43.

Lester, Stephen U. "Questionable Research: The Centers for Disease Control Approach in Studying Areas Where Dioxins and Other Chemicals Have Been Used Leads Many to Question the Agenda of the Agency." *American Legion Magazine* July 1991: 30+.

McMillion, Dave. "Methane Seeping From Dump." *The Morning Herald* 20 Apr. 1992, sec. B:1.

Revkin, Andrew C. "Love Canal Cleanup Settled for $129 Million. A Polluter Agrees to Help Pay the Bill to Clean an Infamous Chemical Dump." *The New York Times* 24 Dec. 1995, Metro sec.:24.

Riechmann, Deb. Detrick Cleanup Costly: Price Tag for Toxic Removal at Least $3 Million." *The Daily Mail* 29 Apr. 1993, sec. B:5.

————. "EPA Expects to Play Role in Site Cleanup. Tests Pending on Possible Runoff at Central Chemical." *The Daily Mail* 24 Feb. 1995, sec. A:1+.

"Town Fights EPA Lead Cleanup." *The Daily Mail* 14 Apr. 1993, sec. C:5.

"Toxic Site Cleanup Reported Lagging: Only 34 of the Worst Facilities Are Dealt With in 8 Years, Rand Study Concludes." *The New York Times* 10 Sept. 1989:32.

United States Environmental Protection Agency. Office of Public Affairs (A-107.) *Environmental Backgrounder: Hazardous Chemicals: Emergency Planning and Community Right-to-Know.* Washington, D.C.: Oct. 1988.

Van Voorst, Bruce. "Toxic Dumps: The Lawyers' Money Pit. Superfund Was Meant to Clean Up the Worst Hazards. It Hasn't. But Lawsuits Have Gobbled Billions of Dollars." *Time* 13 Sept. 1993: 63-64.

3. Lawn Care Pesticides
a. Problems

Alvarado, Emilia. "Lawn Products With Chlordane Sold at Auction. Area Residents Who Bought Banned Chemical Alerted." *The Daily Mail* 15 July 1988, sec. B.

American Defender Network Presents Questions and Answers About Lawn Chemical Dangers. Lake Zurich, IL: The American Defender Network, Mar. 1989.

Belisle, Richard F. "Safer Lawn Care Takes Root. Following Directions for Pesticide Application and Keeping Spraying to a Minimum Help Reduce Dangers to Humans and Animals, Say Experts." *The Herald-Mail* 17 Mar. 1996, sec. C:1+.

Blodgett, Nancy. "Lawn Care Firms: Let Us Spray. But Suits Allege Misleading Ads, Unsafe Pesticides." *ABA Journal* 1 Sept. 1988: 20-21.

Briggs, Shirley A. and Nathan Erwin. *Pesticides and Lawns.* Chevy Chase, MD: Rachel Carson Council, Inc., 1991.

Clarke, C. H. D., Dr. *Pesticides and the Naturalist.* Chevy Chase, MD: Rachel Carson Council, Inc., 1963.

Kyriakos, Marianne. "The Greening of America's Lawns." *The Washington Post* 3 Sept. 1994, sec. E:1+.

"People Hoping to Return to Homes." *The Daily Mail* 10 May 1991, sec. A:6.

Reuter. "Lawn-Care Chemical Tied to Cancer. Dog Study May Show Humans Are at Risk." *Washington Post* 4 Sept. 1991.

Sherman, Janette, M.D. "Pesticide and Lawn Chemicals." *Chemical Exposure and Disease: Diagnostic and Investigative Techniques.* New York: Van Nostrand Reinhold, 1988.

Skow, John. "Can Lawns Be Justified? Awash in Fertilizers and Pesticides, They May Be a Hazard to Howeowners—and Children, Pets and Neighbors." *Time* 3 June 1991: 63-64.

Tronet, Lorens. "Housecalls to Main Street: Doctoring the Nation's Lawns With Chemicals." *Not Man Apart* May/June 1986. In *The Home Book* (Washington, D.C.: Center for Study of Responsive Law): 151-152.

United States General Accounting Office. Report to the Chairman, Subcommittee on Toxic Substances, Research and Development, Committee on Environment and Public Works, U.S. Senate. *Lawn Care Pesticides: Reregistration Falls Further Behind and Exposure Effects Are Uncertain.* Washington: Apr. 1993.

"Victims Urge Control on Lawn Chemicals." *The Daily Mail* 10 May 1991, sec. A:6.

b. Alternatives

Bean, George A., Dr. *Healthy Lawns Without Toxic Chemicals.* Chevy Chase, MD: Rachel Carson Council, Inc., 1971.

"4 Steps to a Non-Toxic Lawn. You Can Have a Beautiful, Healthy Lawn Without Harmful Pesticides." Lakewood, Ohio Environmental Task Force.

Husain, Taher, et al. *Alternative Pest Controls for Lawns and Gardens.* Chevy Chase, Maryland: Rachel Carson Council, Inc., 1994.

Schultz, Warren. *The Chemical Free Lawn.* Emmaus, Pennsylvania: Rodale Press, 1989.

D. Food Pollution
1. Some Problems

"Agency: Better Guard Needed Against Bad Chemicals in Food. Four Million Bushels of Contaminated Oats Had Been Turned Into Cheerios, Frankenberry, Kix and Other Cereals. After the Discovery, All Were Thrown Out." *The Daily Mail* 29 Sept. 1994, sec. A:5.

Berkson, Jim. Affidavit for United States of America, et al., v. State of Oregon, et al. U.S. District Court for the District of Oregon Civil No. 68-513 MA (1994).

"Chemical-Food Hauls Worry Food Processors." *The Daily Mail* 6 Oct. 1989, sec. C:18.

Colborn, Theo, Ph.D. "Tainted Water, Tainted Fish: Stewardship of the Great Lakes Basin." Hearing before the Senate Governmental Affairs Committee, 7 Apr. 1992.

Darnton, John. "The Logic of the 'Mad Cow' Scare." (London.) *The New York Times* 31 Mar. 1996, sec. 4:1+.

"Don't Eat the Fish: 46 Waterways Listed." *The Daily Mail* 20 Nov. 1992, sec. A:10.

Doyle, Jim. "Court Ruling Could Ban Many Pesticides in Food." *San Francisco Chronicle* 9 July 1992, sec. A:1+.

Egan, Timothy. "Bracing for Worst in West Coast Salmon Country." *The New York Times* 5 Apr. 1992, National sec.:18.

_____. "Salmon Fishing Greatly Limited But Not Banned. Fishery Officials Impose Smallest Harvest Ever." *The New York Times* 12 Apr. 1992, National sec. 1:26.

"E.P.A. to Ignore Small Risks in Banning Pesticides." *The New York Times* 17 Feb. 1991, National sec.:29.

"Exporting Banned and Hazardous Pesticides: A Preliminary Review." *FASE Reports*, vol. 9, no. 1, Winter/Spring 1991: 1+.

"Genetically Engineered Foods? Not in *Their* Kitchens!" *The New York Times* 30 July 1992.

Gorman, Christine. "Environment: Getting Practical About Pesticides. Clinton's Eco-Team Grapples With an Inflexible 35-Year-Old Law That Bans Carcinogens in Food." *Time* 15 Feb. 1993: 52.

"Great Lakes Fish Said Risky." *The Daily Mail* 8 Apr. 1992, sec. A:2.

Henneberger, Melinda. "The Last Catch on the Hudson: Sturgeon Limits Upset Fishermen." *The New York Times* 20 June 1993, Metro sec.:34.

Horton, Tom. "The Last Skipjack: After a Century of Overfishing, Mismanagement, Pollution and Disease, the Chesapeake Bay Oyster Is Fast Becoming an Endangered Species." *The New York Times Magazine* 13 June, 1993: 33-36+.

Howe, Marvine. "Moynihan Falls Ill After He Eats Fish During Flight Home." *The New York Times* 19 Jan. 1992, sec. 1:26.

Johnson, Bradley. "Biotech-Created Tomatoes Ripe for Controversy: Marketers Brace for Activists' Knife." *Advertising Age* 19 Oct. 1992.

Krimsky, Sheldon. "Tomatoes May Be Dangerous to Your Health." *The New York Times* 1 June 1992, sec. D:3.

Lehrman, Sally. "Biotech Tomato Bruised: Campbell Soup Backing Away from Calgene's Genetically Engineered Food." *San Francisco Examiner* 10 Jan. 1993.

Lewis, Franca. "General Mills Offers Refunds for Cereals." *The Daily Mail* 31 Mar. 1995, sec. B:1.

MacVean, Mary. "Health food Regulation Is Hot Topic." *The Daily Mail* 8 June 1993, sec. B:8.

Meyerhoff, Al. "No More Pesticides for Dinner." *The New York Times* 9 Mar. 1993, sec. A:19.

Nazario, Sonia. "EPA Under Fire for Pesticide Standards. Agency Is Slow to Revise Rules, Critics Charge. *The Wall Street Journal* 17 Feb. 1989, sec. B:1.

"New Jersey Turkey Franks Recalled." *The Herald-Mail* 7 Nov. 1992, sec.A:2.

"Northwest Salmon Disappearing." *The Daily Mail* 8 Apr. 1992, sec. A:10.

"Report Says Chesapeake Bay Oysters Near Extinction." *The Daily Mail* 26 July 1990, sec. B:6.

Riley, Becky. "General Mills Dumps Contaminated Cereals." *Journal of Pesticide Reform* 14.3 (Fall 1994): 10.

Safety of Your Food Is Under Attack: Do You Want Cancer Causing Pesticides in Your Food? If You Do Not Make Your Voice Heard Now, You Will Have No Choice!, The. Washington, D.C.: National Coalition Against the Misuse of Pesticides, Feb. 1993.

Schneider, Keith. "E.P.A. Plans to Ask Congress to Relax Rule on Pesticides. Chief Calls Law Outdated. She Says New Data Undermine Law Banning Carcinogenic Chemicals in Foods." *The New York Times* 2 Feb. 1993, National ed, sec. A:1+.

_____. "A Trace of Pesticide, an Accepted Risk." *The New York Times* 7 Feb. 1993, sec. E:6.

Seabrook, John. "Tremors in the Hothouse: The Battle Lines Are Being Drawn for the Soul of the American Consumer as Agribusiness Launches the First Genetically Altered Supermarket Tomato." *The New Yorker* 19 July 1993: 32-41.

Shabecoff, Philip. "House Backs Bill Speeding Removal of Some Pesticides: Health Threat Is Feared. Measure Sets 9-Year Deadline for Testing Chemicals and Reduces E.P.A. Costs." *The New York Times* 21 Sept. 1988, Late ed. sec. A:1+.

"Some Md. Crab-Processing Plants Don't Check Meat for Bacteria Contamination." *The Daily Mail* 2 Nov. 1992, sec. C:3.

"This Cupcake Can Kill. Severe Allergic Reactions From 'Hidden' Food Additives May Be Rising." *Time* 17 Aug. 1992: 18.

"*Untested, Unlabeled,* Genetically Engineered Hormones Are in Your Milk, Dairy Products, and Beef!" *Consumer Alert.* Washington, D.C.: Pure Food Campaign. 1130 17th Street, NW, Suite 630, Washington, D.C. 20036. Phone: (202) 775-1132.

"USDA: Pesticide Traces Found in 97% of Apples." (Washington [AP].) *The Daily Mail* 29 Aug. 1995, sec. A:3.

Watanabe, Anne and Scott Welch. "Toxic Pollution: Environmental Estrogens—the New Gender Catalyst." *Wana Chinook Tymoo.* 2-3 (1994). Columbia River Inter-Tribal Fish Commission. 729 N.E. Oregon, Portland, Oregon 97232.

"What's for Dinner?" *The New Yorker* 19 July 1993: 4+.

2. Some Remedies

Berthold-Bond, Annie. "Let's Talk Turkey." *The Green Guide for Everyday Life* 17 (7 Nov. 1995): 1+.

Burros, Marian. "U.S. Is Taking Aim at Farm Chemicals in the Food Supply. Emphasis is on Children. Policies of Three Agencies and a New Study Signal a Shift in Government's Stance." *The New York Times* 27 June 1993, National sec.:1+.

Coleman, Eliot. *The New Organic Grower: A Master's Manual of Tools and Techniques for the Home and Market Gardener.* Chelsea, Vermont: Chelsea Green, 1989.

"Court Bans Pesticides in Processed Foods." *The Daily Mail* 9 July 1992, sec. A:1+.

"EPA Rescinds Grape-Pesticide Approval." *The Arizona Daily Star* 17 Jan. 1993.

Feldman, Jay, and Samuel S. Epstein, M.D. "Get the Cancerous Pesticides Out of Our Food." *The New York Times* 19 Feb. 1993, Editorials/Letters sec.

Fresh Fields Good for You Foods: A Guide to a Whole New World of Food. ADVT.

Gordon, Wendy. "Healthy Farms, Food and Families By Choice, Not Chance. Special Report." *The Green Guide for Everyday Life* (A Publication of Mothers & Others) 13 (14 July 1995): 1+.

Healthway Natural Foods, 4113 John Marr Drive, Annandale, Va. Phone: 703-354-7782.

Interior Design Nutritionals. Automatic Delivery Program, 75 West Center, Provo, Utah 84601-4483.

Jaffe, Russell M., M.D., Ph.D., Director. *Food Combining for Better Digestion.* A service of Serammune Physicians Lab, 1890 Preston White Dr. (AMSA Building, 2nd Floor), Reston, Va. 22091. Phone: (800) 553-5472

"Keep Cancer-Causing Pesticides Out of Food! Add Your Voice Calling for Cancer Prevention." *Pesticide Action Alert.* Eugene, Oregon: Northwest Coalition for Alternatives to Pesticides, Aug. 1993.

Lee, Gary. "Administration Urges Overhaul of Food Safety Laws." *The Washington Post* 22 Sept. 1993, sec. A:1+.

Liebman, Bonnie, M.S., and Jayne Hurley, R.D. *Nutrition Action's Eating Smart Shopping guide. A Factbook of Practical Suggestions on Nutrition and Food From the Pages of Nutrition Action Healthletter.* Washington, D.C.: *Nutrition Action Healthletter*/Center for Science in the Public Interest, 1995.

McDowell, Jeanne. "A Race to Rescue the Salmon. Farmers, Fishermen and Others in the Northwest Will Have to Change Their Ways Under a Federal Plan Being Designed to Save the Region's Cherished Fish." *Time* 2 Mar. 1992: 59-60.

Null, Gary. *Clearer, Cleaner, Safer, Greener: A Blueprint for Detoxifying Your Environment.* New York: Villard Books, 1990.

_____. *Nutrition and the Mind.* New York: Four Walls Eight Windows, 1995.

"Organic Farmer Followed Her Dream to West Virginia." *The Herald-Mail* 11 Jan. 1994, sec. B:6.

Schechter, Steven R., N.D. *Fighting Radiation & Chemical Pollutants With Foods, Herbs, & Vitamins: Documented Natural Remedies That Boost Your Immunity & Detoxify.* Encinitas, California: Vitality, Ink, 1991.

Steinman, David. *Diet for a Poisoned Planet: How to Choose Safe Foods for You and Your Family.* New York: Harmony Books, 1990.

_____ and Samuel S. Epstein, M.D. *The Safe Shopper's Bible: A Consumer's Guide to Nontoxic Household Products, Cosmetics, and Food.* Macmillan USA, 1995.

"Supreme Court Upholds Ban on Cancer-Causing Pesticides." *The Herald-Mail* 23 Feb. 1993, Sec. A:6.

"Tougher Restrictions on MSG Sought." *The Daily Mail* 9 Apr. 1993, sec. A:6.

Traditional Provisions. Purveyors of Chemically-Free Food, Clean Water, and Earth-Friendly Cleaning Products. Catalog. 412 N. Fairfax Blvd., Ranson, WV 25438. Phone: (304) 725-6322. Fax: (304) 725-6422.

United States EPA. Office of Pesticide Programs. *The Federal Insecticide, Fungicide, and Rodenticide Act as Amended.*. Washington, D.C.: Oct. 1988.

United States General Accounting Office. *TestimonyBefore the Subcommittee on Human Resources and Intergovernmental Relations, Committee on Government Operations, House of Representatives. Food Safety: Fundamental Changes Needed to Improve Monitoring of Unsafe Chemicals in Food.* Washington, D.C.: 28 Sept. 1994.

_____. *Report to the Chairman, Human Resources and Intergovernmental Relations Subcommittee, Committee on Government Operations, House of Representatives. Food Safety: Changes needed to Minimize Unsafe Chemicals in Food.* GAO/RCED-94-192. Washington, D.C.: Sept. 1994.

Weil, Andrew, M.D. *Natural Health, Natural Medicine. Completely Revised & Updated.* New York: Houghton Mifflin Company, 1995

E. Catastrophes
1. Global Catastrophes

Barringer, Felicity. "Chernobyl: Outside, the Danger Persists." *The New York Times Magazine* 14 Apr. 1991, sec. 6.

_____. "The Word 'Safety' Was Banned." *The New York Times Magazine* 30 May 1993: 12.

"Bhopal Nightmares Still Linger." *The Herald-Mail* 2 Dec. 1990, sec. A:6.

Clines, Francis X. "A New Arena for Soviet Nationalism: Chernobyl." *The New York Times* 30 Dec. 1990, sec. A:1+.

Crossette, Barbara. "Bhopal's Tragedy Revisited: 10 Years After the Gas, No End to Tears." *The New York Times* 11 Dec. 1994, sec. E:5.

Elmer-Dewitt, Philip. "A Man-Made Hell on Earth: The Ecological Devastation of Kuwait Is Worse Than Anyone Imagined, but it is Not the Planetwide Catastrophe That Some Predicted." *Time* 18 Mar. 1991: 36-37.

"Environmental Death in Eastern Germany: Ecological Cleanup Moves Slowly in Bitterfeld." *The Daily Mail* 20 May 1992, sec. A:8.

"Four Years Later, Valdez Update Grim." (Anchorage, Alaska [AP].) *The Daily Mail* 23 Mar. 1993, sec. A:2.

Ivleva, Victoria. "Chernobyl: Pictures Inside the Reactor." *The New York Times Magazine* 14 Apr. 1991, sec. 6.

Karliner, Joshua. "The Bhopal Tragedy: Ten Years After." *Global Pesticide Campaigner* 4.4 (Dec. 1994): 1+.

Keeva, Steve. "After the Spill: New Issues in Environmental Law." (Exxon Valdez.) *ABA Journal* Feb. 1991: 66+.

Lacayo, Richard. "A War Against the Earth: Torching Oil Wells and Disgorging Crude Into the Gulf, Saddam Makes the Planet His Latest Victim." *Time* 4 Feb. 1991: 32-33.

"Mishap Casts Pall Over Big Atomic Waste Site." (Richland, Wash. [AP].) *The New York Times* 15 Aug. 1993, National sec.:18.

"More Blasts Rock Tanker; Fears Rise About Environment." (Genoa, Italy [AP].) *The Herald-Mail* 14 Apr. 1991, sec. A:3.

"Nigeria Hangs Playwright, Activist." (Lagos, Nigeria [AP].) *The Herald-Mail* 11 Nov. 1995, sec. C:6.

Read, Piers Paul. *Ablaze: The Story of the Heroes and Victims of Chernobyl.* Random House, 1993.

"Report Links Agent Orange With Diseases." (Washington, D.C. [AP].) *The Daily Mail* 2 May 1990, sec. A:6.

Shenon, Philip. "A Pacific Island Nation Is Stripped of Everything." (Yaren; Nauru.) *The New York Times* 10 Dec. 1995, sec. 1:3.

Solzhenitsyn, Aleksandr I. "To Tame Savage Capitalism." *The New York Times* 28 Nov. 1993, sec. E:11.

Specter, Michael. "10 Years Later, Through Fear, Chernobyl Still Kills in Belarus. A Wasted Land. A Special Report." *The New York Times* 31 Mar. 1996, sec. 1:1+.

"Toxic Cloud Floats Over Residential Area." (Cape Town, South Africa [AP].) *The Daily Mail* 18 Dec. 1995, sec. A:3.

Tyler, Patrick E. "A Tide of Pollution Threatens China's Prosperity." *The New York Times* 25 Sept. 1994, International sec.:3.

Van Biema, David. "Prophet of Poison. After Tokyo Suffers a Nerve-Gas Attack, Suspicion Focuses on the Leader of an Apocalyptic Cult." *Time* 3 Apr. 1995: 26-33.

Wald, Matthew L. "Kuwaitis, Having Survived Hussein, Now Find Their Environment Toxic." *The New York Times* 28 Apr. 1991, International sec.:14.

Wright, Angus. "Where Does the Circle Begin? The Global Dangers of Pesticide Plants." *Global Pesticide Campaigner* 4.4 (Dec. 1994): 1+.

2. Regional and Local
a. Evacuations

"Acid Cloud in East Bay Sends 3,200 to Hospitals." *San Francisco Chronicle* 27 July 1993, sec.: 1.

"Chemical Plant Explosion Causes Injuries, Evacuations." (Bristol, Pa. [AP].) *The Morning Herald* 22 June 1994, sec. B:6.

"Chlorine Cloud Forces Palm Springs Evacuation." (Calif.) *The Herald-Mail* 9 Oct. 1988, sec. A:8.

Fagan, Kevin and Peter Fimrite. "New Furor Over Leaky Rail Tanker." *San Francisco Chronicle* 27 July 1993, sec. A:1.

Ford, Clyde. "Fumes Force Nursing Home Evacuation." (Boonsboro, Md.) *The Herald Mail* 6 Mar. 1993, sec. A:1+.

"Hundreds Flee Fumes From Pa. Fire." (Coplay, Pa. [AP].) *The Daily Mail* 24 Feb. 1993, sec. B:4.

"Thousands Flee Cloud of Chlorine Gas." (Simi Valley, Calif. [AP].) *The Daily Mail* 6 Jan. 1989, sec. A:2.

b. Spills

"Chemical Spill Forces Evacuation." (Hammond, Ind. [AP].) *The Daily Mail* 14 Dec. 1995, sec. A:3.

"Chemical Waste Spills in W.Va. Wreck." (Medina, W.Va. [AP].) *The Herald-Mail* 18 Nov. 1995, sec. D:8.

"Crude Oil Spills into Alaskan Inlet." (Kenai, Alaska [AP].) *The Daily Mail* 6 Dec. 1995, sec A:3.

Easton, Robert. *Black Tide: The Santa Barbara Oil Spill and Its Consequences.* New York: Delacorte Press, 1972.

"Elusive Oil Slick Reported Off Northwest Washington Coast. *The Herald-Mail* 25 Sept. 1994, sec. A:10.

"Pa. Sees One Toxic Spill Per Week." (Philadelphia [AP].) *The Herald-Mail* 3 Sept. 1994, sec. D:14.

Rhodes, Dave. "Toxic Spill Temporarily Closes I-81 Rest Area." (Chambersburg, Pa.) *The Daily Mail* 21 May 1992, sec. B:3.

"Spill Forces 50 From Homes." (Rosedale, Md. [AP].) *The Daily Mail* 25 July 1990, sec. D:8.

"Toxic Spill: 1,000 Evacuated After Spill." (Ferndale, Md. [AP].) *The Herald Mail* 21 Apr. 1996, sec. C:4.

"Toxins Found in Wells That Supply Harford Residents With Water." *The Daily Mail* 21 May 1992, sec. B:4.

c. Leaks

Chua-Eoan, Howard. "Burning Up the Road. NAFTA Is About to Unleash Unsafe Mexican Trucks That May Become a Nightmare for Border States." *Time* 11 Dec. 1995: 52.

"Crews Neutralize Poison Leaking From Train Tank Car." (Bogalusa, La. [AP].) *The Daily Mail* 26 Oct. 1995, sec. A:2.

"Crews Transfer Leaking Cargo." (Halfway, Md.) *The Herald- Mail* 19 Apr. 1992, sec. F:2.

Ford, Clyde. "Leak Forces Evacuation: Residents on Vale Street Return to Homes After Gas Dissipates." *The Daily Mail* 27 Aug. 1992, sec. B:1.

————. "Chemical Leak at Valley Mall Forces Evacuation. Fire-fighters on Scene Until 2 A.M." *The Daily Mail* 7 May 1993, sec. B:1.

Goodwin, M. David. "La. Paper Mill Fallout: 2nd Toxic Cloud, Fear." *USA Today* 25 Oct. 1995, sec. A:3.

"Hazardous Liquid Leaks From Truck." (Greencastle, Pa.) *The Daily Mail* 6 Aug. 1993, sec. B:3.

"Hundreds Treated After Leak at Plant." (Bogalusa, La. [AP].) *The Daily Mail* 24 Oct. 1995, sec. A:3.

"Hundreds Work to Contain Spill." (Salvador, Brazil [AP].) *The Herald-Mail* 19 Apr. 1992, sec. A:8.

Turgeon, Marc, and Rufus Morison. "Science Quality and Risk Assessment: The Leaking Landfill." Presented at the 1989 Annual Meeting of the Society for Risk Analysis in San Francisco, Calif., 30 Oct. 1989.

II. Some Victims and Their Stories
A. Individuals

Arminger, Jared. Baltimore, Maryland. Student. Son of Marian Arminger.

Carson, Larry. "Chemical Aversion Makes Boy Sue School." *The Evening Sun* 20 Dec. 1990, sec. B:1+.

Armstrong, Donna. Minneapolis, Minnesota. School receptionist.

Souder, William. "A Fragrant Violation? You Won't Believe the Stink a Little Perfume Caused at this Midwestern School." *The Washington Post* 11 Dec. 1994, sec. F:1.

Ballou, Laurel. Bothell, Washington. Office worker.

Taylor, Rob. "An Invisible Disability: Chemical Sensitivity Victims Want Recognition, Treatment." *Seattle Post-Intelligencer* 23 Dec. 1993, sec. A:1+.

*Barker, Robert T. Hagerstown, Maryland. Former Navy officer.

Barker, Robert T. Letter to Jacob B. Berkson. 6 Apr. 1995.

*Barrell, Ruth Ann. San Diego, California. Minister's wife, accounting clerk.

Stimson, Eva. "The Poisoning of Ruth Ann Barrell." *Presbyterian Survey* Oct. 1991: 27-29.

Berkson, Jacob. Hagerstown, Maryland. Attorney.

Berkson, Jacob. "Patient Statement: A Canary's Tale." *Toxicology and Industrial Health* 10.4/5 (1994): 323-326.

_____. "A Canary's Warning: The Link Between Pesticides and MCS." *Rachel Carson Council News No.* 86 Oct. 1995: 1+.

_____. "MCS: A Case Study." *American PIE* 2.1 (Winter 1996): 8.

Callen, Bill. "Waging One Final Battle: Berkson Writing Book on Chemical Pollution." *The Herald-Mail* 18 Apr. 1993, sec. F:1+.

Rosenthal, Norman E., M.D., and Christine L. Cameron, B.S. "Letters to the Editor: Exaggerated Sensitivity to an

Organophosphate Pesticide." *American Journal of Psychiatry* 148.2 (1991): 270.

Snodgrass, Will. *Who Poisoned Jacob Berkson.* Video. 1994.

*Berman, Ronald M., M.D. San Pablo, California. Medical doctor.

"Acid Cloud in East Bay Sends 3,200 to Hospitals." *San Francisco Chronicle* 27 July 1993, sec.: 1.

Bierly, John and Karen. Baltimore, Maryland. Engineer.

Bowie, Liz. "Prolonged Battle With Pesticide Costs Family Their Home. Misapplied Chlordane Contaminates Their House." *Baltimore Sun* 19 May 1991, sec. A:1+.

*Blakeman, Brenda. Clarksburg, West Virginia. Antique Dealer.

Berkson, Jacob B. Personal interview. 8 Nov. 1995.

Bonhage-Hale, Myra. Alum Bridge, West Virginia. Retired.

"Organic Farmer Followed Her Dream to West Virginia." (Alum Bridge, W.Va. [AP].) *The Herald-Mail* 11 Jan. 1994, sec. B:6.

*Bormel, Lurie. Baltimore, Maryland. Attorney at Law, CPA.

Berkson, Jacob B. Personal interview. 7 Aug. 1995.

*Bower, Lynn. Bloomington, Indiana. Artist, Author.

Biever, Richard G. "Healthy Home Zone. Couple Finds New Life in 'Healthy House.'" *Electric Consumer* 43.8 (Feb. 1994): 8-10+.

Unthank, Kitty. "Hoosier Creates 'Safe' Homes. This Builder Knows All About Ecological Illness." *Indianapolis Star* 19 Mar. 1985: 1+.

*Bready, Bill. Clarksburg, West Virginia. Construction project safety coordinator.

Berkson, Jacob B. Personal interview. 8 Nov. 1995.

*Canfield, Diane. Winston, New Mexico.

Canfield, Diane. Letter to Jacob B. Berkson. 31 Mar. 1995.

_____. Letter. 1 Aug. 1995.

Carpenter, Christine. Fairfax County, Virginia. Secretary.

Davis, Patricia, and D'Vera Cohn. "Va. Woman Wins Case, but Still Has Toxic House. *The Washington Post* 21 Feb. 1992, sec. B:1+.

Channing, Carol. Actress.

Scott, Walter. "Personality Parade." *Parade* 11 Oct. 1992: 2.

Chuda, Colette. California. Infant, deceased.

Roan, Shari. "From the Pain, a Passion. James and Nancy Chuda* Lost Their Little Girl to a Rare Cancer. Now They Are on a Mission to Protect Other Children." *Los Angeles Times* 20 Nov. 1994, sec. E:1+.

*Clarke, Susan. Concord, Massachusetts. Musician, Orchestra Conductor, President, ENHALE, Environmental Health Advocacy League.

Clarke, Susan. Telephone conference and letter to Jacob B. Berkson. 30 Nov. 1995.

Cochran, Jerry. Albany, Georgia. Sailor.

Schmitt, Eric. "Dying Former Sailor Battles Navy in Search for Afflicted Shipmates." *The New York Times* 27 Sept. 1992, National sec.:1+.

*Cohen, Debora. Portland, Oregon. Writer, editor, video producer.

Cohen, Debora. *Canary in a Mine: A Documentary*. Portland, Oregon: Raspberry Wood Productions.

*Conrad, Richard H., Ph.D. Point Reyes Station, California. Biochemist, consultant.

Conrad, Richard H., Ph.D. Symposium talk to CDHS/ATSDR. Berkeley, 5 May 1994.

Dadd, Debra Lynn. California. Author.

Castleman, Michael. "This Place Makes Me Sick. Doctors Tell Them It's All in Their Heads. But Sufferers From Environmental Illness Know That the Cause—Like the Cure—Lies in the World Around Them. *Sierra* Sept./Oct. 1993: 106-119.

Dadd, Debra Lynn. *Nontoxic, Natural, & Earthwise: How to Protect Yourself and Your Family from Harmful Products and Live in*

Harmony With the Earth. Los Angeles: Jeremy P. Tarcher, Inc., 1990.

Dauble, Janet. Executive director.

Dauble, Janet. Letter to Whom It May Concern Regarding Multiple Chemical Sensitivity. 21 June 1995.

*Davis, Earon S. Illinois. Attorney, MPH.

Davis, Earon S., J.D., M.P.H. "The New Chemical Victims." Reprinted from the "Ecological Illness Law Report," July/October, 1985, by permission from Editor, Earon S. Davis, J.D., M.P.H., in *The Human Ecologist* 32 (1986): 19-22.

DiPetrillo, Terry. Rhode Island.

"Man Wins $1.2 Million in Agent Orange Suit." (Providence, R.I. [AP].) *The Herald-Mail* 25 May 1996, sec. A:2.

*Doyle, Edward R. Robbinsville, North Carolina. Sign Painter and Manufacturer

Doyle, Theresa C. Letter to Jacob B. Berkson, including enclosures of medical records, reports, and Dr. Allan Lieberman's evaluation. 18 Jan. 1995.

Social Security Adminstration. *Retirement, Survivors and Disability Insurance Notice of Award*. 23 Nov. 1993.

*Duehring, Cindy. Williston, North Dakota. Housewife, writer, editor, author.

Duehring, Cindy. "Trapped By Her Sensitivity. She Is Unable to Tolerate Chemicals All of Us Are Exposed to Every Day." *The Lutheran* 20 Feb. 1991: 10-13.

Duehring, Cindy, and Cynthia Wilson. *The Human Consequences of the Chemical Problem*. White Sulphur Springs, Mont.: TT Publishing, 1994.

Dupriest, Marlene and Carroll. California.

Pegg, Judy. "Dream Home Turns Into a Nightmare: Insecticide Contamination by a California Pest Control Operator." *Journal of Pesticide Reform* 12.2 (Summer 1992): 24.

*Eill, Dr. Bryna. New York. Educator.

NYCAP representative. Participant, NCAMP Forums.

*Enger, Laurie. Idaho. Writer, Business Executive.

Enger, Laurie. Correspondence and phone conferences with Jacob B. Berkson beginning 29 May 1995.

Enright, Jean. Alberta, Canada. Author.

Rousseau, David, W. J. Rea, M.D., and Jean Enwright. "Chapter 24 Living with Environmental Illness." *Your Home, Your Health, & Well-Being.* Berkeley, California: Ten Speed Press, 1988, pp. 217-231.

Farr, Heather. Deceased. Golfer.

"Golfer Farr Remains Critically Ill." (Scottsdale, Ariz. [AP].) *The Herald-Mail* 20 Nov. 1993, sec. B:3.

Potter, Jerry. "Farr's Frightening Foe. LPGA Learns Realities of Breast Cancer." *USA Today* 7 Nov. 1991, sec. C:1.

Reisner, Mel. "Funeral Services Held for LPGA Member Farr. Professional Golfer Lost Four-Year Battle Against Cancer." (Phoenix [AP].) *The Daily Mail* 24 Nov. 1993, sec. D:4.

*Fischer, Siegfried. Duesseldorf, Germany. Engineer, ret.

Dinant, Hans. TV Documentary. RTL—German National Television.

*Fischer, Ellen. Duesseldorf, Germany. Bilingual secretary, ret.

Dinant, Hans. TV Documentary. RTL—German National Television.

*Forbes, William. Clear Spring, Maryland. Writer, Pest Management Specialist.

Forbes, William. "Jared's Story: Least Toxic Approaches to Managing Pests in Schools." In Norma L. Miller, Ed.D., ed. *The Healthy School Handbook. Conquering the Sick Building Syndrome and Other Environmental Hazards In and Around Your School.* Washington, D.C.: NEA Professional Library, June 1995, p. 243-254.

Fried, Diane. Writer.

Fried, Stephen. "Prescription for Disaster." *The Washington Post Magazine* 3 Apr. 1994: 13-15+.

*Fuzzell, Frank. Florida. Farmer.

> Levesque, William R. "Benlate: Phantom on the Farm. A Special Report. 'A Tragic Mess': The Story of the Fungicide Benlate Is a Tale Without Equal in Modern Agriculture, Leaving Florida Farmers With Little to Do Other Than Watch As Their Crops Wither and Die." Lakeland, Florida *The Ledger* 15-19 Nov. 1992: 6.

*Gariazzo, Anne. Maryland. Federal government analyst, editor newsletter: "The Chemical Sensitivity Connection."

> Berkson, Jacob B. Personal interviews. 1994-1995.

*Golos, Natalie. Maryland. Author, consultant.

> Golos, Natalie, and William J. Rea, M.D. *Success in the Clean Bedroom: A Path to Optimal Health.* Rochester, New York: Pinnacle Publishers, 1992.

> _____, and Frances Golos Golbitz. *Coping With Your Allergies.* New York: Simon & Schuster, Inc. (Fireside Division), 1986.

*Gorman, Nancy. Maryland. Retired Federal attorney, MCS Disability consultant.

> Lieberman, Allan D., M.D., F.A.A.E.M. Letter to Ms. Barbara P. Lawrence. Re: Nancy Gorman. 15 May 1991.

> Gorman, Nancy W., Esquire. Letter to Hillary Rodham Clinton. Re: Task Force on Health Care Parity. 28 Apr. 1993.

Green, Nancy Sokol. Author.

> Green, Nancy Sokol. *Poisoning Our Children: Surviving in a Toxic World.* Chicago: The Noble Press.

*Hamman, Doris. Denton, Texas. Former Daycare Owner and Operator.

> Berkson, Jacob B. Telephone interview. 7 Dec. 1995. Letter. 13 Dec. 1995.

Hareld, Bethna. Colorado. Science researcher.

> Halbrook, David. "Life Is Killing Bethna Hareld. The Problem of MCS—Multiple Chemical Sensitivities—Has Polarized Science,

Medicine and Industry." *American Legion Magazine* Jan. 1992: 34+.

*Harper, Sheila M. Hendersonville, North Carolina. School teacher.

Harper, Sheila M. Letter to Jack Berkson. 12 Sept. 1991, 13 Dec. 1995.

*Hawks, Shelley. Bendon City, Washington. Farmer's wife and mother.

Casey, Kenneth R., M.D., F.C.C.P. Letter to John S. Moore. Re: Shelly Hawks. 2 Oct. 1992.

Monroe, David H., M.S.P.H., Ph.D. Letter to John S. Moore. Re: Shelley Hawks, draft report. 5 Mar. 1992.

*Hayes, J. Clark, Rev. Hagerstown, Maryland. Pastor—Salem Reformed Church, Hagerstown, Maryland.

Berkson, Jacob B. Personal interviews. 1988-.

*Hayes, Jane. Hagerstown, Maryland. Wife of Rev. J. Clark Hayes.

Heminway, Aaron. New York. Student. Son of Diane.

*Heminway, Diane. "The Great Big FMC Corporation and a Schoolyard." *Journal of Pesticide Reform* 9.1 (Spring 1989): 2+.

*Hollingsworth, Kimo. Gulf War Vet, Marine. National Headquarters, American Legion, Washington, D.C.

Berkson, Jacob B. *A Canary's Tale*, Vol I, Part 9, Chapter 4.

*House, Steve. Algonac, Michigan. Disabled Terminix PCO.

House, Steve. Speech before NCAMP Thirteenth National Pesticide Forum. 17 Mar. 1995.

*Howard, Pat. Waldorf, Maryland. Bank employee.

Berkson, Jacob B. Telephone conference. 10 Aug. 1995.

*Hue, Margaret. Kennewick, Washington. Farmer's wife and mother, Activist.

Hue, Margaret. Rt. 4, Box 4250, Kennewick, WA 99337. Tri-Citians Against Chemical Trespass.

*Ingram, Iris. Florida. Retired.

Golos, Natalie, and William J. Rea, M.D. *Success in the Clean Bedroom: A Path to Optimal Health.* Rochester, New York: Pinnacle Publishers, 1992. pp. 9-10.

*Jackson, Jim. South Carolina. Retired Airline executive, consultant.

Jackson, Jim. Letter to Jacob B. Berkson. Re: Summerville Safe Haven. 8 Sept. 1992.

*Kahn, Jack. Santa Fe, New Mexico. Radio producer, host.

"It's a Matter of Health—The Environment and Your Well-Being." A 50 minute health talk show extraordinare on AM radio in Santa Fe, New Mexico—KVSF AM1260. 9 Dec. 1994.

Kehoe, Denise. Nashua, New Hampshire.

Lambert, Wade. "More Claim Chemicals Made Them Ill." *Wall Street Journal* 18 Jan. 1995, sec. B:1+.

*Keplinger, Helen. Maryland. EPA attorney, speaker at ATSDR Conference, Baltimore, Maryland 1994.

Keplinger, Helen. "Patient Statement: Chemically Sensitive." *Toxicology and Industrial Health* 10.4/5 (1994): 313-317.

*Kinnear, Ellen. Baltimore, Maryland. School teacher.

Berkson, Jacob B. Personal interviews, correspondence, and meetings. Sept. 1995-.

*Lachman, Tessa. Leesburg, Virginia. Former computer programer, consultant.

Lachman, Tessa. Owner and designer of less toxic home.

*Lamielle, Mary. Vorhees Township, New Jersey. Activist, advocate.

Burke, Adrienne, Senior Associate Editor. "Safety Perspectives: The Advocate. What Makes an Activist Tick? Here's the Story of One Determined Woman." *Industrial Safety & Hygiene News* Sept. 1993.

*Latimer, Tom. Dallas, Texas. Petroleum engineer.

Allen, Frank Edward. "Lonely Crusade: One Man's Suffering Spurs Doctors to Probe Pesticide-Drug Link. Tom Latimer, Tagamet User, Fell Ill After He Mowed Lawn That Was Treated.

A Problem Little Understood." *The Wall Street Journal* 14 Oct. 1991, eastern ed, sec. A:1+.

Latimer, J. R., Jr. "Thomas L. Latimer Written Statement. Senate Subcommittee on Toxic Substances." 9 May 1991.

Latimer, Thomas L. "Poisoned." 1993.

————. Correspondence with Jacob B. Berkson. 1992-.

*Lawson, Lynn. Illinois. Author, medical editor, teacher.

Lawson, Lynn. *Staying Well in a Toxic World: Understanding Environmental Illness, Multiple Chemical Sensitivities, Chemical Injuries, and Sick Building Syndrome.* Chicago: The Noble Press, Inc., 1994.

Lebens, Melinda. Vienna, Virginia. Former teacher's aide.

Bates, Steve. "Vienna Renter Finally Gets No-Spray Zone. Woman Had Suffered Reaction to Pesticides." *The Washington Post* 12 Jan. 1995, sec. B:5.

*Lescs, Cecile M. Virginia. Attorney.

Cecile M. Lescs v. William R. Hughes, Inc., *et al.*, Virginia Circuit Court, City of Winchester 90-L-272 (1992). Case nonsuited voluntarily. Case refiled in Federal District Court for the Western District of Virginia. File No. 94-0091 (H). 5 Dec. 1994.

*Light, Joseph. Florida. Former Executive, New York, New York.

Berkson, Jacob B. Personal interview. Jan. 1993.

*Lynch, Glenda. Dallas, Georgia. Cosmetologist.

Berkson, Jacob B. Telephone interview. 31 Oct. 1995.

Lynch, Glenda. Letters to Jacob B. Berkson. 1 Nov. 1995-.

Lynch, Susan. Dallas, Georgia. Daughter of Glenda Lynch.

Magidson, Peggy. Princetown, New York. Telemarket firm president.

Esch, Mary. "Chemically Respondent: Isolated Setting Heals Victim of Multiple Sensitivity." *Albuquerque Journal* 7 Nov. 1994, sec. B:1+.

Markee, Pat. Oregon. Truck driver.

Hope, Rose-Ellen. "Delivering Pesticides: One Driver's Story." *Journal of Pesticide Reform* 13.2 (Summer 1993): 13-15.

Martinez, Jose Campos. California. Farmworker, deceased.

"Farm Worker's Death Fueled Fight to Ban Deadly Pesticide." (Fresno, Calif. [AP}.) *The Daily Mail* 6 Sept. 1991, sec. A:8.

*Martz, JoAnn K. Williamsport, Maryland. Sales representative.

*Mason, Ann. Sarasota, Florida. Realtor, activist, director, board member.

Berkson, Jacob B. Telephone interview. 11 Dec. 1992.

*Matthews, Bonnye. Seattle, Washington. Federal employee supervisor, author.

Matthews, Bonnye. *Chemical Sensitivity: A Guide to Coping With Hypersensitivity Syndrome, Sick Building Syndrome and Other Environmental Illnesses.* Jefferson, N.C.: McFarland & Co., Inc., 1992.

McCauley, Ann. Norcross, Georgia. Mother.

Fernandez, Maria Elena. "'I Have Always Taken Care of My Children.' Mom With Questionable Illness Fights State to Keep Daughters." *Atlanta Constitution* 6 Mar. 1995.

*McVicker, Marilyn. Baltimore, Maryland. School teacher, musician, author.

McVicker, Marilyn G. "Customizing a Van for MCS Accessibility." *The Human Ecologist* 69 (Spring 1996): 11-14.

*Meek, Earle. Berkeley Springs, West Virginia. School teacher, housing consultant.

Berkson, Jacob B. Personal interview, correspondence and meetings. Sept. 1995-.

*Mogus, Joe. Peach Bottom, Pennsylvania.

Wallace, Brian. "Poisoning of Well Leaves Owner With Bitter Taste." *Intelligencer Journal* 17 Dec. 1994, sec. A:1+.

*Molloy, Susan. Marin City, California; Snowflake, Arizona. Editor: "The Delicate Balance," activist, AZ Governor's Council.

Molloy, Susan. *Home Ownership with Section 8.* Prescott Valley, Arizona: New Horizons.

Reinhold, Robert. "When Life Is Toxic: They Suffer Agonizing Reaction From Contact With Almost Anything Chemical, Forcing Them Into Protective Cocoons. They Call It a Disease, But Is It? Not All Doctors Are Convinced." *The New York Times Magazine* 16 Sept. 1990: 50-51+.

*Morison, Rufus, Ph.D. Virginia. Ecologist, EPA employee.

Hirzy, J. William, and Rufus Morison. "Carpet/4-Phenylcyclohexene Toxicity: The EPA Headquarters Case." *Advances in Risk Analysis.* Vol. 9: *The Analysis, Communication, and Perception of Risk.* Ed. B. John Garrick and Willard C. Gekler. Society for Risk Analysis. New York: Plenum Press, 1991.

Morris, Charles. Washington State. Commercial painter.

Taylor, Rob. "An Invisible Disability: Chemical Sensitivity Victims Want Recognition, Treatment." *Seattle Post-Intelligencer* 23 Dec. 1993, sec. A:1+.

Nonnon, Patricia. Bronx, New York. Mother of three, activist extraordnaire.

Dreifus, Claudia. "Battling Mount Trashmore." *McCall's* Apr. 1991: 79-82+.

*Noren, Nancy. New Mexico.

Noren, Nancy. *Report on New Mexico Safe Housing & MCS/EI Communities.* 25 Apr. 1991.

*Orselli, Janet. North Carolina. Teacher.

Orselli, Janet. "Chemically Poisoned, Please...Not 'Sensitive.'" *The Wary Canary* 8: 14.

"Page, Betty." Pennsylvania. Medical doctor.

Roueché, Berton. "Annals of Medicine: The Fumigation Chamber." *The New Yorker* 4 Jan. 1988: 60-65.

_____. "Department of Amplification." *The New Yorker* 2 Feb. 1988: 80-81.

Parks, Roger. Registered nurse and Army reservist.

> Scharnberg, Ken. "Gulf War Syndrome: A Case Study in Despair." *The American Legion* 140.5 (May 1996): 30.

*Plumlee, Lawrence A., M.D. Bethesda, Maryland. President, CSDA

> Berkson, Jacob B. Telephone interviews, correspondence and meetings. 1992-.

Radtke, Donald and Linda. Stone Mountain, Georgia.

> "Family Has Home Hauled to Toxic Waste Dump." *The Herald-Mail* 23 Apr. 1989, sec. A:8.

Rea, William J., M.D. Dallas, Texas. Surgeon, Professor of Medicine, Author, Activist.

> Environmental Health Center—Dallas.

> Rea, William J., M.D., F.A.C.S., F.A.A.E.M. "Part II: Tracing the Roots of the 20th Century Illness." *The Human Ecologist* 41: 24-25.

> _____. *Chemical Sensitivity*. 2 vols. Boca Raton, Fla.: Lewis Publishers, 1994.

Reed, John, his three children, and family friend, Karen Smith. Cleveland, Ohio. Deceased.

> "Carbon Monoxide Victims Thought Gas Was in Their Home. Doctor Told Family They Had the Flu. 'My Nephew, John Michael, Was Not in This World. He Was Delirious, Tired, Non-Functional. This Doctor Should Have Known by the Symptoms of John Michael Alone.'—Mark Reed." (Cleveland [AP].) *The Herald-Mail* 24 Dec. 1995, sec. A:8.

Registry of Pesticide Sensitive Persons. Florida.

> Mulrennan, John A., Jr., Ph.D. Memorandum No. 624 to all commercial pest control licensees and limited certificate-holders. Subject: Registry of pesticide sensitive persons. 25 Jan. 1993.

*Rozines, Jennifer. Columbus, Ohio. Former schoolteacher.

> Rozines, Jennifer. *What the Heck Is Wrong With* _____? Columbus, Ohio: Jennifer Rozines.

Ruff, Sandi. Washington State. Former runner.

> Taylor, Rob. "An Invisible Disability: Chemical Sensitivity Victims Want Recognition, Treatment." *Seattle Post-Intelligencer* 23 Dec. 1993, sec. A:1+.

Saro-Wiwa, Ken. Ogoni, Nigeria. Playwright, African Environmentalist

> "Nigeria Hangs Playwright, Activist." (Lagos, Nigeria [AP].) *The Herald-Mail* 11 Nov. 1995, sec. C:6.

Scanlon, Sarah, R.N., and 46 other registered nurses. Boston, Massachusetts.

> *Can Buildings Make You Sick?* Mike Tomlinson, producer. Robin Brightwell, ed. NOVA, PBS, Boston, 26 Dec. 1995.

Schneider, Susan. San Francisco, California.

> Piller, Charles and Michael Castleman. "Is Your Office Making You Sick?" *Redbook* Apr. 1990: 114, 115+.

Scott, Margie. Connecticut. Former employee of lawn care company, environmental activist.

> Scott, Margie. "My Pesticide Story." *NYCAP News* 4.4 (Late Winter 1994): 26+.

See, Todd. Gulf War vet.

> Cowley, Geoffrey. "Coming Home to Pain: Why Are So Many Gulf War Veterans So Sick?" *Newsweek* 28 June 1993: 58-59.

Selph, Marvin and Carol. Jasper, Florida. Wife is school teacher.

> "A House No One Wanted to Touch." *The New York Times* 18 Dec. 1993.

*Shannon, Anne. Boulder, Colorado. Nurse, RN. Deceased.

*Shannon, Katherine. Boulder, Colorado. Student, NCAMP Activist.

*Shannon, Robert. Boulder, Colorado. CPA. Deceased.

*Sills, Gene and C. E. Kosciusko, Mississippi. Realtor and Landowner.

> Sills, Gene and C. E. Telephone conference and letter to Jacob B. Berkson. 27 Nov. 1995.

Smith, Herb, Lt. Col. Green Beret, Gulf War Vet.

> Scharnberg, Ken. "What's Wrong With Me? Sick Gulf War Veterans Ask and Ask, But Medical Researchers and VA Have Few Answers...and the Pentagon Isn't Talking." *The American Legion* Jan. 1995: 33-37+.

*Snodgrass, Will. Missoula, Montana. Missoulians for Clean Environment.

> Snodgrass, Will. *Who Poisoned Jacob Berkson*. Video. 1994.

*Spear, Judy. Lancaster, Massachusetts. Art History Editor.

> Spear, Judy. "Chemical Sensitivity." *Boston Phoenix* 8 Sept. 1995, Letters sec.

Steingraber, Sandra. Illinois. Author, teacher.

> Steingraber, Sandra. *Post-Diagnosis*. Ithaca, New York: Firebrand Books, 1995.

Sweigard, Sylvia. Halifax, Pennsylvania. Employee—Pennsylvania Lottery.

> "Workers Say They're Sick of Being in Sick Building." *The Daily Mail* 17 Feb. 1992, sec. D:8.

Taylor, Elizabeth. Bel-Air, California. Actress.

> "Shocked Liz Taylor Told By Docs: Your Home Gave You Life-Threatening Illness. She's Living in Hotel While Experts Try to Clear Mystery Bug From Her $5M Mansion." *Star* 10 July 1990: 5.

Taylor, Krissy. Florida. Model.

> Gorman, Christine. "Medicine—Asthma: The Hidden Killer. Model Krissy Taylor's Death Underscores How Lethal and Deceptive This Common Ailment Can Be." *Time* 7 Aug. 1995: 56.

*Taylor, Sharon. Los Banos, California. Educator, writer, NCAMP Board Member.

> Taylor, Sharon. "Pest Control Without Poisons." *Home Magazine* June 1994.

Thompson, Laura. Rarden, Ohio. Elementary school student.

Berkson, Jacob B. Telephone conference with mother, *Susan Thompson. 9 Aug. 1995.

*Tvedten, Stephen L. Marne, Michigan. Get Set, Inc., Stroz Services, Inc.

Tvedten, Stephen L. *The Best Control (An Integrated Pest Management Manual.* 1994.

————. Speaker, Thirteenth National Pesicide Forum, NCAMP. 17 Mar. 1995.

*Vassallo, Margaret. Neshamie, New Jersey. Seamstress.

Berkson, Jacob. Telephone conference with husband, Philip. 10 Jan. 1996.

Watson, Hubert and Freida. Deceased. Galax, Virginia.

Arch, Mary Ellin. "Orkin Held Responsible for 2 Fumigation Deaths. Company Fined $500,000 in Virginia Case." *The Washington Post* 1988, sec. D:1+.

Weaver, Blanche and Ward. Mount Vernon, Virginia.

Cohn, D'Vera. "Pesticide Fears Leave Pair a House That's Not Home. Virginia Couple Stay in Backyard Trailer." *The Washington Post* 6 Apr. 1989, sec. D:1+.

*Weidner, Christine. Newtown Square, Pennsylvania. Activist.

President, Grow, Inc., Grass Roots the Organic Way.

*Wilson, Cynthia. White Sulphur Springs, Montana. Builder, author, editor.

Duehring, Cindy, and Cynthia Wilson. *The Human Consequences of the Chemical Problem.* White Sulphur Springs, Mont.: TT Publishing, 1994.

Wilson, Cynthia, ed. *Our Toxic Times.*

————. *Chemical Exposure and Human Health.* Jefferson, N.C.: McFarland & Co., Inc., 1994.

————. "Patient Statement: Chemical Sensitivity—One Victim's Perspective." *Toxicology and Industrial Health* 10.4/5 (1994): 319-321.

*Wilson, Linda. Florida. Executive assistant—stock brokerage firm, writer, housewife, mother, consultant.

Circeill, Deborah. "Sensitivity Isolates Victims From World." *Clay Today* 16 Apr. 1991: 1+.

Wimberley, Texas residents.

Belkin, Lisa. "Seekers of Clean Living Head for Texas Hills." *The New York Times* 2 Dec. 1990, National sec.:1+.

_____. "The Cleanest town in Texas: It Is a Haven for the Chemically Sensitive—But How Long Will It Last?" *San Francisco Chronicle/Examiner* 16 Dec. 1992.

Hall, Stephen S. "In Wimberley, Texas, Some People Live in Houses Lined With Aluminum Foil, Wear Gas Masks in Public, and Shun Newspapers, Deodorant, and Most Things Man-Made. They're Crazy Right? Or Maybe They're Allergic to the 20th Century." *Health* May/June 1993: 74+.

Monday, Susan McAtee. "A Chemical Cage: 'Canary' Issues Warning Against Toxic Terrors." *San Antonio Light* 26 Jan. 1992, sec. J:1+.

_____. "Victim Avoids Exposure, Tries to Maintain Mainstream Life." *San Antonio Light* 26 Jan. 1992, sec. J:9.

_____. "'Save Comanche Hill' Group Sets Organizational Meeting." *San Antonio Light* 26 Jan. 1992, sec. J:12.

*Yingling, Ronald. Spring Grove, Pennsylvania. Accountant.

Berkson, Jacob B. Personal interview. 19 Aug. 1995.

Young, Marsha L. Missouri. Army nurse.

Young, Marsha L. "Women in Combat." *The American Legion* Oct. 1994: 6+.

Note: Asterisk * indicates that the author personally met with and/or communicated with and/or corresponded with the individual listed or his representative.

B. Gulf War Vets
1991

Lacayo, Richard. "A War Against the Earth: Torching Oil Wells and Disgorging Crude Into the Gulf, Saddam Makes the Planet His Latest Victim." *Time* 4 Feb. 1991: 32-33.

Schmitt, Eric. "After the War: Military, Political and Environmental Repercussions. The Environment: Fouled Region Is Casualty of War. Cleanup Workers Confronting Gritty, Longlasting Battle on Land, Sea and Air." *The New York Times* 3 Mar. 1991, International sec.:1.

1992

Kong, Dolores. "Learning From Agent Orange: Government Preparing for Gulf War Health Questions." *The Daily Mail* 5 Aug. 1992, sec. B:9.

"Military Probes Oil Fire Fumes." (Raleigh, N.C. [AP].) *The Daily Mail* 10 Aug. 1992, sec. A:2.

Sherman, Janette D., M.D. Letter to Richard Christian. Re: Gulf War Veterans. 15 Aug. 1992.

"Vets Hospital Sets Up Clinic for Gulf Soldiers." (Durham, N.C. [AP].) *The Daily Mail* 19 Aug. 1992, sec. B:8.

"Petrochemicals Suspected in Gulf War Ills." *The American Legion* Oct. 1992: 36.

Schwarzkopf, General H. Norman. *General H. Norman Schwarzkopf: The Autobiography: It Doesn't Take a Hero/Written With Peter Petre.* New York: Linda Grey Bantam Books, 1992, pp. 291-503.

1993

"Gulf War Vets at Risk From Radiation." (Boston [AP].) *The Daily Mail* 19 Mar. 1993, sec. A:8.

Berkson, Jacob B. Letter to Hillary Rodham Clinton. Task Force on National Health Care Reform. The White House. Re: Request for Health Care Reform. 28 Apr. 1993.

Chris Wallace for Ted Koppel. "Desert Storm Syndrome." *Nightline.* ABC. 8 June 1993.

Miller, Claudia S. "Testimony of Claudia S. Miller, M.D., M.S." For the Committee on Veterans' Affairs Subcommittee on Oversight and Investigations, Washington, D.C. 9 June 1993.

Cowley, Geoffrey. "Coming Home to Pain: Why Are So Many Gulf War Veterans so Sick?" *Newsweek* 28 June 1993: 58-59.

Wilson, Cynthia. Letter to Jacob B. Berkson. 30 Aug. 1993. Listing the following Gulf War Vets: SSG Tom Yuppa, c/o 115th MP Co., Pawtucket, RI 02860; St. Sgt. Steve Robertson, American Legion, Washington, DC 20006, (202) 861-2740; Alan Fostoff, Pomonia, NY 10970; John K. Ryan, Selton, DE 19943.

"Doctor Says Chemicals Used in Gulf War." (Washington [AP].) *The Daily Mail* 29 Oct. 1993, sec. A:1.

"Vets Claim Chemical Exposure." (Washington, D.C.) *The Daily Mail* 10 Nov. 1993, sec. A:2.

"Pentagon: Chemicals Not to Blame. Mysterious Health Problems Plague Gulf War Vets." (Washington [AP].) *The Daily Mail* 11 Nov. 1993, sec. A:9.

Gorman, Christine. "The Gulf Gas Mystery: Evidence Suggests That Troops Were Indeed Exposed to Chemical Agents, But Were the Iraqis Responsible?" *Time* 22 Nov. 1993: 43.

"Gulf Veterans to Get Treatments." (Washington, D.C.) *The Daily Mail* 22 Dec. 1993, sec. A:2.

1994

Lamielle, Mary. Statement before the Institute of Medicine Committee to Review Health Consequences of Service During the Persian Gulf War. 28 Feb. 1994.

"Gulf Vets Suffer Mysterious Illnesses." (Washington [AP].) *The Daily Mail* 1 Mar. 1994, sec. A:2.

Barrett, Jim. "The War and Dr. Miller: Faculty Physician Wins a Battle for Research in Her Quest to Solve the Mystery of Gulf War Syndrome." *The Mission* Spring 1994: 3-7.

Roberts, Lyman W., Ph.D. Facsimile Transmittal Header Sheet— Department of the Army, Office of the Surgeon General, Professional Services Directorate to Dr. Olsen. 6 Apr. 1994.

Sherman, Janette D., M.D. Letter to Dr. Patricia Olson, DVM. Re: Gulf War Veterans. 11 Apr. 1994.

Quindlen, Anna. "Casualties of War." *The New York Times* 5 Oct. 1994, sec. A:23.

"Veterans' Issues." *The Delicate Balance* vol. v, nos. 3-4 (1994): 21-25.

"Chemical Arms Didn't Make Gulf Vets Ill: Expert." (Bethesda, Md.) *The Daily Mail* 28 Apr. 1994, sec. A:8.

Front Page. Re: Persian Gulf Syndrome. Channel 5. 26 Apr. 1994.

National Institutes of Health Workshop Statement. NIH Technology Assessment Workshop on the Persian Gulf Experience and Health. 27-29 Apr. 1994.

Sherman, Janette D., M.D. Letter to Jacob B. Berkson, Esquire. Includes "List of Pesticides Procurred During Desert Shield/Storm (Acquired Through the Federal Supply System)." 29 Apr. 1994.

"Rockefeller: Vaccines Could Be Cause of Gulf Vets' Sicknesses." (Washington [AP].) *The Daily Mail* 6 May 1994, sec. A:5.

"Gulf Vets Blame Pills. Defense Department Denies Drug Caused Sickness." (Washington [AP].) *The Herald-Mail* 7 May 1994, sec. A:14.

"'Gulf Syndrome' Vets to Be Paid." (Mobile, Ala.) *The Daily Mail* 10 June 1994, sec. A:2.

"Panel: No One Answer to Gulf Vets' Ills. But V.A. Promises Medical Care Available." (Washington [AP].) *The Daily Mail* 24 June 1994, sec. A:10.

"Gulf Ills Treatment Supported. VA Secretary Backs House Bills. Also, a Senate Report Says GIs May Have Been Exposed to U.S.-Made Chemical and Biological Materials." *The American Legion* Aug. 1994: 32.

"Gulf War Vets Hit With Health Problems." (Washington, Pa. [AP].) *The Daily Mail* 28 Sept. 1994, sec. A:9.

"Benefits Ordered for Ailing Gulf Vets." (Washington [AP].) *The Herald-Mail* 9 Oct. 1994, sec. A:2.

Young, Marsha L. "Women in Combat." *The American Legion* Oct. 1994: 6+.

1995

Scharnberg, Ken. "What's Wrong With Me? Sick Gulf War Veterans Ask and Ask, But Medical Researchers and VA Have Few Answers...and the Pentagon Isn't Talking." *The American Legion* Jan. 1995: 33-37+.

Kincaid, Cliff. "Russia's Dirty Chemical Secret. Russia May Have Developed a New Kind of Weapon and Tested it on Our Troops in the Gulf War." *The American Legion for God and Country* Feb. 1995: 32-34+.

Sherman, Janette D., MD. "Gulf War Illnesses: The Need for a Toxicology Investigation." *Health & Environment Digest* 8.11 (Mar. 1995): 87-89.

Harris, John F. "Clinton Woos Lukewarm Veterans; Vows to Fight VA Cuts, Study 'Gulf War Syndrome' Thaws VFW's Mood." *The Washington Post* 7 Mar. 1995, sec. A:7.

Bradley, Ed, reporter. "Gulf War Syndrome." *60 Minutes* CBS, 12 Mar. 1995.

"Chemical Cocktail Given Gulf War Soldiers Cause of Mysterious Illnesses?" (Durham, N.C. [AP].) *The Daily Mail* 11 Apr. 1995, sec. A:7.

Bradley, Ed, reporter. "Gulf War Syndrome." *60 Minutes* CBS, 20 Aug. 1995.

"VA Study Begins on Gulf War Illnesses." (Washington [AP].) *The Daily Mail* 9 Nov. 1995, sec. A:2.

"Legion Forms Task Force for Gulf Veterans, If You Want It Done Right..." *The American Legion* 139.6 (Dec.1995): 42.

Powell, Colin L. *My American Journey/With Joseph E. Persico*. New York: Random House, 1995, pp. 459-542.

1996

"The Gulf War, Part I." *Frontline*. MPT. 9 Jan. 1996.

"The Gulf War, Part II." *Frontline*. MPT. 10 Jan. 1996.

"The Gulf War +5." *CBS Reports*. Dan Rather, reporter. 18 Jan. 1996.

"Talking With David Frost." Interview of former President George Bush. PBS video. 29 Jan. 1996.

Miller, Claudia S., M.D., M.S. Presentation Before Presidential Advisory Committee on Gulf War Veterans' Illnesses Meeting. San Antonio, Texas. 27 Feb. 1996.

"Gulf Disease. Research funded by the U.S. Army and conducted at Jerusalem's Hebrew University is expected to shed light for the first time on the puzzling 'Gulf War Syndrome' that appeared among thousands of American soldiers in the wake of the 1991 war against Iraq." *Congregation B'Nai Abraham* 4.6 (Mar. 1996).

"Sick Gulf War Veterans Say VA Slow to Help." (Washington [AP].) *The Daily Mail* 12 Mar. 1996, sec. A:2.

Puglisi, Matthew L., Assistant Director, Gulf War Veterans, The American Legion. Letter to Jacob B. Berkson. 27 Mar. 1996.

"Veterans of the Gulf War. They Came Home Victorious, But Their Battles Aren't Over. Gulf War Legacies: Chemical Nightmares, Birth Defects, How the Legion Helps." *The American Legion* 140.5 (May 1996): cover.

Scharnberg, Ken. "Interview: Jonathan Tucker: Saddam's Toxic Plot. Did Iraqi Military Planners Hatch a Secret Scheme to Debilitate Our Troops With Low Levels of Chemical and Biological Weapons?" *The American Legion* 140.5 (May 1996): 26-27+.

Shellenberger, Michael. "In Defense of Gulf War Syndrome." *Our Toxic Times* 7.5 (May 1996): 17-18. Reprinted from the *San Francisco Chronicle*, April 9, 1996.

C. Agricultural Workers

Blair, Aaron, Ph.D. *An Overview of Potential Health Hazards Among Farmers From Use of Pesticides*. Cincinnati, Ohio: National Institute for Safety and Health, 1991.

"Excess Cancers Among Farmers." *NYCAP News* Early spring 1993: 5.

"Farm Worker's Death Fueled Fight to Ban Deadly Pesticide." (Fresno, CA [AP].) *The Daily Mail* 6 Sept. 1991, sec. A:8.

Fryzek, Glen Paul. Hickory Hills, Illinois. Deceased. Landscaping, Lawn, and Sod Field Maintenance.

Fryzek, Pat. "In Memory." *NYCAP News* 5.2 (Fall 1994): 19.

Levesque, William R. "Benlate: Phantom on the Farm. A Special Report. 'A Tragic Mess': The Story of the Fungicide Benlate Is a Tale Without Equal in Modern Agriculture, Leaving Florida Farmers With Little to Do Other Than Watch As Their Crops Wither and Die." Lakeland, Florida *The Ledger* 15-19 Nov. 1992: 1-12.

Long, Becky. "Oregon Farmworkers Union Boycotts Two Food Processing Companies. *Journal of Pesticide Reform* 13.1 (Spring 1993): 20.

Rodriguez, Arturo S., President. United Farm Workers of America AFL-CIO. Letter dated 10 Nov. 1995. Re: Cesar Chavez and Farmworkers' fight for social justice. National Headquarters: La Paz, P.O. Box 62, Keene, California 93531.

Schemo, Diana Jean. "The Price of Bananas." *The New York Times* 10 Dec. 1995, sec. 4:2.

D. Firefighters

"Carroll Co. Blaze Destroys Apartments." *The Daily Mail* 6 Dec. 1994, sec. A:7.

Ford, Clyde. "Firefighters Left Woozy." (Berkeley Springs, W.Va.) *The Daily Mail* 7 May 1991, sec. A:1.

Kilburn, Kaye H., M.D., Raphael H. Warsaw, and Megan G. Shields, M.D. "Neurobehavioral Dysfunction in Firemen Exposed to Polychlorinated Biphenyls (PCBs): Possible Improvement After Detoxification." *Archives of Environmental Health* 44.6 (Nov./Dec. 1989: 345-350.

"Public Nuisance and Injury." *Syracuse Post Standard* 23 Mar. 1993. In *NYCAP News* Summer 1993: 27.

Shields, Megan, M.D., Shelley L. Beckmann, Ph.D., and Ginny Cassidy-Brinn, R.N.P. "Improvement in Perception of Transcutaneous Nerve Stimulation Following Detoxification in Firefighters Exposed to PCBs, PCDDs and PCDFs." *Clinical Ecology* VI.2 (1989): 47-50.

E. Infants and Children

Center for Disease Control. "Pesticide Poisoning in an Infant— California." *MMWR—Morbidity and Mortality Weekly Report* 29.22 (6 June 1990).

"Child Cancer Risk Linked to Home Pesticide Use." (Washington [AP].) *The Daily Mail* 27 Feb. 1995, sec. A:2.

Children's Health Environmental Coalition (CHEC). *Our Children's Health Is at Risk...They Need Our Help.* Brochure. Malibu , California: CHEC, 1995.

Davis, James R., Ph.D. "Childhood Brain Cancer Linked to Consumer Pesticide Use." *Pesticides and You* Spring 1993: 18+.

Fenske, Richard A., Ph.D., M.P.H., et al. "Potential Exposure and Health Risks of Infants Following Indoor Residential Pesticide Applications." *American Journal of Public Health* 80 (1990): 689-693.

"Home Pesticide Use Linked to Child Cancer." *The New York Times* 27 Feb. 1995, National sec. B:7.

Landrigan, Philip J., M.D., and Joy E. Carlson. "Protecting Children's Health from Environmental Toxics. Understanding Children's Vulnerability and What Needs to Be Done." *Pesticides and You* 15.4 (Winter 1995-1996): 8-11.

Lefferts, Lisa Y. "Children, Pesticides, & Food: Federal Policies Provide Inadequate Protection." *Pesticides and You* 14.1 (Spring 1994): 15-18.

McMillion, Dave. "Infant Deaths Linked to Passive Smoking." (Charles Town, W.Va.) *The Herald-Mail* 27 Dec. 1992, sec. F:1+.

Mott, Lawrie, Farrel Vance, and Jennifer Curtis. *Handle With Care: Children and Environmental Carcinogens*. Natural Resources Defense Council, Oct. 1994.

"Parents Urged Not to Smoke in Homes." (Washington [AP].) *The Daily Mail* 21 July 1993.

"Pesticides and Children: What the Pediatric Practitioner Should Know." 1985 Nobel Peace Prize Physicians for Social Responsibility. Case Western Reserve University Department of Pediatrics. 1995. Physicians for Social Responsibility, 1101

Fourteenth Street Northwest, Suite 700, Washington D.C. 20005. Phone: (202) 898-0150.

"Pesticides Found in 50% of Baby Food. 'Pesticides Should Not Be Allowed in Baby Food Until They Have Been Proven Safe for Infants.'" *Pesticide Watch* 6.3 (Winter 1996): 2.

Protecting Children and Families From Pesticides. National Coalition Against the Misuse of Pesticides. Materials. Thirteenth National Pesticide Forum, 17-20 Mar. 1995

Rachel Carson Council. *A Parent Alert: Children at Risk From Household Pesticides.* Chevy Chase, Maryland: Rachel Carson Council, Inc.

Scharnberg, Ken. "Do Babies Dream? Perhaps More Than Anything— the Mysterious Illnesses, Staggering Medical Bills and Shattered Lives—Desert Storm Gis Are Tormented by the Thought That They Have Caused Their Children's Birth Defects." *The American Legion* 140.5 (May 1996): 28-30+.

"Study Finds Covered Pickup Trucks Can Expose Kids to Deadly Fumes." (Chicago [AP].) *The Daily Mail* 22 Jan. 1992, sec. A:6.

United States EPA—Office of Prevention, Pesticides, and Toxic Substances. *Background Questions and Answers—National Academy of Sciences Report: Pesticides in the Diets of Infants and Children.* Washington, D.C.: 28 June 1993.

United States General Accounting Office. *Report to the Honorable Gerald D. Kleczka, House of Representatives. Social Security: Rapid Rise in Children on SSI Disability Rolls Follows New Regulations.* Washington, D.C.: Sept. 1994.

Zwiener, Robert J., M.D., and Charles M. Ginsburg, M.D. "Organophosphate and Carbamate Poisoning in Infants and Children." *Pediatrics* 81.1 (Jan. 1988): 121+.

F. Golfers

"Golf Course Pesticides: Is Death Stalking the Links?" *Pesticides and You* 14.1 (Spring 1994): 9-10.

"Golfer Farr Remains Critically Ill." (Scottsdale, Ariz. [AP].) *The Herald-Mail* 20 Nov. 1993, sec. B:3.

"Health Tips." *The Johns Hopkins Medical Letter, Health After 50* 7.4 (June 1995): 8.

Jaffe, Susan, Special Assistant, et al. *Toxic Fairways: Risking Groundwater Contamination From Pesticides on Long Island Golf Courses.* New York: New York State Environment Protection Bureau, Robert Abrams, Attorney General, July 1991.

Lind, Pollyanna. "News From Around: Playing With Poisons? More Cancer Deaths Among Golf Course Superintendents." *Journal of Pesticide Reform* 14.2 (Summer 1994): 27.

Potter, Jerry. "Farr's Frightening Foe. LPGA Learns Realities of Breast Cancer." *USA Today* 7 Nov. 1991, sec. C:1+.

Prior, George M., Lieutenant, U.S. Navy. Deceased.

"The George M. Prior Memorial Fund." *NCAMP's Tenth Anniversary Commemorative Book:* 16.

*Lucy, Liza Prior. Widow. NCAMP Board of Directors.

Reisner, Mel. "Funeral Services Held for LPGA Member Farr. Professional Golfer Lost Four-Year Battle Against Cancer." (Phoenix [AP].) *The Daily Mail* 24 Nov. 1993, sec. D:4.

G. Miners/Industrial Workers

Buder, Leonard. "Verdict Upheld in Assault Case Over Mercury. Thermometer Makers Endangered Workers." (Brooklyn, N.Y.) *The New York Times* 29 Oct 1989, Metropolitan sec.:37

"Carbon Monoxide Kills 13 at Slovak Steel Plant." (Bratislava, Slovakia, Oct. 28 [Reuters].) *The New York Times* 29 Oct. 1995, International sec.:17.

Eldredge, Niles. *The Miner's Canary: Unraveling the Mysteries of Extinction.* New York: Prentice Hall Press, 1991.

"Silicosis Found in Lungs of Eight Surface Miners." (Pittsburgh [AP].) *The Daily Mail* 20 Apr. 1995, sec. A:6.

*Stewart, Rex. West Virginia. Former DuPont employee. NCAMP speaker 1993.

Jacob B. Berkson. Personal interview. Mar. 1993.

*Stinson, Doris. Neshanic Station, New Jersey. Former industrial worker. Correspondence with Jacob B. Berkson. Apr. 1995-.

H. Vietnam Vets/Agent Orange Victims

"Admiral Zumwalt Speaks on Dioxin and Scientific Conflict of Interest."
    Pesticides and You 15.4 (Winter 1995-96): 4.

*Agent Orange Coverup: A Case of Flawed Science and Political
    Manipulation, The. Twelth Report by the Committee on Government
    Operations Together With Dissenting Views.* 101st Congress, 2d
    Session. House Report 101-672. 9 Aug. 1990.—Committed to
    the Committee of the Whole House on the State of the Union
    and ordered to be printed. Washington, D.C.: U.S. Government
    Printing Office, 1990.

"And Justice for (Not Quite) All..." *The American Legion* Mar. 1996:
    38.

Gorman, Christine. "Agent Orange Redux: Reversing Previous
    Findings, Experts Link Hodgkin's Disease, Among Others, to the
    Vietnam-Era Defoliant." *Time* 9 Aug. 1993: 51.

"Report Links Agent Orange With Diseases." (Washington, D.C. [AP].)
    The Daily Mail 2 May 1990, sec. A:6.

"Two More Diseases Linked to Herbicide Used in Vietnam. Vietnam
    Veterans With Hodgkin's disease or With a Liver Disorder Called
    Porphyria Cutanea Tarda Will Become Eligible for Disability
    Payments Under a Proposed Rule." (Washington [AP].) *The Daily
    Mail* 27 July 1993, sec. A:5.

Zumwalt, E. R., Jr., Admiral, U.S. Navy (Ret.), Chairman, Agent
    Orange Coordinating Council. *Statement Before the Science
    Advisory Board, Executive Committee Meeting, U.S. Environmental
    Protection Agency.* 21 Sept. 1995.

————. *Statement Before the House Subcommittee on Energy and
    Environment.* 13 Dec. 1995.

————. Letter to Jacob B. Berkson. 1 Apr. 1996.

————. *Report to the Secretary of the Department of Veterans Affairs on
    the Association Between Adverse Health Effects and Exposure to Agent
    Orange.* 5 May 1990.

I. Nurses

McFarling, Usha Lee. "For Brigham Nurses, Health Woes Persist. 'I Had
    Chest Pain for Four Months Before I Went Out. They Were

Assuring Us It Was Getting Better.' Kathy Sperrazza, Nurse." *Boston Globe* 23 July 1994.

Scanlon, Sarah, R.N., and 46 other registered nurses. Boston, Massachusetts. *Can Buildings Make You Sick?* Mike Tomlinson, producer. Robin Brightwell, ed. NOVA, PBS, Boston, 26 Dec. 1995.

Young, Marsha L., Army nurse. "Women in Combat." *The American Legion* Oct. 1994: 6+.

III. Links—Cause and Effect
A. Acute—Non-Controversial

"Ammonia Leak Forces Evacuation." (Kindred, N.D.) *The Daily Mail* 23 Oct. 1992, sec. A:2.

Belisle, Richard F. "Tanker Leak Sends 10 to Hospital, Closes Truck Stop." (Martinsburg, W.Va.) *The Daily Mail* 28 May 1992, sec. B:3.

Berkson, Jacob B. "A Canary's Warning: The Link Between Pesticides and MCS." *Rachel Carson Council News No. 86* Oct. 1995: 1+.

Briggs, Shirley A. *Basic Guide to Pesticides: Their Characteristics and Hazards*. Rachel Carson Council. Washington, D.C.: Taylor & Francis, 1992.

"Carbon Monoxide Poisoning Sends Team to Hospital." (Dallas.) *The Daily Mail* 20 Jan. 1992, sec. A:1.

"Exterminator Charged in Redwood City Death." *San Francisco Chronicle* Aug. 1992.

"Family Treated for Burning Eyes." *The Daily Mail* 3 Jan. 1994, sec. B:2.

"Firm Stops Making Chemical After Leak." (Westover, W.Va.) *The Herald Mail* 15 Dec. 1990, sec. B:10.

"Five Injured in Hazardous Spill in W.Va." (Marlowe, W.Va.) *The Daily Mail* 27 May 1992, sec. B:3.

Ford, Clyde, and Laura Ernde. "Chemicals Hospitalize at Least 8." *The Daily Mail* 12 June 1992, sec. A:1+.

"4 Injured By Leak at Dry Cleaners." (Frederick, Md.) *The Daily Mail* 9 Mar. 1993, sec. B:4.

"Fumes Kill Boys in Trash Bin." (Tampa, Fla.) *The Daily Mail* 15 June 1992, sec. A:2.

"Lead Poisoning Death Prompts Call for Testing." (Atlanta.) *The Daily Mail* 29 Mar. 1991, sec. A:8.

McFadden, Nancy. "Terminix Strikes Again." *NYCAP News* 5.2 (Fall 1994): 19.

McMillion, Dave. "Infant Deaths Linked to Passive Smoking." (Charles Town, W.Va.) *The Herald-Mail* 27 Dec. 1992, sec. F:1+.

_____. "Poison Gas Sickens Hood Students at Party." (Frederick, Md.) *The Daily Mail* 15 Oct. 1990, sec. B:1.

Morgan, Donald P., M.D., Ph.D. *Recognition and Management of Pesticide Poisonings.* 4th ed. Washington, D.C.: United States Environmental Protection Agency, Mar. 1989.

"Pa. Man Dies in Garage Accident." (McConnellsburg, Pa.) "A 34-year-old Dublin Township man died of apparent carbon monoxide poisoning while working on a car at his home near Burnt Cabins Monday evening, according to Pennsylvania State Police.

"Police said Bruce Allan Snyder was overcome around 7 p.m. while working on a running car in a closed garage." *The Daily Mail* 6 Feb. 1996, sec. B:1.

"PCB Is Keeping 120 From Indiana Homes." (Highland, Ind.) *The New York Times* 9 Dec. 1990, International sec.:25.

"Pesticide Spray Kills Stowaways." (San Juan, Puerto Rico [AP].) *The Daily Mail* 20 June 1990, sec. A:9.

"Toxic Fumes Blamed in Disco Tragedy: 2,000 Attend Mass for 43 Victims." (Zaragoza, Spain.) *The Daily Mail* 15 Jan. 1990, sec. A:1.

"Toxic Gases Kill One, Sicken 37." (Sea Isle City, N.J.) *The Daily Mail* 27 Aug. 1992, sec. A:7.

"Toxic Smoke Kills 43 at Disco." (Zaragoza, Spain [AP].) *The News* (Frederick, Maryland) 15 Jan. 1990.

Turner, Dan. "New State Rules on Fumigation. Second Person Dies in Apartment Building That Had Been Treated." *San Francisco Chronicle* 4 Apr. 1992.

"Turpentine Spill at Westvaco Sends 56 to Area Hospitals." (Piedmont, W.Va.) *The Daily Mail* 26 July 1990, sec. C:4.

"Zoos Take Action on Antifreeze." (San Diego, Oct. 8 [AP].) *The New York Times* 8 Oct. 1995, National sec.:32.

B. Acute—Being Studied

Grossman, Laurie M. "The Smell of Chanel May Be No. 2 Issue After Cigarettes. Strong Odors of All Sorts Make People Sick or Merely

Mad; Now: Aroma-Free Zones." *The Wall Street Journal* 13 May 1993, eastern ed, sec. A:1+.

"Mustard Gas Tests." *The American Legion* Apr. 1993: 32.

"Refinery Release Problem: Residents Say Chemical Leak Made Them Sick." (Crockett, Calif. [AP].) *The Daily Mail* 14 Dec. 1994, sec. D:5.

"Registry Update." *The American Legion* Apr. 1993: 34.

Rowland, Tim. "Bad Sludge Caused Stir for Campers." (Williamsport, Md.) *The Daily Mail* 19 May 1992, sec. B:2.

"Runoff From Slaughterhouses May Be Source of Illness." (Milwaukee [AP].) *The Daily Mail* 9 Apr. 1993, sec. A:2.

Van Biema, David. "Prophet of Poison. After Tokyo Suffers a Nerve-Gas Attack, Suspicion Focuses on the Leader of an Apocalyptic Cult." *Time* 3 Apr. 1995: 26-33.

"Widely Used Pesticide Is Blamed for Illnesses." (Harrisburg, Pa. [AP].) *The Record Herald* 24 Feb. 1995, sec. B:6.

C. Chronic
1. Established/Recognized

"Government Plans Effort to Rid Nation of Lead Poisoning." (Washington, D.C.) *The Evening Sun* 20 Dec. 1990, sec. A:11.

Holloway, Lynette. "Lead Paint Is Removed From School. Queens Parents Get Action on Weekend." *The New York Times* 27 Sept. 1992, Metro sec. 1:36

"Maryland's Number One Public Health Problem." Winter 1994. The Coalition for a Smoke Free Maryland. 7401 Osler Drive Suite 206, Townson, Maryland 21204.

Pear, Robert. "U.S. Orders Testing of Poor Children for Lead Poisoning: Millions Under 6 at Risk, But Directive to Medicaid Will Let States Use Inaccurate Method of Screening." (Washington, D.C.) *The New York Times* 13 Sept. 1992, late ed:1+.

Perl, Rebecca. "Cover Story—Cigarettes: Lethal Little Packages." *The Washington Post* 11 Jan. 1994.

"Report Links Agent Orange With Diseases." (Washington, D.C. [AP].) *The Daily Mail* 2 May 1990, sec. A:6.

Rowland, Tim. "Lead Paint Not Just a Baltimore Problem." (Annapolis, Md.) *The Herald-Mail* 8 Mar. 1992, sec. A:1+.

"30,000 Baltimore Children May Have Lead Poisoning." *The Daily Mail* 13 Oct. 1989, sec. C:8.

"Two More Diseases Linked to Herbicide Used in Vietnam. Vietnam Veterans With Hodgkin's disease or With a Liver Disorder Called Porphyria Cutanea Tarda Will Become Eligible for Disability Payments Under a Proposed Rule." (Washington [AP].) *The Daily Mail* 27 July 1993, sec. A:5.

U.S. Department of Health and Human Services. Public Health Service. Centers for Disease Control. Center for Chronic Disease Prevention and Health Promotion. Office on Smoking and Health. *Smoking and Health: A National Status Report. A Report to Congress.* 2nd ed. Rockville, Maryland: Feb. 1990.

2. Being Studied

Colborn, Theo, Frederick S. vom Saal, and Ana M. Soto. "Developmental Effects of Endocrine-Disrupting Chemicals in Wildlife and Humans." *Environmental Health Perspectives* 101.5 (1993): 378-384.

"Company Recalls Leather Spray." (Minneapolis.) *The Daily Mail* 29 Dec. 1992, sec. A:2.

Filips, Janet. "Experts Study Links Between Chemicals, Ailments. Youngsters' Smaller Bodies May Be Less Able to Weather Pesticides' Effects." *The Sunday Oregonian* 14 May 1995, sec. A:18.

Guillette, L. J., Jr. "Endocrine-Disrupting Environmental Contaminants and Reproduction: Lessons From the Study of Wildlife." *Women's Health Today: Perspectives on Current Research and Clinical Practice* (D. R. Popkin and L. J. Peddle, eds.) New York: Parthenon Publ. Group, 1994. pp. 201-207.

Hirzy, J. William, and Rufus Morison. "Carpet/4- Phenylcyclohexene Toxicity: The EPA Headquarters Case." *Advances in Risk Analysis*. Vol. 9: *The Analysis, Communication, and Perception of Risk*. Ed.

B. John Garrick and Willard C. Gekler. Society for Risk Analysis. New York: Plenum Press, 1991.

Kong, Dolores. "Learning From Agent Orange: Government Preparing for Gulf War Health Questions." *The Daily Mail* 5 Aug. 1992, sec. B:9.

Landrigan, Philip J. "Pesticides May Be Doing Double Damage to Children." *The Herald-Mail* 25 July 1993, sec. F:6.

Laurence, Leslie. "Toxins May Be Cause of Rising Infertility Cases." *The Daily Mail* 30 Oct. 1995, sec. C:1.

"Lead Plant Workers Studied." (Pennsville Township, N.J.) *The Daily Mail* 28 Aug. 1992, sec. B:6.

Lemonick, Michael D. "Not So Fertile Ground: Some Scientists Fear That Pollutants Are Damaging Human Reproductive Systems." *Time* 19 Sept. 1994: 68-70.

_____. "What's Wrong With Our Sperm? Men's Reproductive Cells Seem to Be in Serious Decline Worldwide. One Possible Cause: Chemical Pollution." Photo: "Spreading Infertility? Pesticides Sprayed By Crop Dusters Like This One Are Among Suspects Being Investigated." *Time* 18 Mar. 1996: 78-79.

McMillion, Dave. "Attorney Cites School Library Health Threat. Jefferson Co. Officials Argue Ranson Elementary Work Safe." (Ranson, W.Va.) *The Morning Herald* 10 Jan. 1992, sec. B:1.

_____. "Ranson School to Remove Controversial Wooden Beams." (Charles Town, W.Va.) *The Daily Mail* 11 Mar. 1992, sec. B:2.

_____. "Beams Librarian Said Made Her Sick Coming Down." (Ranson, W.Va.) *The Herald-Mail* 6 Aug. 1992, sec. C:8.

Sherman, Janette D. "Structure-Activity Relationships of Chemicals Causing Endocrine, Reproductive, Neurotoxic, and Oncogenic Effects—A Public Health Problem." *Toxicology and Industrial Health* 10.3 (1994): 163-179.

_____. Organophosphate Pesticides—Neurological and Respiratory Toxicity. *Toxicology and Industrial Health* 11.1 (1995): 33-39.

_____. "Chlorpyrifos (Dursban)—Associated Birth Defects: A Proposed Syndrome, Report of Four Cases, and Discussion of the Toxicology." *Internation Journal of Occupational Medicine and*

Toxicology 4.4 (1995): 417-431. Copyright © 1995 Princeton Scientific Publishing Co., Inc.

Smith, Linda Wasmer. "Falling Sperm Counts and Chemicals." *Medical & Legal Briefs* 1.1 (July/Aug. 1995: 1-3.

"Suit Links Bugspray and Birth Defects: NY Couple Fights Dow." *Pesticides and You* Dec. 1990: 4.

"Vets Hospital Sets Up Clinic for Gulf Soldiers." (Durham, N.C.) *The Daily Mail* 19 Aug. 1992, sec. B:8.

3. Chemical Exposure and Cancer

Angier, Natalie. "A Special Risk for Leukemia Patients." *The New York Times* 7 Nov. 1991, National sec. B:14.

Brown, David. "Cancer Risk Up Sharply in This Era: New Study Suggests Preventable Causes Are Still Unidentified." *The Washington Post* 9 Feb. 1994, sec. A:1+.

Callahan, Daniel. "Lab Games: A Look at the Way Interest Groups Use and Abuse Cancer Research for Their Own Ends." *The New York Times* 9 Apr. 1995, Book Review sec.: 15.

"Child Cancer Risk Linked to Home Pesticide Use." (Washington [AP].) *The Daily Mail* 27 Feb. 1995, sec. A:2.

Davidoff, Linda Lee, Ph.D. Letter to Physician on subject of lawn care pesticides. 3 Apr. 1989.

Davis, Devra Lee, Ph.D., M.P.H., Gregg E. Dinse, Sc.D., and David G. Hoel, Ph.D. "Decreasing Cardiovascular Disease and Increasing Cancer Among Whites in the United States From 1973 Through 1987: Good News and Bad News." *JAMA* 271.6 (9 Feb. 1994): 431-437.

Davis, James R., et al. "Family Pesticide Use and Childhood Brain Cancer." *Archives of Environmental Contamination and Toxicology* 24 (1993): 87-92.

"DDT Linked to Cancer in Workers." (Philadelphia.) *The Daily Mail* 26 July 1990, sec. A:9.

"Effects of Chemical Pesticides on Human Health." *NYCAP News* 3.4 (Late Fall, 1992): 12.

Epstein, Samuel S., M.D. *The Politics of Cancer.* San Francisco, California: Sierra Club Books, 1978.

_____. "Smoking Declines, Yet Cancers Multiply." *The New York Times* 30 Sept. 1994.

_____. "Environmental and Occupational Pollutants Are Avoidable Causes of Breast Cancer." *International Journal of Health Services* 24.1 (1994): 145-150.

_____, and Marvin S. Legator. *The Mutagenicity of Pesticides: Concepts and Evaluation.* Cambridge, Massachusetts: The MIT Press, 1971.

"Excess Cancers Among Farmers." *NYCAP News* 4.1 (1993): 5.

"Factors That Might Lead to the Development of Cancer." *Cancer Crusader* Winter 1992.

Gorman, Christine. "Agent Orange Redux: Reversing Previous Findings, Experts Link Hodgkin's Disease, Among Others, to the Vietnam-Era Defoliant." *Time* 9 Aug. 1993: 51.

Hansen, Mark. "Second-Hand Smoke Suit: Flight Attendants Blame Tobacco Companies for Cancer, Risk of Illness." *ABA Journal* Feb. 1992: 26.

Hilts, Philip J. "Breast Implant Tied to Cancer By the F.D.A. Hundreds of Thousands Are Using the Devices." *The New York Times* 14 Apr. 1991, National sec. 1:18.

"Husband Wins Claim in Secondhand Smoke Death." *The New York Times* 17 Dec. 1995, sec. 1:28.

"In Harm's Way." *The New York Times* 9 Feb. 1992, XII-L1:4.

Kay, Jane. "Chemicals Likely Link to Breast Cancer." *Co Examiner* 23 Feb. 1994, sec. A:1+.

_____. "Cancer Linked to Use of DDT: But Some Dispute Israeli Findings." *Co Examiner* 2 Mar. 1994, sec. A:4.

Malakoff, David. "Breast Cancer & Pesticides: What's the Connection?" *Pesticides and You* 13.3 & 4 (1993-1994):16- 17+.

Margolis, Simeon, M.D., Ph.D., and Hamilton Moses, III, M.D., ed. "Industrial Agents and Chemicals" in "Chapter 1: Cancer." *The*

Johns Hopkins Medical Handbook; The 100 Major Medical Disorders of People Over the Age of 50. New York: Rebus, Inc., 1992. p. 22.

"Men Link Tumors to 'Sick' Building. State Investigating Rare Brain Cancers in Former Environmental Crime Fighters." *The Daily Mail* 23 Mar. 1992, sec. C:3.

Nash, J. Madeleine. "Stopping Cancer in Its Tracks: New Discoveries About Wayward Genes and Misbehaving Proteins Show Cells Become Malignant—and Perhaps How to Bring Them Under Control." *Time* 25 Apr. 1994: 54+.

"Neighbors Say Factory Contaminated Town." (Atlanta) *The New York Times* 15 Aug. 1993, National sec.:19.

"New Research Links Breast Cancer to Pesticides Yet Federal Regulators May Permit Carcinogenic Pesticides in Food!" *Pesticide Action Alert* May 1993.

"Pollution Blamed for Sharp Climb in Cancer." (New York.) *The Daily Mail* 10 Dec. 1990, sec. A:2.

Post, Diana, VMD. "Breast Cancer and Pesticides." *Rachel Carson Council News No. 82* Mar. 1994: 1.

Proctor, Robert N. *Cancer Wars. How Politics Shapes What We Know About Cancer.* New York: Basic Books, 1995.

Quindlen, Anna. "Public & Private: Mother and Child—the Legacy and Lesson of DES." *The New York Times* 9 May 1993, Op-ed sec.

"Relentless DDT: Years Later, Residual Amounts of the Pesticide May Trigger Breast Tumors." *Time* 3 May 1993: 24.

Snyder, George. "Yuroks Fear Cancer From Spraying." *San Francisco Chronicle* sec. A:1.

Ubell, Earl. "Stepping Up the Fight Against Breast Cancer. Despite Scientific Breakthroughs, Cure Rates Remain Disappointing. But Women Have Lobbied for More Research Funds, and New Studies May Bring Answers." *Parade Magazine* 11 Sept. 1994: 24+.

Watson, Traci. "Breast Cancer's Deadly Masquerade? A Controversial Theory Says That Ubiquitous Toxic Chemicals may Mimic a Natural Hormone." *U.S. News & World Report* 7 Feb. 1994: 59-60.

"What You Need to Know About Breast Cancer." Informational advertisement. America's Pharmaceutical Research Companies.
Phone: 1-800-862-4110.

"Workers' Comp Case Linked to Smoke." Indianapolis [AP].) *The
Herald-Mail* 16 Dec. 1995, sec. A:2.

4. Chemical Exposure and the Lungs and Respiratory System

"Asthma Death Rate Climbed 46% in '80s." (Atlanta.) *The Daily Mail*
5 Oct. 1992, sec. B:4.

Burton, Sandra. "Environment: Taming the River Wild. The World's
Largest Dam Is Under Way in China, But It Won't Solve the
Country's Giant Energy Problems." *Time* 19 Dec. 1994: 62+.

"Chemicals and Tobacco Smoke." *Breathing Easy With Asthma.* Kansas
City, Mo.: Marion Merrell Dow, Inc., 1991.

Gorman, Christine. "Medicine—Asthma: The Hidden Killer. Model
Krissy Taylor's Death Underscores How Lethal and Deceptive This
Common Ailment Can Be." Time 7 Aug. 1995: 56.

"Lung Cancer Is Always Treatable." *The Johns Hopkins Medical Letter,
Health After 50* 7.6 (Aug. 1995): 1-2.

Margolis, Simeon, M.D., Ph.D., and Hamilton Moses, III, M.D., ed.
"Asthma" in "Chapter 11: The Lungs and Respiratory System."
*The Johns Hopkins Medical Handbook; The 100 Major Medical
Disorders of People Over the Age of 50.* New York: Rebus, Inc.,
1992. pp. 324-328.

_____. "Chronic Bronchitis" in "Chapter 11: The Lungs and
Respiratory System." *The Johns Hopkins Medical Handbook; The
100 Major Medical Disorders of People Over the Age of 50.* New
York: Rebus, Inc., 1992. pp. 328-330.

_____. "Emphysema" in "Chapter 11: The Lungs and Respiratory
System." *The Johns Hopkins Medical Handbook; The 100 Major
Medical Disorders of People Over the Age of 50.* New York: Rebus,
Inc., 1992. pp. 330-331.

Pennybacker, Mindy. "Breathing Space: What You Can Do to Stop the
Rise of Asthma." *The Green Guide* 21 (1 Mar. 1996): 1-3+.

Understanding Asthma. Denver, Colo.: National Jewish Center for Immunology and Respiratory Medicine, 1992.

5. Chemical Exposure and the Ears, Nose and Throat

Margolis, Simeon, M.D., Ph.D., and Hamilton Moses, III, M.D., ed. "Sinusitis" in "Chapter 6: The Ears, Nose, and Throat." *The Johns Hopkins Medical Handbook; The 100 Major Medical Disorders of People Over the Age of 50*. New York: Rebus, Inc., 1992. pp. 220-223.

_____. "Smell and Taste Disorders" in "Chapter 6: The Ears, Nose, and Throat." *The Johns Hopkins Medical Handbook; The 100 Major Medical Disorders of People Over the Age of 50*. New York: Rebus, Inc., 1992. pp. 223- 225.

_____. "Sore Throat" in "Chapter 6: The Ears, Nose, and Throat." *The Johns Hopkins Medical Handbook; The 100 Major Medical Disorders of People Over the Age of 50*. New York: Rebus, Inc., 1992. pp. 226-228.

6. Chemical Exposure and the Brain and Nervous System

Daly, Helen B. "Chapter 7: The Evaluation of Behavioral Changes Produced by Consumption of Environmentally Contaminated Fish." *The Vulnerable Brain and Environmental Risks, Volume 1: Malnutrition and Hazard Assessment*. Ed. Robert L. Isaacson and Karl F. Jensen. New York: Plenum Press, 1992. pp. 151-171.

Margolis, Simeon, M.D., Ph.D., and Hamilton Moses, III, M.D., ed. "Dementia" in "Chapter 3: The Brain and Nervous System." *The Johns Hopkins Medical Handbook; The 100 Major Medical Disorders of People Over the Age of 50*. New York: Rebus, Inc., 1992. pp. 97-101.

_____. "Alzheimer's Disease" in "Chapter 3: The Brain and Nervous System." *The Johns Hopkins Medical Handbook; The 100 Major Medical Disorders of People Over the Age of 50*. New York: Rebus, Inc., 1992. p. 105.

_____. "Headache" in "Chapter 3: The Brain and Nervous System." *The Johns Hopkins Medical Handbook; The 100 Major Medical Disorders of People Over the Age of 50*. New York: Rebus, Inc., 1992. p. 126.

7. Chemical Exposure and the Digestive System

Margolis, Simeon, M.D., Ph.D., and Hamilton Moses, III, M.D., ed. "Inflammatory Bowel Disease" in "Chapter 5: The Digestive System." *The Johns Hopkins Medical Handbook; The 100 Major Medical Disorders of People Over the Age of 50.* New York: Rebus, Inc., 1992. pp. 195-199.

8. Pesticides and the Immune System

Repetto, Robert, and Sanjay S. Baliga. *Pesticides and the Immune System: The Public Health Risks.* Washington, D.C.: World Resources Institute, 1996.

● ● ●

Note: For overall coverage of this section, III. Links—Cause and Effect, see:

Sherman, Janette D., M.D. *Chemical Exposure and Disease: Diagnostic and Investigative Techniques. The Professional and Layperson's Guide to Understanding, Cause and Effect.* Princeton, New Jersey: Princeton Scientific Publishing Co., Inc., 1994.

IV. Multiple Chemical Sensitivity/MCS
Symptoms, History, Definition, Controversy

Ashford, Nicholas A., Ph.D., J.D., and Claudia S. Miller, M.D., M.S. *Chemical Sensitivity: A Report to the New Jersey State Department of Health.* Dec. 1989.

_____. *Chemical Exposures: Low Levels and High Stakes.* New York: Van Nostrand Reinhold, 1991.

Baker, Gordon P., M.D. "Medical Up-Date: A Rebuttal to the Simon Study." *Our Toxic Times* 93 4(6):3-4.

Barrett, Stephen, M.D. *Unproven "Allergies": An Epidemic of Nonsense.* New York: American Council on Science and Health, Inc., 1993.

Bascom, Rebecca, M.D., M.P.H. *Chemical Hypersensitivity Study.* Prepared in response to Maryland Senate Joint Resolution 32. 8 Dec. 1988.

Bell, Iris R., M.D., Ph.D. "White Paper: Neuropsychiatric Aspects of Sensitivity to Low-Level Chemicals: A Neural Sensitization Model." Proceedings of the Conference on Low-Level Exposure to Chemicals and Neurobiologic Sensitivity. *Toxicology and Industrial Health* 10(4/5) (July-October 1994): 277:312.

Berkson, Jacob B. "Patient Statement: A Canary's Tale." Presented to the Conference on Low Level Exposure to Chemicals and Neurobiologic Sensitivity, ATSDR, Baltimore, MD, 6-7 Apr. 1994. *Toxicology and Industrial Health* 10.4/5 (1994): 323-326. Copyright © 1994 Princeton Scientific Publishing Co., Inc.

_____. "A Canary's Warning: The Link Between Pesticides and MCS." *Rachel Carson Council News No.* 86 Oct. 1995: 1+.

Conrad, Richard H., Ph.D. Symposium talk to CDHS/ATSDR. Berkeley, 5 May 1994.

Council on Scientific Affairs, American Medical Association. "Clinical Ecology." *Issue One* 1993: 20-23. Originally published in *The Journal of the American Medical Association (JAMA)* 23/30 Dec. 1992, 268.24: 3465-3467.

Davidoff, Linda L., Ph.D. *Multiple Chemical Sensitivities: Research on Psychiatric/Psychosocial Issues.* Paper presented at the symposium Multiple Chemical Sensitivity and the Environment II: Diagnosis and Therapy. American Public Health Association, Atlanta, GA, 13 Nov. 1991.

Davidoff, Ann L., and Linda Fogarty. "Psychogenic Origins of Multiple Chemical Sensitivities Syndrome: A Critical Review of the Research Literature." *Archives of Environmental Health* 49.5 (Sept./Oct. 1994): 316-325.

Davis, Earon S., J.D., M.P.H. "The New Chemical Victims." *The Human Ecologist* 32 (1986): 19+.

Duehring, Cindy and Cynthia Wilson. *The Human Consequences of the Chemical Problem.* White Sulphur Springs, Mont.: TT Publishing, 1994.

Gibson, Pamela Reed. "Environmental Illness/Multiple Chemical Sensitivities: Invisible Disabilities." *Women & Therapy* Vol. 14, No. 3/4, 1993: 171-185 and *Women with Disabilities: Found Voices* (ed: Mary E. Willmuth, and Lillian Holcomb) The Haworth Press, Inc., 1993: 171-185.

Heuser, Gunnar, M.D., Ph.D., F.A.C.P. "*Editorial:* Diagnostic Markers in Clinical Immunotoxicology and Neurotoxicology." *Journal of Occupational Medicine and Toxicology* 1.4 (1992): v-x.

Hilleman, Bette, and Owen Washington. "Multiple Chemical Sensitivity." *Chemical & Engineering News* 22 July 1991: 26-42.

Jaffe, Russell, M.D., Ph.D., FASCP, FACN, FAIAIS, and Marshall Hoffman, B.S., M.S. *16 Million Americans Are Sensitive to Pesticides.* Reston, VA: Health Studies Collegium, Report 90100, Mar. 1990.

Lambert, Wade. "More Claim Chemicals Made Them Ill." *The Wall Street Journal* 17 Jan. 1995, sec. B:1+.

Larson, David, E., M.D., ed-in-chief. "Twentieth-Century Allergy: Fact or Fiction?" in "Part II: The World Around Us." *The Mayo Clinic Family Health Book.* New York: William Morrow and Co., Inc., 1990. p. 332.

_____. "20th Century Syndrome: Can You Be Allergic to Modern Times?" in "Allergies." *The Mayo Clinic Family Health book.* New York: William Morrow and Co., Inc., 1990. p. 455.

Lawson, Lynn. *Staying Well in a Toxic World: Understanding Environmental Illness, Multiple Chemical Sensitivities, Chemical Injuries, and Sick Building Syndrome.* Chicago: The Noble Press, Inc., 1994.

Matthews, Bonnye. *Chemical Sensitivity: A Guide to Coping With Hypersensitivity Syndrome, Sick Building Syndrome and Other Environmental Illnesses.* Jefferson, N.C.: McFarland & Co., Inc., 1992.

Miller, Claudia S., M.D., M.S. "White Paper: Chemical Sensitivity: History and Phenomenology." *Toxicology and Industrial Health* 10.4/5 (1994): 253-276.

Mitchell, Frank L., D.O., M.P.H., ed. *Proceedings of the Conference on Low-Level Exposure to Chemicals and Neurobiological Sensitivity, 6-7 April, 1994, Baltimore, Maryland.* Princeton, New Jersey: Princeton Scientific Publishing Co., Inc.

Morton, William, M.D., Dr. PH. "Chronic Porphyrias' Role in MCS." *Our Toxic Times* 6.8 (Aug. 1995): 22-24.

Multiple Chemical Sensitivities: Addendum to Biologic Markers in Immunotoxicology. Washington, D.C.: National Academy Press, 1992.

Multiple Chemical Sensitivities at Work: A Training Workbook for Working People. New York: The Labor Institute, 1993.

"Multiple Chemical Sensitivity." *Rachel's Hazardous Waste News #165* 24 Jan. 1990.

"Multiple Chemical Sensitivity: Disorders of Porphyrin Metabolism: New Protocol Helps Patients Get Tested." *NYCAP News* 5.3 (Summer 1995): 27.

Orselli, Janet. "Chemically Poisoned, Please…Not 'Sensitive.'" *The Wary Canary* 8: 14.

Randolph, T. G. *Environmental Medicine—Beginnings and Bibliographies of Clinical Ecology.* Fort Collins, CO: Clinical Ecology Publications, Inc., 1987.

_____, and R. W. Moss. *An Alternative Approach to Allergies.* New York: Harper and Row, 1989.

Rea, William J., M.D., F.A.C.S., F.A.A.E.M. "Part II: Tracing the Roots of the 20th Century Illness." *The Human Ecologist* 41: 24-25.

_____. *Chemical Sensitivity.* 2 vols. Boca Raton, Fla.: Lewis Publishers, 1994.

Recognition of Multiple Chemical Sensitivity (Albert Donnay, compiler and ed. Desert Storm Veterans Coalition and MCS Referral and

Resources, Apr. 1994) reprinted in *The New Reactor* July/Aug. 1994: 14.

Reinhold, Robert. "When Life Is Toxic: They Suffer Agonizing Reaction From Contact With Almost Anything Chemical, Forcing Them Into Protective Cocoons. They Call It a Disease, But Is It? Not All Doctors Are Convinced." *The New York Times Magazine* 16 Sept. 1990: 50-51+.

Rest, Kathleen M., ed. "Proceedings of the Association of Occupational and Environmental Clinics (AOEC) Workshop on Multiple Chemical Sensitivity." *Toxicology and Industrial Health: An International Journal, Special Issue* 8.4 (July-Aug. 1992).

Rogers, Sherry, M.D. "*Environmental Medicine Update:* Is It Senility or Chemical Sensitivity?" *The Healer* Fall 1992: 14.

Rosenthal, Norman E., M.D., and Christine L. Cameron, B.S. "Letters to the Editor: Exaggerated Sensitivity to an Organophosphate Pesticide." *American Journal of Psychiatry* 148.2 (1991): 270.

Schacker, Stephen A., M.D. "Kindling and Chemical Sensitivity." *Our Toxic Times* Vol 5, No. 1, Jan. 1994.

Selner, John C., M.D. "Chemical Sensitivity." *Current Therapy in Allergy, Immunology and Rheumatology.* Ed. Lawrence M. Lichtenstein, M.D., Ph.D., and Anthony S. Fauci, M.D. Toronto: B. C. Decker, Inc., 1988.

Thrasher, Jack D., Roberta Madison, and Alan Broughton. "Immunologic Abnormalities in Humans Exposed to Chlorpyrifos: Preliminary Observations." *Archives of Environmental Health* Vol. 48, No. 2, Mar./Apr. 1993: 89-93.

Twombly, Renee. "MCS: A Sensitive Issue." *Environmental Health Perspectives: Journal of the National Institute of Environmental Health Sciences* 102.9 (Sept. 1994): 746-750.

Weisskopf, Michael. "Hypersensitivity to Chemicals Called Rising Health Problem. Some Cannot Adapt to Low Doses of Toxics, Study Says." *The Washington Post* 10 Feb. 1990, sec. A:2.

Wilson, Cynthia. "CFS—FM—MCS: Are They One and the Same Illness?" *Our Toxic Times* 6.7 (July 1995): 1+.

_____. "MCS: A World-wide Problem." *Our Toxic Times* 6.8 (Aug. 1995): 1+.

_____. "Porphyrinopathies in the MCS Community." *Our Toxic Times* 7.3 (Mar. 1996): 1+.

Ziem, Grace, M.D., Dr. P.H., and Linda L. Davidoff, Ph.D. "Editorial— Illness From Chemical 'Odors': Is the Health Significance Understood?" *Archives of Environmental Health* 47.1 (Jan./Feb. 1992): 88-91.

V. Environmental Medicine
A. Explanation
History, Definition, Diagnosis, Controversy

Baker, Gordon P., M.D. "Porphyria and MCS Overlap Symptoms: Another Chemical Connection." *Our Toxic Times*, vol 5, no. 8, Aug. 1994: 1+.

"Clinical Ecology: Council on Scientific Affairs, American Medical Association." *The Journal of the American Medical Association*, vol. 268, no. 24, 23/30 Dec. 1992: 3465-3467.

Crook, William G., M.D. *The Yeast Connection: A Medical Breakthrough.* Jackson, Tenn.: Professional Books, 1984.

Duehring, Cindy. "Chemical Injury, CFIDS and Chemical Sensitivity: A Crossroads for Industry and Society. An Interview With Gunnar Heuser, M.D., Ph.D., F.A.C.P." *Informed Consent* Nov./Dec. 1993: 3-5.

_____. "Medical Interview—Pesticides and Human Health: An Interview With Dr. Marion Moses." *Informed Consent* May/June 1994: 21+.

_____. "Profile by Cindy Duehring: *Chemical/Chemical Sensitivity: Objective Tests and Findings.*" *Our Toxic Times*, vol. 4, no. 4, Apr. 1993: 5-6.

_____. "Medical Interview—Parallels Between Seasonal Affective Disorder and Multiple Chemical Sensitivity: An Interview With Norman Rosenthal M.D." *Informed Consent* Nov./Dec. 1994: 40-43.

_____. "Case-Controlled Neurospect Brain Scan Study Shows Impairment in Chemically Exposed Patients." *Our Toxic Times* 7.2 (February 1996): 13+.

_____, and Cynthia Wilson. "Medical Challenges in Toxic Health Issues." *The Human Consequences of the Chemical Problem.* White Sulphur Springs, Mont.: TT Publishing, 1994.

Environmental Physician, The. Medical journal published by the American Academy of Environmental Medicine. P.O. Box 16106, Denver, CO 80216. Phone: (303) 622-9755.

Frank, Arthur W. "Illness Is Us: The Author Sees His Asthma as an Occasion to Connect Body, Self and Society." (Book review of

Brookes, Tim. *Catching My Breath: An Asthmatic Explores His Illness*. New York: Times Books/ Random House.) *The New York Times* 25 Sept. 1994, sec. 7:23.

Heuser, Gunnar, M.D., Ph.D., F.A.C.P. *"Editorial:* Diagnostic Markers in Clinical Immunotoxicology and Neurotoxicology." *Journal of Occupational Medicine and Toxicology* 1.4 (1992): v-x.

_____, Ismael Mena, M.D., and Francisca Alamos, Ph.D. of the Division of Nuclear Medicine, Harbor-University of California Los Angeles (UCLA) Medical Center in Torrance, California. "Neurospect Findings in Patients exposed to Neurotoxic Chemicals." *Toxicology and Industrial Health* 10(4/5) (1994): 561-571.

Jaffe, Russell M., M.D., Ph.D., Director, Serammune Physicians Lab. *Chronic Fatigue Protocol—Clinical Suggestions*. Reprinted from *International Clinical Nutrition Review*, 1991; 11:85-91.

_____. *Effective Therapies for Treatment Resistant Patients*. Seminar. Bethesda, Maryland. 22 May 1993. Serammune Physicians Lab. Providers of the Elisa/Act™. 1890 Preston White Drive, Suite 201, Reston, VA 22091. Phone: (800) 553-5472.

Lieberman, Allan D., M.D. *Introduction: Concepts of Environmental Medicine*. North Charleston, SC: Center for Environmental Medicine, 1 Mar. 1991.

Rea, William J., M.D., F.A.C.S., F.A.A.E.M. "Part II—Tracing the Roots of the 20th Century Illness." *The Human Ecologist* 41: 24-25.

_____. *Outpatient Information*. Dallas, TX: Environmental Health Center—Dallas, Oct. 1988.

Rogers, Sherry, M.D. "Total Load." *The Human Ecologist* 32 (1986): 7-8.

Roueché, Berton. "Annals of Medicine: The Fumigation Chamber." *The New Yorker* 4 Jan. 1988: 60-65.

Sherman, Janette D., M.D. *Chemical Exposure and Disease: Diagnostic and Investigative Techniques. The Professional and Layperson's Guide to Understanding, Cause and Effect*. Princeton, New Jersey: Princeton Scientific Publishing Co., Inc., 1994.

Snyder, Clovis, M.D. "Other Allergic Disorders/Multiple Chemical Sensitivities." *Antietam Medical Associates: Allergy Services*.

Ziem, Grace, M.D. "Diagnosing and Treating Chemically Injured People." *Pesticides and You* Summer/Fall 1993: 8+.

B. Treatment
1. Avoidance—Education—Recognition—Prevention

Universally accepted by all authorities

2. Medical

Lieberman, Allan D., M.D., F.A.A.E.M., and Hildegarde L. A. Sacarello, Ph.D. *Center for Environmental Medicine: Program for Biodetoxification—Designed to Reduce the Body's Burden of Toxic Environmental Chemical Contaminants.* North Charleston, SC: Center for Environmental Medicine.

Randolph, Theron G., M.D., and R. Michael Wisner. *Detoxification: Personal Survival in a Chemical World.* HealthMed, Inc., 1988.

Rea, William J., M.D., F.A.C.S., et al. *Environmental Control of Indoor Air Pollution in Hospital and Home Environment in Relation to Cardiovascular Disease.* Dallas, TX.

United States EPA. *Recognition and Management of Pesticide Poisonings.* 4th ed. Donald P. Morgan, M.D., Ph.D. Washington: Mar. 1989.

Weil, Andrew, M.D. *Spontaneous Healing: How to Discover and Enhance Your Body's Natural Ability to Maintain and Heal Itself.* New York: Alfred A. Knopf, 1995.

Ziem, Grace E., M.D., Dr. PH. "Multiple Chemical Sensitivity: Treatment and Followup With Avoidance and Control of Chemical Exposures." *Toxicology and Industrial Health*, vol. 8, no. 4, 1992: 73-86.

_____, and Albert Donnay, M.H.S. MCS Referral & Resources. 2326 Pickwick Road, Baltimore MD 21207-6631.

3. Change of Lifestyle
a. Food—Nutrition—Organic—Rotation Diet

Ashford, Nicholas A., and Claudia S. Miller. "Mechanisms, Diagnosis, and Treatment." *Chemical Exposures: Low Levels and High Stakes.* New York: Van Nostrand Reinhold, 1991: 138-140.

Golos, Natalie, and William J. Rea, M.D. *Success in the Clean Bedroom: A Path to Optimal Health*. Rochester, New York: Pinnacle Publishers, 1992.

Schechter, Steven, R., N.D. *Fighting Radiation & Chemical Pollutants With Foods, Herbs, & Vitamins: Documented Natural Remedies That Boost Your Immunity & Detoxify*. Encinitas, CA: Vitality, Ink, 1991.

Steinman, David. *Diet for a Poisoned Planet: How to Choose Safe Foods for You and Your Family*. New York: Harmony Books, 1990

b.   Clothing—Natural Material, No Synthetics

Schneider, Paul. "The Cotton Brief: Really Now, How Green Is Your Underwear? Is It Organically Grown Cotton, Unprocessed Cotton, or Hide-the-Label Synthetic? So Many Choices. What's an Eco-Shopper to Do?" *The New York Times* 20 June, 1993, sec. 9:1+.

c.   Shelter—A Healthy Less Toxic Home

Bower, Lynn Marie. *The Healthy Household: A Complete Guide for Creating a Healthy Indoor Environment*. Bloomington, Indiana: The Healthy House Institute, 1995.

Snyder, Clovis M., M.D., F.A.C.A. *Guide to "Desensitizing" a Room*. Richmond, Virginia: A.H. Robbins Company, n.d.

d.   Products—Environmentally Sound

Dadd, Debra Lynn. *Nontoxic, Natural, & Earthwise: How to Protect Yourself and Your Family from Harmful Products and Live in Harmony With the Earth*. Los Angeles: Jeremy P. Tarcher, Inc., 1990.

Elkington, John, Julia Hailes, and Joel Makower. *The Green Consumer*. Penguin Book, 1990.

e.   Exercise—Essential

Peterson, James A., Ph.D., and Cedric X. Bryant, Ph.D. *Ten Reasons Why Aerobic Exercise Is Important*. Parley International, 1989.

f. Alternatives

Rochlitz, Prof. Steven. *Allergies and Candida with the Physicist's Rapid Solution. Towards a Science of Healing.* Vol. 1. 3rd ed. New York: Human Ecology Balancing Sciences, Inc., 1991.

Note: Additional material in Section XII of this volume.

VI. Mystery Illnesses

Altman, Lawrence K. "Mystery Illness Slows in Cuba, But Cause Still Eludes Experts." *The New York Times* 4 July, 1993, International sec.:12.

_____. Poison Gas Attacks: Why a Diagnosis Is So Difficult. *The New York Times* 18 Sept. 1988: 14.

_____. "U.S. Scientists Baffled By a Cuban Epidemic." *The New York Times* 30 May 1993, International sec.:17.

Barnhart, Marlo. "Sewer Odor a Mystery. Four Overcome By Fumes; Tests Planned Today." *The Daily Mail* 11 Sept. 1992, sec. A:1+.

Belisle, Richard F. "Mystery of Fallen Firefighters Continues." (Berkeley Springs, W.Va.) *The Daily Mail* 8 May 1991, sec. B:3.

Brazil, Eric. "Gambling With Pesticides: Casino Hit By Mystery Illness. Workers Blame Cockroach Spray for Nausea, Seizures at Harvey's Tahoe." (South Lake Tahoe.) *San Francisco Examiner* 5 Apr. 1992, sec. B:1+.

"Farm Worker's Death Fueled Fight to Ban Deadly Pesticide." (Fresno, Calif. [AP}.) *The Daily Mail* 6 Sept. 1991, sec. A:8.

Ford, Clyde. "Firefighters Left Woozy." (Berkeley Springs, W.Va.) *The Daily Mail* 7 May 1991, sec. A:1.

"Goo Surfaces in Refinery Town; Attention Turns to Old Oil Pit." (Baytown, Tex., Sept. 9 [AP].) *The New York Times* 10 Sept. 1995, National sec.:39.

Hedges, Chris. "Girls in Egypt Faint By Score in Classrooms." *The New York Times* 18 Apr. 1993, International sec.:9.

"Illnesses at Firehouse Under Investigation." (Queens, New York.) *The New York Times* 27 Sept. 1992, Metro sec.

"Irritant Affects 5 at School." *The Washington Post* 13 Dec. 1994, sec. D:3.

Johnson, Marguerite. "Valley Fever: A Dust-Borne Fungus Is Causing an Epidemic of Misery and Rising Mortality in Central California." *Time* 1 Feb. 1993: 59.

Kolata, Gina. "It's Science Against Nature's Cruel Imagination. It Seems That There Is a New Disease Under the Sun in the Southwest." *The New York Times* 6 June 1993, sec. 1:23.

"Military Probes Oil Fire Fumes." (Raleigh, N.C.) *The Daily Mail* 10 Aug. 1992, sec. A:2.

"Moscow Shrouded in Gray Smog." *The Daily Mail* 10 Aug. 1992, sec. A:2.

"Mystery Fumes Strike Again? Another Patient Apparently Makes Medics Sick." (Bakersfield, Calif.) *The Daily Mail* 28 Feb. 1994, sec. A:1.

"Mystery Illnesses in Albany Still Under Investigation." *The New York Times* 30 Aug. 1992, Weather sec.:43.

"Report Discounts Mystery Fumes." (Los Angeles.) *The Herald-Mail* 3 Sept. 1994, sec. A:2.

Saltus, Richard. "Hospital Staffers Battle Mystery Malady. Airborne Irritants Are Targeted for Cleanup." *The Boston Sunday Globe* 21 Nov. 1993, MetroRegion sec.:37+.

Toufexis, Anastasia. "Evil Over the Land: A Deadly Illness Plagues the Navajo Nation." *Time* 14 June 1993: 57.

VII. Environmental Issues—Public Policy—Public Debate
A. Global

"Agreement Is Reached on Replacing Chernobyl." *The New York Times* 28 May 1995, International sec.:8.

Behr, Peter. "Environmental Issues Emerge As Key to Trade Pact on Hill." *The Washington Post* 17 Mar. 1993.

Cullen, Robert. "The True Cost of Coal: Coal Accounts For More Than Half of America's Electricity Because It Is So Cheap—and It Remains Cheap Because No One Pays the Very Large Hidden Costs of Its Mining and Burning." *The Atlantic Monthly* Dec. 1993: 38+.

Cushman, John H., Jr. "Owl Issue Tests Reliance on Consensus in Environmentalism." *The New York Times* 6 Mar. 1994, National sec.:28.

Elmer-Dewitt, Philip. "Environment: Not Just Hot Air: Clinton Promises to Curb Global Warming. Now He Has to Figure Out How to Do It, Which Won't Be Easy." *Time* 3 May 1993: 59.

Erlanger, Steven. "U.S. Aid for Huge Russian Lake Is in Jeopardy." *The New York Times* 3 Sept. 1995, International sec.:3.

"Exporting Banned and Hazardous Pesticides, 1991 Statistics—The Second Export Survey by the FASE Pesticide Project." *FASE Reports—Foundation for Advancements in Science and Education* 11.1 (Spring 1993):S-1-S-8.

Gore, Al, Senator. *Earth in the Balance: Ecology and the Human Spirit.* New York: Houghton Mifflin Company, 1992.

Gould, Jay M. and Benjamin A. Goldman. *Deadly Deceit: Low Level Radiation High Level Cover-Up.* New York: Four Walls Eight Windows, 1990.

Greenpeace. "Banned Pesticide Producer—Global Polluter." Greenpeace Pesticides Campaign, Sept. 1992.

Kinzer, Stephen. "Europe's Leaders See Green." *The New York Times* 9 Apr. 1995, sec. E:16.

Linden, Eugene. "The Century Ahead: Too Many People. If the Environment Is Already Threatened By Overpopulation, What

Would the World Be Like With Twice As Many Inhabitants? You Wouldn't Want to Be There." *Time* Fall 1992: 64-65.

_____. "Environment: Who Lost the Ozone? How the World Waited Too Long to Rescue the Shield That Protects Earth From the Sun's Dangerous UV Rays." *Time* 10 May 1993: 56-58.

McKibben, Bill. "Not So Fast. The Environmental Optimists Are Wrong: There Is No Market-Oriented, Technological Fix. Simply, and Radically, People Have to Change Their Lives." *The New York Times Magazine* 23 July 1995: 24- 25.

Moore, Monica. "The First Word." *Global Pesticide Campaigner* 5.4 (Dec. 1995): 2.

"Nobel Prize Proves Political Hot Potato." (Stockholm, Sweden [AP].) *The Daily Mail* 12 Oct. 1995, sec. A:3.

"Nobels: Of Ozone and Fruit Flies—A German, a Dutchman and Seven Americans Win the Science Prizes." *Time* 23 Oct. 1995: 82-83.

Pitt, David E. "U.N. Talks Combat Threat to Fishery. Seek to Control Overfishing That Is Said to Be Wiping Out Several Species." *The New York Times* 25 July 1993, International sec.:13.

Rich, Bruce. *Mortgaging the Earth: The World Bank, Environmental Impoverishment, and the Crisis of Development.* Boston: Beacon Press, 1994.

Ridgeway, James. *The Politics of Ecology.* New York: E. P. Dutton & Co., Inc., 1970.

Schneider, Keith. "Dolphins vs. Dollars: Balancing Nature's Claims and International Free Trade." *The New York Times* 19 Jan 1992, sec. E:5.

Shenon, Philip. "French Tow Ships Off Side of Atom Test: Dozens of Protesters Placed Under Arrest." *The New York Times* 3 Sept. 1995, International sec.:9.

Stevens, William K. "Developing Ourselves to Death: Are the World Bank's Policies Despoiling the Environment?" *The New York Times* 6 Mar. 1994, sec. VII, 29:1.

_____. "Experts Confirm Human Role in Global Warming." *The New York Times* 10 Sept. 1995, sec. A:1+.

————. "Keeping the Ozone Whole." *The New York Times* 15 Oct. 1995, sec. E:4.

Suro, Roberto. "Ideas & Trends: In Search of a Trade Pact With the Environment in Mind." *The New York Times* 14 Apr. 1991, sec. E:4.

United States Environmental Protection Agency. Office of Public Affairs (A-107). *Environmental Backgrounder: Global Issues: Acid Rain, Greenhouse Effect, Stratospheric Ozone, Transboundary Movement of Hazardous Waste, Pesticides Export Notification, Ocean Dumping, Environmental Emergencies, Other Initiatives.* Washington, D.C.: Mar. 1989.

B. National

"After 20 Years, Navy Prepares for Disposal of Napalm Stockpile." (Fallbrook, Calif.) *The New York Times* 18 Dec. 1994, National sec.:46.

Berke, Richard L. "Greening of the Presidency: Clinton Reverses Bush on Global Warming and Biodiversity Pacts." *The New York Times* 25 Apr. 1993, sec. E:2.

Browner, Carol M. "After 100 Days, a 'Legacy of Unfairness' or a 'Bolder Direction'?" *The New York Times* 9 Apr. 1995, National sec.:22.

Buchanan, Patrick. "Free Trade Folly. We're Paying Price for Deceitful Pact." *Dallas Morning News* 31 Aug. 1995.

Burleigh, Nina. "Small Ants, Tall Tales: The Republicans Are Wielding Dubious Personal Anecdotes in Their War Against Federal Regulations." *Time* 18 Sept. 1995: 53.

Callahan, Daniel. "Lab Games: A Look at the Way Interest Groups Use and Abuse Cancer Research for Their Own Ends." *The New York Times* 9 Apr. 1995, Book Review sec.: 15.

"Clinton Blames Special Interests During Address." (Washington [AP].) *The Herald-Mail* 9 May 1993, sec. A:8.

Cooper, Kenneth J. "Gingrich Pledges Major Package of Spending Cuts Early Next Year." *The Washington Post* 13 Dec. 1994, sec. A:1+.

Cushman, John H., Jr. "Environmental Lobby Beats Tactical Retreat." *The New York Times* 30 Mar. 1994, National sec. B:7.

_____. "A Clinton Cutback Upsets Environmentalists." *The New York Times* 26 Sept. 1993, National sec.:33.

_____. "Timber! A New Idea Is Crashing. Ecosystem Management Was the Trend, Until Republicans Repopulated the Government's Habitat." *The New York Times* 22 Jan. 1995, sec. E:5.

_____. "Conservatives Tug at Endangered Species Act. The Question Is Not Whether to Revise a Major Environmental Law, But How Much." *The New York Times* 28 May 1995, National sec.:26.

_____. "Earth Day at 25: Promoting a Cleaner Environment and a More Effective Bureaucracy." *The New York Times* 23 Apr. 1995, National sec.:24.

Dominguez, Alex. "Carpet Fumes Fuel Debate at Indoor Air Pollution Conference." *The Daily Mail* 23 Apr. 1993, sec. A:8.

Dowie, Mark. "Hostile Environment: What Happens When Insider Trading Collides With the Great Outdoors? *The New York Times Book Review* 28 Jan. 1996, sec. 7:12.

Durnil, Gordon K. *The Making of a Conservative Environmentalist. With Reflections on Government, Industry, Scientists, the Media, Education, Economic Growth, the Public, the Great Lakes, Activists, and the Sunsetting of Toxic Chemicals.* Bloomington: Indiana University Press, 1995.

Engelberg, Stephen. "Packwood Diaries: A Rare Look at Washington's Tangled Web. Chronicle of Abuse: The Packwood Papers, a Special Report." *The New York Times* 10 Sept. 1995, sec. A:1+.

Gingrich, Newt. "Tending the Gardens of the Earth: Scientifically Based Environmentalism." Chapter 21 in *To Renew America.* New York: Harper Collins Publishers, Inc., 1995.

Goodman, Howard. "Politically Incorrect: Peter Kostmayer Is So Upstanding, Candid and Compassionate, He Has Trouble Holding a Public Job." *Inquirer* 11 Feb. 1996: 12+

Greider, William. *Who Will Tell the People: The Betrayal of American Democracy.* New York: Simon & Schuster, 1992.

Harris, David. *The Last Stand: The War Between Wall Street and Main Street Over California's Ancient Redwoods.* New York: Times Books/Random House, 1996.

Holton, Deborah. "Pest Problems Need to Be Put in Perspective." *The Oregonian* 15 May 1995, sec. A:1+.

Kinsley, Michael. "Essay: You Still Can't Have It All." *Time* 21 Sept. 1992: 72.

Lacayo, Richard. "This Land Is Whose Land? From Out of the West Comes a Strike Force of Congressmen and Senators Who Think Natural Resources Ought to be Exploited, Not Coddled." *Time* 23 Oct. 1995: 68-71.

Linden, Eugene. "Environment: The Green Factor—Does Protecting the Planet Destroy Jobs? Bush Says Yes, Clinton Says No, and Their Running Mates Fight It Out on the Stump." *Time* 12 Oct. 1992: 57+.

————. "Essay: Will the System Defeat Al Gore?" *Time* 1 Feb. 1993: 74.

Mayer, Nancy. "Fouling Our Nests." *The Sunday Oregonian* 14 May 1995, sec. A:1+.

Noble, Kenneth B. "Ecology War Brews in California Desert. Squatters Vow to Defeat a Waste Site." *The New York Times* 19 Nov. 1995, National sec.:18.

Ohman, Jack. "Gore in the Balance." Cartoon. *The New York Times* 25 Apr. 1993, sec. E:6.

Philips, Kevin. *Arrogant Capital: Washington, Wall Street, and the Frustration of American Politics*. Little, Brown and Co., 1994.

————. "Book Excerpt—Fat City: Americans Have Good Reason to Hate Washington. It's Bloated, Arrogant and Ruining the Country, Argues a Noted Political Analyst, Who Contends That Democracy Needs an Overhaul." *Time* 26 Sept. 1994: 48-57.

"Politics Trumps Ecology: To Protect His Budget, Clinton Retreats on Land Use, Then Talks Trees." *Time* 12 Apr. 1993: 16-17.

Proctor, Robert N. *Cancer Wars. How Politics Shapes What We Know About Cancer*. New York: Basic Books, 1995.

Raines, Howell. "The 100-Day Hurricane." *The New York Times* 9 Apr. 1995, sec. E:13.

Roush, Jon, President, the Wilderness Society. "Healthy Environment Aids the Economy." *The New York Times* 7 Jan. 1996, sec. E:18.

Sarbanes, Paul S. U.S. Senator. Letter to Jacob B. Berkson. 31 Oct. 1995. Re: Artic National Wildlife Refuge (ANWR).

Schneider, Keith. "New View Calls Environmental Policy Misguided." *The New York Times* 21 Mar. 1993: 1+.

_____. "Clinton the Conservationist Thinks Twice." *The New York Times* 4 Apr. 1993, sec. 4:1+.

_____. "Loggers Listen to What Michigan Forests Say." *The New York Times* 25 July 1993, National sec.:20.

_____. "As Earth Day Turns 25, Life Gets Complicated." *The New York Times* 16 Apr. 1995, sec. E:6.

_____. "The Green Republican. One Day, Gordon D. Durnil Woke Up and Smelled the Chlorine. *The New York Times Book Review* 27 Aug. 1995, sec. 7:17.

Spalt, Allen. "'Adopt a Chemical.'" *Agricultural Resources Center.* 15 Mar. 1991.

Taylor, Elizabeth. "Al's O.K., You're O.K." *Time* 12 Oct. 1992: 60.

Templet, Dr. Paul H. "Does a Cleaner Environment Mean More Jobs? An Empirical Analysis of the Positive Relationship Between Jobs, Environment and the Economy." *Pesticides and You* 15.1 (Spring 1995): 17-24.

Thompson, Dick. "Congressional Chain-Saw Massacre: If Speaker Newt Gingrich Gets His Way, the Laws Protecting Air, Water and Wildlife May Be Endangered." *Time* 27 Feb. 1995: 58-60.

United States Environmental Protection Agency. Office of Public Affairs (A-107). *Environmental Backgrounder: Ozone and Carbon Monoxide.* Washington, D.C.: Jan. 1989.

_____. Policy, Planning and Evaluation (PM-223). *Hazardous Substances in Our Environment: A Citizen's Guide to Understanding Health Risks and Reducing Exposure.* EPA 230/09/90/081. Washington, D.C.: Sept. 1990.

Worsnop, Richard L. "Water Quality: Should Safety Standards for Drinking Water Be Tougher in the U.S.?" *CQ Researcher* 4.6 (11 Feb. 1994): 121+.

C. Regional

Brown, Phil, and Edwin J. Mikkelsen. *No Safe Place: Toxic Waste, Leukemia, and Community Action.* University of California, 1990.

"Cement Firm Ordered to Stop Kiln-Burning of Hazardous Waste. State: Keystone Covered up Violations." (Allentown, Pa. [AP].) *The Daily Mail* 2 Apr. 1992, sec. C:4.

Diringer, Elliot. "Big Industry Under Fire in East Bay. Contra Costa Homeowners Live in Fear of Toxic Disaster." *San Francisco Chronicle* 6 July 1992, sec. A:1+.

Schneider, Keith. "Ohio Incinerator Spared. E.P.A. Increases Oversight of Hazardous Waste Makers." *The New York times* 23 May 1993.

_____. "A Test for Gore: The Environmental Fix With a Legion of Doubters." *The New York Times* 20 Dec. 1992, sec. E:5.

"2,000 Protest Chemical Plant." (Taipei, Taiwan [AP].) *The Herald-Mail* 2 Dec. 1990, sec. A:9.

D. Local

Amdur, Daniel M. "ICC Outlines Tire-Burning Plan." *The Daily Mail* 6 Aug. 1993, sec. B:2.

Berkson, Jacob B. "Save the Earth." Opinion. *The Daily Mail* 22 Apr. 1992.

Blodgett, Nancy. "Lawn Care Firms: Let Us Spray. But Suits Allege Misleading Ads, Unsafe Pesticides." *ABA Journal* 1 Sept. 1988: 20-21.

Callen, Bill. "Sludge Proposal Prompts Public Outcry." *The Herald-Mail* 27 Dec. 1992, sec. F:1+.

Fletcher, Guy. "Residents Near Dump Want Action." *The Daily Mail* 22 May 1992, sec. A:1+.

_____. "Quarry Neighbors Question Proposal: Rockdale Expansion Would Mine Deeper, Pump Out Water." *The Daily Mail* 15 Apr. 1993, sec. B:1.

Ford, Clyde. "Md. Officials Can't Explain Why Stream Ran Blood Red." *The Daily Mail* 19 May 1992, sec. B:2.

Homeowners Opposed to Pit Encroachment. "The Burning Issue at ICC." *Washington County Network* 3.2 (Mar.-Apr. 1991): 1+.

Maginnis, Bob. "Trust the Regulators?" Opinion/Editorial. *The Daily Mail* 14 Apr. 1992, sec. A:4.

Reuter. "Lawn-Care Chemical Tied to Cancer. Dog Study May Show Humans Are at Risk." *The Washington Post* 4 Sept. 1991.

Schwartz, Don. "Fighting the Weed Wars. Time, Money Needed to Battle Perennial Problem." *The Daily Mail* 30 May 1995, sec. B:5.

Skow, John. "Can Lawns Be Justified? Awash in Fertilizers and Pesticides, They May Be a Hazard to Homeowners—and Children, Pets and Neighbors." *Time* 3 June 1991: 63+.

E. Human Behavior

Baker, Beth. "The Art of Being Unreasonable. David Brower Still Agitates to Save the Earth, Though He Himself Has Mellowed." *AARP Bulletin* 36.10 (Nov. 1995), Washington, D.C. ed.: 20+.

"Cipollone v. Liggett: Legal Costs Doom Suit Against Tobacco Industry." *The New York Times* 8 Nov. 1992, sec. IV:4.

Cousins, Norman. *Head First: The Biology of Hope.* New York: E. P. Dutton, 1989.

Eldredge, Niles. *The Miner's Canary: Unraveling the Mysteries of Extinction.* New York: Prentice Hall Press, 1991.

Goodman, Ellen. "Mother Nature's Pain: Irag's Deliberate Oil Spill a Crime Against Humanity." *The Herald-Mail* 2 Feb. 1991, sec. A:4.

Kaplan, Robert D. "The Coming Anarchy. How Scarcity, Crime, Overpopulation, Tribalism, and Disease Are Rapidly Destroying the Social Fabric of Our Planet." *The Atlantic Monthly* Feb. 1994: 44+.

Mydans, Seth. "Forget About Lotus Land. Thank You for Not Smoking." *The New York Times* 8 Aug. 1993, sec. E:16.

Power, Thomas Michael, and Paul Rauber. "The Price of Everything: The Market Speaks on Environmental Protection. Put Up or Shut Up, It Says." *Sierra* 78.6 (Nov./Dec. 1993): 86+.

Ridley, Matt, and Bobbi S. Low. "Can Selfishness Save the Environment? *The Atlantic Monthly* Sept. 1993: 76-86.

Russell, Dick. "Conversations: Ed Begley, Jr. When This Screen Veteran Talks About His Commitment to the Environment, He Isn't Acting." *E Magazine* VII.1(Jan./Feb. 1996): 10-13.

Wilson, Edward O. "Is Humanity Suicidal? If Homo Sapiens Goes the Way of the Dinosaur, We Have Only Ourselves to Blame." *The New York Times Magazine* 30 May 1993: VI, 24+.

F. Risk/Benefit

Castleman, Barry I., Sc.D., and Grace E. Ziem, M.D., D.Ph. *Corporate Influence on Threshold Limit Values.* Alan R. Lies, Inc., 1988. Cited in *American Journal of Industrial Medicine* 13 (1988): 531-559.

Feldman, Jay. "Pesticides in Food: Assessing the Risks." *Trial* Oct. 1994: 32.

Ginsburg, Robert. "Quantitative Risk Assessment and the Illusion of Safety." *New Solutions* Winter 1993: 8-15.

Gregory, Michael. "Some Unacceptable Risks of Risk Assessment." *Pesticides and You* 15.1 (Spring 1995): 14- 16.

Riley, Becky. "Risks of Cancer-Causing Chemicals Aren't Negligible." *The Register-Guard* 7 Aug. 1992.

United States Environmental Protection Agency. *EPA: For Your Information— Risk/Benefit Balancing Under the Federal Insecticide, Fungicide, and Rodenticide Act (FIFRA).* Washington, D.C.: Aug. 1991.

_____. Policy, Planning and Evaluation (PM-223). *Hazardous Substances in Our Environment: A Citizen's Guide to Understanding Health Risks and Reducing Exposure.* EPA 230/09/90/081. Washington, D.C.: Sept. 1990.

_____. *Understanding Environmental Health Risks and Reducing Exposure: Highlights of a Citizen's Guide.* Washington, D.C.: Sept. 1990.

Wartenberg, Daniel, and Caron Chess. "The Risk Wars: Assessing Risk Assessment." *New Solutions* Winter 1993: 16-25.

G. Preventive Medicine

Califano, Joseph A., Jr. *Radical Surgery: What's Next for America's Health Care*. New York: Times Books/Random House, 1994.

"Group Seeks Physician Involvement." *FASE (Foundation for Advancements in Science and Education) Reports* 7.2 (Winter, 1988): 1+.

Moyers, Bill. *Healing and the Mind*. New York: Doubleday, 1993. pp. 44, 55, 57, 58, 64, 233, 234.

"Panel: Do Labels on Cigarette Packs Deceive Smokers?" (Bethesda, Md. [AP].) *The Daily Mail* 6 Dec. 1994, sec. A:6.

Toner, Robin. "It's Not Enough to Mend the Ill and Injured. Joseph A Califano Envisions a Health Care Plan Aimed at Prevention." *The New York Times* 15 Jan. 1995, sec. VII:14.

Weisskopf, Michael. "AMA Buses Doctors to Practice Preventive Medicine at Capitol." *The Washington Post* 26 Mar. 1993, sec. A:10.

H. Chemical/Biological Warfare

Cole, Leonard A. *Clouds of Secrecy: The Army's Germ Warfare Tests Over Populated Areas*. Totowa, New Jersey: Rowman & Littlefield, 1988.

Douglass, Joseph D., Jr., and Neil C. Livingstone. *America the Vulnerable. The Threat of Chemical/Biological Warfare: The New Shape of Terrorism and Conflict*. Lexington, Massachusetts: Lexington Books, 1987.

McDermott, Jeanne. *The Killing Winds: The Menace of Biological Warfare*. New York: Arbor House Publishing Company, 1987.

Seagrave, Sterling. *Yellow Rain: A Journey Through the Terror of Chemical Warfare*. New York: M. Evans and Company, Inc., 1981.

Smolowe, Jill. "Chemical Time Bombs. The Race Is On to Destroy Weapons Filled With Deadly Toxins—Before They Destroy Us." *Time* 12 Feb. 1996: 42.

Thompson, Mark. "The Battle for Poison. In a Public Relations Duel, Alabama and Missouri Squabble Over a Nerve-Gas Training Facility." *Time* 22 May 1995: 48.

I.   Earth Day '95 Books Reviewed

"'A Moment on the Earth.'" Letters to the editor. *The New York Times Book Review* 28 May 1995: 23.

Dowie, Mark. *Losing Ground: American Environmentalism at the Close of the Twentieth Century*. Cambridge, Massachusetts: The MIT Press, 1995.

Earle, Sylvia Alice. *Sea Change: A Message of the Oceans*. New York: G. P. Putnom's Sons, 1995.

Easterbrook, Gregg. *A Moment on the Earth: The Coming Age of Environmental Optimism*. New York: Viking, 1995.

Mann, Charles C., and Mark L. Plummer. *Noah's Choice: The Future of Endangered Species*. New York: Alfred A. Knopf, 1995.

O'Reilly. "Troubled Waters: A Distinguished Biologist's Elegy for the Biggest Place on Earth." *The New York Times Book Review* 23 Apr. 1995: 14.

Quammen, David. "Live and Let Die: We're the Ones Who Decide Which Species Get to Come Aboard the Ark." *The New York Times Book Review* 23 Apr. 1995: 16.

Schneider, Keith. "Back to the Grass Roots: Has the Environmental Movement Turned Into Just Another Special Interest?" *The New York Times Book Review* 23 Apr. 1995: 15.

Specter, Michael. "Not That Hard Being Green. Gregg Easterbrook Says Things Are Looking Up for the Environment—Despite What the Environmentalists Say." *The New York Times Book Review* 23 Apr. 1995: 13.

VIII. Environmental Law—A Few Examples
A. Legislation

"Clean Air Act Amendments." *1990 CQ Almanac*. 248-279.

"Government Actions Aimed at Reducing Your Exposure to Hazardous Substances." Part II, Chapter 5. United States Environmental Protection Agency. Policy, Planning and Evaluation (PM-223). *Hazardous Substances in Our Environment: A Citizen's Guide to Understanding Health Risks and Reducing Exposure*. EPA 230/09/90/081. Washington, D.C.: Sept. 1990.

Public Law 88-206 and Public Law 101-549: Clean Air Act. USC 1988 Title 42 sec. 7401 et seq.

Public Law 91-190: National Environmental Policy Act of 1969 (NEPA). USC 1988 Title 42 sec. 4321 et seq.

Public Law 95-217: Clean Water Act. USC 1988 Title 33 sec. 1251 et seq.

Public Law 101-336: The Americans With Disabilities Act of 1990 (As Amended). 104 STAT.327. 42 USC 12101 note. 26 July 1990.

U.S. Congress. House, amendment to the *Federal Insecticide, Fungicide, and Rodenticide Act*. 102d Cong., 1st sess., H.R. 3742. 7 Nov. 1991.

U.S. Congress. House, *The Federal-State Pesticide Regulation Partnership Act of 1991*. 102d Cong., 1st sess., H.R. 3850/S 2085. 21 Nov. 1991

U.S. Environmental Protection Agency. Office of Pesticide Programs *The Federal Insecticide, Fungicide, and Rodenticide Act as Amended*. Washington, D.C.: Oct. 1988.

B. Regulations

Federal Register: Part III—Department of Justice. Office of the Attorney General. 28 CFR Part 36. Nondiscrimination on the Basis of Disability By Public Accommodations and in Commercial Facilities; Final Rule 56.144 (26 July 1991).

Federal Register: Part IV—Department of Justice. Office of the Attorney General. 28 CFR Part 35. Nondiscrimination on the Basis of

Disability in State and Local Government Services; Final Rule 56.144 (26 July 1991).

Setting, Mary Ellen, Chief, Pesticide Regulation Section. Letter to Mr. Jacob B. Berkson. 26 Apr. 1993.

"FDA Comes Up With New Rules to Reduce Seafood Poisonings." (Washington [AP].) *The Daily Mail* 8 Dec. 1995, sec. A:8.

C. Legal Opinions

Weidenfeller, George L., Deputy General Counsel (Operations). Memorandum for all regional counsel, subject Multiple Chemical Sensitivity Disorder and Environmental Illness as Handicaps. 14 Apr. 1992. U.S. Department of Housing and Urban Development, Washington, D.C. 20410-1000.

Wilson, Carole W., Associate General Counsel for Equal Opportunity and Administrative Law. Memorandum for Frank Keating, General Counsel, subject Multiple Chemical Sensitivity Disorder and Environmental Illness as Handicaps. 5 Mar. 1992.

D. Decisions

Exterminator's Tort Liability for Personal Injury or Death Directly Resulting From Operations. Whatley v. Cardinal Pest Control. Sct Ala. (1980) 388 So 2d 529, 29 ALR4th 981.

In the Matter of Nancy W. Gorman and Equal Employment Opportunity Commission, Washington, D.C. Employees' Compensation Appeals Board, U.S. Department of Labor. Docket No. 92-1563. Decision and Order. Issued 17 May 1993.

"Judge Upholds Penalty on Dow Chemical." (Reno, Nev., Feb. 10 [AP].) "A judge on Friday rejected a request by the Dow Chemical Company to throw out a $14 million jury award to a woman who said leaky breast implants had made her seriously ill..." *The New York Times* 11 Feb. 1996, sec. 1:31.

"Smoking Ban Ruling Put Off." (Annapolis, Md. [AP].) *The Daily Mail* 6 Dec. 1994, sec. A:5.

Steinberg, Jacques. "Judge Backs Plan to Ship Sewage. Westchester Sludge to Go to New Jersey." *The New York Times* 18 Dec. 1994, Metro sec.:60.

Wisconsin Public Intervenor and Town of Casey, Petitioners v. Ralph Mortier, et al. on Petition for a Writ of Certiorari to the Supreme Court of Wisconsin in the Supreme Court of the United States, Oct. Term, 1990 No. 89-1905.

E. Legal Notices

Important Notice of Proposed Settlement of Class Action and Fairness Hearing. Notice to U.S. workers with on-the-job exposure to Galecron®. In *The Daily Mail* 16 Sept. 1994, sec. A:9.

F. Enforcement

"Businessmen Convicted of Environmental Crimes." (Newark, N.J. [AP].) *The Herald-Mail* 24 Oct. 1992, sec. B:6.

"Prison Term for Inspector in Bribe Case. He Imported Seafood That Was Rotting." (Newark.) *The New York Times* 18 Dec. 1994, Metro sec.:55.

Revkin, Andrew C. "Nuclear Plants Are Safe, Northeast Utilities Says. After Federal Rebukes, a Company Promises to Reshape Management." *The New York Times* 10 Mar. 1996, Metro sec.:36.

Sanjour, William. "Citizens Could Improve Feeble Enforcement at U.S. Environmental Protection Agency." *Rachel's Environment & Health Weekly #484* 7 Mar. 1996.

"Special Investigation: Blowing the Whistle on Nuclear Safety—How a Showdown at a Power Plant Exposed the Federal Government's Failure to Enforce Its Own Rules. George Galatis at Millstone in Connecticut." *Time* 4 Mar. 1996: cover.

U.S. Department of Justice. Civil Rights Division. Public Access Section. *Enforcing the ADA: A Status Report From the Department of Justice* 4 Apr. 1994.

United States General Accounting Office. Report to the Chairman, Committee on Governmental Affairs, U.S. Senate. *Environmental Enforcement: EPA Cannot Ensure the Accuracy of Self-Reported Compliance Monitoring Data.* Washington, D.C.: Mar. 1993.

G. Books

Braverman, Nathan, et al. *Environmental Law and You: A Guide for Compliance in Maryland*. Eau Claire, Wisconsin: National Business Institute, Inc., 1993.

Environmental Compliance in Maryland. Connecticut: Business & Legal Reports, Inc.

Gingrich, Newt. "Tending the Gardens of the Earth: Scientifically Based Environmentalism." Chapter 21 in *To Renew America*. New York: Harper Collins Publishers, Inc., 1995.

Gray, Oscar S. *Cases and Materials on Environmental Law*. 2nd ed. Washington, D.C.: Bureau of National Affairs, 1973.

Greider, William. "Chapter 5: Hollow Laws." In *Who Will Tell the People: The Betrayal of American Democracy*. New York: Simon & Schuster, 1992. pp. 123+.

Harr, Jonathan. *A Civil Action*. New York: Random House, 1995.

H. Bar Association Publications

Arnold, James R., and Gerald J. Buchwald. "Superfund=Superliability. Are Lawyers the Next Deep Pocket?" *ABA Journal* Sept. 1993: 117.

Blum, Fred M. Carmen A. Trutanich, and Timothy C. Cronin. "Continuing Legal Education—Defending Environmental Crimes: Pretrial Considerations Are Crucial to an Effective Defense." *California Lawyer* Sept. 1992: 57- 60.

DeBenedictis, Don J. "Few Like Pollution Guidelines. Business 'Up in Arms' Over Proposed Fines for Corporate Environmental Crimes." *ABA Journal* June 1993: 25-26.

Duncan, Laura. "Cigarette Makers Race Attorneys General to Court. Industry Suits Aimed at Stopping Expected Litigation. The Cost of Treating Smoking-Related Illnesses Is Causing Some States to Seek Recompense From Cigarette Makers. Smoking Guns. Five States Have Filed Lawsuits Against Tobacco Companies to Recover medical Costs for Smoking-Related Illnesses." *ABA Journal* Mar. 1996: 38.

Evans, James. "Through the Revolving Door. The Allure of Big Money Draws Environmental Lawyers From the Public Sector Into Private Practice." *California Lawyer* Apr. 1991: 45+.

Fulton, William. "Environmental Law—Toxics Complicate Real Estate Practice: Real Estate Lawyers Today Can't Close a Deal Without a Little Help From the Environmental Department." *California Lawyer* May 1990: 45+.

Granader, Robert. "Privilege an Obstacle in Groom Lake Suit. Government Refuses Even to Name Secret Air Base in Litigation Over Pollution." *ABA Journal* Sept. 1995: 28.

Hansen, Mark. "To Lawyer's Surprise, Cancer Suit Lost. Judge Rules Cigarettes Unreasonably Dangerous, But Jury Doesn't Find Causation." *ABA Journal* Sept. 1993: 40.

_____. $15 Billion in Punitives Sought. If Exxon Verdict Sets Record, It's Unlikely to Stand. *ABA Journal* Sept. 1994: 30-31.

_____. "Record Punitives: $5 Billion Award Unlikely to Stand." Re: Exxon Valdez. *ABA Journal* Dec. 1994: 41.

Keeva, Steve. "After the Spill: New Issues in Environmental Law." *ABA Journal* Feb. 1991: 66-69.

Marcotte, Paul. "The Asbestos Claim—Who Pays? Four-Year San Francisco Case Could Provide the Answer." *ABA Journal* Jan. 1989: 28.

McKinnon, John D. "Flight Attendants' Secondhand Smoke Suit Gets Go-Ahead. A Florida Appeals Court Has Upheld a Class Action By Flight Attendants Who Say They Were Sickened By Secondhand Smoke." *ABA Journal* Mar. 1996: 39.

Possehl, Suzanne René. "Keeper of the Green. Just as His Father Went After Organized Crime, Robert Kennedy Jr. Is Waging War on Polluters...and Winning." *ABA Journal* Jan. 1996: 56+.

Pressman, Steven. "Environmental Law—Whose Toxics Are They? California's Hazardous Waste Law Will Be Tested in a Case Involving Shipyard Dumping." *California Lawyer* Feb. 1990: 26+.

Prestley, Peter B. "The Future of Superfund: After the Rio Summit, Domestic Policy Won't Be the Same." *ABA Journal* Aug. 1993: 62+.

Reske, Henry J. "Record EPA Prosecutions. But Polluters More Likely to Get Civil, Rather Than Criminal, Sanctions." *ABA Journal* Mar. 1992: 25.

————. "Judge Gets Tough in Fungicide Trials. Disputed Evidence, Attorney's Sarcastic Remarks Cited in New Trial Orders." *ABA Journal* Aug. 1995: 28.

Reuben, Richard C. "Stringfellow's Toxic Shocks." *California Lawyer* May 1993: 26-27.

Rutter, Nancy. "The Greening of Corporate America. Northern California Lawyers Helped Invent Environmental Practice. Now Many of Them Are Grinding Out Billables for the People They Used to Sue." *California Lawyer* Apr. 1991: 33+.

Simon, Joel. "Dirty Work: With Approval of the Free Trade Agreement Hanging in the Balance, Mexico and the United States Struggle to Stop Border Pollution." *California Lawyer* Feb. 1993: 40+.

State Bar of California. "State Bar Report—Crime Against the Environment: Does It Even Exist?" *California Lawyer* Aug. 1993: 88+.

Thaler, Jeffrey A. "Protecting the Environment: Assessing a Toxic Tort Case." *Trial* Sept. 1991: 43-49.

Walters, Dan. "Compensation's Complications: Workers' Comp Laws Are Now Under Their Greatest Pressure for Reform." *California Lawyer* May 1993: 29-30.

I. Journals

Adler, Robert. "The Clean Water Act: Has It Worked? We Have a Long Way to Go." *EPA Journal* 20.1-2 (Summer 1994): 10+.

McCabe, Martha. "Pesticide Law Enforcement: A View From the States." *Journal of Environment Law and Litigation* 4 (1989): 35+.

Migliorini, Al M., Executive Director. *Medi/Legal Journal* 15301 Ventura Blvd., Suite 300, Sherman Oaks, CA 91403.

J. Environmental Organizations' Publications

"A Golden Opportunity to Repeal 'Logging Without Laws'." *AFSEEE Activist* Dec. 1995.

Anderson, Sarah, et al., eds. *The Scorecard. League of Conservation Voters. National Environmental Scorecard. October 1994. 103rd Congress, Second Session.* Washington, D.C.: The League of Conservation Voters®, Oct. 1994.

Cartwright, Raymond W., director, Housing Division, Pennsylvania Human Relations Commission. *Filing/Maintaining and/or Preventing Complaints Based on Handicap and/or Disability (H/D) Multiple Chemical Sensitivity (MCS) (H/D - C/S)*. Presentation for National Committee Against the Misuse of Pesticides. 29 Mar. 1992.

Feldman, Jay. "Congress Emasculates Environmental Laws." *Pesticides and You* 15.2 (Summer 1995): Inside front cover.

National Coalition Against the Misuse of Pesticides. *Preserving the Authority of Local Governments to Regulate Pesticides.* 701 E Street, SE, Suite 200, Washington, D.C. 20003

_____. *Technical Report* in Law and on Immune System Effects 5.6 (June 1990). 530 7th St., S.E., Washington, D.C. 20003.

_____. *Technical Report* on DDT and Cancer...on Chlorpyrifos 5.9 (Sept. 1990). 701 E Street, SE, Suite 200, Washington, D.C. 20003.

Natural Resources Defense Council. *Litigation Dispatch—Re: Court Action to Make Texaco Pay for Polluting Our Environment.* 40 West 20th Street, New York, NY 10011.

Sierra Club Legal Defense Fund Docket: 1995. 180 Montgomery St., Suite 1400, San Francisco, CA 94104-4209. Phone: (415) 627-6700.

"Suit Links Bugspray and Birth Defects: NY Couple Fights Dow." *Pesticides and You* Dec. 1990: 4.

Wilson, Cynthia. "Boeing Workers Win Their Day in Court." *Our Toxic Times* 6.12 (Dec. 1995): 1+.

K. Announcements—Courses

Environmental Breakfast Series. 7 Feb. 1996 - 7 May 1996. Radisson Plaza Lord Baltimore Hotel. 20 W. Baltimore Street, Baltimore, Maryland. MICPEL. The Maryland Institute for Continuing Professional Education of Lawyers, Inc., Suite 830 Candler

Building, 111 Market Place, Baltimore, Maryland 21202-4012. Phone: (410) 659-6730 or (800) 787-0068.

Environmental Regulation Course. Washington, D.C., 8-10 January 1996. Executive Enterprises, 22 West 21st Street, New York, NY 10010-6990. Fax: 212-645-8689.

L. Newspapers/Magazines

Arch, Mary Ellin. "Orkin Held Responsible for 2 Fumigation Death. Company Fined $500,000 in Virginia Case." *The Washington Post* 16 Nov. 1988, sec. D:1+.

Barnhart, Marlo. "Pair Charged in Chemical Dumping." *The Daily Mail* 24 June 1994, sec. B:3.

Bates, Steve. "Vienna Renter Finally Gets No-Spray Zone. Woman Had Suffered Reaction to Pesticides." *The Washington Post* 12 Jan. 1995, sec. B:5.

"Bud Shuster's Dirty Water Act." *The New York Times* 2 Apr. 1995, sec. E:14.

"Businessmen Convicted of Environmental Crimes." (Newark, N.J. [AP].) *The Herald-Mail* 24 Oct. 1992, sec. B:6.

"Cipollone v. Liggett: Legal Costs Doom Suit Against Tobacco Industry." *The New York Times* 8 Nov. 1992, sec. IV:4.

"Company fined $100,000 for Raising Stink." (Houston [AP].) *The Daily Mail* 2 Sept. 1992, sec. A:10.

"Court Bans Pesticides in Processed Foods." (San Francisco [AP].) *The Daily Mail* 9 July 1992, sec. A:7.

Cushman, John H., Jr. "The Environment: E.P.A. Bill, Modified, Still Faces Veto Threat." *The New York Times* 19 Nov. 1995, National sec.:21.

_____. "Environment" in "Congress at Midpoint: To the Left or the Right, Gridlock Everywhere." *The New York Times* 21 Jan. 1996, sec. 1:14

Dao, James. "Dropping of Curb on DEET Blocked by Court." *The New York Times* 9 July 1995, Metro sec.: 29.

Davis, Patricia, and D'Vera Cohn. "Va. Woman Wins Case, but Still Has Toxic House. *The Washington Post* 21 Feb. 1992, sec. B:1+.

DePalma, Anthony. "Law Protects Mexico's Workers But Its Enforcement Is Often Lax." *The New York Times* 15 Aug. 1993, International sec.:1+.

"Du Pont's Enemy in Lawsuit: Its Own Papers." *The New York Times* 1 Aug. 1993, National sec.:36.

"8 Are Accused of Demolishing Rapids on Salt River in Arizona." *The New York Times* 16 Oct. 1994, National sec.:36.

Elkins, Deborah. "'Toxic Torts' Bubble Up in Virginia." *Lawyers Weekly* X.8 (31 July 1995): 1+.

"Employee Death Cases Going to Court." (Elk Grove Village, Ill. [AP].) *The Daily Mail* 27 Oct. 1989, sec. A:16.

Engelberg, Stephen. "Tall Timber and the E.P.A.: 3 Companies and 3 Strategies." *The New York Times* 21 May 1995, sec. 3:1+.

"Environmental Deadlines Violated." (New York.) *The Daily Mail* 1 Oct. 1992, sec. A:2.

Feder, Barnaby J. "Dow Corning's Bankruptcy: The Impact on Implant Suits." *The New York Times* 21 May 1995, sec. F:9.

Ford, Clyde. "Wal-Mart Files Suit Over 1993 Chemical Fire." *The Herald-Mail* 17 Nov. 1994, sec. B:2.

Geyelin, Milo. "Scorched Earth. DuPont Draws Fire for Stonewall Defense of a Suspect Fungicide. It Resists Giving Plaintiffs Tests Bearing on Whether Benlate Was Poisonous. Allegation of Fraud in Court." *The Wall Street Journal* 3 May 1995, eastern ed, sec. A:1+.

"Headaches, Heartaches Remain. Residents Lose 12-Year Battle With Chemical Firm." (Sturgeon, Mo. [AP].) *The Daily Mail* 20 June 1991, sec. B:7.

Hicks, Jonathan P. "In Council, Bill Gains to Restrict Smoking." *The New York Times* 8 Dec. 1994, sec. B:2.

Lambert, Wade. "More Claim Chemicals Made Them Ill." *The Wall Street Journal* 17 Jan. 1995, sec. B:1+.

"Man Wins $1.2 Million in Agent Orange Suit." (Providence, R.I. [AP].) *The Herald-Mail* 25 May 1996, sec. A:2.

Pooley, Eric. "Special Investigation: Nuclear Warriors. Two Gutsy Engineers in Connecticut Have Caught the Nuclear Regulatory Commission at a Dangerous Game That It Has Played for Years: Routinely Waiving Safety Rules to Let Plants Keep Costs Down and Stay Online." *Time* 4 Mar. 1996: 47-54.

"Rep. Gilchrest Becomes Major Player on Environmental Issues. The Once-Obscure Eastern Shore Congressman Is a Leader of the So-Called 'Green Republicans,' Who Are Capable in Coalition With Democrats of Prevailing on Key Environmental Votes." (Kennedyville, Md. [AP].) *The Daily Mail* 24 Aug. 1995, sec. A:6.

"Safety Lapses Net Firm $119,295 Fine." *The Herald-Mail* 2 Feb. 1991, sec. A:3.

Schneider, Keith. "Ex-Mine Official Is Under Inquiry. Chief of Bush's Strip Mining Office Accused of Blocking Enforcement of Laws." *The New York Times* 18 Apr. 1993, National sec.:28.

Sullivan, Charles. "Lobbyists Working to Gut Environmental Law." *The Herald-Mail* 16 July 1995, sec. F:3.

"Vermont Passes Sweeping No-Smoking Law." *The New York Times* 2 May 1993, National sec.:44.

IX. Call to Action
A. Organization Campaigns

A Woman's Cancer Agenda. The Women's Community Cancer Project, c/o The Women's Center, 46 Pleasant Street, Cambridge, MA 02139. 617-354-9888.

Babbitt, Bruce. Letter to "Friend." Re: League of Conservation Voters, 1707 L Street, N.W., Washington, D.C. 20036.

Beyond Pesticides. 701 E Street, SE, Washington, D.C. 20003. 202-543-5450.

Cesar E. Chavez' United Farm Workers of America AFL-CIO. Re: Farmworkers' fight for social justice. National Headquarters: La Paz, P.O. Box 62, Keene, California 93531.

Common Cause. *People vs. PACs Campaign*. P.O. Box 98058, Washington, D.C. 20077-7209.

_____. *Campaign to End Corporate Welfare*. P.O. Box 98057, Washington, D.C. 20077-7208.

Earth Day 1995. Free the Planet. *An Environmental Petition to Newt Gingrich*. 218 D Street, SE, Washington, D.C. 20003. 202-546-0263.

International Wildlife Coalition. *Whale Adoption Request*. Re: Rescue, nurture & protect marine mammals. 634 North Falmouth Highway, P.O. Box 388, North Falmouth, Massachusetts 02556-0388.

Maddy, Jim. League of Conservation Voters. Letter to Jacob B. Berkson. Re: To the polls and vote. 17 Oct. 1994.

Marks, Marcia F., Board Chair, "Stop Smoking Children," Maryland Coalition to Stop Illegal Sales of Tobacco to Minors. Letter to Jacob B. Berkson. Re: The illegal sale of tobacco to minors in "over the counter" sales.

McGinn, Chris. "Activist Alert: NAFTA Threatens Public Health Protections." *Public Citizen* July-Aug. 1993: 31.

National Forests Campaign. The Wilderness Society™, 900 Seventeenth Street, N.W., Washington, D.C. 20006-2596.

NYZS The Wildlife Conservation Society. *Forest Elephant Campaign*. Re: To join the Wildlife Conservation Society's fight to save Africa's mysterious forest elephants. International Programs, Bronx, NY 10460.

Pens, Letters, Action! Mothers & Others/The Green Guide for Everyday Life, 40 West 20th Street, New York, NY 10011. Phone: 212-242-0010.

San Francisco BayKeeper. Building A-Fort Mason Center, San Francisco, CA 94123.

"Sensitive Issue." (Coalition for Disability Rights.) *Albuquerque Journal* 25 Jan. 1995.

Sierra Club Legal Defense Fund. *Save Yellowstone Now! Campaign*. 180 Montgomery Street, Suite 1400, San Francisco, CA 94104-4209.

Talbert, Terry. "Don't Smoke Today: Cancer Society Holding Its Great American Smokeout." *The Daily Mail* 17 Nov. 1994, sec. B:2.

Union of Concerned Scientists. *World Scientists' Warning to Humanity* Apr. 1993. Two Brattle Square, Cambridge, MA 02238-9105.

Zero Population Growth, Suite 320, 1400 Sixteenth Street NW, Washington, D.C. 20077-6640.

B. Pesticide Action Alerts

Feldman, Jay, and Samuel S. Epstein, M.D. "Get the Cancerous Pesticides Our of Our Food." *The New York Times* 19 Feb. 1993, Editorials/Letters sec.

National Coalition Against the Misuse of Pesticides (NCAMP) and more than 70 organizations. *National Toxic Poisoning Prevention Platform*. 701 E Street, S.E., Washington, D.C. 20003.

Northwest Coalition for Alternatives to Pesticides. "Let's Get Hazardous and Cancer-Causing Pesticides Out of Our Food!" *Pesticide Action Alert* June 1994.

_____. "New Research Links Breast Cancer to Pesticides Yet Federal Regulators May Permit Carcinogenic Pesticides in Food!" *Pesticide Action Alert* May 1993.

_____. "Flyer Beware! Airlines Spray Unsuspecting Passengers With Insecticides on International Flights! Speak Out Now!" *Pesticide Action Alert* Mar. 1994.

C. Government and Other Reports

New York State Department of Law. Robert Abrams, Attorney General. *Pesticides in Schools: Reducing the Risks*. New York: March 1993.

NOAA. *Our Water Planet Is Becoming Polluted with Plastic Debris...* Newport, Oregon: National Marine Fisheries Service Marine Refuse Disposal Project. Marine Debris Information Offices: Atlantic Coast and Gulf of Mexico Office—1725 DeSales Street, NW, #500, Washington, DC 20036. Pacific Coast Office—580 Market Street, Suite 550, San Francisco, CA 94104.

Public Citizen's Congress Watch. *Pesticide Reports*. Department N, 215 Pennsylvania Avenue SE, Washington, D.C. 20003.

Sierra Club. Pennsylvania Chapter. *Getting Pesticides Out of Schools*. P.O. Box 135, Cogar Station, Pa. 17728.

U.S. Department of Health and Human Services. Public Health Service. Centers for Disease Control and Prevention. *It's Time to Stop Being a Passive Victim*.

U.S. Environmental Protection Agency. Office of Pesticide Programs. *Pest Control in the School Environment: Adopting Integrated Pest Management*. Washington, D.C.: Aug. 1993.

_____. Prevention, Pesticides and Toxic Substances. *Pesticides Industry Sales and Usage. 1992 and 1993 Market Estimates*. Washington, D.C.: June 1994.

_____. Prevention, Pesticides and Toxic Substances. *Status of Pesticides in Reregistration and Special Review*. Washington, D.C.: June 1994.

_____. Prevention, Pesticides, and Toxic Substances. *Pesticide Reregistration Progress Report*. Washington, D.C.: Oct. 1994.

United States General Accounting Office. *Report to Congressional Requesters. Superfund: Improved Reviews and Guidance Could Reduce Inconsistencies in Risk Assessments*. Washington, D.C.: Aug. 1994.

D. Religious Forces

Coalition on the Environment and Jewish Life. 443 Park Avenue South, 11th floor, New York, NY 10016. Phone: (212) 684-6950. "Deuteronomy 20:19 prohibits the destruction of the trees of our enemies in a time of war. Why, in a time of peace, are we destroying our own last remaining ancient forests?"

Committee on the Environment of the Diocese of Maryland,The. "'We must proclaim the power of the Gospel to those in power.' Presiding Bishop Edmond L. Browning." For information on the Episcopal Public Policy Network call 1-800-228-0515.

Cornell, George W. "Religious Forces Moving to Safeguard Environment." *The Herald-Mail* 23 May 1992, sec. A:6.

Diocesan Committee on the Environment Contacts: Chris Glennon, Committee Chair. (301) 874-5147.

"Greening the Small Congregation." *Reform Judaism* Winter 1995: 62.

"Is the Earth a Jewish Issue? The Shalom Center Says Yes and Needs Your Help." *Moment* Oct. 1992: 25. Shalom Center, 7318 Germantown Ave., Philadelphia, PA 19119. (215) 247-9700.

Rabinowitz, Charles P. *Shirai Gan: A Family Service for Tu B'Shevat,* revised ed. 1996.

Sagan, Carl. "Religion and Science, Old Antagonists, Forge a New Alliance to Avert a Common Danger." *Parade Magazine* 1 Mar. 1992: 10-15.

To Build a Just Society. Episcopal Church Public Policy Network. New York: The Public Policy Network.

E. Conferences/Seminars

"Alligators, Organics & You. Advancing Alternative to Pesicides." 1995 PAN North America Conference. 17-19 Sept. 1995. Vallombrosa Center, Menlo Park, California.

ATSDR Conference on Low Level Exposure to Chemicals and Neurobiologic Sensitivity. Baltimore, Md. 6-7 Apr. 1994.

Ernde, Laura. "Allaying Fears—Parents Want Environmental Tests; Board Tries to End Rumors of Health Risks at Lincolnshire." *The Herald-Mail* 3 Sept. 1994, sec. A:3.

"Healthy Environment: Healthy People." The Metropolitan Washington Public Health Association. 30 Apr. 1993.

"Rio: Coming Together to Save the Earth." *Time* 1 June 1992: 40-46+.

F. Editorials—OpEd—Columnists

Duffield, Linda. "Saddam, the Earth and Regular Folks." *The Herald-Mail* 17 Feb. 1991, sec. D:1.

"Environment Unites Us All." *USA Today* 9 Nov. 1992, sec. A:15

"Politics and Science in the House." *The New York Times* 14 May 1995, sec. E:14.

Reese, Charley. "To Save Earth, We Must Change Our Lives." *The Daily Mail* 3 Feb. 1992, sec. A:4.

Roush, Jon, President, the Wilderness Society. "Healthy Environment Aids the Economy." *The New York Times* 7 Jan. 1996, sec. E:18.

Sagan, Carl. "Is There Intelligent Life on Earth? What an Alien Spaceship Might Reveal About Our Planet—and Ourselves." *Parade Magazine* 6 June 1993: 4-6.

Spalt, Allen. "Commentary: Social Justice Lies at the Heart of Environmentalism." *The Chapel Hill News* 7 Jan. 1996, sec. A:5.

Talbert, Terry. "Mother Earth, the Government and Pollution." *The Herald-Mail* 24 May 1992, sec. F:1+.

————. "Trying to Spread a Word of Warning About Mother Earth, the Environment." *The Herald-Mail* 6 June 1993, sec. C:2.

Wicker, Tom. "A More Desperate Struggle." *The New York Times* 29 Dec. 1991, Op-Ed sec.:9.

Wilson, Edward O. "Is Humanity Suicidal? We're Flirting With the Extinction of Our Species." *The New York Times Magazine* 30 May 1993: VI, 24+.

G. Books

"Air Pollution: Is the Air a Common Resource or a Common Sewer?" *The 1992 Information Please Environmental Almanac.* Comp. World Resources Institute. Boston: Houghton Mifflin Company, 1992. pp. 147-156.

Apex Press, The, 1994 Catalog, Council on International and Public Affairs, 777 United Nations Plaza (Suite 3C) New York, NY 10017. (212) 953-6920 or (914) 271-2039. Publication Office: P.O. Box 337, Croton-on-Hudson, NY 10520. (914) 271-6500.

Caplan, Ruth, and the staff of Environmental Action. *Our Earth, Ourselves: The Action-Oriented Guide to Help You Protect and Preserve Our Environment.* New York: Bantam Book, 1990.

Carson, Rachel. *Silent Spring.* 25th anniv. ed. Boston: Houghton Mifflin Company, 1962, 1987.

Colborn, Theo, Dianne Dumanoski, and John Peterson Myers. *Our Stolen Future: Are We Threatening Our Fertility, Intelligence, and Survival? A Scientific Detective Story.* New York: Dutton, 1996.

Commoner, Barry. *The Closing Circle: Nature, Man, and Technology.* New York: Alfred A. Knopf, 1971.

Douglas, William O. *Farewell to Texas: A Vanishing Wilderness.* New York: McGraw-Hill Book Company, 1967.

_____. Review of *Silent Spring* by Rachel Carson. *Book of the Month Club News* 1962. "This book is the most important chronicle of this century for the human race."

Duehring, Cindy, and Cynthia Wilson. *The Human Consequences of the Chemical Problem.* White Sulphur Springs, Mont.: TT Publishing, 1994.

Gibbs, Lois Marie, and the Citizens Clearinghouse for Hazardous Waste. *Dying From Dioxin: A Citizen's Guide to Reclaiming Our Health and Rebuilding Democracy.* Boston: South End Press, 1995.

Gore, Al, Senator. *Earth in the Balance: Ecology and the Human Spirit.* New York: Houghton Mifflin Company, 1992.

Greenfield, Ellen J. *House Dangerous: Indoor Pollution in Your Home and Office—and What You Can Do About It!* New York: Interlink Books, 1991.

Greider, William. *Who Will Tell the People: The Betrayal of American Democracy.* New York: Simon & Schuster, 1992.

Lappé, Marc, Ph.D. *Chemical Deception: The Toxic Threat to Health and the Environment.* San Francisco: Sierra Club Books, 1991.

Steingraber, Sandra. *Post-Diagnosis*. Ithaca, New York: Firebrand Books, 1995.

Titles in Industrial Hygiene. Lewis Publishers, 2000 Corporate Blvd., N.W., Boca Raton, FL 33431.

Wiley Professional Books-By-Mail, John Wiley & Sons, Inc., Somerset, New Jersey 08875-9977.

H. News Reports and Magazine Articles

"'Dirty Dozen' Consumer Items: Cancer Group Faults Crest, Hotdogs; Companies, Feds Insist Products Safe. (Washington [AP].) *The Daily Mail* 21 Sept. 1995, sec. A:5.

"Eastern States Plan to Curb Emissions From Smokestacks." *The Daily Mail* 27 Sept. 1994, sec. B:6.

Grier, Norma. "Spreading the Word About Pesticide Hazards and Alternatives." *Journal of Pesticide Reform* 13.4 (Winter 1993): 2+.

Gup, Ted. "The Land Lord: Bruce Babbitt Aims to Protect Millions of Federal Acres That Have Long Been Commercially Exploited." *Time* 8 Mar. 1993: 38.

"Hagerstown Lawyer Hopes His Book Alerts Public to Dangers of a 'Chemical Society.'" *The Maryland Lawyer* 15 May 1993: 9.

Kaplan, Robert D. "The Coming Anarchy. How Scarcity, Crime, Overpopulation, Tribalism, and Disease Are Rapidly Destroying the Social Fabric of Our Planet." *The Atlantic Monthly* Feb. 1994: 44+.

Shenon, Philip. "French Tow Ships Off Side of Atom Test: Dozens of Protesters Placed Under Arrest." *The New York Times* 3 Sept. 1995, International sec.:9.

Simons, Marlise. "Europeans Begin to Calculate the Price of Pollution." *The New York Times* 9 Dec. 1990, sec. E:3.

Van Voorst, Bruce. "A Thousand Points of Blight. From Fuel Spills and Toxic Wastes to Live Shells and Lethal Landfills, the U.S. Military Is the Nation's No. 1 Polluter." *Time* 9 Nov. 1992: 68-69.

Wald, Matthew L. "Smuggling of Polluting Chemicals Is Described. Environmentalists Warn That an Accord to Protect the Ozone

Layer Is Being Circumvented." *The New York Times* 17 Sept. 1995, National sec.:30.

I. Industry

Council of Better Business Bureaus' Foundation. *Grocery Stores—Access Equals Opportunity: Your Guide to the Americans With Disabilities Act.* U.S.A.: Council of Better Business Bureaus' Foundation, 1992.

_____. *Medical Offices—Access Equals Opportunity: Your Guide to the Americans With Disabilities Act.* U.S.A.: Council of Better Business Bureaus' Foundation, 1992.

_____. *Restaurants & Bars—Access Equals Opportunity: Your Guide to the Americans With Disabilities Act.* U.S.A.: Council of Better Business Bureaus' Foundation, 1992.

Department of Justice, and National Rehabilitation Hospital's ADA Health Care Facility Access Project. *ADA—The Americans With Disabilities Act (ADA): Answers to Questions Commonly Asked by Hospitals and Health Care Providers.* Washington, D.C.

Holusha, John. "Dow Chemical's Cleanup Czar Unlocks the Gates. Dave Buzzelli Has the Clout to Bring Environmentalists in as Advisers." *The New York Times* 20 Sept. 1992, sec. F:3.

National Center for Access Unlimited. *Americans With Disabilities Act: Answers for Foodservice Operators.* Washington, D.C.: National Restaurant Association, 1992.

Salmen, John P. S., AIA. *Accommodating All Guests: The Americans With Disabilities Act and the Lodging Industry.* Washington, D.C.: The American Hotel & Motel Association, 1992.

X. Blueprints for Obtaining Recognition of MCS
A. Medical
1. Mind/Body Connection

Moyers, Bill. *HEALING AND THE MIND.* New York: Doubleday (a division of Bantam Doubleday Dell Publishing Group, Inc.), 1993.

2. Psychoneuroimmunology

Cousins, Norman. *HEAD FIRST: THE BIOLOGY OF HOPE.* New York: E. P. Dutton (now Dutton Signet, a division of Penguin Books USA Inc.), 1989.

3. Seasonal Affective Disorder (SAD)

Duehring, Cindy. "Medical Interview—Parallels Between Seasonal Affective Disorder and Multiple Chemical Sensitivity: An Interview With Norman Rosenthal M.D." *Informed Consent* Nov./Dec. 1994: 40-43.

Rosenthal, Norman E., M.D. *Seasons of the Mind: Why You Get the Winter Blues & What You Can Do About It.* New York: Bantam Books, 1989.

_____. *Winter Blues: Seasonal Affective Disorder—What It Is and How to Overcome It.* New York: Guilford Press, 1993.

4. Time Dependent Sensitization

Antelman, Seymour M., Ph.D. "TDS as a Possible Model for MCS." *Our Toxic Times* 6.4 (April 1995): 1+.

5. A Neural Sensitization Model

Bell, Iris R., M.D., Ph.D. "White Paper: Neuropsychiatric Aspects of Sensitivity to Low-Level Chemicals: A Neural Sensitization Model." Proceedings of the Conference on Low-Level Exposure to Chemicals and Neurobiologic Sensitivity. *Toxicology and Industrial Health* 10(4/5) (July-October 1994): 277:312.

6. The Metabolic Factor for MCS

Duehring, Cindy. "A Place to Start: Toward a Unifying Metabolic Factor for MCS." *Our Toxic Times* 7.3 (Mar. 1996): 15-20+.

B. Government
1. Multiple Chemical Sensitivity (MCS)

Recognition of Multiple Chemical Sensitivity (Albert Donnay, compiler and ed. Desert Storm Veterans Coalition and MCS Referral and Resources, Apr. 1994) reprinted in *The New Reactor* July/Aug. 1994: 14.

Weidenfeller, George L., Deputy General Counsel (Operations). Memorandum for all regional counsel, subject Multiple Chemical Sensitivity Disorder and Environmental Illness as Handicaps. 14 Apr. 1992. U.S. Department of Housing and Urban Development, Washington, D.C. 20410-1000.

Wilson, Carole W., Associate General Counsel for Equal Opportunity and Administrative Law. Memorandum for Frank Keating, General Counsel, subject Multiple Chemical Sensitivity Disorder and Environmental Illness as Handicaps. 5 Mar. 1992.

2. Pesticide Poisonings

Morgan, Donald P., M.D., Ph.D. *Recognition and Management of Pesticide Poisonings.* 4th ed. Washington, D.C.: United States Environmental Protection Agency, Mar. 1989.

XI. Some Environmental Organizations/Publications

American Environmental Health Foundation (AEHF). William Rea, M.D., Director. 8345 Walnut Hill Lane, Suite 200, Dallas, Texas 75231. Phone: (214) 361-9515.

American Lung Association of Maryland, Inc. 814 West Diamond Avenue, Suite 270, Gaithersburg, Maryland 20878. Phone: (301) 990-1207 or (800) 445-6016 (toll free in Maryland).

American PIE, American Public Information on the Environment. 31 North Main Street, P.O. Box 460, Marlborough, Connecticut 06447-0460. Phone: (800) 320-APIE. Brad Easterson, Executive Director.

Association of Forest Service Employees for Environmental Ethics. P.O. Box 11615, Eugene, Oregon 97440. Phone: (541) 484-2692. *Inner Voice*.

Bio-Integral Resource Center, The, (BIRC). P.O. Box 7414, Berkeley, California 94707. Phone: (510) 524-2567. *Common Sense Pest Control Quarterly*.

Center for Environmental Medicine. Allan Leiberman, M.D., Director. 7510 North Forest Drive, North Charleston, South Carolina 29420. Phone: (803) 572-1600.

Center for Marine Conservation. 1725 DeSales Street, N.W., Washington, D.C. 20036.

Center for Science in the Public Interest. Suite 300, 1875 Connecticut Avenue, N.W., Washington, D.C. 20009-5728. *Nutrition Action Healthletter*.

Chemical Injury Information Network. P.O. Box 301, White Sulphur Springs, Montana 59645. *Our Toxic Times*. Cynthia Wilson, ed.

Chemical Injury Research Foundation. 3639 North Pearl Street, Tacoma, Washington 98407. Phone: (206) 752-6677. Matt Sweeting, Executive Director. Donald Dudley, M.D., Medical Director.

Chemical Sensitivity Disorders Association (CSDA). P.O. Box 24061, Arbutus, Maryland 21227. *The Chemical Sensitivity Connection*.

Chesapeake Bay Foundation. 162 Prince George Street, Annapolis, Maryland 21401.

Chicago-area Environmental Illness/Multiple Chemical Sensitivities Support Group. 1404 Judson Avenue, Evanston, Illinois 60201-4722. Phone: (847) 866-9630. *CanaryNews*. Lynn Lawson, coordinator and editor.

Children's Health Environmental Coalition (CHEC). P.O. Box 846, Malibu, California 90265. Phone: (213) 656-8715.

Citizens' Environmental Coalition. 33 Central Avenue, Albany, New York 12210. Phone: (518) 462-5527. *Toxics in Your Community Newsletter*.

Citizens Clearing House for Hazardous Waste. Lois Marie Gibbs, Executive Director. P.O. Box 6806, Fall's Church, VA 22040. Phone: (703) 237-2249.

Colette Chuda Environmental Fund, The. 8409 Yucca Trail, Los Angeles, CA 90046. Phone: (213) 656-8715.

Columbia River Inter-Tribal Fish Commission. *Wana Chinook Tymoo*. 729 N.E. Oregon, Portland, Oregon 97232.

Common Cause. 2030 M Street, NW, Washington, D.C. 20036-3380. Phone: (202) 833-1200. "Action Alerts and legislative updates on the status of our fights to clean up Congress."

Co-Op America. 1612 K Street NW, Suite 600, Washington, D.C. 20006. *National Green Pages*.

Cooperative Extension Service. University of Maryland System. Washington County Office. 1260 Maryland Avenue, Hagerstown, Maryland 21740. Phone: (301) 791-1604.

E *The Environmental Magazine*. Subscription Department, P.O. Box 699, Mount Morris, Illinois 61054-7590.

EDF—Environmental Defense Fund. 257 Park Avenue South, New York, New York 10010. *1995-96 Calendar*.

Environmental Access Research Network. Cindy Duehring, Director of Research. P.O. Box 426, Williston, North Dakota 58802. Branch Office: 315 7th Ave. W., Sisseton, South Dakota 57262. Phone: (701) 859-6367. *Medical & Legal Briefs: A Referenced Compendium of Chemical Injury*.

Environmental Health Network. P.O. Box 1155, Larkspur, California 94977. *The New Reactor: The Newsletter of the Environmental Health Network (EHN)*.

Environmental Research Foundation. P.O. Box 5036, Annapolis, Maryland 21403-7036. Phone: (410) 263-1584. *Rachel's Environment & Health Weekly* (formerly *Rachel's Hazardous Waste News*). Peter Montague, Ph.D., ed.

Foundation for Advancements in Science and Education. Park Mile Plaza, 4801 Wilshire Boulevard, Los Angeles, California 90010. Phone: (213) 937-9911. Foundation for Toxic Free Dentistry. P.O. Box 608010, Orlando, Florida 32860-8010. *Dental Health Facts*.

Friends of the Earth. 1025 Vermont Avenue, NW, Third Floor, Washington, D.C. 20005. Phone: (202) 783-7400. *National Survey U.S. Environmental Policy*.

Grass Roots the Organic Way. Grow, Inc. 38 Llangollen Lane, Newtown Square, Pennsylvania 19073. Phone: (215) 353- 2838. MD Brochures.

Greenpeace USA. 1436 U Street N.W., Washington, D.C. 20009

Healthy House Institute, The. 430 N. Sewell Road, Bloomington, Indiana 47408. Phone: (812) 332-5073. *Reports "The Unhealthy House No. 101*.

Human Ecology Action League. P.O. Box 49126, Atlanta, Georgia 30359. Phone: (404) 248-1898. *The Human Ecologist*.

Izaak Walton League of America. 1701 N. Fort Myer Drive, Arlington, Virginia 22209. Phone: (703) 528-1818.

League of Conservation Voters. Frank E. Loy, Chair, 1707 L Street, N.W., Suite 750, Washington, D.C. 20036. Phone: (202) 785-8683. *National Environmental Scorecard, February 1996*.

Maryland Coalition to Stop Illegal Sales of Tobacco to Minors. "Stop Smoking Children." P.O. Box 33, Cabin John, Maryland 20818-0033. Phone: (301) 229-6466.

MCS Referral and Resources. 2326 Pickwick Rd., Baltimore, Maryland 21207-6631. Phone: (410) 448-3319.

Maryland Department of Natural Resources. Forest, Park and Wildlife Service. 14038 Blairs Valley Road, Clear Spring, Maryland 21722.

MBAN—Methyl Bromide Alternatives Network. 116 New Montgomery, No. 810, San Francisco, California 94105. Phone: (415) 541-9140. *Methyl Bromide Briefing Kit.*

Mothers & Others for a Livable Planet. P.O. Box 98111, Washington, D.C. 20077-7319. Phone: (212) 727-4474. *Mothers & Others Action News for a Livable Planet.*

_____. *The Green Guide for Everyday Life*. 40 W 20th St. New York, NY 10011.

National Audubon Society. 700 Broadway, New York, New York 10003.

National Center for Environmental Health Strategies, The. 1100 Rural Avenue, Voorhees, New Jersey 08043. *The Delicate Balance.* Mary Lamielle, ed.

National Coalition Against the Misuse of Pesticides (NCAMP). 701 E Street S.E., Suite 200, Washington, D.C. 20003. Phone: (202) 543-5450. *Pesticides and You.*

National Foundation for the Chemically Hypersensitive. P.O. Box 222, Ophelia, Virginia 25530. Phone: (517) 697- 3989. Fred Nelson.

National Jewish Center for Immunology and Respiratory Medicine. 1400 Jackson Street, Denver, Colorado 80206. Phone: (303) 388-4461 or (800) 222-LUNG. *LungLine® Letter.*

National Poison Prevention Week. P.O. Box 1543, Washington, D.C. 20013. Promotional materials including 1994 Report and List of Materials 1995.

National Wildlife Federation. 1400 Sixteenth Street, N.W., Washington, D.C. 20036-2266.

Natural Resources Defense Council. 40 W. 20th Street, New York, New York 10011. Phone: (212) 727-2700. *Handle With Care: Children and Environmental Carcinogens.*

Nature Conservancy, The®. Maryland Chapter. 2 Wisconsin Circle, Suite 600, Chevy Chase, Maryland 20815. Phone: (301) 656-8673. International Headquarters: 1815 North Lynn Street, Arlington, Virginia 22209. Phone: (703) 841-5300. "The Nature Conservancy is dedicated to preserving plants, animals, and natural communities, which represent the diversity of life on Earth, by protecting the lands and waters they need to survive."

New Horizons Independent Living Center.   8600 E. Valley, Suite B, Prescott Valley, Arizona 86314. Phone: (602) 772- 1266. Susan Molloy.

New York Coalition for Alternatives to Pesticides (NYCAP).   353 Hamilton Street, Albany, New York 12210-1709 Phone: (518) 426-8246. *NYCAP News*.

NCAP—Northwest Coalition for Alternatives to Pesticides. Norma Grier, Dir. P.O. Box 1393, Eugene, Oregon 97440. Phone: (503) 344-5044. *Journal of Pesticide Reform*. Caroline Cox, ed.

Organic Gardening. Rodale Press Inc. 33 E. Minor St., Emmaus, Pennsylvania 18098. Phone: (610) 967-5171.

PAN, Pesticide Action Network.   North America Regional Center. Monica Moore, Dir. 116 New Montgomery Street, #810, San Francisco, California 94105. *Global Pesticide Campaigner*, and *1995 Annual Report*.

Pesticide Education Center. P.O. Box 420870, San Francisco, CA 94142-0870. Phone: 415-391-8511. Marion Moses, MD, President.

Pesticide Watch. Joan M. Clayburgh, Dir. 116 New Montgomery Street, Suite 530, San Francisco, California 94105. Phone: (415) 543-2627. *Pesticide Watch*.

Public Citizen. 1600 20th Street, N.W., Washington, D.C. 20009. Phone: (202) 833-3000. Ralph Nader, Founder.

Public Citizen's Congress Watch. Department N, 215 Pennsylvania Avenue SE, Washington, D.C. 20003.

Rachel Carson Council, Inc. Diana Post, DVM, Dir. 8940 Jones Mill Road, Chevy Chase, Maryland 20815. Phone: (301) 652-1877. *Rachel Carson Council News*.

R.E.A.C.H. International, Inc. 5650 Jackson Loop NE, Rio Rancho, New Mexico 87124. *Reach Review New Mexico*.

Share, Care and Prayer, Inc. P.O. Box 2080, Frazier Park, California 93225.

Sierra Club. 730 Polk Street, San Francisco, California 94109. Phone: (415) 776-2211.

Student Conservation Association, Inc., The. P.O. Box 550, Charlestown, New Hampshire 03603.

Sustainable Agriculture Network. Dr. V. Philip Rasmussen, Jr. Soils and Biometeorology Dept., Utah State University, Logan, Utah 84322-4820. Phone: (801) 750-2179. *Sustainable Agriculture Research and Education Program 1992 National Overview.*

The CRJ Radiation and Public Health Project. 163 Third Avenue, Suite 134, New York, NY 10003. *Radiation and Public Health Report.*

United Farm Workers of America. P.O. Box 62-LA PAZ, Keene, California 93531.

University of Maryland at College Park. School of Public Affairs. Environmental Policy Programs. 2101 Van Munching Hall. College Park, Maryland 20742. Phone: (301) 405-6351.

U.S. Environmental Protection Agency. Information Access Branch. Public Information Center (PIC). 401 M Street, SW, PM-211B, Washington, D.C. 20460. Phone: (202) 260-7751.

U.S. Public Interest Research Group. 215 Pennsylvania Avenue SE, Washington, D.C. 20003. Phone: (202) 546-9707.

Washington County Soil Conservation District. 1260 Maryland Avenue, Suite 101, Hagerstown, MD 21740. Phone: (301) 797-6821. *Conservation News.*

Washington Toxics Coalition (WTC). 4516 University Way NE, Seattle, Washington 98105. Phone: (206) 632-1545.

Whale Adoption Project. 634 No. Falmouth Hwy., North Falmouth, Massachusetts 02556.

Wilderness Society, The. 900 Seventeenth Street, N.W., Washington, D.C. 20006-2596. *Wilderness.*

World Resources Institute. P.O. Box 4852, Hampden Station, Baltimore, Maryland 21211. Phone: (800) 822-0504 or (410) 516-6963.

Worldwatch Institute. 1776 Massachusetts Ave., N.W., Washington, D.C. 20036-1904. *State of the World 1996.*

World Wildlife Fund. 1250 Twenty-Fourth Street, NW, Washington, D.C. 20037.

XII Some Additional Alternatives
A. In the Home

Bower, Lynn Marie. *The Healthy Household: A Complete Guide for Creating a Healthy Indoor Environment.* Bloomington, Indiana: The Healthy House Institute, 1995.

"Clean Humidifier for Safe Use." *LungLine*® *Letter* 7.2 (Winter 1993): 3.

Federal Trade Commission. Office of Consumer/Business Education. Bureau of Consumer Protection. "Buying a Home Water Treatment Unit. *Facts for Consumers* Aug. 1989.

————. Bureau of Consumer Protection. Office of Consumer & Business Education. "Water Testing Scams." *Facts for Consumers* Dec. 1993 (#F027880).

Hazardous Products in Your Home: A Guide to Reduce Pollution. College Park, Maryland: The University of Maryland Cooperative Extension Service, 1988-89.

Heinrich, Brian, et al. "Open a Window!" *The Herald-Mail* 5 May 1993, Letters sec.

Jackson, Jim. Letter to Jacob B. Berkson. Re: Summerville Safe Haven. 8 Sept. 1992.

Lefferts, Lisa Y., M.S.P.H. "Avoiding Hormone-Altering Chemicals, Part I." *The Green Guide for Everyday Life* 15 (21 Sept. 1995): 1-3.

————. "Avoiding Hormone-Altering Chemicals, Part II." *The Green Guide for Everyday Life* 16 (14 Oct. 1995): 1-3.

Moses, Marion, M.D. *Designer Posions: How to Protect Your Health and Home from Toxic Pesticides.* San Francisco: Pesticide Education Center, June 1995.

Remmers, Susan. "'Clear the Air'…Naturally." *The Business Exchange* 3.1 (Jan. 1992): 13.

Salvaggio, Denise. "Variety of Products Aim to Fight Indoor Air Pollution." *The Herald-Mail* 23 Aug. 1990, sec. E:8

United States Environmental Protection Agency. *The Consumer's Handbook for Reducing Solid Waste.* Washington, D.C.: Aug. 1992.

B. Consumer Products

Air Krete®. Cementitious Foam Insulation. Palmer Industries, Inc., 10611 Old Annapolis Rd., Frederick, MD 21701. Phone: 301-898-7848.

Allergy Relief Shop, Inc., 1996. 3371 Whittle Springs Road, Knoxville, Tenn. 37917. Ordering: (800) 626-2810. Consultation: (423) 522-2795.

American Environmental Health Foundation. 8345 Walnut Hill Lane, Suite 225, Dallas, Tex. 75231. Phone: 800-428- 2343 or 214-361-9515.

Austin Healthmate. Air cleaner. Befit Enterprises. P.O. Box 2143, Southhampton, New York 11969. Phone: 800-497- 9516.

"Breathing Easier in the Decade of the Environment." *SAAB* Apr. 1991: 18.

Brower, David. "Kenaf: A Tree-Free Alternative. 'Many Countries, Such as China, Which Killed Its Trees and Settled Its Wilderness Long Ago, No Longer Use Trees for Paper: They Cannot. They Have Been Forced to Find Substitutes, From Rice to Kenaf. I Like to Read. I Like Forests on the Sides of My Mountains. There Is Still a Choice for Many Countries.'—David Brower." *Inner Voice* 7.6 (Nov./Dec. 1995): 1+.

"Cleanest Machine." *Time* 31 Dec. 1990: 51.

Clearing the Air. Mobil Corporation, 1994, 1995.

Elkington, John, Julia Hailes, and Joel Makower. *The Green Consumer: You Can Buy Products That Don't Cost the Earth.* U.S.A.: Penguin Book, 1990.

Foil-Ray® Insulation. Elnathan Thermal 'R' Systems, P.O. Box 7528, Odessa, Texas 79760. Phone: 505-682-3361.

"Furnishings." *Healthy House Reports* 102. Unionville, Ind.: The Healthy House Institute, 1993.

Holusha, John. "Environmentalists Try to Move the Markets." *The New York Times* 22 Aug. 1993, sec. E:5.

Jackson, Tom. "Build It Better With Earth-Friendly Products." *Better Homes and Gardens* Mar. 1993: 76+.

Leary, Warren E. "Use of Hydrogen as Fuel Is Moving Closer to Reality." *The New York Times* 16 Apr. 1995, National sec.:15.

McCarroll, Thomas. "No Fuel Like a New Fuel. Environmentalism and War Spur a Race for Gasoline Alternatives." *Time* 18 Mar. 1991: 66.

"Natural Fungus Could Reduce Insecticide Use." (Washington [AP].) *The Daily Mail* 31 Aug. 1995, sec. A:10.

"Painting." *Healthy House Reports* 103. Unionville, Ind.: The Healthy House Institute, 1993.

"Paints. Stirring Up Innovation. Environmental Improvements in Paints and Adhesives. Brief Survey of Recent Environmental Innovations in Paints and Adhesives." INFORM, Inc., 120 Wall Street, New York, NY 10005-4001. Phone: (212) 361-2400, ext. 233.

Popular Mechanics. "Metal Roofing: Authentic and Durable." *The Herald-Mail* 18 Jan. 1991, sec. C:4.

Scaletta, Sue Ellyn. "Budding Environmental Decade Can Blossom in the Coming Year." *The Herald-Mail* 13 Jan. 1991, sec. D:6.

"SMOG: Pollution Tests on the Run." *Time* 2 Dec. 1991: 29.

Steam Inhalation Therapy. "Get relief from the misery." The Magellan Group advertisement. 800-644-8100.

Steinman, David and Samuel S. Epstein, M.D. *The Safe Shopper's Bible: A Consumer's Guide to Nontoxic Household Products, Cosmetics, and Food.* Macmillan USA, 1995.

3M Filtrete™ Particle Filters. "A 3M innovation lets you breathe clean air inside your car no mattter how bad it is outside." Advertisement. 3M 1995. 1-800 3M HELPS.

C. Pest Control

Bio-Logical Pest Management. Member, N.C.A.M.P. and B.I.R.C. Serving Metro D.C. "Chemical Treatment Is Your Last Option, Not Your First." Alan M. Cohen, President. Phone: (202) 237-7509.

"Controlling Ants Without Poisoning Your Home." *Environmental Health Coalition*. 1717 Kettner Boulevard, Suite 100, San Diego, California 92101. Phone: (619) 235-0281.

"Controlling Fleas Without Poisoning Your Home." *Environmental Health Coalition*. 1717 Kettner Boulevard, Suite 100, San Diego, California 92101. Phone: (619) 235-0281.

"Currie, William E. International Pest Management Institute. P.O. Box 389, Bryans Road, Maryland 20616. Phone: (301) 753-6930.

"Dye Could Become Weapon Against Fruit Flies." (Los Angeles.) *The New York Times* 18 Dec. 1994, National sec.:39.

Feldman, Jay. "Taking the Pesticide Out of Pest Control. The Controversy That Has Plagued Alternatives." *Pesticides and You* 15.4 (Winter 1995-1996): 12-19.

"Flea Control for Your Pet and Home." *Agricultural Resources Center*. 115 West Main Street, Carrboro, NC 27510. Sept. 1990.

Forbes, William. Montgomery County Maryland School System. Phone: 301-840-8100.

Gips, Terry. *Breaking the Pesticide Habit: Alternatives to 12 Hazardous Pesticides*. International Alliance for Sustainable Agriculture. Newman Center. University of Minnesota. 1701 University Ave. S.E., Room 202, Minneapolis, MN 55414. Phone: (612) 331-1099.

Graff, Debra. *Pest Control You Can Live With: Safe and Effective Ways to Get Rid of Common Household Pests*. Sterling, Va.: Earth Stewardship Press, 1990.

Husain, Taher, et al. *Alternative Pest Controls for Lawns and Gardens*. Chevy Chase, Maryland: Rachel Carson Council, Inc., 1994.

IPMI. International Pest Management Institute. High Quality Pest Management Training. IPM is risk reduction. P.O. Box 389, Bryans Road, Maryland 20616. Phone: (800) 484- 3236, Sec. Code 1238; or (301) 246-9499.

Ketrow, Ray. "Integrated Pest Management Helps Environment." *The Herald-Mail* 5 Mar. 1995, sec. E:6.

League of Women Voters of Ligonier Valley. *Gypsy Moth Control: Understanding Your Options*.

"Mosquitoes Immune to Pesticide. A Wet Winter, Along With Mosquitoes Becoming Immune to the Pesticide Malathion, Could Create a Summer Nightmare." (Annapolis [AP].) *The Herald Mail* 21 Apr. 1996, sec. A:1+.

"Natural Predators Replace Pesticides in 'Biocontrol.'" *The Herald-Mail* 25 May 1990, sec. A:13.

Quarles, William, Ph.D., and Christine Bucks. "Non-Toxic Termite Treatments! Here's How to Beat Subterranean and Drywood Termites *Without* Using Dangerous Pesticides!" *Organic Gardening* Dec. 1995: 44-50.

Raver, Anne. "What Horrifies Roaches and Grows on Trees?" *The New York Times* 27 Nov. 1994:75.

Su, Nan-Yao, Ph.D. "Basic Research Keys Development of New Termite Control Bait." *Pest Control* June 1993.

_____. "Baits: Are They in the Future of Termite Control? At Least One Prominent Termite Researcher Thinks So." *PCT: Pest Control Technology* July 1993.

Tim-Bor® Insecticide. Manufacturer: U.S. Borax, Inc., 26877 Tourney Rd., Valencia, CA 91355. Phone: Hot-Line (800) 9-TIMBOR.

Tvedten, Stephen L. Stroz Services, Inc., Get Set, Inc., 2530 Hayes Street, Marne, MI 49435. Phone: (800) 221-6188.

"We Kill 'em With Coldness." Tallon Termite & Pest Control ad. *San Diego Union-Tribune* 28 Oct. 1992, sec. A:9.

World Environmental Technology, Inc. Gerald C. Shirley, CEO. P.O. Box 528, Belleville, IL 6222-0528. Phone: (618) 236-2728. Pest Patrol.

D. Outdoors

"A Surprising Ally in the Fight to Save the Environment—an Oil Company." Sunoco ad. *Time* 1993.

"Fungus May Fight Locusts." *The Daily Mail* 17 Nov. 1993.

McKinley, James C., Jr. "Agreement Is Reached on Pollution. 10 States to Reduce Smokestack Emissions." *The New York Times* 2 Oct. 1994, Metro Report sec.:33+.

Morris, David, and Michael Lewis. "The Energy Tax: Its Time Will Come." *The New York Times* 15 Aug. 1993, sec. F.

Riechmann, Deb. "Bill Would Fund Mine Pollution Cleanup. Sarbanes: Much of the Potomac's North Branch Is Biologically Dead." *The Daily Mail* 3 Sept. 1992, sec. A:8.

Riordan, Teresa. "Rethinking Plastics From the Ground Up. A Chemist's Plan Would Cut Pollution and Add New Materials." *The New York Times* 11 Sept. 1994, sec. F: 7.

Schneider, Keith. "Toxic Messes: Easier Made Than Undone." *The New York Times* 2 Oct. 1994, sec. E:5.

"Sludge Is Said to Hold Answer for Disposal of Mustard Gas." *The New York Times* 14 May 1995, National sec.:26.

E. Planning

Bowermaster, Jon. "Take This Park and Love It. Douglas Tompkins, Esprit Millionaire, Bought a Chunk of Chile to Create the World's Largest Private National Park. But the Reception Has Been... Well, Chilly." *The New York Times Magazine* 3 Sept. 1995: 24-27.

Dominguez, Alex. "Restoring Nature: Entrepreneurs Find Ecological Work Fulfilling and Lucrative. As Interest in the Environment Continues to Grow, So Does the Number of Businesses That Deal in Ecological Restoration. Growing Federal and State Legislation Dealing With Preservation, Restoration or Replacement of Natural Areas Have Made Restoration of Nature Big Business." *The Herald-Mail* 8 Nov. 1992, sec. F:7.

"EI/MCS Public Housing Applications Needed." *Reach Review New Mexico* 1.6 (Dec. 1994-Jan. 1995): 1.

"5 Waterfront Communities Call on Carp to Control Aquatic Weeds in Nearby Peach Lake. A Biological Approach to Correcting a Biological Problem." (North Salem, N.Y., Feb. 11.) *The New York Times* 18 Feb. 1996, Metro sec.:40.

"Hundreds of New Homes Planned at Site of Love Canal Toxic Nightmare." (Niagara Falls, N.Y.) *The Daily Mail* 1 Dec. 1994, sec. A:10.

Lemonick, Michael D. "Environment: Rocky Horror Show. Why Can't Rocky Flats' Plutonium Be Cleaned Up? It's Against the Rules." *Time* 27 Nov. 1995: 69-70.

Noren, Nancy. *Report on New Mexico Safe Housing & MCS/EI Communities*. 25 Apr. 1991.

————. *Update on the Dry Duck Creek Project*. 9 May 1991.

Penenberg, Adam L. "Slick Solutions to an Environmental Scourge. The New Oil-Spill Law May Create a Market for Novel Cleanup Methods." *The New York Times* 15 Aug. 1993, sec. F:11.

"This Year Georgia-Pacific Will Plant 50 Million Trees. Help Us Make It 50 Million and One. 'Who's Going to Make Sure the Trees Will Be Here Tomorrow?'" Georgia-Pacific ad.

"Virginia's Scientific Field Stations: The Natural World as Laboratory." *The College and Graduate School of Arts & Sciences*, The University of Virginia, 11.2 (Spring 1993): 2.

Wald, Matthew L. "Deal Is Likely On Cars Run By Electricity. California May Drop Quotas for Incentive." *The New York Times* 19 Nov. 1995, National sec.:25.

"Wisconsin—Planning Circle of Cities to Aid the Environment." *The New York Times* 5 Jan. 1992, Campus Life sec.:31.

F. Medicine

Crook, William G., M.D. *The Yeast Connection, a Medical Breakthrough*. 2nd ed. Jackson, Tenn.: Professional Books, 1984.

Eng, James L. "Nature's Healing Hands: Herbal Cures More Popular, but Critics Want More Tests." *The Washington Times* 5 May 1993, sec. E:1+.

Environmental Hazards and Biodetoxification. Center for Environmental Medicine, Program for Biodetoxification. North Charleston, S.C. 1 Mar. 1991.

Frobouck, Jo Ann. "Traditional Oriental Medicine Comes to Hagerstown." *The Antietam Advertiser* V.12 (11 Oct. 1995): 2.

Lieberman, Allan D., M.D., F.A.A.E.M., Medical Director. Center for Environmental Medicine, P.A. 7510 Northforest Drive, North Charleston, SC 29420. Phone: (803) 572- 1600.

Liebman, Bonnie. "Dodging Cancer With Diet." *Nutrition Action Healthletter* 22.1 (Jan./Feb. 1995): 1+.

Michaud, Ellen, Alice Feinstein, and the editors of *Prevention Magazine*. *Fighting Disease: The Complete Guide to Natural Immune Power*. Emmaus, Pa.: Rodale Press, Inc., 1989.

Null, Gary. *No More Allergies: Identifying and Eliminating Allergies and Sensitivity Reactions to Everything in Your Environment*. New York: Villard Books, 1992.

Toufexis, Anastasia. "Dr. Jacobs' Alternative Mission: A New NIH Office Will Put Unconventional Medicine to the Test." *Time* 1 Mar. 1993: 43-44.

Weil, Andrew, M.D. *Natural Health, Natural Medicine*. *Completely Revised & Updated*. New York: Houghton Mifflin Company, 1995

_____. *Spontaneous Healing*. New York: Knopf, 1995.

G. Dentistry

Clifford Materials Reactivity Testing Report. Laboratory Services by Clifford Consulting & Research, Inc., CLIA 06D0669295. Clifford Consulting & Research, Inc., 2275-J Waynoka Road, Colorado Springs, CO 80915-1635 U.S.A. Phone: (719) 550-0008.

Fischer, Richard D., D.D.S. Evergreen Professional Center, 4222 Evergreen Lane, Annandale, Virginia 22003. Phone: (703) 256-4441. Mercury Free Dentistry. *Pathways* Winter 95-96.

Gorman, Christine. "Are Your Teeth Toxic? A Colorado Dentist Built a Successful Practice Pulling Out Silver Fillings. Now He's In Trouble." *Time* 11 Dec. 1995: 71.

Ziff, Sam, and Michael F. Ziff, D.D.S. *Dentistry Without Mercury*. Rev. and expanded ed. Orlando, Florida: Bio- Probe, Inc., 1993

_____, Michael F. Ziff, D.D.S., and Mats Hanson, Ph.D. *Dental Mercury Detox*. Rev. and expanded ed. Orlando, Florida: Bio Probe, Inc., 1993.

H. Politics

Birnbaum, Jeffrey H. "Bill's Nemesis: Nader?" *Time* 25 Mar. 1996: 16.

Carmody, Deirdre. "President of Audubon Society Reins in Magazine." ("...Mr. Wicker wrote that environmentalists had often criticized

Mr. Clinton's environmental positions and that they were now taking with a grain of salt the President's recent stance as 'a stand-up fighter for their interests.'…") *The New York Times* 11 Feb. 1996, sec. 1:30.

Cushman, John H., Jr. "Dispirited E.P.A. Is Near Sweeping Tract on Goals." *The New York Times* 24 Sept. 1995, National sec.:26.

_____. "Budget Cuts Leave E.P.A. Facing Layoffs. A Furlough May Turn Into Something More Permanent." *The New York Times* 24 Dec. 1995, sec. 1:14.

_____. "Logs That Glow in the Dark?" *The New York Times* 4 Feb. 1996, sec. E:2.

_____. "Many States Give Polluting Firms New Protections. White House Is Alarmed. Laws in 18 States Are Meant to Encourage Companies to Monitor Themselves." (Washington, April 5.) *The New York Times* 7 Apr. 1996, sec. 1:1+.

DePalma, Anthony. "Blockade of Oil Wells Costs Mexico $8.5 Million in 12 Days." (Mexico City, Feb. 10.) ("…the rush to extract the oil without proper safeguards has turned great sections of the state into a toxic swamp where oil seeps up through the ground and rivers are so polluted they catch on fire…") *The New York Times* 11 Feb. 1996, sec. 1:8.

Gingrich, Newt. "Tending the Gardens of the Earth: Scientifically Based Environmentalism." Chapter 21 in *To Renew America*. New York: Harper Collins Publishers, Inc., 1995.

"G.O.P. Hears Nature's Call. The Party Scrambles on Environmental Policy." *Time* 4 Mar. 1996: 57.

Gore, Al, Senator. *Earth in the Balance: Ecology and the Human Spirit*. New York: Houghton Mifflin Company, 1992.

Leary, Warren E. "Congress's Science Agency Prepares to Close Its Doors." *The New York Times* 24 Sept. 1995, National sec.:26.

Linden, Eugene. "Chicken of the Sea? A 'Dolphin-Safe' Tuna Flap Makes the U.S. Squirm." *Time* 4 Mar. 1996: 57.

Locy, Toni. "Rostenkowski Fraud Plea Brings 17-Month Sentence." *The Washington Post* 10 Apr. 1996, sec. A:1+.

Nader, Ralph. "Letters: Support for Reich." *The New York Times Book Review* 24 Dec. 1995: 4.

Raines, Howell, ed. "A Greener White House." *The New York Times* 26 Nov. 1995, sec E:10.

Ramirez, Anthony. "Consumer Crusader Feels a Chill in Washington. Nader Remains Unbent by Winds of Change. Ralph Nader says a Congressional Measure to Limit Punitive Damages in Civil Liability Suits Would Be the Consumer Movement's Biggest Setback Since the 1970's." *The New York Times* 31 Dec. 1995, sec. 3:1+.

Sanger, David E. "Dilemma for Clinton on Nafta Truck Rule. Enacting a Provision Would Anger States; Stopping It Would Repudiate a Pact." *The New York Times* 17 Dec. 1995, sec. 1:36.

Vote for the Earth: The League of Conservation Voters' Election Guide. Earthworks Press, 1992.

WuDunn, Sheryl. "Accident at A—Plant Leads Japan to Debate." *The New York Times* 17 Dec. 1995, sec. 1:4.

Zumwalt, Elmo R., Jr., Admiral USN (Ret.). *On Watch: A Memoir.* Arlington, Virginia: Admiral Zumwalt & Associates, Inc., 1976.

I. Agriculture

Cesar E. Chavez' United Farm Workers of America AFL-CIO. Re: Farmworkers' fight for social justice. National Headquarters: La Paz, P.O. Box 62, Keene, California 93531.

Clark, Merrill. *Stewardship of the Land and the Food It Grows: A Look at Alternative Agriculture in Michigan.* Washington, D.C.: League of Women Voters Education Fund, Oct. 1992.

Coleman, Eliot. *The New Organic Grower: A Master's Manual of Tools and Techniques for the Home and Market Gardener.* Chelsea, Vermont: Chelsea Green, 1989.

"Couple Pushes Organic Farming in Md." *The Daily Mail* 7 Apr. 1992, sec. A:7.

Cox, Caroline, ed. "Sustainable Agriculture in the Pacific Northwest." *Journal of Pesticide Reform: Northwest Coalition for Alternatives to Pesticides* 13.1 (Spring 1993).

Feder, Barnaby J. "Out of the Lab, a Revolution on the Farm. New Genetic Weapons to Battle Bugs and Weeds." *The New York Times* 3 Mar. 1996, sec. 3:1.

Lewis, Yale. "Idaho Farmer Reduces Pesticide Use. Legume Rotation Saves Time, Money, and the Environment." *Pesticides and You* Fall 1995: 11+.

Mather, Robin. *A Garden of Unearthly Delights. Bioengineering and the Future of Food.* New York: Dutton, 1995.

McGrath, Mike, Editor in Chief. "Why We Grow." *Organic Gardening* Dec. 1992: 5.

Mendoza, Laura, and Cindy Duehring. "National Organic Standards Board Creates More Loopholes." *Our Toxic Times* 6.9 (Sept. 1995): 5-6+.

"Organic Gardening Given Second Look. Rodale Research in Pa. Grabs Interest of USDA." (Kutztown, Pa. [AP].) *The Herald-Mail* 3 Apr. 1994, sec. F:6.

"Prince Charles Becomes a Gentleman Organic Farmer." *The Frederick New-Post* 30 Dec. 1993, sec. C:5.

Raeburn, Paul. *The Last Harvest. The Genetic Gamble That Threatens to Destroy American Agriculture.* New York: Simon & Schuster, 1995.

Schultz, Warren. Garden Design Magazine, 100 Avenue of the Americas, New York, NY 10013. Phone: 212-219-7457.

Spalt, Allen. Agricultural Resources Center, 115 West Main St., Carrboro, NC 27510. Phone: 919-967-1886.

Tallmadge, John. "Cultivating Disaster? Why Modern Farming Methods May Threaten Our Food Supply." *The New York Times Book Review* 13 Aug. 1995, sec. 7:18.

Verhovek, Sam Howe. "King Cotton, Meet Rachel Carson." *The New York Times* 28 Jan. 1996, sec. E:2.

J.   Environmental Architects/Builders/Consultants

Bierman-Lytle, Paul. The Masters Corporation: Architecture and Master Building, P.O. Box 514, New Canaan, Connecticut 06840. Letter to Jacob B. Berkson. 7 Jan. 1992.

Bower, John. The Healthy House Institute, 430 Sewell Road, Bloomington, IN 47408. Phone: 812-332-5073.

Brown, Patricia Leigh. "A House Built to Be 'Healthy.'" *The New York Times* 19 Apr. 1990, sec. C:1+.

Browne, Eichman, Dalgliesh, Gilpin and Paxton, P.C. Architects. P.O. Box 2555, Charlottesville, VA 22902- 2555. Letter to Jacob B. Berkson. 21 Dec. 1995.

Chuda, James. Architect. Environmental, sustainable, architecture. 27450 Pacific Coast Highway, Malibu, CA 90265. Phone: 310-589-5727.

Clarity House. Earle B. Meek and Edward L. Eichman, Jr., AIA, NCARB. 45 Chipmunk Hill, Berkeley Springs, West Virginia 25411. Phone: 304-258-9029.

Hull, Michael G., A.I.A. Noelker and Hull Associates, Inc., Architects. 438 Lincoln Way East, Chambersburg, PA 17201. Phone: 717-263-8464.

Hunter, Linda. Healthy Home Designs. 4423 Kingman Boulevard, Des Moines, Iowa 50311. Phone: 515-255-1425.

Lemonick, Michael D. "Design: Architecture Goes Green: An Array of New Projects Proves That Buildings Can Be Ecologically Correct, Cost Efficient and Beautiful as Well." *Time* 5 Apr. 1993: 38-40.

Morin-Rocco, Inc. Architects, Designers, Constructors. 49 Summit Ave., Hagerstown, Md. 21741. Phone: 301-739- 2300.

Spalding, Steven K. Letter to Jacob B. Berkson. Re: Residential design-build proposal for Jacob Berkson. Toxic-free residential construction. 24 Jan. 1994. Spalding Construction. 609 Ravenswood Drive, Hagerstown, Maryland 21740. Phone: 301- 797-4346.

K. Accommodations for Persons With Disabilities

"Allergic to Life. In the Mysterious, Seductive Safe, Suburbia Can Kill You." *Time* 26 June 1995: 79.

Gorman, Nancy W., J.D. 9042 Canterbury Riding, Laurel, Maryland 20723. Phone/Fax: 301-498-1193. Accommodation/Benefits Representation.

Headlee, Terry. "ADA Five Years Later." *The Herald-Mail* 22 Oct. 1995, sec. F:1+.

King, Warren L., and Jane E. Jarrow, Ph.D. *Testing Accommodations for Persons With Disabilities: A Guide for Licensure, Certification, and Credentialling.* Lexington, Kentucky: UNICOR Print Plant, 1992.

McVicker, Marilyn G. "Customizing a Van for MCS Accessibility." *The Human Ecologist* 69 (Spring 1996): 11-14.

Stansky, Lisa J. "Opening Doors. Five Years After Its Passage, the Americans With Disabilities Act Has Not Fulfilled the Greatest Fears of Its Critics—or the Greatest Hopes of Its Supporters." *ABA Journal* Mar. 1996: 66-69.

L. Education

Parini, Jay. "The Greening of the Humanities. Deconstruction Is Compost. Environmental Studies Is the Academic Field of the 90's. *The New York Times Magazine* 29 Oct. 1995, sec. 6:52-53.

Shaw, Dennis. "Environmental Challenges of the New Year." *The Herald-Mail* 31 Dec. 1995, sec. E:1.

"16th Annual Summer on the Lawn: Earth, Wind, Rain, and Fire—The Changing Global Environment." Sponsored by Division of Continuing Education, College of Arts and Sciences Alumni Association. University of Virginia. Charlottesville, Virginia. 16-20 June 1996.

United States Environmental Protection Agency. Prevention, Pesticides, and Toxic Substances (7501C). *Citizen's Guide to Pest Control and Pesticide Safety.* EPA 730-K- 95-001. Washington, D.C.: Sept. 1995.

_____. Prevention, Pesticides, and Toxic Substances (7506C). *Office of Pesticide Programs Annual Report for 1995.* EPA 730-R-95-002. Washington, D.C.: Dec. 1995.

_____. Prevention, Pesticides and Toxic Substances (7508W). *Pesticide Program Progress Report.* EPA 738-R-95-020. Washington, D.C.: Apr. 1995.

Note: Please refer to all Organizations listed in Section XI, p. 133 et seq for additional Education resources.

M. Business Consultants

John Thompson Environmental Consulting and Marketing Services®.
"Mission Statement:...is dedicated to fighting environmental
degradation with free-enterprise solutions that attract the resources
and problem-solving acumen of business." 2066 Westwood Circle,
Smyrna, Georgia 30080. Phone: (770) 333-8563.

ADDENDUM

Since the publication of A Canary's Tale in August 1996--

1. A 70-page EPA Memorandum reviewing chlorpyrifos (Dursban) poisoning data, dated January 14, 1997, by Jerome Blondell PhD., MPM, and Virginia A. Dobozy VMD, MPH, among other things links Dursban poisoning to MCS. Hallelujah! One reference cited was the Rosenthal/Cameron article about my poisoning reported in Am J Psychiatry and here in Vol. I. p. 127.

2. A three-page letter dated January 14, 1997, by Lynn R. Goldman M.D., Asst. Administrator U.S. EPA, confirmed her concern about Dursban to Mr. John Hagaman, President and CEO Dow Elanco, manufacturer of Dursban, reciting, among other things:

"The EPA strongly supports the notion of the public's right-to-know. In this regard, as I explained, it is EPA's desire to find ways to better educate the public on the use of and exposure to pesticides, particularly indoor/household products."

Endorsing A Canary's Tale is an excellent way to educate the public.

3. A major study of the Gulf War syndrome by Robert W. Haley M.D., Associate Professor of Medicine, and others at The University of Texas, Southwestern Medical Center, Dallas, was published in the January 15, 1997 issue of the Journal of the American Medical Association (JAMA). Dr. Haley stated in a January 7, 1997 letter, to study participants, including my friend, Herbert J. Smith, D.V.M., Col., U.S. Army (Retired):

"The results of our studies indicate that many Gulf War veterans suffered varying degrees of damage to the brain, spinal cord and peripheral nerves, probably from combinations of low-level chemical nerve agents, pyridostigmine bromide in the anti-nerve gas tablets, DEET in highly concentrated insect repellents, pesticides in flea collars, and possibly pesticide spraying. Analysis of the psychological testing data by my colleague, neuropsychologist Dr. Jim Hom, found no evidence of combat stress, post-traumatic stress disorder, or other psychological illnesses."

The Perot Foundation provided funding for the studies. H. R. Perot and the author of this book served together as Naval Officers aboard Destroyer Division 322 on a goodwill mission around the world in 1953-54. Comin' Home by Berkson describes some of their adventures.